The Bastard Instrument

TRACKING POP

SERIES EDITORS: JOCELYN NEAL, JOHN COVACH,
ROBERT FINK, AND LOREN KAJIKAWA

The Bastard Instrument

A Cultural History of the Electric Bass

Brian F. Wright

University of Michigan Press • *Ann Arbor*

For questions or permissions, please contact um.press.perms@umich.edu

Published in the United States of America by the
University of Michigan Press
Manufactured in the United States of America
Printed on acid-free paper
First published July 2024

A CIP catalog record for this book is available from the British Library.

Library of Congress Cataloging-in-Publication Data

Names: Wright, Brian F., author. | Michigan Publishing (University of Michigan),
    publisher.
Title: The bastard instrument : a cultural history of the electric bass / Brian F Wright.
Other titles: Cultural history of the electric bass | Tracking pop.
Description: Ann Arbor : University of Michigan Press, 2024. | Series: Tracking pop |
    Includes bibliographical references (pages 341–261) and index.
Identifiers: LCCN 2024002501 (print) | LCCN 2024002502 (ebook) | ISBN
    9780472076819 (hardcover) | ISBN 9780472056811 (paperback) | ISBN 9780472221707
    (ebook)
Subjects: LCSH: Bass guitar—History. | Bass guitarists. | Popular music—1951–1960—
    History and criticism. | Popular music—1961–1970—History and criticism.
Classification: LCC ML1015.B35 W75 2024 (print) | LCC ML1015.B35 (ebook) | DDC
    787.87/19—dc23/eng/20240206
LC record available at https://lccn.loc.gov/2024002501
LC ebook record available at https://lccn.loc.gov/2024002502

To my wife Amanda Wright, for her love, her insights,
and her unwavering support. I could not have done it without you.

Contents

Digital materials related to this title can be found on the Fulcrum platform
via the following citable URL: https://doi.org/10.3998/mpub.11314397

Acknowledgments

I have been working on this project for nearly twelve years, and over that time, I have been blessed to receive so much wonderful input and advice from friends and colleagues. I am truly grateful to all of you. What follows is but a partial list of people who deserve credit and recognition.

First, I should thank Robert Walser and Susan McClary, who set me on this path after an eventful conversation at the 2011 American Musicological Society conference in San Francisco. It was they who convinced me that the history of the electric bass was a story worth telling.

I would also like to thank everyone who has been gracious enough to read excerpts of this book and lend me their expertise, including Mark Burford, Leah Branstetter, Matt Brennan, John Dougan, Robert Fink, Mark Katz, Sean Lorre, Karl Hagstrom Miller, Darren Mueller, Chris Reali, Travis Stimeling, Elijah Wald, Gayle Wald, Lynn Wheelwright, and Albin Zak. I am particularly indebted to Amy Coddington, Stephanie Doktor, Peter Graff, Andrew Mall, and Sarah Rude for reading (and rereading) multiple drafts of different chapters and for being sounding boards in my moments of doubt. You are all, literally, the best. I also owe a huge debt of gratitude to Steve Waksman, whose own work on the electric guitar paved the way for a book like this to even exist. I am very thankful to Steve for advocating for this project, and I appreciate the time and energy he has put in to helping me improve it. I know that it would not have become what it is without his guidance.

My research on the electric bass began while I was a graduate student, first at the University of Nevada, Reno, and then at Case Western Reserve University, and I would like to thank my graduate school advisers, David Ake, Daniel Goldmark, and Louis Niebur, for helping to shape this project. Thanks especially to Daniel for his kindness and his generosity over these many years, as well as for being a model of the kind of scholar I hope to become.

Since graduating, I have also had the privilege of being mentored by some of the scholars I most respect, including Theo Cateforis, Andrew Flory, Tammy L. Kernodle, and Albin Zak. Tammy, in particular, has remained a never-ending source of inspiration. From her, I learned the value of having a clear mission statement for my work, and through all the ups and downs of my career, her advice has always served as a guiding light.

I developed this project in pieces, presenting it at various academic conferences and symposia, including American Musicological Society conferences, International Association for the Study of Popular Music–US Branch conferences, Society for American Music conferences, the AMS Popular Music Study Group Junior Faculty Symposium, and many more. Through these, I have been lucky enough to meet and engage with a community of scholars that continue to inspire me. In addition to those already named, I would like to thank Erin Bauer, Christa Bentley, David Blake, Matt Carter, Norma Coates, Mike D'Errico, Sara Gulgas, Jack Hamilton, Jason Hanley, Paula Harper, Anthony Kwame Harrison, Robin James, Jake Johnson, Brian Jones, Loren Kajikawa, Lauron Kehrer, Steven Lewis, Joanna Love, Kimberly Mack, S. Alexander Reed, RJ Smith, Victor Szabo, Mikkel Vad, and David Vanderhamm for the formative conversations we've had, both about my work and about popular music in general.

This work also would not have been possible with the support of my institution, the University of North Texas, which provided me the time and funding to pursue such an extended research project. Likewise, I would like to thank my colleagues, especially Andrew Chung, Rebecca Geoffroy-Schwinden, David Heetderks, Sean Powell, April L. Prince, and Vivek Virani, for making UNT such a satisfying place to work. Thanks as well to my students for the many thoughtful and insightful discussions they have had with me, and thanks to my former research assistants Meng Ren and Robbie Segars, for helping me track down increasingly obscure information about bass history.

This book was supported by grants and fellowships from the PCA/ACA, the Rutgers Institute of Jazz Studies, the Society for American Music, the Baker Nord Center for the Humanities, and the American Musicological Society. An earlier version of Chapter 2 was published as "'A Bastard Instrument': The Fender Precision Bass, Monk Montgomery, and Jazz in the 1950s," *Jazz Perspectives* 8, no. 3 (2015): 281–303, and some material from Chapter 6 was previously published in "Reconstructing the History of Motown Session Musicians: The Carol Kaye / James Jamerson Controversy," *Journal of the Society for American Music* 13, no. 1 (February 2019): 78–109.

Research for this book was conducted at the Rutgers Institute of Jazz Studies, the National Association of Music Merchants Library, the Frist Library and Archive of the Country Music Hall of Fame and Museum, the Rock & Roll Hall of Fame and Museum Library and Archive, the Browne Popular Culture Library at Bowling Green State University, the Southern Folklife Collection at the University of North Carolina at Chapel Hill, and the Smithsonian Institution, among others. I therefore owe quite a lot of thanks to the many archivists and librarians who helped me find and consult a wealth of archival material. You are the real unsung heroes of academic research. Similarly, the librarians at UNT have been instrumental throughout this project, and I would like to thank Blaine Brubaker, Susannah Cleveland, and Janelle Foster for accommodating my ever-evolving research requests.

One of the most unexpected developments of the last few years is that I would come to meet and engage with several of my bass heroes, some of whom I discuss in this book. I am especially appreciative of bassists Jack Casady, Jerry Jemmott, Stan Lark, Tony Newton, Norbert Putnam, and Chuck Rainey, who were all kind enough to sit down and discuss their experiences with me. Their stories have made this book infinitely richer.

Many thanks to the University of Michigan Press and its staff for their work shepherding this book through to publication. In particular, I'd like to thank my editor, Sara Jo Cohen, who, even though she inherited this book from a previous editor, has remained a steadfast advocate for it. Thanks as well to Tracking Pop series editor John Covach and to the manuscript's anonymous reviewers for their feedback and advice.

Lastly, I must give thanks to my family, especially my wife Amanda Wright. In many ways, this book is a chronicle of our life together and all the unexpected adventures that have come with it. I have been blessed on this journey to have such a brilliant partner. Your advice and support have been invaluable, as have the endless conversations we've had about my work. No one has had a bigger hand in shaping this book, and no one read as many drafts as you did. I sincerely cannot thank you enough for the years of time and energy you have invested in me and this project. I love you so very much. Thanks as well to my daughter Layla. It's been such a joy watching you grow up, and I hope you know that I am proud of you and that I love you all the universe and beyond.

Introduction

Music History from the Bottom Up

The story of the electric bass is the story of jazz musicians who were mocked for playing an amplified instrument, of touring musicians who made their living on the road, of hometown heroes who never had a hit, of virtuosic session players who redefined rhythm & blues, of rock stars who brought the sound of the instrument to millions of fans, of funk musicians who used it to invent a new approach to rhythm. Like the electric bass itself, these people stand as the foundation of modern popular music, yet their contributions remain undervalued.

Take, for example, the birth of "folk rock," widely celebrated as one of the most significant milestones in popular music history. The style itself can be traced to three hit singles from 1965, the Byrds' "Mr. Tambourine Man," Bob Dylan's "Like a Rolling Stone," and Simon & Garfunkel's "The Sounds of Silence." The electric bass is an essential component of all three recordings: without that slow bass slide in the intro to "Mr. Tambourine Man," the punchy ascending bass line that drives each verse in "Like a Rolling Stone," or the rhythm section's dramatic entrance in "The Sounds of Silence," each would sound and feel profoundly different. Yet even knowledgeable fans likely can't name the musicians who played those bass lines, because, in most tellings, the bass is simply left out of the story.

But revisiting folk rock's history from a bass-centric perspective would force us to recount a slightly different version of events: The Byrds went into the studio to record their rendition of Bob Dylan's "Mr. Tambourine Man" for Columbia Records on January 20, 1965. Unsure about the band's musical abilities, producer Terry Melcher hired Los Angeles session musicians, including electric bassist Larry Knechtel, to record the song's backing track. When the recording climbed to the top of the *Billboard* Hot 100 that summer, it became Columbia's first No. 1 hit single in over two years.[1] This sudden windfall made many in the company stop and take notice, especially Dylan's own producer, Tom Wilson. In June, just as "Tambourine Man" was peaking on the charts, Wilson and Dylan entered a New York recording studio to begin work on a new single, "Like a Rolling Stone." On the session, Wilson pushed Dylan to follow the Byrds' model and adopt a more rock-oriented sound, and like Melcher, he brought in professional session musicians to fill out the rhythm section, including Joe Macho on electric bass.[2] The following month, just as "Like a Rolling Stone" was being released, Wilson decided to repeat this experiment once more. Unbeknownst to Simon & Garfunkel, he hired another session rhythm section (this time featuring electric bassist Bob Bushnell) to overdub electric instruments onto "The Sounds of Silence," an acoustic folk single that had flopped the previous year. Wilson then took the overdubbed master tapes to Columbia engineer Don Meehan, who created a new mono mix. Meehan, an upright bassist who played at bar mitzvahs and local dances around the New York City area, specifically engineered the song so that the bass would be prominently heard, even on the small, tinny speakers found in most car radios at that time.[3] Working behind the scenes, each of these people played an important role in crafting the sound of folk rock, a sound they all agreed should prominently feature the electric bass.

Digging deeper, we would also find that before they came together in 1965, these same people had accumulated years of professional experience working across diverse sectors of the music industry. For example, prior to his work with the Byrds, Terry Melcher had been a pioneer of the California surf rock sound. Tom Wilson, the first Black staff producer at Columbia Records, had begun his career in the mid-fifties recording jazz LPs by Sun Ra and Cecil Taylor. Larry Knechtel had previously worked with both Duane Eddy and Phil Spector. Joe Macho had been part of the house band for Cameo-Parkway Records in Philadelphia, where he had played on hits by Chubby Checker and Bobby Rydell. And Bob Bushnell had gone from playing upright bass in Louis Jordan's Tympany Five to playing electric bass on pop hits such as the Angels' "My Boyfriend's Back" (1963) and the Drifters' "Under the Boardwalk" (1964). Looking at folk rock this way thus situates the music within a rich lineage, one that includes everything from bebop and postwar rhythm & blues, to surf rock and New York bar mitzvah bands.

This brief example encapsulates the benefits of studying popular music history from the perspective of the bass. First, by emphasizing the often-overlooked contributions of bassists and their collaborators, a bass-centric approach complicates the traditional depiction of artists as lone musical geniuses. Second, it gives us new insights into even the most well-worn stories. Third, it highlights how—despite apparent differences in genre, style, and context—popular music remains intricately connected through a complex network of performers, listeners, and music industry personnel. And lastly, it allows us to hear the music of the past with fresh ears, offering new reasons to go back and listen again.

The Bastard Instrument offers the first detailed account of the electric bass's early history. Focusing primarily on developments in the United States and United Kingdom, this book chronicles the instrument from its invention through its acceptance and evolution over the course of the sixties. In so doing, it demonstrates how the electric bass and the people who played it fundamentally altered the trajectory of popular music.

The Electric Bass's Role in Popular Music

The electric bass (Figure 1) was a paradoxical invention. Its creators intended it to solve the underlying disadvantages of the upright acoustic bass, most notably its fragility and limited volume; but they also intended for it to be played like a guitar, not a bass. It was part of a broader disruption within musical instrument manufacturing; yet sonically it was old-fashioned, designed to mimic the quick-decaying sound of an upright as closely as possible. At its inception, it was both radically new and, in many ways, intrinsically conservative, and no one was quite sure what to do with it. It was, in bassist Monk Montgomery's words, a "bastard instrument."

Montgomery's phrase (explored further in Chapter 2) is an apt and useful metaphor for thinking through the electric bass's early history. When it was first introduced, it was considered a strange, debased instrument—an unconventional hybrid of an upright bass and an electric guitar—and those who played it were initially looked down upon and dismissed by other musicians who considered it, at best, a novelty, and at worst, a desecration. Moreover, the instrument's murky ancestry had given it neither a distinct sonic identity nor an obvious musical home. What ultimately saved it from the ash heap of history was its volume. When played through an amplifier, the electric bass was *loud*. Even in its most modest incarnations, it gave an unprecedented audibility to the

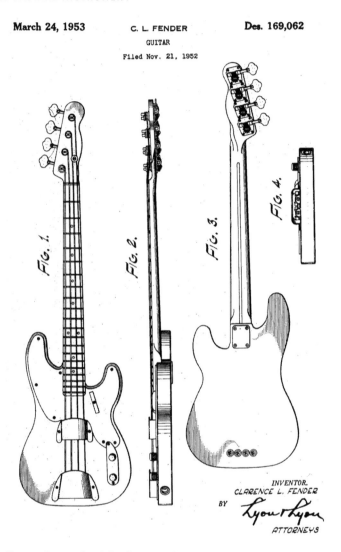

March 24, 1953   C. L. FENDER   Des. 169,062

GUITAR

Filed Nov. 21, 1952

INVENTOR.
CLARENCE L. FENDER

BY

ATTORNEYS

Figure 1. Patent sketch for the original Fender Precision Bass, 1952.
(Source: Google Patents.)

low end. The electric bass's slow but eventual adoption throughout the fifties and sixties came from the widespread appeal (and adaptability) of this concept.

Musically, electric basses operate similarly to their upright predecessors, acting as the primary bridge between the rhythm section and the front-line (or lead) instruments.[4] In most situations, electric bassists take on two simultaneous roles: their rhythm locks in with or accentuates a groove (usually in conjunction with a drummer), while the specific notes they play establish or clarify the music's harmony (which often acts as the musical bedrock on which lead lines are built).[5] In conventional Western musical analysis, the harmonic framework that the bass provides is the lens through which all the other musical elements are interpreted. The bass's role is therefore foundational—it sets up the "rules," so to speak, through which musicians, analysts, and listeners understand other sounds as fitting or not.

Writing in 1969, Lenny Kaye described the bass as "a negative instrument, recognized only when it's not present."[6] In other words, when listening to a song, we most often focus on the singer or the soloist or the beat and we don't think twice about the musical frame surrounding them, no matter how crucial that frame may be. As Sting once remarked, "It's easier for the bass player to lead the band than almost anyone else, because you can lead without seeming to. It's a very powerful yet discreet instrument. You can control the music because you can dictate what the chord is—I mean, it's not a chord until the bass player decides what the root is."[7] Such a description underscores the bass's importance, but it also highlights yet another paradox: the bass's function is essential, yet most listeners do not actively recognize what it is doing.

Writing about Musical Instruments

Arguing for the importance of studying musical instruments, Steve Waksman notes that rather than being "mere tools," instruments simultaneously stand as commodities, technologies, visual icons, and repositories of knowledge—all in addition to their pivotal role as "sound-producing devices, without which music could hardly be said to exist at all."[8] Musical instruments are therefore multifaceted objects that serve as complicated, and at times contested, sites of cultural meaning.[9] Moreover, as Waksman so eloquently demonstrates in his own work on the electric guitar, one of the most substantial advantages of instrument-centric studies is that they necessarily cut across multiple musical genres.[10] For example, modern accounts of popular music from the fifties and sixties tend to treat rock 'n' roll, country and western, rhythm & blues, and jazz as relatively separate phenomena. Although such accounts have been valuable in chronicling these genres' individual developments, by treating them as self-contained cultural spheres, they have also inadvertently reified the boundaries between them.[11] But, because the electric bass was never isolated to any one genre or style, a full account of its history requires an inherently expansive view of popular music. Following Waksman, *The Bastard Instrument* thus has a deliberately cross-genre focus, one that highlights popular music's many overlaps and connections.

While the study of musical instruments in popular culture remains a relatively niche scholarly pursuit, there is a far larger and more significant popular discourse on these instruments dating back decades. Critics, journalists, and fans have long been interested in histories of musical instruments, especially of models that were played by famous musicians. Yet this popular discourse too often idealizes its subject. This is especially true for the history of the electric guitar, which has been so enthusiastically documented and debated that its story has taken on mythological proportions. Consider the 2016 book *Play It Loud: An Epic History of the Style, Sound, and Revolution of the Electric Guitar*. Written by Brad Tolinski and Alan di Perna, two longtime contributors to *Guitar World* magazine, the book narrates popular music history through "twelve landmark guitars." Here is how they describe the instrument in their preface:

> [T]he electric guitar would represent much more than just musical innovation. It would directly and indirectly impact the entertainment industry, politics, art, the economy, and many other facets of our cultural life. The instrument's burgeoning popularity played a small but nonetheless significant role in advancing the cause of racial integration. It became a symbol of the counterculture sixties, rallying opposition to the Vietnam War, as its urgent clangor pushed forward the sexual revolution and progress toward gender equality.[12]

Although there is much to appreciate in *Play It Loud*, I believe this particular framing is problematic. To say that the electric guitar was in some ways responsible for racial integration and gender equality credits inanimate objects for those advances, rather than those who actually fought for them (not to mention that it potentially obscures the real and ongoing racial and gender struggles of musicians and listeners alike). More than that, though, this depiction inherently treats the instrument as a force for good. Tolinski and di Perna never reflect, for instance, on the guitars played by white supremacist hardcore bands or on the guitars played by musicians who use their fame to coerce sex from their underage fans. That is to say that, though instruments may have histories, their meanings (both good and bad) are always bound to their human contexts—they require *people* to play them, to build them, to listen to them, to look at them, and to dance along to the sounds that emanate from them.[13] Musical instruments are interactive. They enable and constrain certain uses, and in that way they shape and mediate musical experiences.[14] But they are not independent. On their own, they lack *intention*. Pretending otherwise only serves to marginalize the real people who have given them meaning.

Admittedly, prior histories of the electric guitar and electric bass have been influential in shaping this book, but by mythologizing instruments and the famous musicians who play them, this work has tended to promote a story about greatness while ignoring (or worse, actively suppressing) any details that might complicate that narrative. As a corrective, this book is an attempt to explain how and why electric bassists mattered, not by deifying them or their instruments but by firmly situating their contributions within each of their distinct historical and cultural contexts.

Methodology and Organization

The Bastard Instrument uses a framework that combines in-depth historical research, close listening, and cultural analysis. Drawing on materials housed at archives across the United States, its narrative privileges firsthand sources and accounts. Furthermore, it foregrounds the perspectives and voices of bassists as much as possible and therefore relies heavily on published interviews, oral histories, memoirs, and other surviving materials in which these musicians described their lives and careers. Lastly, this book is guided by my own background as an electric bassist. Years of actively listening to bass lines has trained me to hear their value, regardless of their complexity or style, and my time spent as a performer has given me insights into both the bass's musical functions and, more practically, how the bass lines discussed in this book were constructed and performed.[15]

This book is organized as a series of overlapping case studies, comprising both longer chapters and shorter interludes. Each full-length chapter (presented roughly in chronological order) explores a significant, well-documented moment in bass history and contextualizes it within the wider cultural backdrop of popular music. The interludes, by contrast, focus on developments for which far less information survives. Rather than omit these stories, or depict them as merely tangential, my goal is to show that they too were significant, even if today they only exist in fragments. Therefore, although they are shorter, the interludes are of no less importance—in fact, they are essential for understanding the subsequent chapters in the book. My hope is that, together, the chapters and interludes form a robust, nuanced portrait of the electric bass's first two decades.

The first of this book's three thematic sections outlines the instrument's various origin stories, focusing on the inventors who originally experimented with electric bass technology and the musicians who played their instruments. Interlude I details the initial attempts to create a viable electric bass in the era surrounding World War II. Chapter 1 then explores Leo Fender's invention of the Fender Precision Bass—the first commercially successful electric bass guitar—and spotlights some of the earliest musicians to play it, including now-forgotten bassists such as Joan Anderson, Shifty Henry, Joel Price, Sonny Jay, and Bob Manners. Interlude II considers Everett Hull's coinciding innovations in electric upright bass technology, which although ultimately unsuccessful, eventually led his company to create a celebrated line of bass amplifiers. These stories culminate in Chapter 2, which examines the career of trailblazing bassist Monk Montgomery and the stigma he faced as a jazz musician playing an electric instrument.

The second section explores how the electric bass first came to be established within multiple popular music cultures. Interlude III traces the instrument's early acceptance in the Texas-based genres of western swing, honky-tonk, and conjunto. Chapter 3 then outlines developments in mid-fifties rock 'n' roll, exploring how the differing requirements of live and studio performance led musicians such as Little Richard, Jerry Lee Lewis, Elvis Presley, and Buddy Holly to incorporate the electric bass into their touring bands. Interlude IV centers on the instrument's adoption by Black musicians associated with the Chicago electric blues scene. Chapter 4 demonstrates how, in the late fifties, teams of musicians and producers collaborated in the studio to finally create distinct sonic identities for the electric bass within the realms of rock 'n' roll, country, and easy listening. Continuing this story into the early sixties, Chapter 5 argues that the instrument was broadly popularized by a mass influx of teenage amateur musicians. Interlude V then examines the parallel history of the electric bass in Europe, showing how a group of German-speaking violin makers escaped ethnic cleansing in Czechoslovakia to establish Europe's first major electric bass manufacturers, which then supplied instruments to England's homegrown skiffle and rock 'n' roll acts.

The third and final section chronicles how the electric bass's role evolved and expanded alongside significant new developments in popular music. Chapter 6 demonstrates how session bassists such as Carol

Kaye, Joe Osborn, James Jamerson, Duck Dunn, Tommy Cogbill, Jerry Jemmott, and Chuck Rainey invented new, intricate bass styles that both dominated the music charts and greatly influenced later generations of bassists. Focusing on British bands, Chapter 7 then analyzes how Paul McCartney, Bill Wyman, and John Entwistle came to develop their own influential approaches to bass playing. Interlude VI focuses on James Brown's band, highlighting how electric bass playing developed within the context of early funk. Lastly, Chapter 8 shows how Jack Casady and Larry Graham ultimately solidified the electric bass's role as a lead instrument.

By the end of the sixties, the electric bass had become indispensable within nearly every genre of popular music. *The Bastard Instrument* is, first and foremost, about the many people who made that happen. At the same time, this book is also intended as an alternate account of popular music's most celebrated era, one that I hope will inspire further discussions about how we tell its history, and, most importantly, whom we include in that story.

PART I

Origin Stories

INTERLUDE I

The Forebears

The impetus for the electric bass was volume. By the end of the twenties, the upright bass had become the standard low-end instrument in American popular music, with dance orchestras, jazz bands, and country combos all utilizing its strong, clear tone to anchor their harmony and rhythm.[1] Yet within the context of a large ensemble, the upright was often difficult to hear, especially for those in the audience. Some bassists, such as Bill Johnson and Pops Foster, overcame this limitation by playing the instrument in a "slap" style, but that too had its drawbacks—most notably a lack of sustain.[2] Seeing a distinct need for a type of bass that could be audible underneath a full band, multiple musical instrument inventors simultaneously set out to develop new designs. An upright bass's potential volume, however, is directly proportional to the size of its wooden body, and since the average upright was already around six feet tall, creating an even larger instrument was simply not practical. Instead, these modern inventors turned to a new concept: amplification. Building on recent innovations in electrical technology, they recognized that if the bass's sound could be generated from an electrical signal, powered via vacuum tubes, and then projected out of an external speaker, its volume would no longer be contingent on the instrument's physical size. In fact, they could do away with the instrument's large, acoustic resonating chamber altogether.

This interlude chronicles the various attempts to create a viable electric bass in the thirties and early forties. Although none of these instruments achieved widespread commercial success, their stories point to a broader discourse, where, for a brief time, multiple amateur and professional instrument builders were simultaneously experimenting with electric bass technology. These initial experiments, in turn, would serve as important precursors to the better-known innovations of the following decade.

The Vivi-Tone V-I Bass Viol

The first electric bass can be traced back to famed luthier Lloyd Loar (1886–1943) and his business partner Lewis A. Williams (1878–1951), who established the Vivi-Tone Company in Kalamazoo, Michigan, in 1932.[3] Prior to forming Vivi-Tone, Loar and Williams had worked together at the Gibson Guitar and Mandolin Company, where they had developed what would become two of the company's most popular instruments— the F-5 mandolin and L-5 acoustic guitar. Unlike their former Gibson colleagues, Loar and Williams presciently believed that the future of musical instrument manufacturing lay in electrical amplification.[4] Vivi-Tone became their attempt to prove the concept, and over the course of the thirties, the company marketed a wide variety of electric instruments, including mandolins, guitars, violins, and pianos—as well as an electric upright bass, the Vivi-Tone Double Bass or Bass Viol—Style V-I.

The V-I featured an upright bass neck and fingerboard joined to a thin, solid, wooden frame; a bridge, pickup, and modified tailpiece were mounted at the lower portion of that frame, all of which sat atop a telescopic endpin (Figure 2). Designed for portability, the instrument featured collapsible side pieces that, when extended, placed the bassist in the customary playing position. It also featured a shorter-than-average scale length (between that of a standard upright and a cello). But the instrument's most revolutionary aspect was Vivi-Tone's signature electromagnetic pickup, designed by Loar, which converted the vibration of the instrument's bridge into an electrical signal.

Describing the instrument's sound and playability, the company's 1934 catalog proudly stated that the V-I provided "instant tonal assertion" and "infinitely pure string tone," and that its shorter scale and lighter gauge strings, "together with [its] extraordinary sensitivity, due to electrical energizing . . . bulk a total in convenience of playing that facilitates technic [*sic*] above any double bass invented."[5] The retail price for the V-I was listed as either $99 for the instrument by itself, $199 for both the instrument and a 6-watt amplifier, or $224 for both the instrument and a 30-watt amplifier.[6] Although payment plans were available for all three options, these were still quite expensive instruments. Today,

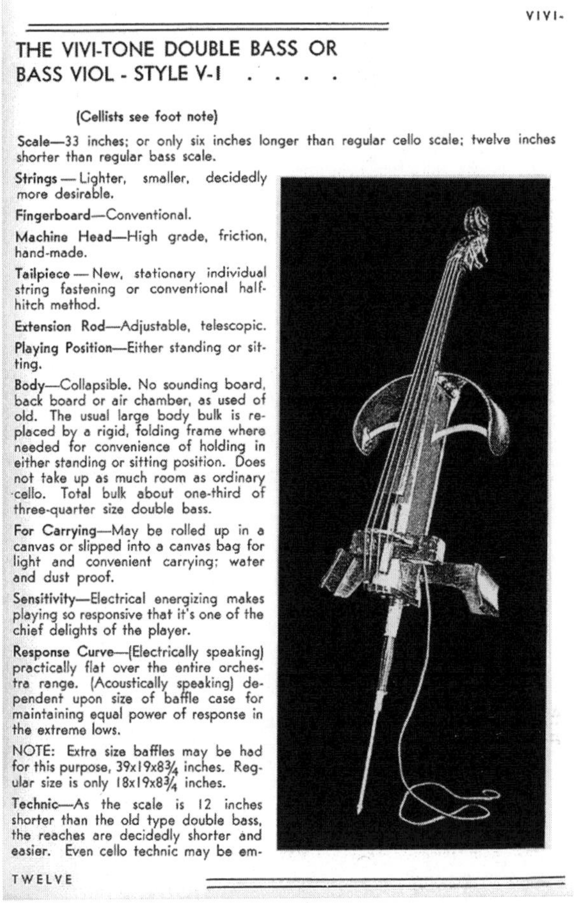

VIVI-

THE VIVI-TONE DOUBLE BASS OR
BASS VIOL - STYLE V-I . . . .

(Cellists see foot note)

Scale—33 inches; or only six inches longer than regular cello scale; twelve inches shorter than regular bass scale.

Strings—Lighter, smaller, decidedly more desirable.

Fingerboard—Conventional.

Machine Head—High grade, friction, hand-made.

Tailpiece—New, stationary individual string fastening or conventional half-hitch method.

Extension Rod—Adjustable, telescopic.

Playing Position—Either standing or sitting.

Body—Collapsible. No sounding board, back board or air chamber, as used of old. The usual large body bulk is replaced by a rigid, folding frame where needed for convenience of holding in either standing or sitting position. Does not take up as much room as ordinary cello. Total bulk about one-third of three-quarter size double bass.

For Carrying—May be rolled up in a canvas or slipped into a canvas bag for light and convenient carrying; water and dust proof.

Sensitivity—Electrical energizing makes playing so responsive that it's one of the chief delights of the player.

Response Curve—(Electrically speaking) practically flat over the entire orchestra range. (Acoustically speaking) dependent upon size of baffle case for maintaining equal power of response in the extreme lows.

NOTE: Extra size baffles may be had for this purpose, 39x19x8¾ inches. Regular size is only 18x19x8¾ inches.

Technic—As the scale is 12 inches shorter than the old type double bass, the reaches are decidedly shorter and easier. Even cello technic may be em-

TWELVE

Figure 2. Entry for the V-I Bass Viol in the 1934 Vivi-Tone catalog. (Image courtesy of Lynn Wheelwright.)

adjusted for inflation, the total cost for a V-I and 30-watt amplifier would be the equivalent of over $5,000.

Competing Innovations

By the late thirties, at least four other companies were also marketing their own versions of an electric bass. The best known of these first appeared in 1936, when the Southern California–based Electro String Instrument Corporation (also known as Rickenbacker) produced their Electro Bass Viol.[7] The instrument, an amplified upright designed by George Beauchamp (1899–1941), was quite similar to Loar's V-I bass, with a few key exceptions: it had the scale length of a full-size upright, it was constructed out of a cast aluminum frame, and—most importantly—it featured Beauchamp's unique electromagnetic pickups, which produced a much stronger electrical signal than Loar's design.

Despite the modern appearance of its metal frame, the Electro Bass Viol was designed to be recognizable and comfortable for upright bassists. Like the Vivi-Tone V-I, the instrument featured an ebony fingerboard, a conventional upright headstock and tuners, an adjustable endpin, and a hinged arm that extended to place the performer in the standard playing position.[8] It therefore offered bassists a sense of familiarity, while promising them the expanded dynamic potential of amplification. Overall, this design represented a substantial step forward in electric bass technology, but in practice it suffered from two fundamental flaws. First, at the time there were no commercially available metal bass strings, a crucial component that was required for the magnetic pickup to properly function. (The company eventually overcame this problem by wrapping the bottoms of the instrument's gut strings in a thin layer of steel, providing just enough metal to activate the pickup.) Second, the instrument's accompanying amplifier was poorly designed.[9] At the time, amplification technology was still in its infancy, and Electro String took a deliberately economical approach, using the same basic amplifier design interchangeably for all their instruments. Thus, while the Bass Viol's amp featured a larger, 12-inch speaker than their standard 8-inch amps, its internal circuitry was not expressly tailored to the lower frequencies produced by an electric bass and was therefore unable to produce a full bass sound. The company released a sleeker, redesigned version of the instrument in 1938, but these problems persisted.[10]

Soon after, other manufacturers brought similar instruments to market. By 1939, Chicago's Regal Musical Instrument Company had produced their Electrified Double Bass and Boston's Vega had released their Electric Bass Viol and Amplifier.[11] Regal's advertising emphasized their instrument's portability and versatility, while Vega's specifically touted the capabilities of their supposedly superior amplifier: "The 18-watt amplifier used with this Bass is supplied with special rubber mounting to handle the heavy bass vibrations and is recommended for perfect response and clarity of tone."[12]

But not all early electric basses were uprights. The Audiovox Manufacturing Company out of Seattle took a fundamentally different approach when, around 1936, it released the #736 Electronic Bass Fiddle.[13] Designed by the company's owner, inventor and travelling musician Paul Tutmarc (1896–1972), the #736 was a compact, fretted, solid-body instrument, and the first electric bass designed to be played horizontally

Figure 3. Lorraine Tutmarc (left) playing an Audiovox #736 with the Tutmarc family band, ca. 1938. (Photo courtesy of Flower Pentecostal Heritage Center.)

like a guitar.[14] Tutmarc, a Hawaiian steel player, developed the bass (and his own pickup) while experimenting with early electric guitar technology, and he incorporated the instrument into his family's Hawaiian music band, where it was played by his wife, Lorraine Tutmarc (1906–1992).[15] The first bass guitarist was therefore likely a woman (Figure 3).[16] It is difficult to determine how many of these basses Audiovox actually produced, but at least three are known to survive. According to Peter Blecha, Tutmarc sold the #736 regionally in the Pacific Northwest, but he never implemented a national distribution strategy, and his innovations were quickly forgotten.[17] Ten years later, Paul's son, Bud Tutmarc, marketed a similar instrument under the Serenader brand name, but it too was unsuccessful.[18]

The electric bass has other potential origin stories as well. Take, for example, the following November 1939 *Down Beat* letter from Springfield, Massachusetts, bassist Jimmy Mack. Responding to a picture of an Electro String Bass Viol from a previous issue, Mack wrote,

> On page 1 [*sic*] of your Oct. 1 issue you have a picture of an electric bass and part of the caption reads, "It's the first electrically-operated bass in the northeast."
>
> This is not true, for I have been playing an electric bass for the

past three years with my own band. This bass of mine is not a commercial instrument, but one I built myself, including associated amplifier. I am a qualified radio and sound engineer as well as being a member of [AFM] Local 171, and I have used my instrument during this time on band jobs and many air shots over both local radio stations.[19]

Had Mack been paying close attention to that October 1 issue, he might have also seen the feature article on page 6 titled "'All-Electric' Bands Cause Big Rivalry in New York," which detailed the competition between bandleaders Tom Adrian Cracraft and Buddy Wagner.[20] As experimenters with an interest in emergent technologies, both Cracraft and Wagner had invented their own electric musical instruments, which they showcased in their respective "All-Electric" orchestras, Buddy Wagner's Electro Swing Band and the Cracraft Electronic Orchestra.[21] Both bands included electric basses.

Measuring the Extent of the Initial Electric Bass Boom

The initial electric bass boom was over by the early forties, hastened by new government restrictions tied to the escalating war effort. In 1942, the US government passed a series of Restrictive Measures specifically targeting musical instrument manufacturers.[22] These measures eventually mandated that new instruments contain less than 10 percent by weight of "critical materials," which included iron, steel, copper, aluminum, and nickel. Sarah Deters Richardson convincingly argues that these restrictions fundamentally transformed the musical instrument industry: production of band instruments was sharply curtailed, piano production ceased entirely, and guitar manufacturers were forced to design new instruments that used as little metal as possible.[23] Additionally, with skilled manufacturing labor suddenly in high demand, most American factories were converted to war-related production. Rickenbacker, for instance, halted all instrument production by June 1942 and repurposed its pickup-winding machinery to instead wind armatures for navigational equipment.[24] During this era, manufacturing electric basses—especially upright models constructed out of large metal frames—was simply no longer possible.

Looking back, it is difficult to judge how prevalent these early electric basses were, although their use was certainly not widespread. There were, however, at least a few notable examples of musicians playing these instruments. For example, when Lionel Hampton parted ways with Benny Goodman to form his own big band, he attempted to set his group apart by consciously embracing the novelty of amplified instruments. A *Metronome* headline from November 1940 boldly proclaimed that "Hampton Now Has Electric Band," and a *Down Beat* feature from the same month specified the instrumentation: "Three reeds doubling on electric violins, Irving Ashby on electric guitar, Vernon Alley on electric bass, which resembles somewhat the mellowness of a bowed bass, and of course Lionel on his electric vibes are to be the nucleus for his new campaign."[25]

Other early adopters include Moses Allen, longtime member of the Jimmie Lunceford Orchestra, and Howard Rumsey, who played with Stan Kenton (Figure 4).[26] In 1941, Rickenbacker secured endorsement deals with Rumsey and Allen, with both bassists agreeing to play a second-generation Electro Bass Viol for one year. According to Rumsey, "It was not a fun instrument."[27] The amplifier, he explained, was especially plagued with difficulties:

> First of all, if we went east of New York, I had to rent a converter because it would only play on alternating current. It wouldn't work on direct current. One night we were playing at a theatre in Brooklyn. [Saxophonist and vocalist] Red Dorris was sitting next to my speaker when all of a sudden, some police calls came through the amplifier and shocked us all. We didn't know what was happening. We're in the middle of a gig and pick up a shortwave broadcast somewhere—what a joke![28]

Nonetheless, these problems did not deter Rumsey from fulfilling his endorsement deal, and he even used the instrument in the recording studio, playing his Electro Bass Viol on some of Kenton's early sessions. As Rumsey recalled,

> When I went into Decca over here in Hollywood with the original Kenton band, Jack Kapp was standing right there, and he saw me coming in with that electric bass, and he said, "Don't you know we've never recorded one of those things successfully?" It scared me so bad, and I said, "Well, this will be the first one." And I ducked under him and went in the studio. I recorded with it. I [also] did the original Kenton library for the McGregor Transcriptions with that.[29]

Figure 4. Howard Rumsey (far left) playing a redesigned Electro Bass Viol onstage with Stan Kenton, 1941. (Source: University of North Texas Music Library Digital Collections.)

As for Kenton, Rumsey explained, "He didn't like the sound of the instrument, but he put up with it. He had a sharp new band, and I was playing a sharp modern-looking bass."[30]

Outside of the musicians discussed in this interlude, few traces remain of anyone actually playing these early electric basses, and in the era before World War II curtailed musical instrument production, none of these instruments appear to have had substantial sales. Had it not been for a renewed interest in electric bass technology in the postwar years, these instruments would likely be remembered as historical curiosities—if they were remembered at all.[31] In hindsight, however, they stand as the forebears to an idea that was just about to come to fruition.

ONE | The Modern Instrument

Leo Fender and the Early Years of the Fender Precision Bass

The man who invented the modern electric bass did not know how to play it. Nor could he play any of the other iconic instruments that bore his name. Instead, Clarence "Leo" Fender (1909–1991) was an inventor and electrical engineer with an abiding interest in technology and experimentation. A constant tinkerer, he placed his faith in the power of trial and error and wasn't afraid to buck conventional wisdom, especially when he thought he had a better idea. What separated him from other postwar electronics hobbyists, however, was his ability to combine his technological fascinations with an entrepreneurial vision—one that would lead him to found one of the most influential guitar manufacturing companies of all time.

Fender's route to the guitar was a circuitous one: in 1938, he founded his own radio repair business, which in effect became a one-stop shop for all electronics needs. Here, he repaired not only radios, but public address (PA) systems for live music, as well as instrument amplifiers. Before long he transitioned from repairing musical equipment to inventing his own, and through his interactions with local musicians, Fender came to believe that he could design a superior electric guitar. Notably, he approached this first and foremost as a technological and manufacturing challenge, attempting to create an instrument that would be reliable but also easy to mass-produce. Working with his partner George Fullerton, Fender spent months toiling away in a sweltering warehouse in Fullerton, California, building and rebuilding his prototype, adjusting and fine-tuning until he felt it was finally ready for wider production.

The result was the single-pickup, solid-body Fender Esquire, which his company officially released in 1950. Even then he continued to redesign the instrument, eventually producing an improved two-pickup version that he called the Broadcaster. Yet, as would become a common theme in Fender's career, it turned out that he was a better engineer than businessman. Almost immediately after Fender began advertising the instrument, the Fred Gretsch Company sent a cease-and-desist letter, arguing that the name of Fender's guitar infringed on their trademarked "Broadkaster" line of drums. Eventually, Fender's business partner Don Randall suggested that they rename the guitar in honor of the most important contemporary trend in technology: the television. Thus, by late 1951, the Broadcaster had become the Telecaster.

The Telecaster was a disruptive force in guitar manufacturing. Steve Waksman claims that it "broke the rules of guitar design; it was distinctly plain in appearance, with no sumptuous curves or eye-catching finishes. Yet this lack of ornamentation also meant the guitar was easy to reproduce, and thus ready for distribution on a scale unheard of for guitars of comparable quality."[1] Although traditional manufacturers mocked the instrument for its inelegant solid slab body and its bolted-on hardware, musicians, especially in the genres of western swing and country, were drawn to its durability and its affordable price. At the same time that his solid-body guitar, in its various incarnations, was challenging the norms of musical instrument manufacturing, Fender was also devoting his time to a new project: the Fender Precision Bass.

This chapter examines the Precision Bass in its moment of newness, before it had become firmly established as the archetype of the modern electric bass.[2] Building on the work of Fender historian Richard R. Smith, I detail the onerous experimentation involved in the creation of both the instrument and the original Bassman amplifier, which together were intended to sonically imitate the sound of an upright. As I argue, although Fender was largely successful, his design also left the electric bass without a distinct sonic identity, and by failing to establish a primary demographic for the instrument, the first musicians to adopt it ultimately represented a diverse (if scattershot) cross section of American popular music, including Shifty Henry with rhythm & blues showmen the Treniers, Joel Price with Grand Ole Opry star Little Jimmy Dickens, Sonny Jay with jump blues saxophonist Louis Jordan, and Bob Manners with Liberace. Collectively, their stories present a snapshot of the modern electric bass in its infancy and foreshadow the practical advantages that would eventually make it a fixture in popular music.

Figure 5. Joan Anderson (second from right) and Patsy Cline (third from left) with Bill Peer and His Melody Boys and Girls. (Source: *Winchester Evening Star*, April 27, 1954.)

A Note on Lost Stories

Before I begin, it is worth noting that the rest of this chapter will be, at best, only a partial account. Although the instruments and their technical details survive, the history of the first-generation of Precision Basses exists only in fragments. For example, it is impossible to know exactly how many of these instruments the company manufactured. A rare sales figure from Leo Fender's records show that the company sold eighty-three Precision Basses in 1951 and was planning on building four hundred more by June 1952.[3] We might then presume that by the time he introduced the second-generation Precision Bass in 1954, there were likely less than fifteen hundred on the market—but we cannot know for certain. More importantly, aside from sales figures, we have very little information about the musicians who originally bought and played these instruments. For each of the bassists discussed in this chapter, there were hundreds of others whose names we simply do not know. The tragedy of this ignorance is more than the irritation of an inexact historical record; it lies in the stories that have been silenced along the way.

Take, for example, Joan Anderson, a woman from Winchester, Virginia. At the very same time that the other musicians discussed in this chapter were performing to audiences across the country, Anderson was playing a first-generation Fender Precision Bass as part of a local country band, Bill Peer and His Melody Boys and Girls. The group never put out a record and likely would have been entirely forgotten if not for the fact that they were one of the first bands to feature a young Patsy Cline (Figure 5). In a short interview from the nineties, Anderson compared her own career with Cline's:

> You know, it wasn't an easy thing to be a woman in country music back then. I was resented as a woman bass player, believe me. But I knew I could do the job, so I just went on and did it. Patsy was the same way, much more so. She had the guts to get what she wanted. She said exactly what she thought. . . . In a lot of ways, Patsy was way ahead of her time.[4]

In this brief passage, Anderson raises tantalizing questions that we simply aren't able to answer (what *was* it like to be a woman playing an electric bass in a country band in 1953?). This single account represents just one of the many rich and insightful stories that have likely been lost—stories that might have greatly enriched our conception of early electric bass history.[5] What follows is therefore an account of the early years of the Fender Precision Bass constructed from the remnants that have survived.

Reinventing the Electric Bass

Leo Fender did not create the Precision Bass in a vacuum. When he began working on his prototype in 1950, he was already aware of the Electro String Bass Viol, as well as large acoustic fretted bass instruments, such as the Gibson Mando-Bass.[6] He took more direct inspiration from the mariachi bands that he heard performing at local Mexican restaurants in Southern California: Listening to these bands, he noticed a loud bass line being supplied by what looked like a large, six-string acoustic guitar (in fact, a *guitarrón*).[7] Drawing on his encounters with these previous instruments, Fender set out to design his own version of an electric bass, one that combined the best aspects of each.

In a *Guitar Player* interview from 1978, Fender described the thought process that led him to create the Precision Bass:

> We needed to free the bass player from the big doghouse, the acoustic bass. That thing was usually confined to the back of the band, and the bass player couldn't get up to the mike to sing. And besides, bands were getting a little smaller . . . and sometimes guitar players would have an advantage if they could have an instrument with frets that would make doubling on bass easier for them. The doghouse was uncomfortable, too, and the player would have to hunch over right next to the peghead to hear whether or not it was in tune. . . . The old bass took up so much room, and it was difficult for the player to haul it all around.[8]

Rather than emphasize the Precision Bass's amplification and therefore its potential for increased volume, Fender appears to have been much more focused on the upright's various limitations. His recollection also highlights another key aspect of the instrument: following the example of the *guitarrón*, he conceived of it as a horizontal bass guitar, one designed specifically to be played by guitarists. For his plan to work, though, the instrument would need to play like a guitar while still *sounding* like an upright.

Fender and his team thus set out to build a fretted, solid-body electric bass guitar—in essence, an enlarged version of the Broadcaster. As Fender designer George Fullerton later recalled, "The challenge of designing an electric bass seemed beyond imagination. Since there was nothing available as far as parts go to produce this new instrument, we realized we would have to make everything from scratch."[9] Starting with nothing more than an idea, it took nearly a year of research and development to create a functional prototype. For example, one of the Precision Bass's most influential features was its now-standard scale length.[10] Tuned a full octave below a standard guitar, the Precision Bass required both thicker strings than a traditional guitar and a longer scale length; however, in order to be played horizontally and still manageably fit the arm span of an average musician, that scale length could not be as long as a standard upright. Fullerton recalled that they originally experimented with a 30-inch, 32-inch, and even 36-inch scale length, before finally settling on 34 inches.[11] While this process of trial and error was an inherent part of the Precision Bass's design, it also encapsulates Fender's peculiar autodidactic process, as he reportedly derived the length after looking through his secretary Elizabeth Nagel Hayzlett's UCLA physics textbook.[12] The Precision Bass's double-cutaway body shape (the first for any Fender instrument) similarly resulted from repeated experimentation to better balance the weight of the instrument's longer neck and heavier tuners.

When the prototype for the first-generation Precision Bass was complete, it was something of a Frankenstein's monster: it featured a flat-pole, single-coil electromagnetic pickup and a plain slab body with no contours; its tuning heads had been taken from an upright bass, cut down, and rebuilt to fit onto a guitar headstock; similar to the Electro Bass Viol, it was strung with gut strings to which a thin layer of steel wire had been glued (as still no commercial manufacturer made electric bass strings); its bridge piece had been modeled on the Broadcaster's design; and like the Broadcaster, the neck was bolted on by four screws. By the time it was brought to market, the company had retooled the design, incorporating custom Kluson tuning heads and flatwound V.C. Squier strings, and adding metal pickup and bridge covers (the latter of which housed a foam rubber mute). Concealing the hundreds of hours of work that had gone into its design, the instrument ultimately reflected the company's modernist aesthetic. It was straightforward, practical, and easily mass-produced. According to Richard R. Smith, it was dubbed the "Precision Bass" both because its "fretted neck offered precise intonation" and because it "paid homage to [Fender's] expensive machines that cut fretboards with the meticulous surgical accuracy of scalpels; it suggested a precise product made in a precise manner."[13]

For his instrument to be successful, however, Fender also had to overcome the problems that had plagued earlier electric bass amplifiers. As Smith explains:

> Leo knew that before an electric bass would be practical, it would have to have a good amplifier; the poor quality of amplifiers before World War II had thwarted Gibson, Rickenbacker, Vega, and Regal. Vega's bass amp, for example, developed a mere 18 watts of power. Although the company claimed the amp had "perfect response and clarity of tone," the output was pathetically inadequate for a professional. . . . Even in the 1930s a rumbling electric bass needed a heavy-duty speaker, a rugged cabinet without rattles, and loud volume.[14]

Figure 6. Ad introducing the Fender Precision Bass and Bassman Amplifier. (Source: *The Music Trades*, April 1952.)

Thus, by early 1952, Fender had produced the first generation of Bassman amplifiers, which the company's ads touted as having "true fidelity bass reproduction," "excellent volume characteristic," and "rugged construction" (Figure 6).[15] The original Bassman featured a "TV-front," a ported back, and a single 15-inch speaker that produced 26 watts of power; it also featured a chassis mounted to the bottom of the cabinet to prevent rattling.[16] At its release, the Precision Bass had a hefty retail price of around $200 with an additional $200 for a Bassman amplifier (a combined equivalent of more than $4,500 today). The company's press materials hailed the pair as a new and unrivaled innovation in bass technology: "This new instrument, when used with the Bassman amplifier, provides considerable [*sic*] more volume than a conventional string bass, and with a great deal less effort on the part of the player. Bass players will find that they are far less tired after a night of playing this instrument than with the older type."[17]

Although Fender's constant tinkering had played a key role in the Precision Bass's development, it also had its downsides—especially when it came to marketing the instrument. Despite officially introducing the Precision Bass in October 1951, the company was unable to produce a demonstration model in time for the July 1951 National Association of Music Merchants (NAMM) trade show in Chicago. Likewise, the company was slow to deliver the first batch of Precision Basses and did not even begin advertising them until April 1952.

When the Precision Bass and Bassman finally debuted at the subsequent 1952 NAMM show in New York, they were met with immediate skepticism from the rest of the industry. As Fender salesman Charlie Hayes recalled the event, "Those who were not sure if Leo was crazy when he brought out the solid-body guitar were darn sure he was crazy now. . . . They were convinced that a person would have to be out of their mind to play that thing."[18] This reception not only highlights how bizarre the Precision Bass seemed within the context of early fifties guitar manufacturing, but also how quickly the idea of an electric bass guitar would spread. Even though they may have ridiculed Fender's concept and design, over the next few years other manufacturers still rushed to create their own versions of the instrument. They may have thought he was crazy, but that didn't mean they were going to let him have the market to himself.

Fender's missed deadlines, haphazard marketing efforts, and bungled rollouts were more than just bad business. They also meant that when the company was finally ready to distribute the Precision Bass nationally, it had yet to secure any musician endorsements—a key aspect in the marketing of musical instruments. In addition to the simple appeal of celebrity, such endorsements serve an important discursive function: they prepare retailers and buyers to associate specific instruments with specific musical contexts. The problem for the Precision Bass was that no one at Fender seemed to have a clear conception of what kinds of musicians would actually be inclined to play an electric bass, let alone what specific types of music it would be best suited for. Operating at the very last minute, Fender and his sales associates decided to take a catchall approach and attempted to drum up support for the instrument simply by visiting nightclubs in New York and Los Angeles to show it off to any and all interested parties. Ironically, this decision not to target a specific musical demographic proved to be a key element of the Precision Bass's early success, as it allowed musicians from different genres to see the instrument as adaptable to their own creative needs.

Shifty Henry and the Treniers

Don Randall recalls giving one of the first Precision Basses to John Willie "Shifty" Henry (1921–1958).[19] Far from a household name, Henry was a jazz bassist, songwriter, and arranger best known at the time for his association with Billy Eckstine. By some accounts, Leo Fender personally selected him to receive the instrument—which is perhaps plausible given Henry's connection to Los Angeles's Central Avenue jazz scene. What was more likely was that Henry was simply the first musician willing to try this strange new invention. Either way, Fender had secured their first official endorsee, and the company quickly ran promotional materials featuring the bassist and the instrument, proudly proclaiming: "SHIFTE HENRI says 'MY FENDER BASS IS THE MOST'" (Figure 7).[20]

Around the same time that he received his Precision Bass, Henry joined the Treniers, a lively rhythm & blues outfit fronted by twins Cliff and Claude Trenier.[21] Refashioning the stage antics they had honed with the Jimmie Lunceford Orchestra, the Treniers' dynamic performances made them one of the most in-demand live acts of the early fifties. (Today they are most often portrayed as a proto-rock 'n' roll act, but their musical style is better thought of as a hybrid of swing, postwar rhythm & blues, and mid-fifties rockabilly.) When Henry joined the band, the Treniers were already a fully-fledged nightclub act, complete with an infectious musical style and energetic choreography. The best surviving remnant of the group's stage show comes from their May 1954 performance of "Rockin' Is Our Bizness" on *The Colgate Comedy Hour*, hosted by Dean Martin and Jerry Lewis.[22] The group starts the song executing synchronized dance steps, before the frontmen literally jump into a break-dancing, "itchy bug" routine. While Henry doesn't participate in the bug dance, he does execute the rest of the group's synchronized choreography: he shuffles from side to side, he gyrates his hips, he tilts forward and back, and by the end he is jumping up and down in unison with his bandmates. All of this is only possible thanks to the portability of the Precision Bass strapped over his shoulder. Not burdened by the cumbersome heft or fragility of an upright, Henry is free to join in, adding a sense of communal excitement to the band's performance.

Although it is difficult to hear Henry's playing in the Martin and Lewis performance, the sound of his Precision Bass is clearly audible on

Figure 7. Fender promotional photo featuring Shifty Henry. (Source: Fender Sales and Radio Tel, ca. 1952.)

the group's recordings. The first Treniers session to feature Henry on electric bass took place on September 9, 1953. Of the two songs recorded that day, his bass is most noticeable on "Rock-a-Beatin' Boogie"—a rock-abilly number written by Bill Haley.[23] Throughout the song, Henry plays a walking bass line that anchors the band through each iteration of its twelve-bar blues form. However, unlike the sound of an upright on a comparable record (such as Haley's own recording of the song from 1955), Henry's Precision Bass and Bassman amplifier allow him to cut through the mix and establish himself on equal musical footing with the saxophone and vocalists. Unlike other early Precision Bass recordings from this era, the electric bass here sounds noticeably distinct from an upright. It is not only loud, it is powerful, giving the sense that it is driving the ensemble, propelling them forward. This is heard most clearly at one minute and fifteen seconds into the recording, when Henry punctuates a brief break in momentum via some downward slides. After a quiet bass fill that leads into the next chorus, the song explodes with energy. Even though the vocalist, drummer, and saxophonist are audible in this section, they all take a back seat to the bass. Henry then dominates the rest of the recording's sonic space, playing more and more elaborate bass fills until the song reaches its eventual conclusion.

Sadly, "Rock-a-Beatin'-Boogie" was not a hit. It was also Henry's last recording with the Treniers. In the end, while his time with the group may have been short-lived, Henry's work with the Treniers nevertheless made him perhaps the first bassist to exploit the practical and musical advantages of a Fender Precision Bass and Bassman amplifier, and his performance on "Rock-a-Beatin'-Boogie" stands as a rare early glimpse into the latent potential of Fender's invention.

Joel Price and Little Jimmy Dickens

Leo Fender loved country-and-western music, and he had hoped that these musicians might adopt the Precision Bass, as many had adopted his solid-body guitars and lap steels.[24] However, the instrument's horizontal design made it less idiomatic for the percussive slap style then prevalent among country bassists, and most chose not to make the switch. One notable exception was bassist Joel Price (1910–2003).

Born in rural Georgia, Price began his professional career playing upright bass, singing, and doing comedy routines as part of Tommy Scott's traveling medicine show.[25] His turn in the national spotlight first came in early 1948, when he replaced bassist Howard Watts in Bill Monroe's Blue Grass Boys. As a sideman for Monroe, Price toured the country, played the Grand Ole Opry stage, and recorded around two dozen sides for Decca (including Monroe's original version of "Uncle Pen" and the blistering instrumental "Raw Hide"). Price played off and on with Monroe until mid-1951, when he left to officially join Little Jimmy Dickens and the Country Boys.

Price switched to a Fender Precision Bass while working as a sideman for Dickens. As he recalled,

The [upright] bass had to travel on the roof of the car. And when it rained or got damp, and then the sun came out, the gut strings would break because of the changes in the weather with the heat and humidity. You got to a date and all the strings would be broke. . . . When I heard about this [electric bass], I went straight out and bought the demonstration model Fender sent to Nashville. I paid $100 for it. . . . I showed a lot of people how to play the electric bass; how I played it or thought it should be played, anyway.[26]

Even though Fender had explicitly designed the Precision Bass for guitarists, most early electric bassists were actually upright players who adopted the instrument for practical reasons—because its portability made it easier to do the choreography, or in this case, because its smaller size and durability made it an easier instrument to travel with on the road.

Price immediately incorporated the instrument into his work with Dickens, becoming both the first musician to play electric bass on the Grand Ole Opry stage and the first to ever record with a Precision Bass. That particular session took place on the afternoon of September 19, 1952, at Nashville's Castle Studio under the direction of producer Don Law. Of the four songs recorded that day, Price's electric bass is best heard on "You Don't Have Love at All."[27] Throughout the song, Price maintains a standard country bass line, mostly alternating between the root and fifth of each chord, and while it is clearly audible, his bass is buried in the overall mix. Unlike the Treniers' later recording, here the band and producer chose to downplay any of the Precision Bass's unique timbral markers and instead treat it simply as if it were an upright. This makes some sense, given that there were no established procedures at the time for recording an electric bass (and, in general, the song as a whole is not particularly well recorded). Yet it also demonstrates an essential fact about first-generation Precision Basses: they were *meant* to sound like uprights. Equipped with flatwound strings and a foam rubber mute, Fender had explicitly designed the instrument to sonically mimic that dampened, quick-decaying sound.[28] His goal was not to create a fundamentally new instrument, but rather a substitution that could plausibly pass as the original.

"You Don't Have Love at All" is likely to disappoint modern listeners looking for a sign of bass history to come. Instead, it stands as an important reminder that early electric bassists existed in a world with substantially different aesthetic priorities—one where the ideal bass timbre was still inherently bound to the sound of an upright.

Sonny Jay and Louis Jordan

While Shifty Henry and Joel Price were enthusiastic about switching to the electric bass, others came to it begrudgingly. One such musician was bassist Thurber "Sonny" Jay (1917–1993), who was compelled to adopt the Precision Bass after he replaced Bob Bushnell in Louis Jordan's Tympany Five.[29] A pioneer of the jump blues style, Louis Jordan was one of the most successful acts of the forties—racking up forty-seven Top 10 hits for Decca Records on *Billboard*'s Race Records chart. Although he was still enjoying a lucrative career as a live performer, by the fifties, his time as a hitmaker had waned as newer and younger acts began to dominate the charts. Finding himself in a position of creeping irrelevance, Jordan began to look for ways to modernize his band without fundamentally changing his signature sound. Incorporating an electric bass was therefore an easy way for Jordan to embrace new developments in the music industry. This decision, however, came as news to Jay, who had joined the Tympany Five in March 1953. As he recalled:

> When we were somewhere in the East [Coast] an accident occurred to my string bass and the neck was broken. I had to borrow a bass from the guy in Woody Herman's band. . . . Louis realized this and suggested that I try one of the electric basses that were just coming in then, but I didn't go for the idea originally. When the tour ended Louis gave me an ultimatum—that I had to play electric bass from now on. He said he'd pay for it, but also said that I only had two weeks to learn it before we started touring again. He got an early model Fender [Precision Bass] direct from the factory somewhere near Santa Ana, California, and to be honest I wasn't at all pleased, but I sat at home in Fresno and taught myself how to play it. I did it the unorthodox way, by sticking the neck up slightly, which made it feel more natural for my left hand.[30]

Jay, like other upright bassists, quickly found out that Fender's instrument was not intuitively designed for his skill set. Playing it required an adjustment in his right- and left-hand technique, changes that Jay attempted to minimize by holding the instrument almost vertically.[31] But, with dedicated practice and a good (if coerced) incentive, he quickly overcame these obstacles.

Jay's first recording session with Jordan—and his first playing electric bass—was also one of Jordan's final sessions for Decca. Commencing on the morning of May 28, 1953, the session produced five sides, all in a classic jump blues style. From these, the sound of Jay's electric bass is most conspicuous on "House Party," an up-tempo twelve-bar blues with a stop-time feel.[32] Just as on Henry's and Price's recordings, Jay's amplified Precision Bass has volume, clarity, and depth. Yet here, within the context of Jordan's seven-piece combo, the instrument's sonic imitation of an upright bass is even more striking, as it is especially difficult to hear the instrument as a distinctly *electric* bass. Rather, in this larger texture, the timbre of Jay's bass is nearly indistinguishable from any of the upright bass lines found in Jordan's forties hits, such "Is You Is or Is You Ain't My Baby?" (1944) or "Choo Choo Ch'Boogie" (1946).

For all of Jordan's insistence that Jay play electric bass, it appears that the net effect was negligible, although this may be merely a historical fallacy. Popular music scholars have long treated recordings as the primary window into the sounds of the past, but the experience of listening to a record and seeing a band perform live were often quite different. On the bandstand, in a large hall playing to dancing bodies, the volume of Jay's Precision Bass and Bassman amplifier would likely have been heard (and felt) much more forcefully than it survives on "House Party." Jay himself was likely very familiar with the differences between these two musical contexts, as he spent the next three years alternately featuring on Jordan's recordings and playing in front of large crowds across the country.

Bob Manners and Liberace

As previously mentioned, Fender and his sales associates initially had no clear conception of what music would best suit the Precision Bass. Even after the instrument had been on the market for a few years, the company remained more focused on getting it in front of the public than on marketing it to a specific demographic. In this era, the best publicity they could hope for was an on-air television endorsement by a musical celebrity—or at least one of the members of their band. This is how the instrument eventually found its way into the hands of bassist Bob Manners (1922–2011).

Manners had gotten his start in the early forties as an upright bassist with the 4 Music Makers, a four-piece accordion-led jazz combo. In 1951, he joined the Harry James Orchestra, with whom he recorded a number of singles, including the hit "You'll Never Know" featuring vocalist Rosemary Clooney. By the end of 1952, he had become the bassist for Lee

Figure 8. Liberace (left) and Bob Manners (center) discuss the Fender Precision Bass. (Source: *The Liberace Show*, January 8, 1954.)

Liberace, accompanying him on tour, on recordings, and on his hit television show. Known for his engaging, family-friendly persona, Liberace was one of the best-selling musicians of the fifties, and his show was the most successful syndicated program on the airwaves, "appearing on 100 stations by October 1953 (more than any network program) and nearly 200 stations a year later."[33] From a publicity standpoint, Fender could do no better than *The Liberace Show*, and Don Randall leapt at the opportunity to have Manners and Liberace endorse the instrument. Out of this deal came a promotional ad campaign featuring both musicians with the caption "BOB MANNERS with the Liberace Orchestra prefers FENDER."[34] Even more important, it meant that the instrument would be a part of a dedicated segment on Liberace's TV show.

While Shifty Henry had played a Precision Bass on *The Colgate Comedy Hour* in May 1954, the instrument's television debut had actually come on the January 8, 1954, episode of *The Liberace Show*. As part of a skit titled "Musical Shopping Tour," Liberace explores a mock music store with a salesclerk, played by actress Joan O'Brien (Figure 8). They have the following exchange:

O'BRIEN: "We have some very unusual instruments too. This just
   came in today." [She picks up a Fender Precision Bass.]
LIBERACE: "Oh, what's that? A new kind of a guitar?"
O'BRIEN: "No. It's a new Fender electronic bass."
LIBERACE: "A bass? Bob!" [He calls over Bob Manners.]
MANNERS: "Yeah, Lee?"
LIBERACE: "Look at this crazy bass."
MANNERS: "Oh, isn't that beautiful?"
LIBERACE: "It's electronic." [He fiddles with the instrument's
   knobs.] "This must be the volume controls here."
MANNERS: "May I try it?"
O'BRIEN: "Certainly." [Manners plays a bass riff.]
LIBERACE: "Oh, that sounds good, doesn't it?"
MANNERS: "Doesn't it sound wonderful?"[35]

After looking at a few other instruments (including a banjo, clarinet,
vibraphone, and violin), Liberace and his band then break out into a
seemingly impromptu Dixieland jazz jam session. Although decidedly
idiosyncratic, even for its time, this one moment likely did more to pub-
licize the Precision Bass than any of the company's previous advertising
combined.[36] On the episode, the sound of Manners's Precision Bass is
not particularly distinct. But that wasn't the point. The instrument was
on *television*, and it was being endorsed by one of the biggest stars of
the day. Fender could now claim Liberace's established musical celebrity
when marketing its instrument, and, in turn, could explicitly associate it
with his wider embodiment of "white, middle-class family values."[37]

Conclusion

The practical and musical advantages that originally attracted musicians
to the Precision Bass were the same that would eventually lead to its
widespread popularity: it was loud, it was portable, it was durable, and it
was easy to transport. These features were all the result of Fender's trial-
and-error process to design the best instrument possible. Yet, once musicians began actually playing it, new problems became apparent. And so,
with input from the diverse cohort of early Precision Bass players, Fender
went back to the drawing board: He redesigned the instrument in 1954,
adding more comfortable, curved contours to the body, as well as a white
pickguard, steel bridge saddles, and an improved pickup that better balanced the volume between strings (Manners can be seen holding an

early one of these second-generation Precision Basses in Figure 8).[38] In 1957, Fender redesigned it again, changing the headstock and bridge and updating the pickup to the split-coil, double-rectangle humbucking design that is most associated with the instrument today. And in 1959, he redesigned the Precision Bass a third time, adding a rosewood fingerboard and a tortoiseshell pickguard. During this same period, he was also continually updating the Bassman amplifier: in 1953, he introduced the now-standard "wide-panel" front, and in 1955, he switched from a single 15-inch speaker design to one with four 10-inch speakers that could produce 40 watts of power. Each of these changes was the result of Fender's ongoing collaborations with bass players; working to address their changing needs, he never stopped improving on his designs.[39]

Fender could not have anticipated it at the time, but the Precision Bass would go on to become the standard by which all subsequent electric basses were judged. In fact, its influence would be so vast that, even into the sixties, all electric basses were generically known as "Fender basses," regardless of manufacturer. While it would take more than a decade for the instrument to supplant the upright bass in American popular music, the seeds of that upheaval had already been sown, thanks to now-forgotten bassists like Joan Anderson, Shifty Henry, Joel Price, Sonny Jay, and Bob Manners. Even if Fender could not play the electric bass, his designs had opened the door for a musical revolution.

Everett Hull and the Amplified Peg

The success of Leo Fender's Precision Bass was not a foregone conclusion. Although the instrument had significant practical advantages—most remarkably its effortless increase in volume—it still represented a fundamental redefinition of what constituted a "bass." Compared to an upright, it looked different, it required a different playing technique, and, at least in small ways, it sounded different. It was, essentially, a guitar, and its design was neither intuitive nor idiomatic for upright players, who nonetheless remained the electric bass's primary consumers in the early fifties. Had the trajectory of music history been ever so slightly different, today we might remember Everett Hull (1904–1981), rather than Leo Fender, as the inventor of the modern electric bass.

This interlude chronicles Hull's own innovations in electric bass technology. As a bassist and inventor, Hull developed an early pickup for upright basses, known as the "Amplified Peg" or "Ampeg." In the mid-forties, he formed his own company based around this product and helped develop a series of amplifiers to pair with it. While the Amplified Peg never found widespread success, it ultimately led Hull's company to produce a stand-alone line of Ampeg amplifiers, including the Portaflex B-15—which was widely considered the best bass amplifier of the early sixties.

Hull's Early Years

Born in rural Wisconsin, Charles Everitt Hull moved to Chicago in the mid-thirties, where he played upright bass in a series of small jazz combos.[1] It was here that he met another Wisconsin native, guitarist Les Paul, who was himself beginning to experiment with electric guitar technology. One night, Paul and Hull found themselves at Cubby's, a local musicians' bar, where they saw someone playing an Electro Bass Viol. Paul later recalled that he told Hull that night, "You ought to make an electrified bass."[2]

Although Paul left for New York in 1938, Hull remained in Chicago, where he formed his own three-piece band, Everett Hull and the Top Notchers, and continued to take on work as a freelance upright bassist. By the early forties, he had landed a lucrative gig performing with bandleader Lawrence Welk, who was in the midst of a ten-year residency at Chicago's Trianon Ballroom. Working with Welk, Hull came to realize that he needed a louder instrument, and after some prompting from his wife, Gertrude, he decided to accept Les Paul's challenge and develop his own electric bass. As he recalled,

> My wife used to say, "Those solos you do are just tremendous. I just think they're wonderful, but nobody hears them." You know, the bass is such a subdued instrument, the people don't know whether you're really doing anything or not. . . . So the wife says, "Being the inventor that you are . . . why don't you do something for the bass? Invent a pickup and an amplifier or something so that those solos will come out." So I went out and bought everything I could get ahold of to amplify the bass. Nothing worked. Finally, I went and bought myself a PA system, a regular PA system, and a microphone . . . on a stand and put it in front of the bass. That gave me the best sound that I'd had. I thought that was wonderful. But there was only one problem; [the microphone] was always in the way. . . . I was always hitting it with my bow. Finally . . . I got to thinking, "Wouldn't it be wonderful if there was a hole in the bottom of the bass big enough that I could set the bass right over the top of the microphone?" So, hey, wait a minute. There's a peg that the bass stands on. Why don't I turn that into a microphone stand? Just make a long peg and let it reach right up into the middle of the bass and put a microphone on the top of that peg, and that will be the answer. It wouldn't touch the bass in any way. It would be standing right in the middle of the bass, and I'd have the pure sound.[3]

After tweaking some of the technical aspects, Hull finalized his prototype for a microphone that could fit inside an upright bass. Once installed, the microphone signal was conducted via a cable that ran from the micro-

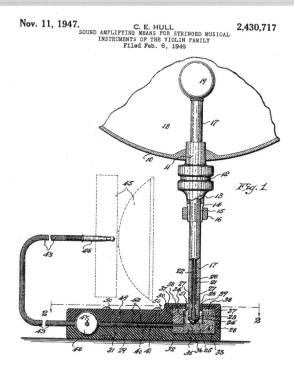

Nov. 11, 1947.   C. E. HULL   2,430,717
              SOUND AMPLIFYING MEANS FOR STRINGED MUSICAL
                   INSTRUMENTS OF THE VIOLIN FAMILY
                        Filed Feb. 6, 1946

Figure 9. Patent sketch
for the original Ampeg.
(Source: Google Patents.)

phone, through the bass's endpin, and out to a stand-alone amplifier
(Figure 9). It was Gertrude who christened this invention the "Ampeg."[4]
Hull filed a patent for the Ampeg on February 6, 1946—a full five and a
half years before Fender's Precision Bass was even in production.

With his new invention and an entrepreneurial vision, Hull moved to
Newark, New Jersey, to be closer to the New York City music scene. But,
as he later recalled, "At the time we started making these things, I was
virtually out of work. . . . I was playing in bands in New York two nights a
week and selling the invention on the other nights."[5] Through persever-
ance and his growing industry connections, the ever-affable Hull slowly
gathered grassroots support for the Ampeg among New York bassists.
He soon came to realize, however, that for his invention to be successful, he would need to pair it with its own, specially designed bass amplifier. To this end, in 1946, Hull partnered with electrical engineer Stanley
Michael, who helped him design the Michael-Hull Bassamp—the first
amplifier voiced specifically for bass frequencies. Featuring 18 watts of
power, the Bassamp was a two-channel tube amp with a single 12-inch
speaker. Although only a handful of these amplifiers survive, Michael

apparently solved the problems that had hindered the success of earlier bass amp designs by Electro String, Regal, and Vega. Evaluating the original Bassamp today, vintage amplifier expert Gregg Hopkins asserts that "It gives a strong first impression, with a remarkably focused, tight sound for such a device. . . . It doesn't have much in the way of volume compared to even modern practice amps, but it has a round bass tone and a swing vibe in spades. It was the first modern bass amplifier, a minor national treasure."[6] By the following year, Michael-Hull Electronic Labs had produced the slightly redesigned Model 770 Bassamp, which maintained the original's wattage but added a pearloid outer wrap, three input jacks, and a ported back. Together, the amp and Ampeg retailed for $245.

Nearly a decade after Les Paul had casually suggested to Hull that he should create an electric bass, Hull's company had a viable system for "electrifying" any standard upright bass and—better still—a quality amplifier that could actually reproduce a full bass sound. And unlike the electric uprights from earlier in the decade, the Ampeg was far more of a hit with musicians: a 1946 *Down Beat* ad listed eighteen jazz musicians in leading orchestras who were currently utilizing the Ampeg pickup and amplifier, including Eddie Safranski (who played with Stan Kenton), Chubby Jackson (who played with Woody Herman), Rolly Bundock (who played with Glenn Miller), and Johnny Frigo (who played with Jimmy Dorsey). Making its selling point as explicit as possible, the ad copy proudly alleged, "Only Ampeg Can Give You Controlled Volume Clarity *Without Harsh Distortion!*"[7]

So why is it, then, that Leo Fender receives all the credit? First and foremost, it is because historians and fans have long celebrated Fender as an electric guitar pioneer, giving him an outsized reputation that has largely overshadowed his contemporaries. It has also not helped Hull's legacy that he actively disdained the distorted sounds of rock 'n' roll and instead ensured that his company's amplifiers emphasized a pure, clean tone. Second, Michael-Hull Electronic Labs lacked the ability to mass-produce their amplifiers. It seems that the company only ever produced a small run of both the original Bassamp and the Model 770, and since Hull's primary consumers were professional upright bassists in the New York City music scene, he spent most of his time trying to drum up local support, rather than focusing on wider distribution. And though he did advertise Ampeg's products in national magazines, he primarily focused on niche publications where he thought he could reach professionals, such as music trade journals, Musicians' Union bulletins, and magazines like *Down Beat*. This process proved successful in securing endorsements among New York's musical elite, but it would be many years before the Ampeg name had broader recognition. Third, and perhaps most importantly, the Ampeg pickup could not live up to Hull's promise of "absolute reproduction."[8] As Peter Dowdall explains,

> Although the microphone placement afforded some degree of isolation from unwanted extraneous sound pickup, it was a less than ideal location for sonic clarity. Some components of the instruments' distinctive sound, like string slap and finger noise for instance, would have been undetectable from inside the body of the bass. Analogous to placing a microphone inside a singer's mouth, this style of amplification had one purpose—to make the bass louder—fidelity was not the primary objective.[9]

While the Ampeg was successful in increasing the bass's overall volume, these limitations ultimately prevented the pickup from reaching a wider audience. As studio guitarist Johnny Smith, an Ampeg endorsee, later stated, "I don't believe that the microphone on a peg inside the bass ever really paid off."[10]

By 1949, internal disputes led to the dissolution of Michael-Hull Electronic Labs, after which "Hull was left with the company, the Ampeg patent, $7,500 in liabilities, and $750 in working capital."[11] Undeterred, Hull restarted the business under a new name, the Ampeg Bassamp Company (eventually shortened simply to the Ampeg Company) and expanded it throughout the fifties by creating a line of dependable bass, guitar, and accordion amplifiers. In 1956, he hired bassist and electrical engineer Jess Oliver (1926–2011), who further solidified the company's reputation in the field of amplification.

One of Oliver's most successful designs was the Ampeg Portaflex B-15. Released in multiple incarnations, the B-15 set the standard for bass amplification throughout the sixties: it delivered a robust bass tone that could be played loudly without distorting. Retailing for $355, the amp originally featured 25 watts of power, a single, rugged 15-inch speaker, and a "flip-top" design in which the head of the amplifier could be neatly stored away inside the cabinet when not in use (Figure 10). Its big sound and reliability made it a particular favorite for session bassists, and B-15s quickly became a mainstay within recording studios across the country.

By 1963, nearly half of all Ampeg amplifiers sales would come from the Portaflex B-15 line.[12] This success is telling: while the redesigned

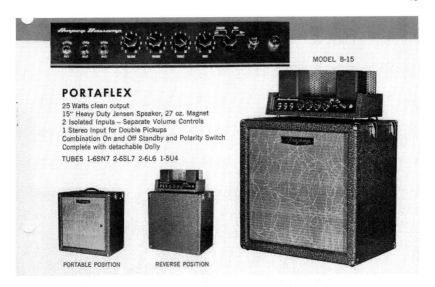

MODEL B-15

PORTAFLEX

25 Watts clean output
15" Heavy Duty Jensen Speaker, 27 oz. Magnet
2 Isolated Inputs — Separate Volume Controls
1 Stereo Input for Double Pickups
Combination On and Off Standby and Polarity Switch
Complete with detachable Dolly

TUBES 1-6SN7 2-6SL7 2-6L6 1-5U4

PORTABLE POSITION   REVERSE POSITION

Figure 10. Ad for the Ampeg Portaflex B-15, demonstrating its "flip top" design. (Source: 1960 Ampeg catalog.)

Fender Bassman eventually served as the inspiration for the Marshall amplifiers that would dominate rock electric guitar playing in the 1970s, they are not particularly remembered as great *bass* amps. This is because, unlike an Ampeg B-15, a 1955 Fender Bassman has far less headroom, meaning that before it is cranked up even halfway, its sound begins to distort. Unlike electric guitarists, who often prize this sort of amplifier-based distortion, early electric bassists had far different aesthetic priorities. Following the sonic template established by the upright, their ideal bass sound was a rich, full, *clean* tone. In this particular contest, Ampeg amplifiers were the clear winners.

History may forever remember Leo Fender as the man responsible for "inventing" the electric bass. Yet Hull also deserves recognition for his innovations. With the Ampeg pickup, he was the first to create a viable approach to amplifying an acoustic upright bass, and while it may have been less successful than he had hoped, those early designs set his company on a path that ultimately made Ampeg amplifiers the gold standard for bass amplification.

TWO | THE NOVELTY INSTRUMENT

Monk Montgomery's Jazz Innovations

"Do you happen to be a bass player, or sympathize with anyone who is? Have you ever lugged your instrument from the bus, up five flights of stairs, or across a crowded street on a hot summer day? Have you ever had to submit to those corny gags about the near-sighted landlady who says you can't take that girl to your room?"[1] So asked jazz critic Leonard Feather in the July 30, 1952, issue of *Down Beat.* For anyone who answered in the affirmative, he presented a new, "sensational instrumental innovation" in jazz bass playing: the Fender Precision Bass. Describing its use in the hands of Lionel Hampton's bassist Roy Johnson, Feather wrote that he was "duly impressed by the deep, booming quality, the ability to make astonishing glissandi, and the way the bass, its volume turned up a little above normal, cut through the whole bottom of the band with surging undertow."[2] Feather envisioned a bright future for this new instrument as a smaller and more powerful replacement for the traditional upright; others would not be nearly as sympathetic.

Although the electric bass appeared in multiple genres in the early fifties, its most prominent, high-profile supporters were two jazz musicians, Lionel Hampton and his bassist Monk Montgomery (older brother of famed guitarist Wes Montgomery). It was through their efforts that the electric bass had its first taste of consistent mainstream exposure. At the same time, this increased visibility led to a backlash from conservative jazz critics and musicians who were outspokenly opposed to the instrument. These detractors stigmatized the electric bass, presenting it as a disreputable instrument that did not belong in jazz. Paradoxically, the instrument's marginal status functioned as a lucrative marketing opportunity for Montgomery, who was able to reap attention, performance opportunities, and financial reward from his perceived novelty. Drawing on commercial recordings, commentaries in contemporary liner notes and periodicals, and Montgomery's own recollections of the era, this chapter details how the electric bass guitar first found its way into jazz and the contested discourse that surrounded its arrival. As I argue, despite claims to the contrary, the electric bass fit comfortably within the sonic landscape of jazz in this era. Its negative reception, therefore, had far more to do with critics' preexisting biases than with the actual sound it produced.

Leo Fender and Lionel Hampton

The electric bass's introduction to jazz was simply a matter of chance. As discussed in Chapter 1, Fender and his associates visited nightclubs to show the Precision Bass directly to musicians. It was their hope that its volume and playability would impress the musicians enough that they would incorporate it into their live acts, which in turn would serve as a form of grassroots publicity for the instrument. According to Christian Fabian, bassist with the Lionel Hampton Big Band in the late nineties, Hampton met Leo Fender during one of these ad hoc nightclub visits, likely in late 1951:

> [Hampton] told me that he was at a jam session with his bassist, Roy Johnson, where they met "the guy who invented that thing," meaning Leo Fender. Roy went up on the bandstand and tried it. Lionel said that *people booed him*, because he was a jazz bassist playing this electric bass. But Lionel really liked the sound, and Leo Fender told him he could keep the bass. Right after that, they took it on a tour of the South. Lionel said that everywhere they played, it got a lot of attention. People would come up afterwards and ask about it. Leo Fender had given Lionel his phone number, and he gave it to the people who were asking about the bass. He said that after a month, Fender must have had 100 orders for the bass.[3]

Even from its earliest appearance in Hampton's band, the Precision Bass was met with scorn and derision. Perhaps this reaction should not be surprising; as Paul Théberge reminds us, "[C]onflicts in musical aesthetics and values have accompanied virtually every development in music technology."[4] Yet, in a group that already included an electric guitarist and a vibraphone player—two amplified instruments already maligned by jazz purists—it was this *electric bass* that specifically elicited boos from the audience.[5] What, then, was so objectionable? The answer likely lies in the Precision Bass's volume (its "deep, booming quality") and, more importantly, its appearance. Rather than the large, wooden acoustic signifier the audience had come to expect, they were suddenly presented with a new, modern-looking electric contraption. Perhaps it was simply that the electric bass was new and different from what audiences were accustomed to. Either way, the stigma surrounding the instrument did not faze Hampton. After his chance encounter with Leo Fender, he immediately incorporated the Precision Bass into his band and the instrument continued to elicit commentary wherever he went (including inspiring Leonard Feather's aforementioned *Down Beat* article). And, unlike Shifty Henry, Fender's other Precision Bass endorsee in this era, Hampton was a bona fide celebrity.

The partnership between Fender and Hampton was mutually beneficial: in exchange for free equipment and maintenance, Fender was able to use Hampton's image in its marketing campaigns, thereby helping the company shed its prevailing association with country-and-western music. As Smith notes, "Virtually no jazz or pop musicians appeared in Fender advertising before the Fender bass. With Lionel Hampton's endorsement, especially, Fender took a major step towards recognition by the national market."[6] But Hampton was not just the first jazz musician to be featured in the company's advertising campaigns, he was also the first African American. Although African American musicians such as Pee Wee Crayton and Oscar Moore had visited Leo Fender's shop and given the inventor feedback on his prototypes, none before Hampton had appeared in national marketing campaigns. According to *The Golden Age of Fender,*

> African American jazz players, who favored the new [Precision Bass], did a lot to help shake Fender's staunchly cowboy image projected by the Telecaster and their range of steel guitars. Don Randall wasted no time in including their pictures in sales literature of the day and these were among the first racially oriented campaigns launched by any instrument manufacturer to promote guitars.[7]

In addition to the complimentary equipment and the attention garnered by the instrument's novelty value, Hampton also benefited from the Precision Bass's ability to produce a sound loud enough to be audible underneath his twenty-piece band. According to a later Hampton bassist,

Hamp liked [the sound of the Precision Bass] because he could hear the bass. Really hear the bass. . . . When there was an upright bass in a band . . . you didn't really hear it as much as you felt it. . . . Hamp used to come back to the [bass] amp. . . . He would come to the amp and turn it up. . . . He'd clap his way over to the amp and turn it up because he wanted more bass. . . . He liked that sound.[8]

Musically, Hampton's band straddled the line between swing, rhythm & blues, and early rock 'n' roll. But his band is perhaps better understood in terms of function, rather than genre. As saxophonist Jerome Richardson recalled,

[Hampton would] criss-cross America playing barns with sawdust on the floor; concert halls, clubs, jook joints—whatever it was—and he'd kill 'em. He'd pound that backbeat on two and four and I don't give a shit who you were, he rocked your ass until you got up on that floor. . . . He'd hit it till he saw pimps standing on oil drums dancing, people flipping each other doing the jitterbug, and every single person hollering, all that kind of stuff. Hamp was wild. He wanted that every night. . . . Hamp's single purpose was to entertain, and if you were in that band, that's what you had to do.[9]

Regardless of how it was classified, the Lionel Hampton Orchestra was first and foremost a dance band, and Hampton knew that in order to be effective his music required a strong, foundational bass. He had even experimented in the 1940s with different bass configurations to provide a more prominent low end—first by having Vernon Alley play an early electric upright (discussed in Interlude I) and then by having two upright bassists in the band. Fender's newer, louder electric bass had made these experiments obsolete, and Hampton made the electric bass a signature component of his live act, even after he replaced Roy Johnson with a new bassist out of Indianapolis, Monk Montgomery.

Monk Montgomery

The oldest of the Montgomery brothers, William Howard "Monk" Montgomery (1921–1982) was the last to become a professional musician. Having only taken up the upright bass in his late twenties, Montgomery didn't find professional work outside of Indianapolis until he was asked to join Hampton's West Coast tour in November 1952.[10] His recollection of this moment is worth quoting at length:

Well, what happened, the very first thing that happened, right there that night, Hamp walked up and handed me an electric bass. Just handed it to me. . . . [He] said, "Gates, this is the sound I want on the band, so . . ." So I said, "Hey, man . . . when I called you, you told me to bring my bass. You told me you wanted me to play the bass. I don't know nothing about electric bass. . . . I came here to play *my* bass; you hired me for it." So he said, well, there'd be no hard feelings if I didn't want to play it, he understood. He said, "Then I'll just give you two weeks' salary and your fare back home." No way. I just *left* home, right? . . . I couldn't go back home; I couldn't think of going back home. . . . I took it. And when I took it, I was very angry inside. I don't know when I've been that bitter inside. . . . I knew I had to stay with Hamp. That's what I came for. I knew that. . . . I knew I had to make a decision to play the instrument if I took it, or go home. . . . But I knew if I was gonna take the instrument and play it, I was gonna play it well, the best I could. There was no time for jiving around. . . . I had my upright bass, and, very naturally, my mind wasn't open to the electric bass. I had not received it in terms of this is what I want to play. It was just the opposite. But he wanted me, right then, to concentrate on playing electric bass. He didn't want the upright bass.[11]

Like Sonny Jay, Montgomery had been given an ultimatum: either learn the electric bass or go home. This stipulation, which had only been revealed *after* he had traveled halfway across the country, left the bassist, understandably, feeling frustrated, especially since he was being asked to play such a disreputable, gimmicky instrument. (He later stated that the first time he saw an electric bass, he "thought it was the worst thing that happened to music.")[12] Nevertheless, the gig represented a life-changing opportunity for the fledgling musician, and he begrudgingly obliged Hampton's request to switch instruments.

With only two weeks to practice and seemingly no other options, Montgomery quickly and zealously set upon mastering his Precision Bass. Although it did not take him long to change his attitude toward the instrument, like other upright players he struggled with the transition physically:

I had to get used to [the electric bass]. I had to get accustomed to . . . playing horizontal rather than up, you know, the whole strength of it, the whole everything was different. And it felt strange and foreign in my hands. So I spent my days . . . practicing. Practicing . . . I had to work with it mentally as well as physically. See, physically I had to make the transition; but mentally, in my mind, there was a quite . . . I had to make . . . a huge change in my mind. . . . Not only that, see, I was like a . . . I was playing a bastard instrument. I was a freak.[13]

Montgomery would repeat these last two metaphors in interviews throughout the fifties: that the electric bass was a "bastard instrument" and that by playing it, he was a "freak." The instrument's prevailing negative reputation, combined with his own reluctance to play it, had led Montgomery to see the electric bass as a stigmatized instrument, and from then on, he began making strategic decisions concerning how he would manage this stigma.[14] Most importantly, he decided to practice his Precision Bass day in and day out, until he felt that his timing and musicality were unimpeachable.

By the time Montgomery left with Hampton's band to tour Europe in the fall of 1953, he had become the public face of the Fender Precision Bass.[15] Don Randall recalled that

Monk [Montgomery] was the guy who really got us off the ground with our electric bass. . . . The Hampton band made a European tour and we got some glowing reports from Monk. He would write me and say boy, it's going down well. In fact he was getting all the notoriety that Hampton should have got, because everybody was overwhelmed by this guy playing an electric bass. We got clippings from all over Western Europe.[16]

Hampton's and Montgomery's endorsement of the Fender Precision Bass was such a lucrative marketing tool that in 1953 Fender's distributors sent their dealers a promotional photo that featured both musicians and prominently proclaimed "MONK MONTGOMERY with LIONEL HAMPTON says FENDER BASS IS BEST" (Figure 11).

Even if Randall's account is exaggerated, evidence does suggest that Montgomery and his Fender Precision were initially well received by European critics, most of whom were captivated by the instrument's novelty. For example, a *Melody Maker* article on Hampton's September 6, 1953, show in Oslo featured a picture of guitarist Billy Mackel standing next to Montgomery with a caption that read, "*Not two guitars.* The duettists are William Mackel on guitar with William Montgomery—on electric bass."[17] Likewise, the Swedish jazz magazine *Estrad* ran a full feature on Hampton's club dates in Sweden and included a prominent picture of

Figure 11. Fender promotional photo featuring both Hampton (center) and Montgomery (right). (Source: Fender Sales and Radio Tel, ca. 1953.)

Montgomery with his Precision Bass; in the article, critic Simon Brehm wrote,

> The accompaniment, of course, swung incredibly with the "electric" bassist Montgomery as the prime mover. Wonderful invention, by the way. When the orchestra performed just as strongly as any possessed Negro orchestra could play, bass tones could be clearly distinguished, which, it must be pointed out, were also selected with most excellent taste. The fellow certainly knew what he was doing.[18]

The French magazine *Jazz Hot* similarly praised Montgomery: "The rhythm section, truncated due to the absence of [pianist] George Wallington, still swung comfortably thanks to the presence of William Montgomery, a great bassist who happily played an electric bass (which was its first appearance in France)."[19] The only less than glowing assessment came from Swedish jazz critic Harry Nicolausson, who mentioned in his review of Hampton's September 14 concert that

One [musician] who was heard really well, not only on one occasion, but throughout the entire concert, was the bassist William Montgomery, who played the electric bass guitar instead of the regular double bass. Even though he played very nice bass runs with both bounce and drive, he became extremely enervating in the long run because his amplifier was dialed up so much that it permeated everything else. It was a rare experience, however, not to hear a single unclean bass note—the tone is given via his instrument, which has some ties to a regular guitar.[20]

Although the European press was generally charmed by this new invention, both it and Montgomery were occasionally met with public hostility, especially by upright bassists. This is most clearly demonstrated in a 1953 *Melody Maker* roundtable interview led by Ivor Mairants, a highly influential British trad jazz guitarist and author.[21] As he wrote, "Chubby Jackson made a big flap about the electric hold-it-in-your-arms bass a couple of years back. And now Lionel Hampton's bassist is towing one around. . . . What, then, are we missing? And are we, in fact, missing *anything*?" The answer to this question, which he informally posed to multiple British bassists, was a decided no: Jack Seymour stated, "It's all right if you are a guitarist who wants to double, then you can make it sound like anything *except* a bass. Frankly I don't see the point." Joe Muddel claimed, "*It looks nothing like a bass* and can only sound like an electric guitar strung an octave lower. . . . It can only be a weak note amplified. And the amplified note can have *none* of the characteristics of a bass." Johnny Hawksworth opined, "It can never produce a perfect sound; *all you get is an amplified plink-plonk.*" Mairants himself ended by claiming, "Colleagues who heard the new instrument in Sweden said it was *ridiculously loud*, a louder *noise* than a guitar, but with no depth." Obviously, these bassists were just as closed off to the thought of playing an electrified instrument as Montgomery had once been, and their reactions to the electric bass were (and to some extent still are) typical of jazz traditionalists. Their implication was that the electric bass violated some of jazz's sacrosanct aesthetic criteria, and they called into question its volume, its appearance, its requisite amplification, and its familial relationship to the guitar. Yet their rhetorical emphasis on jazz's supposedly acoustic, unamplified purity was a facade, and not a particularly good one at that: Mairaints himself was known to occasionally play electric guitar, and in the same article both Seymour and Hawksworth casually admit to using amplification.[22]

This contention that the electric bass, even in its earliest incarnations, sounded like an "amplified plink-plonk" that lacked a "true bass sound" seems to display an implicit bias against electric instruments—one that is perhaps predictable given the trad jazz style these musicians favored. Likewise, this bias appears, in part, to have stemmed from a distaste for the mass-production process that these instruments embodied. For example, the Kay K-162 Electronic Bass is indirectly referenced in the roundtable (it was the model that Chubby Jackson endorsed).[23] At the time, Kay was one of the world's leading musical instrument manufacturers and was known specifically for its budget instruments.[24] The K-162 was the company's attempt to compete with the Fender Precision Bass by offering an inexpensive alternative. Released in 1952—debuting at the same NAMM Show in New York where the Precision Bass was finally unveiled—the K-162 was priced at $150, a full $50 less than the Fender Bass, and featured a shorter 30.25-inch scale and a semihollow body. For those aghast at Fender's solid-body instruments with bolted-on hardware, Kay's shoddy construction materials were equally appalling and reinforced the belief that electric basses weren't to be taken seriously. This point was made explicitly, if erroneously, in Mairants's roundtable, which features a subheading claiming that electric basses have "plastic" necks, a deliberate exaggeration intended to depict them as toys rather than actual musical instruments. This hostility toward the electric bass, however, may also have betrayed an unspoken fear: as fretted instruments similar to electric guitars, electric basses were designed to make it easy for *guitarists* to double on bass, thereby potentially jeopardizing gigs for upright players. As the ads for the K-162 succinctly stated: "Now, any guitarist can learn to play bass almost overnight" (Figure 12).

When a *Melody Maker* reporter asked Montgomery to comment on this debate, the bassist came to the instrument's defense by describing his own experiences: "[Hampton] said I ought to get [an electric bass]. I didn't like the idea at all. But I got one. Boy was I glad! I had to start learning all over again, but there's nothing like it. . . . The whole thing about it is that you get a *better* tone."[25] Like Leonard Feather and Lionel Hampton, Montgomery also appreciated the bass's increased sonic presence: "Since George Wallington left the band I've found even further advantages. The electric [bass] seems to fill in a lot of the missing piano. It gives a kind of depth to the rhythm that's missing when the piano's not there."[26] He wasn't the only one to notice this depth. Drummer Alan Dawson later recalled, "Well, you know, [the electric bass] was really a godsend in Lionel's band because Lionel's band was a pretty heavy

Figure 12. Kay Electronic Bass ad. (Source: *Down Beat*, February 24, 1954.)

band, you know. And Monk [Montgomery] certainly anchored the band. I mean it hardly mattered who was playing drums heavy, you know. . . . I'll tell you I blessed him every day."[27]

Since more than sixty years have passed, it is unlikely that we will be able to fully resolve the debates concerning early electric basses' timbre and sound quality, though we do have a valuable tool with which to analyze the sound of the instrument: the 1953 recordings of Lionel

Hampton and His Paris All Stars, featuring Monk Montgomery on his first-generation Fender Precision Bass and Bassman amplifier.[28]

Lionel Hampton's Paris All Stars

On September 28, 1953, Lionel Hampton and his band went into the studio and cut ten tracks for the British-based Vogue label. Organized by French jazz impresario Hugues Panassié, the session was recorded live at the École Normale de Musique in Paris in front of an audience of critics and fans. Vogue eventually released the recordings as *Jazz Time Paris Vol. 4*, *Jazz Time Paris Vol. 5*, and *Jazz Time Paris Vol. 6*—which were so enthusiastically received in France that they were reportedly awarded the Grand Prix du Disque in 1954.[29]

In the album's liner notes, *New Musical Express* contributor Mike Butcher described the recording process: "As for Hamp and his colleagues—they just blew! Anything they liked, for as long as they wished. No repertoire restrictions or time limits were imposed by those supervising the date. Everything was as informal as a hipster's party after the glow has set in."[30] Ralph Berton, a *Melody Maker* reporter present at the session, further attested to the band's unrehearsed approach: "'How many sides are you cutting?' I asked [Hampton]. . . . Hamp bent his intense grin on me. 'Hell, man nobody knows,' he said in his rapid stammer. 'This-this-this here's a-a-a-a LP, man; we-we-we-we just goin' keep on cuttin' em like we feel it. Just whatever way it-it-it-it come out man, that's it!'"[31]

Despite the critics' earlier descriptions, Montgomery's electric bass does not sound like an "amplified plink-plonk." Instead, like the recordings by Joel Price and Sonny Jay from the same year, what is most striking about listening to these recordings today is how closely Montgomery's first-generation Precision Bass is able to imitate the sound of an upright, an imitation he further emphasizes by playing the instrument with his thumb; as he later described in an interview with *Guitar Player* magazine, "When I began playing the electric bass, my approach to the instrument was to play with my thumb, because technically I was after the downstroke. I played the electric as if it were an upright, and it came out in the music."[32] Listening to these recordings today actually highlights how successful early Precision Basses were at copying this sound and, in turn, how comfortably they fit within the larger sound world of fifties jazz.

Montgomery's Precision Bass is best represented on the session's four twelve-bar blues jams, most notably "Real Crazy."[33] Listening to the recording today, it is easy to understand why Hampton might have liked this sound: heard clearly at all times, the electric bass adds a strong foundation to the music. Its increased volume also allows it to drive the band, creating an energy that was likely captivating for both listening audiences and dancing bodies. At least that was how Panassié himself heard the recording, as he described in a detailed review in the December 1953 issue of the *Bulletin du Hot Club de France*:

> There is another musician who "responds" admirably to every Lionel brainwave: William Montgomery. I know of few discs where one can hear a bass part with as lively, as biting, overflowing swing. Make no mistake: William Montgomery is not a good bass player, he is a GREAT bass player. And on "Real Crazy" (meaning "really crazy" in the sense of "really great"), his bass part is "really crazy," especially during the long vibraphone solo, which obviously creates real musical jubilation in him. Rhythmically and harmonically, Montgomery vibrates with Lionel, becomes one with him; he sometimes performs a real counterpoint to the vibraphone part, and its rhythmic nuances are directly related to Lionel's. Listen to the breaks that Montgomery performs toward the end of several choruses; they are as charged with dynamite as the breaks of the great drummers. At the beginning of several choruses (for example, in the fifth, seventh, and ninth), there are, during the first four measures, veritable melodic "flights" in Montgomery's phrases. And his first four measures of Lionel's tenth chorus! That, that's the best! What is astonishing, among other things, is the ease with which he executes very moving phrases. . . . In any case, there are few discs where we hear a bass part swinging in the same way.[34]

Writing about the LP in general, Panassié also concluded,

> As for William Montgomery, his bass parts excite me more than I can say. His playing is admirably tranquil, calm in mobility, at once impetuous and easy; his notes are always suited to what the soloists improvise, and his swing is phenomenal. It is enchanting to follow his bass parts from one end of the interpretation to the other. Unlike the electric guitar, which is more difficult to record than the ordinary guitar, the electric bass renders well on record, judging by this recording session.[35]

Unrestrained by instrumental bias or notions of genre purity, Panassié simply liked the music. That his description stands in direct opposition to Mairants's roundtable only further confirms that the critics' harsh characterizations of the electric bass were influenced by their preexisting prejudice.

It is also important to note that Montgomery plays a standard walking bass line throughout "Real Crazy." This deliberate choice not to break with jazz convention can be read as a further attempt to sidestep the stigma surrounding the electric bass, as he actively attempts to succeed within an aesthetic value structure inherited from upright bass traditions.[36] This single recording therefore embodies the inherent tensions in how Montgomery chose to navigate this stigma: he plays a new instrument but chooses to play it in an old-fashioned way; he takes advantage of his instrument's increased volume but chooses to sound as much like an upright as possible. As his career continued, however, Montgomery became less concerned with following the old rules.

The Mastersounds

After he came back from Europe, Montgomery left Hampton's band and spent a few months in Los Angeles before eventually returning to Indianapolis. Back in his hometown, he formed the Montgomery-Johnson Quintet, featuring tenor saxophonist Alonzo "Pookie" Johnson and drummer Robert Johnson alongside his younger brothers, guitarist Wes Montgomery and vibraphonist Charles "Buddy" Montgomery. The quintet, however, was short-lived, and by late 1956 Monk Montgomery had formed the Mastersounds and set out for the Pacific Northwest. This new group—an integrated jazz combo in a vein similar to the Modern Jazz Quartet—featured Monk Montgomery on electric bass, Buddy Montgomery on vibes, Richard Crabtree on piano, and Benny Barth on drums. They found some early success in Seattle but didn't gain traction nationally until they began an unlimited engagement at the Jazz Showcase in San Francisco.

World Pacific Records released the Mastersounds' first album, *Jazz Showcase Introducing The Mastersounds*, in November 1957.[37] Unlike the frenetic energy of Hampton's larger ensemble, the Mastersounds' four-piece lineup and more subdued, straight-ahead style gave Montgomery more space to stretch out. Consequently, the timbre of his Fender Precision is far easier to distinguish from an upright than it had been on his recordings with Hampton. This is especially evident on their version of the

Figure 13. Cover of *Jazz Showcase Introducing The Mastersounds*. (Source: World Pacific Records, 1957.)

Rodgers & Hart standard "Lover." On the recording, Montgomery's new, second-generation Precision Bass maintains the same sonic presence it had on "Real Crazy" but now has noticeably greater sustain; the instrument also sounds far less booming and percussive, and Montgomery no longer sounds like he is trying as hard to mimic the muted, acoustic sound of an upright.

The album's visual material further highlights Montgomery's embrace of the electric bass. On the cover of the album (Figure 13), Montgomery is placed in the center of the frame, proudly displaying his second-generation Fender Precision Bass in a visual imitation of an upright (note, also, that none of the other musicians are pictured with their instruments). This deliberate use of Montgomery's electric bass as a signifier appears to be a fairly blatant attempt at capitalizing on the instrument's novelty—deliberately associating the Mastersounds with the electric bass and vice versa.

While their first album was moderately successful, their next releases—a series of jazz interpretations of Broadway musicals—were smashes.[38] Over the next three years, the Mastersounds released eight albums on the World Pacific Records label and were even named Best New Combo in the 1959 *Down Beat* Critics' Poll, beating out both Ray Charles's and Thelonious Monk's groups.[39] During his tenure with the Mastersounds, Montgomery continued to be a prominent supporter of the electric bass, and Fender reciprocated by running full-page ads for the group in *Down Beat*. In 1957, in support of their first album, Fender ran a two-page ad that prominently displayed Montgomery and his Fender Precision Bass alongside a caption that read, "With Monk Montgomery playing the versatile Fender Precision Bass. Listen especially to 'Spring is Here' . . . you'll quickly see why this remarkable instrument is rapidly becoming the favorite of bassmen playing with the nation's leading musical organizations."[40] The next year, following the release of their *King & I* album, Fender ran a similar ad featuring the covers of both Mastersounds albums, an oft-used sketch of Montgomery holding a Fender Bass, and a caption stating, "More and more fine bassists are discovering the remarkable playing qualities and versatility of the Fender Precision Bass. Hear it on record; try it at your leading music dealer."[41] By simultaneously promoting the Precision Bass and the Mastersounds' records, Fender was again deliberately associating their instrument with professional jazz musicians.

Negotiating the Stigma

In spite of jazz purists' repudiation of the electric bass, Montgomery was able to turn the stigma surrounding the instrument into a profitable gimmick. This is clear from the liner notes to the first Mastersounds album, in which Ralph Gleason writes,

> On hearing the Mastersounds in person you are at once struck by the *odd-looking* bass Monk plays. . . . "You can make it swing," Monk says. "*It won't replace the upright bass* . . . but it has its advantages. For one thing, I don't get tired playing it. It's so much less work, it's more accurate and you have more speed. I can't play a tempo that's too fast for it."[42]

This depiction of Montgomery's electric bass as "the odd-looking bass" points to the instrument's ongoing marginalization in jazz. His statement that the electric bass "won't replace the upright," however, is more complicated. Throughout his career, Montgomery used interviews to carefully construct a unique space for himself. His comments, confusingly, took on many forms, as he would adapt his narrative to suit each given moment. For instance, recall his response to critics in 1953, arguing that the electric bass actually produces "a *better* tone" than the upright. Now, four years later, when it is clear that the instrument is not likely to catch on in jazz, he positions the electric bass not as superior to the upright per se, but as a different kind of instrument altogether—one that won't replace the upright and therefore is really of no threat to upright bassists. Although he embraced his own novelty in the late fifties, this situation changed radically in the seventies as the electric bass became a major component of jazz fusion.[43] Following a brief return to playing upright in the mid-sixties, Montgomery tried to distance himself from his de facto position as the spokesperson for the electric bass. Here is how he reframed his history in January 1977:

> Lionel Hampton wanted that sound in his band in 1951 so I played it. The reaction all over the world was the same. It was a bastard instrument. . . . It attracted a lot of attention and that's probably what Lionel was after, you know, the commercial value, the novelty. I felt like a freak playing an instrument that wasn't an instrument. [But] The musicians in the band really dug it because it was a strong, solid sound.[44]

Not mentioning his own previous attempts to capitalize on the instrument's novelty, Montgomery attempts to strip away some of his own agency by claiming that it was really *the other musicians* who wanted him to play electric. And yet, just eight months later, his story changed again; this time, when asked why he originally switched to electric, Montgomery positioned this move as a break with "convention": "The electric bass was considered a bastard instrument. Conventional bass players despised it. It was new and a threat to what they knew. In fact, by being new, it *was* jazz."[45] All of these statements demonstrate Montgomery's various attempts to manage his uneasy position as an electric bassist in jazz. First, he argued that the electric bass was better than the upright, then that it was not a threat to the upright but rather a separate instrument entirely, then that it was a novelty that he was forced to play, and eventually, that, because it was progressive, the electric bass had actually been *more legitimate* than the upright the entire time. This self-positioning was always highly personal and designed to serve his short-term goals, yet these choices also demonstrate the inherent complexity of Montgomery's position: as a musician playing a stigmatized instrument, he was forced by position and circumstance to carve out a tenuous space for himself in jazz, a space that he then had to defend throughout his entire career.

Conclusion

Eight years after Leonard Feather's *Down Beat* article hailed the revolutionary potential of the Fender Precision Bass, his predictions had already proven incorrect. Monk Montgomery, he wrote in his 1960 *Encyclopedia of Jazz*, "is the only bassist with a major jazz combo to make use of the Fender electric bass."[46] Although this is a slight exaggeration, relatively few jazz musicians had adopted the electric bass, and by the end of the fifties, the instrument still had not yet established a firm foothold in the genre.[47]

But this was not the case in other genres, where the electric bass was slowly overtaking the upright as the favored low-end instrument. As a louder and more versatile instrument, not to mention one that was easier to pick up (both literally and figuratively), the electric bass soon found a home among a diverse cross section of popular musics. In jazz, by contrast, it would be another decade before the electric bass would take on anything resembling a substantive role.

Like many early electric bassists, Montgomery was caught in the middle of a push-and-pull between tradition and innovation, and because he was not willing to wholly abandon one or the other, he was denied the benefits of either—his decisions not to break with convention undercut his legacy as an innovator, and his conscious embracing of his own novelty ultimately barred him from the legitimacy he so desired.[48] Yet, while he never overcame the stigma of the electric bass, he was able to turn it into his greatest asset, finding a steady income and, eventually, personal worth from his position as the electric bass's first real pioneer.

PART II

The Road to Legitimacy

Deep in the Heart of Texas

Located outside of America's major music industry centers, the state of Texas has long been a hotbed of musical innovation. Partly, this is an effect of the diverse cultures that coalesce within the American Southwest. As Gary Hartman contends,

> No other region of the country has had quite the same variety and configuration of ethnic cultures coexisting in such proximity and interacting in the same ways that they have in the Southwest. This has resulted in a distinct cultural environment in which a broad array of ethnic genres drawn from Spanish, Mexican, African, Caribbean, English, Irish, German, Czech, French, Jewish, Polish, and other influences have been woven together to create a remarkably eclectic regional music unlike that found anywhere else.[1]

The benefits of such cultural mixings have never been equally shared. Nonetheless, they have contributed to numerous key developments in popular music history, including in the mid-fifties, when multiple Texas-based musicians began to adopt the electric bass.

This interlude focuses on the music and careers of three Texas bandleaders: Leon Gibbs, Ray Price, and Tony de la Rosa. Although they operated within distinct musical styles (western swing, honky-tonk, and conjunto, respectively), each was profoundly shaped by the diverse cultural climate of the American Southwest, and of Texas in particular. It is therefore likely not a coincidence that, within just a few short years, each of their bands became among the first in the nation to feature electric bass players. As I argue, the particularities of Texas's regional musical cultures and their bands' shared emphasis on accompanying dancing led all three bandleaders to buck prevailing trends and embrace the electric bass's increased volume and sonic presence. Taken together, their stories represent one of many initial phases in the instrument's burgeoning acceptance.

The Miller Brothers Band and Western Swing

In the thirties, Texas had been the birthplace of western swing, a style that, according to Bill C. Malone, "reflected the diverse mingling of musical cultures (Cajun, Tex-Mex, German, Bohemian, Black, cowboy, Anglo) that prevailed in the Southwest."[2] Combining blues, big-band jazz, and the country fiddle tradition, western swing established a new form of dance music, one whose unique instrumentation (twin fiddles, drum kit, horns, electric guitar, steel guitar, and upright bass) was designed to fill the large dance halls scattered across Texas, Oklahoma, and California. The western swing style was epitomized by the work of Bob Wills and His Texas Playboys, whose band had more than twenty Top 10 country hits and drew massive crowds throughout the forties. By the following decade, however, both Wills's and western swing's national reach appeared to be on the decline, and with little support from country radio stations and the new country music establishment in Nashville, western swing was quickly downsized back into a regional phenomenon.[3] Despite these setbacks, however, there was still money to be made in live performance, and western swing bands continued to fill dance halls across the Southwest.[4] Its continued local popularity also led younger musicians to adopt the style, including the Miller Brothers Band from Wichita Falls, Texas. Originally formed by three brothers, Leon, Nat, and Sam Gibbs ("Miller" was a pseudonym), the group developed a strong local reputation before the onset of World War II.[5] Returning home after the war, the brothers reformed the band, leased their own club in Wichita Falls, and found success by explicitly modeling themselves on the Texas Playboys.

The Miller Brothers' reputation as a dance band grew throughout the fifties, although both Nat and Sam had left the band by 1950. In 1952, the Miller Brothers Band was broadcasting a daily show on local, 5,000-watt KWFT and had opened their own dance hall, the M-B Corral, right off State Highway 240. Built on ten acres, the Corral could eventually hold up to a thousand paying patrons, with plenty of room for parking.

Figure 14. Promotional photo of the Miller Brothers featuring Pascal Williams (third from right) playing a second-generation Fender Precision Bass. (Source: Miller Brothers Band, ca. 1954.)

It soon became the place to be on a Saturday night in north Texas, acting both as the home base for the Miller Brothers and as an important hub for other touring bands as well.[6] Emboldened by their success on regional radio and at the Corral, the Miller Brothers went on the road, further expanding their reach. They even secured a recording contract with the California–based 4 Star Records.

With success also came changes to band's personnel, including the addition of a new bassist from Winters, Texas, named Pascal Williams. Little information survives about Williams's life and career, but multiple photos of the Miller Brothers Band from this era show him playing a second-generation Fender Precision Bass (Figure 14).[7] While the exact reasons why Williams decided to play electric bass are unknown, it is likely that, as with Joel Price and Little Jimmy Dickens, the Miller Brothers benefited from the instrument's easier transportability and its increased volume, which helped fill out the band's sound as they played in large dance halls.[8]

Thanks to their grueling touring schedule, the Miller Brothers Band reached national attention in the mid-fifties and received positive write-ups in music industry trade magazines. For instance, a 1955 *Cash Box* poll of disc jockeys listed the Miller Brothers as the fourth most promising "up and coming dance band," and the following year they placed second.[9] Similarly, in 1956, the overall *Cash Box* poll named them the fifth "best country band" in the nation, and by 1957, they had climbed to third, with a total of 19,233 votes.[10]

The Miller Brothers made their living on the road, playing strings of one-nighters across the country. Their fan base came to dance and gladly paid the price of admission, but they were ultimately less interested in buying their records, and so, of the fifty-two sides they recorded for 4 Star, none became a national hit.[11] To complicate matters further, the Miller Brothers Band, like the Texas Playboys, did not fit neatly into any of the music industry's established marketing categories. As Jean A. Boyd notes, "The Miller Brothers Band is still difficult to study and classify because it was so many different bands combined into one. The Miller Brothers was a southwestern swing band, a mainstream jazz band, a country band, and by the mid-1950s, a rock 'n' roll band."[12] As a live band, the Miller Brothers prided themselves on their stylistic eclecticism and their ability to meet the requests of any audience across the country. Yet if this adaptability helped them become a huge success in their own time, it has also inadvertently made it challenging to fully convey the Miller Brothers' place in American popular music. As early adopters of the electric bass, however, the Miller Brothers—and Pascal Williams specifically—should be remembered as musical innovators that brought the sound of the instrument to hundreds of people, night after night.

Ray Price's Texas Shuffle

By 1956, country music was in the midst of stylistic upheaval, as the explosive popularity of rock 'n' roll among American teenagers had pushed the sound of rockabilly onto the top of the country airwaves and music charts. According to Diane Pecknold, rockabilly's mainstream popularity represented "the ultimate triumph of the country industry," as Elvis Presley and his success were depicted as emanating primarily from within country music and helped foster new financial investments in Nashville as a recording center. At the same time, this success sat uneasily with conservative industry insiders—notably country DJs—who were uncomfortable with the music's often sexually charged lyrics, its incorporation of Black rhythm & blues styles, and its emphasis on youthful mass audiences.[13] At the very height of the rockabilly craze, however, a new style emerged that would have a much longer-lasting impact on the direction of country music: in May 1956, Ray Price released "Crazy Arms," a honky-tonk hit that spent eleven weeks at No. 1 on *Billboard*'s Country Best Sellers in Stores Chart and single-handedly ushered in the era of the Texas Shuffle.

Born near Perryville, Texas, Price grew up in the Dallas area. After serving in World War II, he returned home and decided to try to make it as a country singer, eventually adopting the honky-tonk musical style and vocal mannerisms of his hero, Hank Williams. In late 1951, Price met Williams in Nashville, and the two became close friends. Williams brought Price on tour with him, and on the occasions when Williams was too drunk to perform, Price would sometimes front Williams's band, singing Williams's songs to audiences that hopefully wouldn't know the difference. After Williams's untimely death on New Year's Day, 1953, Price formed his own band, the Cherokee Cowboys, and set out in search of his own musical style. In a conscious attempt to distance himself from his former mentor, Price drew on the music of his youth, combining the hard-driving rhythm of honky-tonk with the fiddle-forward sound of western swing.

Entering Nashville's Bradley Film & Recording Studio late on March 1, 1956, with his band and producer Don Law, Price decided to record a version of Ralph Mooney's "Crazy Arms," a song about a lonely man distraught over a lost love. Lyrically, the song trod on well-worn honky-tonk ground. But Price added an updated rhythmic feel that foregrounded a four-beat walking bass line (instead of the more common two-feel). As he later recalled, "The sound they had going at the time in country was a 2/4 sound and a double-stop fiddle. I added . . . a 4/4 bass and shuffle rhythm and the single-string fiddle. We came up with it right there on the session. I don't know why or where from; that's just what I wanted."[14] According to upright bassist Buddy Killen,

In those days they didn't like for a bass player to play 4/4. . . . They wanted it to be 2/4. . . . And I knew that song needed something, so I just started playing 4/4. Don Law got on the intercom. He said, "Buddy, stop playing 4/4. Play 2/4." I said okay, and when he started the tape I started playing 4/4 again. And boy, the record felt so good, he didn't realize I played 4/4.[15]

One reason that Law might not have noticed the change was that Price had added another musical component to emphasize this new rhythm. In likely the earliest example of what would come to be known as "tic-tac bass" style, Price added an additional *electric* bass line. "Back then it was hard to get the bass to pick up [on the microphones]," he remembered, "so I thought it might be a good idea to have an [upright] and electric bass double on the same note."[16] Sonically, this pairing fostered a compelling new bass sound, merging the traditional, recognizable timbre of the upright bass with the added clarity and presence of the electric.

When "Crazy Arms" was released in May 1956, it was an immediate commercial success. It also solidified Price's career, becoming his first in a string of hit singles. Drawing on his Texas roots in honky-tonk and western swing, and operating outside the norms of both mainstream country and prevailing rockabilly trends, Price established a new sound—what would come to be known as the "Texas Shuffle" or the "Ray Price Beat." Whereas rockabilly would prove to be a passing fad in country music, the Texas Shuffle has gone on to become, as Rich Kienzle notes, "a permanent part of country's musical lexicon."[17] And though it has largely gone unremarked by modern histories, "Crazy Arms" was also likely the first hit record to feature electric bass.

Tony de la Rosa and the Modernization of Conjunto

At the same time that western swing and honky-tonk bands were gaining traction with country music audiences, a different set of musicians were developing a distinct regional style along the Texas-Mexican border. Featuring an accordion soloist backed by a small combo, the style now known as *conjunto* (literally "group") first coalesced in the thirties with the music of accordionists such as Narciso Martínez and Santiago Jiménez Sr. Its sound was the result of previous generations of cultural mixing—combining elements of traditional Mexican music, such as the acoustic twelve-string *bajo sexto*, with the inexpensive accordions and dance forms, notably the polka and waltz, that German settlers had brought to northern Mexico in the late nineteenth century. In the postwar era, conjunto's growing popularity within the working-class segment of Texas's Tejano community was fostered by the rise of small independent labels, such as Ideal and Falcon Records. Ideal, formed by Armando Marroquín and Paco Betancourt in 1946, was a low-budget operation that recorded artists on a one-track tape machine in Marroquín's living room. Working within these limitations, however, the company filled a neglected niche in the popular music industry for Mexican American music, and, by 1950, it "had become the leading producer of Chicano music in the Southwest."[18]

In the fifties, the conjunto style would be radically upended by a young accordionist from south Texas named Tony de la Rosa. Inspired by Martínez, de la Rosa purchased his first accordion from a Sears catalog when he was fourteen years old.[19] According to Cathy Ragland, "As a second-generation Texas-Mexican, La Rosa had a style that was as much influenced by Martínez's early recordings as it was by other regional North American musical elements."[20] As he explained to Ragland:

> I would listen to the Spanish program and that's where I heard my first accordion, and it was Narciso Martínez. . . . And there's a lot of other people involved in it, but my strong point was country. . . . It was during the time of Bob Wills, Gene Autry, Roy Rogers, Roy Acuff, and Cajun, you know, Harry Choates, The Texas Top Hands, Adolph Hofner, quite a few of these people, they were traveling around the state and I saw them all. There's a whole bunch of 'em . . . Lefty Frizzell . . . all that western [swing] stuff. My music was a mixture of all that.[21]

Drawing on these eclectic influences, de la Rosa established his own conjunto in 1949, specializing in polkas. The following year, his group began recording for Ideal and, on the basis of their recordings and live performances, they soon became the most popular conjunto in all of Texas.[22]

As Manuel Peña notes, the band's popularity was the result of a number of key innovations.[23] First, following the model of bandleader Valerio Longoria, de la Rosa's group included a drummer. Second, de la Rosa also slowed the music down, creating more space for precise articulation on the accordion. Third, given his position on the US side of the Texas-Mexican border, de la Rosa was able to obtain the latest music technology, which eventually allowed him to fully amplify his band: he purchased a PA system to project his vocals and the sound of his accordion, his brother began to play an electric *bajo sexto*, and his bassist, Adan Pérez (Figure 15), switched from the *tololoche* to electric bass. The introduction of the electric bass freed the *bajo sexto* player from having to reinforce the bass line and instead let them concentrate on filling out the harmony, which in turn freed the accordionist to concentrate primar-

Figure 15. Adan Pérez (far right) playing a second-generation Precision Bass with Amadeo Flores's band. (Source: Conjunto Ideal de Amadeo Flores, *Una Miradita*, Ideal Records, 1954.)

ily on melody. Together, these changes in instrumentation and musical style transformed conjunto into a vehicle for virtuoso accordionists and established the formula "that would set the standard for all Texas-based [conjunto] ensembles to come."[24]

The motivation for these changes, however, was likely just as practical as it was aesthetic. Originally, conjuntos most often performed in small cantinas, but by the early fifties, they had become a regular feature in Texas's large public dance halls. In fact, one of the most important factors in the growing popularity of conjunto music within Tejano communities, according to Guadalupe San Miguel Jr., was the rise of conjunto "dance promoters, public dance halls, and paid admission dances," which demonstrated the newfound "probability of profit in the promotion of all forms of Tejano music, especially conjunto."[25] Of these, none was more famous than La Villita Dance Hall in Alice, Texas, which came to be known as the Grand Ole Opry of conjunto music.[26] The fifteen-thousand-square-foot venue was established in 1952 by Marroquín as a showcase for Ideal's recording artists, including de la Rosa, and with his new, louder instrumentation, de la Rosa's four-piece conjunto could now project across La Villita or any other large sized hall. As with other styles, the introduction of electric bass didn't fundamentally change the bass's role in the music. It simply made it louder. Yet this, in and of itself, provided the music a powerful foundation that reinforced the beat, making it especially easy to dance to.

Just as in western swing, the introduction of electric bass into conjunto was originally intended to better serve the needs of live performance, and it would therefore be many years before the instrument became equally established in the recording studio. According to Peña,

> The four-man conjunto ensemble may have been introduced into the dance halls earlier than the mid-1950s. Indeed, it is likely that it was, but in their totality all the elements—accordion, *bajo sexto*, electric bass, drums, and P.A. systems—probably did not become standardized until 1956. Certainly, in recordings, where a slightly different practice seems to have prevailed, the electric bass did not replace the *tololoche* until the late 1950s.[27]

Here, again, de la Rosa would be a pioneer, as he was eventually able to persuade Ideal to record his conjunto with its live instrumentation. For example, on his best-known recording, "Atotonilco" (1958), Pérez's electric bass rings out clearly and forcefully; it sonically overpowers the drum kit and accentuates each beat of the polka's 2/4 meter with a punch that dominates the recording's midrange. Thanks to de la Rosa's musical innovations, the electric bass became an essential part of conjunto, and Adan Pérez's work, in turn, paved the way for the next generation of conjunto electric bassists, such as Pepe Maldonado.[28]

Conclusion

Collectively, the music of the Millers Brothers Band, Ray Price, and Tony de la Rosa encapsulates a significant, if often overlooked, moment in electric bass history. While jazz musicians like Monk Montgomery may have been the public face of the instrument, and later rock 'n' roll musicians would ultimately get the credit for popularizing it, western swing, honky-tonk, and conjunto musicians deserve recognition for establishing the electric bass within each of their respective styles. Deep in the heart of Texas, it seems, musicians were embracing the electric bass before nearly anyone else.

THREE | The Practical Instrument

Rock 'n' Roll Live and In-Studio

Rock Around the Clock (1956) was the first rock 'n' roll film. Produced by B-movie legend Sam Katzman, the film was an attempt to capitalize on the recent popularity of Bill Haley and His Comets' recording of the same name, which had unexpectedly shot to No. 1 on *Billboard*'s Best Sellers in Stores Chart the previous summer.[1] With a budget of only around $300,000, *Rock Around the Clock* was filmed on a series of studio backlots in just thirteen days. Shot quickly and on the cheap, the film's appeal rested entirely on its musical sequences, which featured bands lip-syncing to their recordings while clean-cut, nonthreatening white teenagers danced along. The Comets alone have six numbers, including performances of "Rock Around the Clock," "See You Later Alligator," and "Rock-A-Beatin' Boogie" (the song Haley had given the Treniers to record back in 1953); the Platters, one of the most successful Black vocal groups of the mid-fifties, perform their No. 1 rhythm & blues hits from the previous year, "Only You (and You Alone)" and "The Great Pretender"; and Freddie Bell and the Bellboys, an unknown white Las Vegas lounge act, perform two choreographed numbers, "Teach You to Rock" and "Giddy Up a Ding Dong."

These on-screen performances fundamentally expanded teenage audiences' exposure to rock 'n' roll, making it accessible even to small-town America. David E. James contends that

> the jukebox musicals [like *Rock Around the Clock*] gave rhythm and blues and other forms of early rock 'n' roll a wide social audibility, visibility, and publicity, bringing to the whole nation a cultural devel-

opment founded on regional Black music and dance. Their fundamental attraction was the audio-visual spectacle of the stars as they
lip-synced to their current or recent hit records, which provided the
opportunity to hear them and see them, respectively, over a theatrical sound system much louder than a domestic record player and in
larger-than-life unobstructed theatrical projection, and perhaps even
to dance along with them.[2]

The loud, freer social space of the movie theater was thus a safe haven
both for teens and for the music itself. Away from most adult supervision,
teens could spend fifty cents to see and hear the latest rock 'n' roll bands
performing in the middle of their hometowns. And, at a time when television had decimated the film industry's adult market, these low-budget
"teenpics" proved surprisingly profitable, as youngsters turned out in
droves to see their musical idols on the silver screen.

In addition to spreading the sound of rock 'n' roll across America,
these teenpics also chronicled a different revolution: in scene after scene,
many of these rock 'n' roll acts were now featuring electric bass players—
including in *Rock Around the Clock*, where keen observers would have
noticed Freddie Bell and the Bellboys' bass player, Frankie Brent (1934–
2002), playing a first-generation Fender Precision Bass (Figure 16).

Formed in 1951, Freddie Bell and the Bellboys directly patterned
themselves on the Treniers.[3] Adopting not only their sound, but also
their eccentric performance style, the Bellboys were one of the first white
outfits to perform in this particular postwar rhythm & blues idiom.[4] They
honed their routine on the road, mostly touring the Midwest, before
landing a lucrative residency at the Sands Hotel in Las Vegas, where their
nightclub act became an overnight sensation—not only attracting the
attention of A&R man Bob Shad (who signed the group to a deal with
Mercury records), but also Sam Katzman, who was in Vegas looking for
groups to put in his upcoming rock 'n' roll teenpic.

The band's cool attitude and synchronized choreography made them
an easy choice for Katzman. In *Rock Around the Clock*, the Bellboys—decked
out in matching suits—snap, clap, and shuffle along with their two musical
numbers, adding a striking visual spectacle that matches their energetic
music. In both songs, Brent's Precision Bass provides the music's primary
harmonic support via quick, continuous bass lines, and as it had with
Shifty Henry, the instrument's over-the-shoulder portability also frees him
up to execute the group's synchronized choreography. Even if moviegoers
didn't specifically notice a difference between the Comets' upright bass

Figure 16. Frankie Brent (second from left) playing a Fender Precision Bass with Freddie Bell and the Bellboys. (Source: *Rock around the Clock*, dir. Fred F. Sears, 1956.)

and Frankie Brent's electric, the Bellboys' performances in *Rock Around the Clock* were part of a wider sea change in bass history: rock 'n' roll bands—especially bands like the Bellboys that made their living on the road—were now increasingly embracing the electric bass.

This chapter explores this first generation of rock 'n' roll electric bassists and their careers, both on-screen and off. While the upright continued to dominate in the recording studio throughout the fifties, the electric bass was slowly being adopted by touring musicians. This disconnect between live and recorded musical practices has largely been overlooked by modern scholarship, which still privileges recordings as the definitive representation of popular music history. Yet, in this era, many musical innovations were developed on the road, and even if the practices of live music-making are difficult to trace concretely, it is clear that for rock 'n' roll musicians the electric bass was introduced on the bandstand long before it was brought into the recording studio.

Through an exploration of the careers of Freddie Bell and the Bellboys' bassist Frankie Brent, Little Richard's bassists Frank Fields and Basie Robinson, Jerry Lee Lewis's bassist J. W. Brown, Elvis Presley's bassist Bill Black, Buddy Holly's bassist Joe B. Mauldin, and Gene Vincent's bassists Bill Mack and Bobby Lee Jones, I examine how and why the electric bass came to be introduced in early rock 'n' roll. As I argue, rather than stemming from a desire to change the sound of their music, most of these musicians were instead initially drawn to the instrument for practical reasons, most notably its volume, portability, and durability. Operating independently of each other, these musicians then brought the sight and sound of the electric bass to audiences across the United States, allowing the instrument to gain a foothold in rock 'n' roll that paved the way for its wider acceptance in American popular music.

This Thing Called "Rock 'n' Roll"

Rock 'n' roll was, by design, an imprecise genre. More of a marketing category than a description of shared musical practices, the term was popularized by radio disc jockey Alan Freed as an attempt to rebrand postwar rhythm & blues as music for white teenagers. In so doing, Freed successfully de-emphasized the music's racial origins, making it socially acceptable for young white listeners to openly embrace the music of Black performers. Once the category was established (and shown to be highly profitable), "rock 'n' roll" expanded into a catchall description, encompassing performers from a variety of musical styles—including pop, rhythm & blues, country-and-western, rockabilly, doo-wop, girl groups, and any others that were aimed primarily at a teen demographic.

In his book *Live Music in America*, Steve Waksman notes,

> Given the expansive range of media outlets that coexisted with and facilitated the commercial rise of rock 'n' roll, live performance has generally been accorded secondary importance by historians and critics of the music. This tendency has given rise to a growing critical orthodoxy in some quarters that the essence of rock 'n' roll, the aesthetic basis of the music, lies in the recorded work.[5]

However, as he demonstrates, early rock 'n' roll culture was inherently shaped by live music promoters, especially those responsible for the multi-artist package tours popular in this era. These tours, Waksman argues, gave young people across the country a sense of what exactly rock 'n' roll "was," and they were therefore significant in establishing the music's loose boundaries.

Rock 'n' roll concerts were significant for musical reasons as well, as they allowed musicians to try out small-scale creative experiments with very little risk. As Ian Inglis argues, "In its ability to simultaneously reflect and influence patterns of socio-cultural activity, [live performance] is one of the principal avenues along which musical change and innova-tion can be introduced and recognized."[6] In the middle to late fifties, live concerts allowed rock 'n' roll musicians to constantly tweak their approaches, to find out what sounds and styles might generate the most excitement and enthusiasm from their audiences. Through this process, they honed their sense of what young people responded to, and some then transferred this knowledge to the studio, using their recordings to capture some of what was already working well on the bandstand. The electric bass's entrance into early rock 'n' roll stands as one of the most significant by-products of this practice.

Frank Fields and Basie Robinson

The split between recorded and live performance in this era is best wit-nessed in the work of Little Richard and his bassists, Frank Fields and Basie Robinson. Collectively, their stories demonstrate the electric bass's journey from the bandstand to the studio, the loose, ever-fluctuating nature of early rock 'n' roll aesthetics, and the important role that teen-pics played in shaping both.

Frank Fields (1914–2005) was a respected upright bassist. A jazz musician with a penchant for understated grooves, Fields was a long-time member of Dave Bartholomew's band, perhaps the most influential rhythm & blues band of the late forties and early fifties.[7] Today, Fields is most remembered as the in-house bassist at Cosimo Matassa's J&M Studio, which at the time was the only recording studio in New Orleans. Here is how producer Robert "Bumps" Blackwell described a typical J&M session:

> Those things we did at Cosimo's were on tape, but they were all done straight ahead. The tracks you heard were the tracks as they were recorded from beginning to end. . . . The studio was just a back room in a furniture store, like an ordinary motel room. For the whole orchestra. There'd be a grand piano just as you came in the door. I'd have the grand's lid up with a mike in the keys and [saxophonists] Alvin Tyler and Lee Allen would be blowing into that. Earl Palmer's drums were out of the door, where I had one mike as well. The [bass player] would be way over the other side of the studio. You see, the bass would cut and bleed in, so I could get the bass.[8]

Working at J&M, Fields and other members of Bartholomew's band would go on to record a number of historic rhythm & blues hits, including Fats Domino's "The Fat Man" (1950)—a No. 2 hit on the *Billboard* Rhythm & Blues Chart that is sometimes described as the first rock 'n' roll record—and Lloyd Price's crossover hit "Lawdy Miss Clawdy" (1952)—which was named the No. 1 rhythm & blues "Record of the Year" by both *Billboard* and *Cash Box*.[9] Specialty Records' owner, Art Rupe, never forgot his label's success with Price's single, and after he signed "Little" Richard Penniman in 1955, he knew exactly where to send him.

Little Richard's first recording session at J&M did not get off to a promising start. But after taking a break to eat at the Dew Drop Inn, Blackwell saw Richard ham it up in front of an audience, playing on the club's piano. Suddenly he broke into a racy song he had been playing in white clubs across the South: "Awop-Bop-a-Loo-Mop Alop-Bam-Boom / Tutti Frutti, good booty!"[10] After seeing Richard's energetic live performance (and the crowd's enthusiastic reaction to it), Blackwell decided they should record the song when they got back to the studio and brought in songwriter Dorothy La Bostrie to clean up the song. After recording a few other numbers, La Bostrie came in with the rewritten lyrics, and, with just fifteen minutes left on the session, the band recorded "Tutti Frutti" in three takes.

With Little Richard on vocals and piano and the J&M studio band behind him, "Tutti Frutti" became an instant smash when it was released in November 1955. Even if La Bostrie replaced the overtly sexual and even queer lyrics with nonsense words ("Tutti Frutti, Aw-Rootie") and vague descriptions of women ("I got a girl, named Sue / She knows just what to do"), none of that mattered—the song's underlying energy was still infectious. Listening to the recording, it is the rhythm and Little Richard's voice (emphatic, but slightly fatigued from a six-hour recording session) that really sell it. Hovering somewhere around 184 beats per minute, the song is a fast, up-tempo dance number. Moreover, there is a sense of urgency built into the rhythm itself, with Richard pounding out straight-eighth notes on the piano as drummer Earl Palmer plays a clashing shuffle beat underneath him.[11] Yet if "Tutti Frutti" points to an unyielding rhythmic conflict between Richard and Palmer, it is Fields's laid-back, quarter-note walking bass line that ultimately bridges the two. Alvin "Red" Tyler, who played baritone sax on the session, best summarized Fields's style: "Frank Fields was about the most steady bass player I've ever worked with. If you set a tempo, he's got it. He plays correct, nothing fancy, very strong and dominant in his bass playing."[12] Altogether, the recording exudes a fun, youthful excitement, held together by Fields's steady groove—if just barely.

As "Tutti Frutti" was climbing to No. 2 on the *Billboard* Rhythm &

Blues Chart (and eventually crossing over to the Top 100, where it peaked at No. 21), Little Richard was on the road with his touring band, the Upsetters. As he recalled:

> I had signed a very bad deal with Specialty. If you wanted to record you signed on their terms or you didn't record. I got a half cent for every record sold. . . . It didn't matter how many records you sold if you were Black. The publishing rights were sold to the record label before the record was released. "Tutti Frutti" was sold to Specialty for fifty dollars. . . . So we knew that to make money we had to go on the road, and it had to be with the best show in the U.S.[13]

Richard's touring band thus not only played Richard's music (and often at even faster tempos than on his recordings), but they also had to be a spectacle unto themselves.[14] According to Upsetters drummer Charles Connor:

> Richard wanted his band to be excitin'. He wanted to do things no one had ever done before. He had us dress in loud clothes, like himself, all matchin'. Richard would wear the loudest clothes of all, makin' a point to match against our colors. He introduced us to a makeup called Pancake #31, which smoothed out our skin and made us look lighter. The band became Richard's tapestry, and he wanted our every appearance to be tailor-made to his vision. . . . Richard made sure to consider every detail. He knew that the crowd would settle for nothin' less. Bein' the best-dressed was as important as bein' the best rockin.' Havin' the best dance steps was as important as playin' on time. So we spent a lot of rehearsals workin' on dances, on smiles. We had never thought of music that way before.[15]

Richard and his band made their living on the road. They therefore needed to be as sharp, as loud, and as energetic as possible. Musically, this meant that while Fields's "nothing fancy" upright bass aesthetic worked in the studio, Richard's live shows had substantially different priorities— ones that were better met by the newest additions to the Upsetters: Olsie "Basie" Robinson and his Gibson Electric Bass.

Released in late 1953, the Electric Bass (later dubbed the EB-1) was part of Gibson's attempts to counter Fender's near total dominance of the electric bass market. Priced at $235, plus $312.52 for its accompanying amplifier, the Gibson Electric Bass was a slightly more expensive alternative to the Precision Bass. It featured a violin-shaped body, faux f-holes, and an attachable endpin that allowed it to be played vertically—features all designed to specifically appeal to upright players. However, it also featured a substantially shorter scale length than a Precision Bass (30.5 inches instead of Fender's 34″), which was likely intended to appeal to guitarists. These inconsistencies prevented the instrument from achieving widespread popularity, and by the time Gibson discontinued it 1958, they had produced only 546 of them.[16] As guitar historian Walter Carter explains, "Bassists never warmed up to the 'thuddy' tone of the short scale [Gibson Electric Bass], and Gibson would always struggle in the bass market."[17] After joining the Upsetters, Basie Robison quickly became the most famous—and most visible—musician to play the instrument.

As Connor recalls,

> I was glad we finally got a full-time bass player. Before then, I had been slammin' extra hard on my bass drum to compensate for the lack of a bass player. It worked, but it certainly wasn't ideal, not for me or the sound. It took time for Basie to learn to play the way Richard wanted. . . . We also had to teach him the dance steps that we were doin'. It wasn't easy for him to learn all of that—the chord changes Richard used were very different—and to couple that with dance routines, it took a lot of practice. But, once he got it, we had a real powerful rhythm section. We looked fresh, man.[18]

It is easy to see why Robinson's Gibson Electric Bass would be more practical for Little Richard's road band. First, like other electric basses, the instrument was louder, almost effortlessly so. Second, it was smaller, less fragile, and easier to transport than an upright. And third, it hung from your shoulders, making it possible for Robinson to join in on the choreography. The earlier complaints that jazz purists had leveled against the instrument's "tone" and "depth" were irrelevant in this context. Little Richard's music was meant to be fun, flashy, and danceable—all other concerns were secondary.

By the time the rock 'n' roll teenpic craze hit, the Upsetters were in full force, and their powerful stage show made them an obvious choice to star in the next wave of rock 'n' roll films. The group eventually appeared in three: *Don't Knock the Rock* (1956), *The Girl Can't Help It* (1956), and *Mister Rock 'n' Roll* (1957). In *Don't Knock the Rock*, Sam Katzman's quasi-sequel to *Rock Around the Clock*, the Upsetters appear alongside Bill Haley and the Treniers (now featuring electric bassist Jimmy Johnson), with each band performing to prerecorded studio tracks. This situation causes an audiovisual dissonance during Little Richard's performance, as we *hear* the J&M band but *see* the Upsetters. More specifically, when they break into "Tutti Frutti," we hear Fields's upright bass but see Robinson playing electric. This disconnect would surely have gone unnoticed by most audience members, but it perfectly captures this moment in bass history: the upright prevailed in the studio sight unseen, while the electric was becoming a standard and visible component of the touring band. This situation repeats itself in *The Girl Can't Help It*, with one minor exception: this time audiences actually got to hear Robinson's electric bass.

By 1956, Richard was a consistent hitmaker. So when it was decided that *The Girl Can't Help It* would feature music specifically rewritten for the film, Richard used the opportunity to insist that he record at least one of the songs with the Upsetters. As he recalled,

> I told Art Rupe that my band was the greatest in the world, better than those studio musicians in New Orleans. I didn't see why the Upsetters couldn't back me on my records the same way they did on stage. The Upsetters were good, and I wanted them on my records, too. . . . Rupe told me I had to make the record in New Orleans. . . . I told him I would break my contract if he insisted. He was really mad, but there was nothing he could do.[19]

The song Little Richard recorded with the Upsetters, "She's Got It," was in fact a revised version of "I Got It," a song he had recorded earlier at J&M that went unreleased until 1959. This was the first of Little Richard's records to feature either Basie Robinson or the sound of an electric bass.

In *The Girl Can't Help It*, Little Richard and the Upsetters are presented in four-track stereophonic sound and shot in Cinemascope in full Technicolor.[20] Although they wear the same outfits as in *Don't Knock the Rock*, the vibrant color enriches the effect of their lively performance (Figure 17).[21] "She's Got It" opens with a stop-time feel. Little Richard's voice, drenched in reverb, takes up most of the sonic space before the full band kicks in. Unlike "I Got It," which has a nearly identical arrangement, the saxophones and drums are much more poorly recorded, and the entire band is much quieter in the final mix. Yet even among his bandmates, Robinson's electric bass is still prominent. Anyone listening through a good set of speakers—such as those found in a mid-fifties movie theater equipped for CinemaScope—would have clearly heard (and felt) Robinson's deep, booming bass line cut through.

Figure 17. Olsie Robinson (third from right) playing a Gibson Electric Bass with Little Richard. (Source: *The Girl Can't Help It*, dir. Frank Tashlin, 1956.)

Released in October 1956 as the B-side to "Heeby-Jeebies," "She's Got It" became a hit on the *Billboard* Rhythm & Blues Chart, climbing all the way to No. 9, and by the time *The Girl Can't Help It* hit theaters in December, Little Richard and the Upsetters were at the height of their popularity. Richard recorded at J&M only two more times after that—both sessions commencing in mid-October 1956. After that, he insisted on recording with his road band, and his final two recording sessions from the fifties both featured the Upsetters. From these sessions, one single in particular stands out, both for its lasting influence on rock 'n' roll and for the sound of Robinson's electric bass.

"Keep a Knockin'" was recorded at a Washington, DC, radio station on January 14, 1957. The song dates back at least to the twenties, and the most famous version prior to Richard's was by Louis Jordan in 1939. Unlike Jordan's laid-back jump blues feel, however, Little Richard's is a barnburner. The song is remembered today for Connor's introductory drum solo (which John Bonham would later rework as the opening to Led Zeppelin's "Rock and Roll"). This intro, however, also presents Robinson's electric bass in its most prominent form to date, and overall, the song stands as the closest recorded approximation of Little Richard's live show: it is fast, high energy, and features the Upsetters at their peak as a collective unit. Robinson's electric bass is heard prominently throughout, adding a propulsive energy that had been part of Richard's live act for years. Thanks in no small part to Robinson's bass line, "Keep a Knockin'" reached No. 8 on the *Billboard* singles chart and No. 2 on the Rhythm & Blues Chart, making it one of Richard's last Top 10 hits of the decade.

J. W. Brown

A similar trajectory can be traced through Jerry Lee Lewis's collaborations with his bassist and cousin, J. W. Brown (1927–2022).[22] Brown had grown up playing music. By the age of ten, he was singing Gene Autry songs and accompanying himself on guitar, and by fourteen, he was playing upright bass in a local country-and-western band. He decided to pursue music professionally in 1956, after an on-the-job electrical accident left him with a year's pension and time on his hands. Looking to start a band, he purchased a Silvertone guitar and went in search of his younger cousin, singer/piano player Jerry Lee Lewis, who was then playing small clubs around northeastern Louisiana. Eventually, Brown convinced Lewis to travel to his home in Memphis, where they might be able to secure a contract with Sam Philips's Sun Records.

With Brown acting as Lewis's manager, the cousins walked into Sun Studio unannounced in mid-November and were disappointed to find out that Philips was on vacation. Instead, Jack Clement, Sun's other in-house producer and engineer, took a chance and scheduled a last-minute session for Lewis with guitarist Roland Janes and drummer Jimmy Van Eaton.[23] This first session produced Lewis's version of "Crazy Arms," a cover of Ray Price's hit remade in a slow rock 'n' roll style. Convinced that the song would be a smash, Lewis quickly formed a touring band to promote the single, hiring Russell Smith on drums and Brown to double on upright bass and rhythm guitar. Ultimately, "Crazy Arms" proved to be only modestly successful, but it helped establish the Jerry Lee Lewis Trio as a touring act, which, in turn, gave Lewis the time he needed to hone his frenzied onstage persona.

In early 1957, after some equipment mishaps on the road, Brown decided to switch to electric bass. As he recalled,

> Jerry complained that I needed to find something else to play because I kept breaking the strings on my 6-string guitar. And I'll never forget the day shortly thereafter when we went to Berl Olswanger's music store in Memphis, and I laid eyes on my very first electric bass. It was a Fender Precision . . . which allowed for amplification at higher volumes without the feedback that I normally got from acoustic double basses . . . Jerry looked at it and said to me, "Don't you play the upright?" And I bought the bass and a Fender Bassman.[24]

Like other rock 'n' roll bassists in this era, J. W. Brown switched from upright to electric bass for practical reasons: it was not only a more durable instrument, but it was loud enough to provide the group's music a solid harmonic foundation (all while allowing him to avoid the feedback that would otherwise thwart those higher volumes). Brown's Bassman also helped the band develop a unique sound: the amplifier was equipped with two input jacks (designated "bright" and "normal"), designed to accommodate both an electric bass and an electric guitar simultaneously; through a series of experiments, Brown discovered that he could play his Precision Bass through the normal channel and then use an old microphone to amplify Lewis's piano through the other. This meant that live, the manic aggressions of Lewis's playing style would be further enhanced, as the sound of his piano playing was doubled via a distorted bass amplifier. According to Brown, "The sound we got out of my bass and Jerry's piano just blew us away. We knew this was something special, and as far as I know it had never been done before. We tried out this arrangement at the next show . . . and the response from the crowd was unbelievable; they went crazy."[25]

Still looking for something to set Lewis's recordings apart, Brown and the group paid close attention to their audiences' reactions, especially as they tried out new material. Not long after Brown switched to electric bass, the trio performed at the Rebel Room in Osceola, Arkansas, where they broke into an impromptu rendition of "Whole Lotta Shakin' Goin' On"—a twelve-bar blues first recorded by Big Maybelle. Their performance was such a sensation that the crowd demanded that they play the song over and over again. At the end of the night, Lewis reportedly turned to Brown and said, "Well, there it goes J.W. Think we got a hit?"[26] Returning to Memphis shortly thereafter, Lewis recorded the song for Sun, again featuring Roland Janes on guitar and Jimmy Van Eaton on drums; this time, however, they also included Brown and his new Precision Bass.

Listening back to the final mix, Sam Philips was less than enthusiastic. Contrary to Big Maybelle's version, in which the song's raunchy implications were somewhat obscured by the lyrics, Lewis's version was overtly and unapologetically sexual. He commanded, "Shake, baby, shake" again and again, before slowing the whole song down and explaining, "All you gotta do honey is kinda stand in one spot / Wiggle around just a little bit." Despite his reservations, Philips released the song in April 1957, but just as the single was taking off, his fears came true: some radio stations across the country began banning the record for its sexually explicit content. Concerned about the state of his investment (especially if he'd have to reimburse retailers for thousands of returned records), Sam Philips brought in his brother Jud to salvage the situation. Jud Philips recognized that Lewis was at his best when he was riling up a live audience and decided to take the singer and his touring band to New York City in hopes of getting them on television. After Jud exploited his various industry connections, Lewis, Brown, and Smith were booked to perform as the last act on the *Steve Allen Show* for July 28, 1957. Lewis's performance that night—complete with frenetic piano playing, increasingly unkempt hair, and a chair kicked halfway across the stage—successfully stemmed the growing backlash against the single. By September 16, "Shakin'" was No. 1 on the *Billboard* Country & Western Chart, No. 1 on the Rhythm & Blues Chart, and No. 3 on the Top 100.

As with Little Richard, film studios wasted no time in putting Lewis in the movies. The Jerry Lee Lewis Trio appeared first in the 1957 teenpic *Jamboree*, lip-syncing to a version of Lewis's latest hit, "Great Balls of Fire." In the film, Brown and his Precision Bass are on prominent display in crisp black and white, although again there is an audiovisual dissonance: while Brown appears in the film, he did not play on the session. Instead, according to Brown, the bassist was Al Stangler, a guitarist and friend of Janes and Van Eaton (much to Brown's later chagrin, Stangler allegedly played Brown's Precision Bass on the recording).[27] The next year, the band also appeared in *High School Confidential*, where they played the film's title song during the opening credits.[28]

Initially, Brown had adopted the electric bass because he needed a more reliable, louder instrument for the road. But this instrument and its amplifier also facilitated new sonic experiments on the bandstand, experiments that led Lewis to develop his signature performing style. This style, and the sound of the electric bass, then became a part of Lewis's recorded output, which itself was further spread through the group's appearances on film and television.

Bill Black

The electric bass's initial introduction to rock 'n' roll was not considered revolutionary. This is because, at the time, the upright and electric bass were thought of as fundamentally similar instruments, with the latter just considered a lesser substitute for the former. However, as touring musicians began to explore the electric bass's practical advantages, the instrument became increasingly seen as a more useful alternative, although it did not supplant the upright overnight. The electric bass's emerging, in-between status is perhaps best encapsulated in the work of Elvis Presley and his bassist, Bill Black (1926–1965).

On July 4, 1954, Presley met Black and guitarist Scotty Moore for the first time during a rehearsal at Moore's home. The three musicians had come together at the suggestion of Sam Philips, who had set up a recording session for them on the following day. During the session, the trio recorded a variety of songs, none of which struck Philips as commercially viable. After hours of trial and error, however, they accidentally stumbled on the sound that would catapult them to stardom. Rockabilly, as it was soon to be called—a hybrid of country, gospel, and rhythm & blues—met Phillips's commercial sensibilities and ultimately fulfilled his infamous dictate that "If I could find a white man who had the Negro sound and the Negro feel, I could make a billion dollars."[29] The trio's first single, a version of Arthur Crudup's "That's All Right," was light-hearted and spontaneous, exhibiting the youthful energy that was at the heart of Presley's appeal. Backed by the rhythmic foundation of Black's upright, slap bass style, "That's All Right" became a regional hit and foreshadowed Presley's immense popularity in the years to come.

Black was the oldest member of the band. He was also the only member to have been born and raised in Memphis. In his early years he had cut his teeth playing upright bass in a wide variety of local styles, including pop, country, and blues. By the time he met Presley, Black had already solidified his hard-slapping style and comedic onstage persona. Musically, his presence is especially evident during those early Sun sessions, where his percussive style filled in the gap left by the absence of a drummer.[30] As Moore later recalled, Black's bass technique was "very, very important because the things we were doing was mostly rhythm. It wasn't a thing where he had to hit the correct note; it was just a blending, an overall sound, you know."[31] This emphasis on rhythm over pitch is a recurring theme in descriptions of Black's style. For example, Sam Phillips once went as far as to claim that "Bill was one of the worst bass players in the world, *technically*, but, man, could he slap that thing!"[32] These dismissals of Black's abilities are likely overstated. Yet they highlight that Black's function in the band was understood primarily in rhythmic terms. This role would gradually evolve as Elvis moved to a major label and the band grew to include drummer D. J. Fontana.

In November 1955, Presley and his manager, "Colonel" Tom Parker, made a deal with RCA-Victor to buy out his contract from Sun Records for an unprecedented $40,000. Beginning in January 1956, Presley and his band—now featuring Fontana on drums—recorded a string of nationwide hits, including five songs that made it into the year-end *Billboard* "1956 Top Tunes": "Don't Be Cruel," "Heartbreak Hotel,"

"Love Me Tender," "Hound Dog," and "I Want You, I Need You, I Love You." Of these "Hound Dog" remains the most notable, both because it topped the Country & Western, Rhythm & Blues, and Top 100 Charts simultaneously, and because it introduced Presley's swinging hips to national audiences.[33]

Originally performed by Willie Mae "Big Mama" Thornton, "Hound Dog" had been written in 1952 by Jerry Leiber and Mike Stoller—two white, Jewish teenagers with a love for Black music.[34] Thornton's version is bluesy, nuanced, and sexual, a shot across the bow to a no-good man. Presley's version is none of those things. In fact, the latter version is so different that it's almost difficult to consider them the same song. This is because Elvis wasn't covering Thornton, he was doing a cover *of a cover*—specifically, he was covering Freddie Bell and the Bellboys' version of the song.

As mentioned earlier, the Bellboys were making waves early in 1956 as a top nightclub draw at the upscale Sands Hotel in Las Vegas. The year before, while still working as a touring band, they had recorded their send-up of "Hound Dog" for Bernie Lowe's Teen Records. For it, Lowe had prompted them to sanitize Leiber and Stoller's lyrics, and thus it was Bell who rewrote the song to be about an actual hound dog rather than a freeloading gigolo. The Teen single received modest airplay and became a regional hit, but it failed to chart nationally. Still, the Bellboys kept honing the song in their live act, and by the time they reached the Sands, the song had become the highlight of their show.

Presley first saw their act in April 1956 while on a last-minute, two-week engagement at the New Frontier Hotel in Las Vegas. While Bell's professional, choreographed rock 'n' roll group was consistently met with high praise from Vegas audiences, Presley's act (as part of Freddy Martin's show) was met with, at best, indifference.[35] Nonetheless, the engagement gave Presley the chance to catch other Vegas acts, including both Liberace (whom he admired) and the Bellboys. According to Peter Guralnick, the Bellboys' high-energy rendition of "Hound Dog" "sparked a determination on Elvis's part to incorporate it into his own show," and, as Moore told the writer, "We stole it straight from them. . . . He already knew it, knew the song, but when we seen those guys do it, he said, 'There's a natural.' We never did it in Las Vegas, but we were just looking on it as comic relief, if you will, just another number to do onstage."[36] After the show, Presley apparently pulled Bell aside and asked him if he could record the Bellboys' version of "Hound Dog." Bell not only agreed, but went back into the studio in May to rerecord the song himself with the hopes of riding Presley's coattails.[37]

Even though Presley's band—Moore on guitar, Black on bass, Fontana on drums, and the Jordanaires singing backup—was smaller than Bell's saxophone-led, seven-piece ensemble, much of Presley's arrangement is lifted straight from Bell. The rewritten lyrics, the handclaps, and most importantly, the rhumba-inflected bass line can all be found on Bell's 1956 version, which was recorded two months prior to Presley's. Aside from the machine-gun snare hits that add excitement and energy to the end of every twelve-bar cycle, Presley's recording is primarily powered by the bass. No longer playing in a distinctively percussive, slap bass style (which Fontana's drums had made redundant), Black—as Roy Brewer discusses—drives the band with his idiosyncratic take on an Afro-Cuban bass line.[38] A similar bass line resides at the core of Bell's version too, with one key difference: just as in *Rock Around the Clock*, Bellboys bassist Frankie Brent performed it on electric bass, while Black played his version on upright. The decision to use one instrument or the other boiled down to practicality. Brent played electric in the Bellboys' stage show, so it made sense for him to play it in the studio; Black had only ever played upright and would have seen no reason to switch to electric just for this one song. For Black, however, circumstances would change during the recording sessions for the film *Jailhouse Rock*, as he would explicitly be asked to abandon his upright.

Presley, like the other rock 'n' rollers, began his film career in 1956. However, unlike his contemporaries, all of his thirty-one feature films were backed by major studios. His first role was in the western *Love Me Tender*, followed by *Loving You* (1957), a star vehicle in the mold of Katzman's *Rock Around the Clock*. The latter film was a box office smash, earning $3.7 million by the end of the year. It also produced a hit single, "(Let Me Be Your) Teddy Bear," cowritten by Bernie Lowe—the onetime owner of Teen Records. Two other songs from the film, "Loving You" and "Hot Dog," had been written by none other than Leiber and Stoller. Although they had disliked Presley's version of "Hound Dog," that hadn't stopped them from cashing their royalty checks or from submitting new songs to the singer, and when they were offered the commission to write new material for Presley's third film, the duo gladly accepted.[39]

The songs for *Jailhouse Rock* (1957) were written quickly and under duress. According to Leiber and Stoller, they had been running around New York City, procrastinating on the project by visiting local jazz clubs; that is, until they were confronted by Presley's publisher, Jean Aberbach:

He came over to lecture us on fidelity in delivering work, and we hadn't done *anything*. And he came over, and he stalked around the room, and he talked about the necessity of being on time, etcetera. And finally he shoved the sofa against the door. And he stretched out on the sofa and said, "Boys, I'm gonna stay here until you give me the score."[40]

Within a few hours of being barricaded in their room, Leiber and Stoller had four songs: "Treat Me Nice," "I Want to Be Free," "(You're So Square) Baby I Don't Care," and "Jailhouse Rock." The recording sessions for the soundtrack took place at Radio Recorders in Hollywood just a few weeks later, with the songwriters present to teach the band the songs and supervise the sessions. As Leiber recalls,

> We jumped right into "Jailhouse Rock." The initial idea was just to show up at the studio to meet Elvis. But, as naturally as the winter turns to spring, we found ourselves in charge of the session. We were producing the guy. Mike worked out the arrangement with Elvis's band— Bill Black on upright bass, Scotty Moore on guitar, D.J. Fontana on drums, and Dudley Brooks on piano. As far as the vocals went, I was amazed to see that Elvis was happy to hear me sing the song with what I considered the right attitude. He was following my vocal cues.[41]

On May 3, 1957, three days after the session that produced "Jailhouse Rock," Presley, his band, and Leiber and Stoller reentered the studio to work on more material for the soundtrack, including "(You're So Square) Baby I Don't Care."[42] Although it is unclear exactly who made the decision, it was determined that an electric bass was essential to "Baby I Don't Care," making it one of the first rock 'n' roll recordings on which the electric bass was included for purely musical reasons. As previously detailed, a number of prior recordings had already featured the instrument; yet, they all appear to be at least partially based on practicality: J. W. Brown, Basie Robinson, and Frankie Brent were playing electric on the road, so it made sense for them to use it when they later entered the studio. Here, Bill Black, an upright bassist, was being asked to switch because the song required the electric bass's unique *sound*. The only issue was Black himself.

The morning of the session, a Fender Precision Bass and amplifier were brought into the studio. With such little time to practice, Black struggled with the necessary shift in technique and style required to play the instrument successfully. Guralnick's depiction of the incident is worth quoting at length:

[During the *Jailhouse Rock* sessions] Bill Black was feeling increasingly frustrated not just at the indifference with which he saw himself and Scotty being treated but by his own difficulties in trying to learn how to play the electric bass. . . . Bill had only recently gotten a Fender bass of his own, and he couldn't get the ominous, rhythmic intro to Leiber and Stoller's "(You're So Square) Baby, I Don't Care," one of the highlights of the film score. He tried it again and again, got more and more pissed off and embarrassed by his failure, and finally slammed the bass down, slid it across the floor, and stormed out of the studio, while everyone watched in disbelief. "Most artists," said [Jordanaire] Gordon Stoker, "would have said, 'You pick that bass up and play it, buster, that's your job,' but not Elvis. You know what Elvis did? Elvis thought it was funny. He picked it up and played it himself. He just picked up that bass, put his foot up on my chair, and played that song all the way through."[43]

This particular story is often used to emphasize Presley's diverse talents while downplaying the musical contributions of his sidemen. Yet it differs from both Scotty Moore's and D. J. Fontana's recollections. For example, Fontana is quick to point out that Black had only received the instrument that morning and had

tried it one time. Elvis wanted this song for him to do . . . "Baby I Don't Care"? Was that the name of it?. . . . *And they had just brought the bass in that morning to the studio and Bill had never picked up an electric bass in his life.* And Elvis was like here look Bill . . . and he tried and he tried and he finally got disgusted after about an hour and threw the bass down and walked out. Elvis said, "Let me have the damn thing, I'll play it." And that's him on that record.[44]

Moore, by contrast, remembers the incident as far less heated:

[A]fter several tries, [Black] finally said, "I can't play the damn thing!" laid down the bass and walked away. He did not slam or slide it. Elvis played it without comment or acting mad, and Bill was not mad at Elvis, but just aggravated that he had not yet mastered the [electric] bass. There was no conflict, no bad feelings afterward.[45]

Since the electric bass had originally been designed for guitarists rather than upright players, it is perhaps understandable why Presley might have had an easier time picking it up than Black. But, regardless, the bass line to "Baby I Don't Care" remains likely the first rock 'n' roll song where the electric bass was chosen expressly for the distinctive sonic possibilities it offered.

The recording opens just with the electric bass, loud and full, as Presley hammers on from a B to a C.[46] Notably, Presley plays the line with a pick, giving the sound of his electric bass a much stronger attack than heard on most other early electric bass recordings (albeit one that is dampened somewhat by the instrument's rubber mute). As the band breaks into the first verse, the other instruments cover over the bass, which remains largely buried in the mix from then on. But, as Guralnick suggests, it is that opening bass riff that really sells the song, and it is difficult to imagine the line having the same sonic presence if played on an upright.

This watershed moment in electric bass history seems, unsurprisingly, to have gone almost completely unnoticed. Aside from being overshadowed by the success of "Jailhouse Rock" and "Treat Me Nice," this moment was further obscured by the film itself: never once does an electric bass appear in the final cut, and—like the audiovisual dissonance of earlier rock 'n' roll films—when "Baby I Don't Care" is played on-screen, Black is simply shown miming along on upright.

Irrespective of the difficulties he experienced in the studio, Black did adopt the electric bass for the subsequent *Jailhouse Rock* tour. Running from August through November 1957, the tour was a big success for Presley, if not for his sidemen. The first show was held in Spokane, Washington, on August 30, with the local paper later declaring that "Presley Whips 12,000 into Near-Hysteria."[47] Photographs of the concert show Black playing a new Fender Precision Bass, which Presley had purchased in mid-August.[48] The tour then ran through four cities—Vancouver, Tacoma, Seattle, and Portland—over the next three days. A session had been scheduled for Presley to record a holiday LP at the end of this first leg—what would become *Elvis' Christmas Album* (1957)—with an added agreement that Moore and Black could also record some instrumentals, which they could release to earn a little extra money. When Parker reneged on this latter agreement, the musicians were livid. The next day, exhausted and underpaid, Black and Moore turned in letters of resignation. Guralnick explains that "they had expected more from Elvis, they had expected to *share* in his success, and here they were making two hundred dollars a week on the road and responsible for their own expenses. They were in debt, they needed financial help, they just wanted some fucking respect."[49] Their resignation sparked a bitter back-and-forth in the local Memphis press, creating a public embarrassment for Presley. By October, however, all parties had reconciled and Black and Moore rejoined the tour; again, photographs from their two-night event at Los Angeles's Pan Pacific Auditorium on October 28 and 29 clearly show Black playing a second-generation Fender Precision Bass with a Bassman amplifier. After that, Black and Moore finished out the remaining shows in Hawaii. This would be Black's last tour with Presley. As for why Black had switched to electric bass full-time, Moore recalled that, in the end, it came down to a different practical concern: "All the people going along on the trips with Elvis' group got to take up so much room that there was no longer room for the big bass, so he began to play an electric."[50]

Joe B. Mauldin

Although "(You're So Square) Baby I Don't Care" has a prominent place in *Jailhouse Rock*, the song was never put out as a single in the United States. However, one year after the film was released, it was given new life when it was recorded by Buddy Holly. Like Presley and Black, Holly and his bassist Joe B. Mauldin exemplified the ongoing negotiation over the bass's role in early rock 'n' roll.

One year younger than Presley, Holly was a self-avowed Elvis fanatic who had witnessed the birth of rock 'n' roll firsthand. His professional music career began in 1956 with two failed singles for Decca Records. After being released from his contract, Holly sought out musician and producer Norman Petty, who owned and operated an independent recording studio out of Clovis, New Mexico. Petty became his manager and producer, and with his help, Holly recorded his first hit, "That'll Be the Day," in February 1957. Holly had previously recorded the song for Decca, but the company had decided not to release it. Even though his contract had been terminated, their agreement still stipulated that Holly wasn't allowed to rerecord any of his Decca songs for five years; to get around this, Holly and his band renamed themselves "The Crickets."

Before "That'll Be the Day" was even released, the band underwent a significant personnel change when bassist Joe B. Mauldin (1940–2015) joined the Crickets, replacing Larry Welborn. According to Philip Norman,

On March 3, bass player Larry Welborn had been unable to make a $65 gig at the Elks Club in Carlsbad, New Mexico. To take his place, Buddy had borrowed the Four Teens' bass player, a diminutive, round-faced sixteen-year-old named Joe B. (for Benson) Mauldin. Compared with Welborn and [previous bassist] Don Guess, Joe B. was anything but a wizard on bass. His great virtue was that he had his own instrument and didn't have to rent or borrow one each time a gig came up. It was to bring that impressive piece of furniture into the Crickets, more than for the sound Joe B. was likely to conjure from it, that Buddy asked him to replace Larry Welborn permanently.[51]

Mauldin recalls the situation somewhat differently: "I remember the first time I was asked to play with Buddy and [drummer] Jerry [Allison] for a dance in Carlsbad . . . I didn't know what they expected of me, so I kept it conservative. That seemed to work out well and I pretty much kept it that way."[52] Either way, Mauldin's relaxed, minimalistic style became a hallmark of the Crickets' sound, and he recorded a string of hits with the group, including "Peggy Sue," "Oh, Boy!," "Maybe Baby," and more.

Mauldin's bass style is clearly captured on the Cricket's cover of "(You're So Square) Baby I Don't Care," which was recorded in Clovis on December 19, 1957. The song opens with Allison (revisiting a gimmick he had used on "Not Fade Away") beating out the rhythm on a cardboard box. This is followed by the entrance of Holly's strummed guitar and Mauldin's simple quarter-note bass line, which alternates between the root and fifth of each chord. Dave Laing and others have been quick to point out that on this recording, Holly is doing something of an Elvis impression—most noticeably at the end of the refrain, when Holly drops down into his chest voice as he sings, *"Baby I don't care."*[53] Yet, while Holly vocally mimics the original recording, musically, almost everything else about the arrangement is different. First, the Crickets forgo the original's signature opening (what Guralnick referred to as the song's "ominous, rhythmic intro"); instead, Presley's bass riff is replaced by Allison's muffled cardboard box. Second, even when Holly's guitar eventually enters, the song lacks the original's full, low-end sound. And third, not only does Mauldin play upright bass on the recording, but he also plays a completely different country-and-western-style, oompah bass line. The sound and function of the electric bass in Presley's version—what was thought to be such an essential component of the recording—is here wholly absent. The Crickets simply recast the song in their own musical style. Which is to say that, in this era, rock 'n' roll aesthetics were in a

Figure 18. Joe B. Mauldin (left) onstage with Buddy Holly and the Crickets, 1958. (Photo Courtesy of Dick Cole, Waterloo, IA.)

constant state of flux, and even though the electric bass was slowly finding its way into the genre, it was not yet fully established.

However, Mauldin did occasionally play electric bass—but only on the road. As he later explained, "The electric [bass] gives you more control and more volume, but it also makes your mistakes stick out. Buddy didn't seem to mind that I wanted to use an electric on the road, but he definitely didn't want to use it in the studio. He was tickled over the sound we were getting with the [upright], and he wanted to keep it that way."[54] In fact, Mauldin only played electric bass on one brief tour with Holly in the summer of 1958. In response to ongoing disputes over royalty payments, Holly wanted to break away from Norman Petty and relocate the band to New York City. Strapped for cash, a "Summer Dance Party" tour was planned as a quick way to earn money. Taking place over the course of ten days in July 1958, the tour wound through Illinois, Michigan, Iowa, Minnesota, and Wisconsin. Photographs, such as the ones taken at their July 8 show in Waterloo, Iowa (Figure 18), stand as the only record of Joe B. playing his third-generation Fender Precision Bass while on tour with Holly.[55]

Like the others before him, Mauldin's decision to play electric was primarily based on practical considerations: just as with Black, they didn't have enough room in the car. John Gribbin notes that,

> With such a small touring party, there was no tour bus involved this time. The three Crickets travelled in Buddy's latest car, a blue Lincoln, while the four members of the Western Swing Band (including Tommy Allsup) officially travelled in a yellow DeSoto station wagon purchased with money from the Crickets' account, although Tommy often rode in the Lincoln. The travelling was made easier because for this trip Joe B. had switched from upright to electric bass.[56]

The electric bass simply took up less room while still serving (for all intents and purposes) the same musical function as the upright. On the road, what mattered was space and volume; there, practicality was king, and thus so was the electric.

The tour on which Mauldin played electric bass would be his last with Holly.[57] Unwilling to move to New York, Allison and Mauldin chose to stay in Lubbock and leave Holly's band. Holly's next bass player, a young Waylon Jennings, would also play electric bass on tour, but for yet another practical reason: he was a guitarist and not a bassist, and the electric made those skills transferable.

Bill Mack and Bobby Lee Jones

Despite the various bands that had come to adopt the electric bass in the middle to late fifties, the instrument remained a rare sight in rock 'n' roll. It is thus best to think of its growing popularity more as a series of coinciding, small-scale shifts in musical practices rather than as a rapidly expanding national trend. This much is evident from the surviving anecdotal accounts of Gene Vincent's bassists, Bill Mack and Bobby Lee Jones.

Born and raised in Greenville, South Carolina, William E. McCreight (1933–2011) began playing upright bass at fourteen. He started working as a professional musician in his early twenties, and by the mid-fifties he and his childhood friend Paul Peek had moved to Washington, DC, and joined the Tunetoppers, a country band led by Red Redding. Just prior to joining the group, McCreight had purchased a second-generation Precision Bass, and his gig with the Tunetoppers allowed him to switch to electric bass full time.

In May 1956, Gene Vincent and His Blue Caps released "Be-Bop-a-Lula," a rockabilly hit that made it to No. 9 on the *Billboard* Hot 100. That September, Vincent and his band were playing a gig in DC, and Peek and McCreight went to hear them rehearse. As McCreight recalls,

> On one of our breaks, Paul and I took a walk down the street and just by chance, Gene Vincent and The Blue Caps were playing at The Casino Royale. . . . So the next day we went into town, and . . . they were rehearsing at the club. The club was on the second floor of the building. So we went up and we walked in, and we introduced ourselves as musicians, and [mentioned] that we were playing at The Metropole. . . . Gene said to us that he needed a rhythm guitarist. He said that Wee Willie was quitting. Paul told Gene that he could play rhythm. So, Gene said come on over and let's see what you can do. Cliff Gallup helped Paul with the chords, and Gene thought that Paul could do the job. So Gene hired Paul right then.[58]

Within days, Peek was on a plane to California, where he and the rest of the Blue Caps would film their appearance in *The Girl Can't Help It*. Before he left, however, McCreight told his friend to keep him in mind if the bass position in the Blue Caps ever opened up:

> I had told Paul if Jack Neal ever quit The Blue Caps, to remind Gene that I was available, and that I would like to have the job playing bass. I did tell Gene when we were conversing, that I played electric bass with Paul at the Metropole. Jack was playing upright bass at the time.[59]

Vincent's second LP, *Gene Vincent and the Blue Caps*, was released on March 4, 1957. In order to promote the album, Vincent formed a new iteration of the Blue Caps and Peek convinced him to hire McCreight as the group's bass player. They went on tour right away, joining a "Rockabilly Spectacular" package that wound through Ohio and included Carl Perkins, Roy Orbison, and Eddie Cochran, followed by the "Rock 'n' Roll Jubilee of Stars," a weeklong tour through Pennsylvania. The practical advantages of McCreight's electric bass were a welcome addition on the road. As Susan VanHecke explains, "Gene was thrilled to have an electric bass in the band, it was so loud and different and took up much less space on stage and in travel than the bulky [upright] bass."[60] McCreight also remembered that to my knowledge I was the only one out there with an electric bass, especially on the shows that I played. Marshall Grant asked me if the electric bass was hard to play. I told him that I thought that it was easy. Later when we played a show with Johnny Cash, Marshall Grant was playing an electric bass.[61]

According to McCreight's recollection, the electric bass was still a relatively novel sight in 1957, but one that spread as other musicians saw and heard the instrument and decided to get one themselves, even if just for live gigs. For McCreight, however, his initial tenure with the Blue Caps was short-lived, as he was let go from the band after less than a month and was replaced by another of Peek's former bandmates, Bobby Lee Jones.

Like McCreight, Jones (b. 1934) played a Fender Precision Bass. Also from Greenville, Jones got his start playing guitar in local country bands, before switching to electric bass in 1956. He joined the Blue Caps in April 1957 and went on to record forty sides with them, including the hit "Lotta Lovin."[62] Recorded on June 19, 1957, at Capitol Recording Studios in Hollywood, the single eventually climbed to No. 7 on the *Billboard* Rhythm & Blues Chart and No. 13 on the Best Sellers in Stores Chart. Jones recalled that he was the first electric bass player to record for Capitol; as he described the session,

> We were on our way to the studio, and the road manager says well, you won't get to play with the band, they'll have to have a staff musician play the [upright] bass. I said oh my goodness. Well, we got there and set up anyway and started playing, and the engineer says he's not picking me up well enough, can't I use a pick? I was playing my Precision with my thumb. So I said well yes, I guess I can, and I started using a pick . . . [After that,] I played with a pick till the day I quit playing.[63]

Listening to the recording today, the timbre of Jones's bass is quite similar to Presley's on "Baby I Don't Care": both musicians pick stock Precision Basses, and this stronger attack creates a fat, muted tone that makes their basses sound noticeably distinct from an upright. Contrary to Presley's recording, however, Jones's rhumba-inflected bass line is featured much more prominently in the overall mix.

In-between recording sessions, Jones continued to tour with the Blue Caps. In October 1957, he participated in the infamous package tour of Australia on which Little Richard unexpectedly decided to give up rock 'n' roll, and in mid-1958, he filmed scenes with the Blue Caps for the teenpic *Hot Rod Gang*. Yet before the film was released, Jones decided to leave the group and return to South Carolina. In May 1958, he was replaced by returning bassist William McCreight, who subsequently adopted the stage name Bill Mack. This version of the Blue Caps only lasted until November.

Mack's and Jones's stories highlight how the electric bass came to be involved in early rock 'n' roll: Rather than being influenced by a critical mass of their contemporaries who were suddenly adopting the instrument, Mack and Jones appear to have come to the electric bass independently, drawn primarily to its practical advantages. As members of the Blue Caps, they both demonstrated the electric bass's usefulness on the road, which eventually led Vincent to bring it into the studio as well. But, from their accounts, this appears to have been a haphazard, spontaneous process.

Conclusion

By 1958, there were a handful of rock 'n' roll recordings that featured electric bass. Although it is possible to see this moment as a fundamental turning point in bass history, really these recordings were just exceptions to a rule. The electric bass had not yet been fully embraced within the studio. It lived on the bandstand.

Live performances are inherently ephemeral. They exist only for a moment. And while some information survives about particular concerts (their dates, locations, lineups, etc.), music historians can only speculate about what those moments were actually like. The lack of documentation surrounding the history and practices of live music-making has led critics and scholars to instead rely on recordings as the definitive texts of popular music.[64] Though I do not mean to discount the benefit of recordings, this approach has fostered the all-too-common misconception that what we hear on records represented what audiences heard live. Moreover, it discounts the key role live performance played in allowing musicians to experiment. At a time when the electric bass was still largely deemed inappropriate for recording, it was actually considered an advantage on the road, where its smaller size, louder volume, and increased durability made it a better practical choice for live music-making. The cumulative result of this process was that the electric bass slowly came to be considered a legitimate musical instrument—at least within specific settings.

Like the rock 'n' roll teenpics craze, by the end of the 1950s, the first wave of rock 'n' roll was over: Bill Haley's popularity waned as younger stars rose to prominence; Little Richard abruptly abandoned rock 'n' roll and entered the ministry; the *Jailhouse Rock* tour was Presley's last before he was drafted into the military; Jerry Lee Lewis was blackballed by the media after marrying his thirteen-year-old cousin (J. W. Brown's daughter);[65] Buddy Holly was killed in a plane crash while on tour in Iowa; and Gene Vincent left the United States due to tax troubles. And within a few years, the entire landscape of popular music shifted, as new musical crazes captured the attention of American teenagers. One of the most prominent of these was "the Twist," a novelty dance that took the nation by storm. The electric bass was a part of this history too. The song had originally been recorded in November 1958 by Hank Ballard & the Midnighters, with electric bassist Navarro Hastings (formerly of Etta James's band). It was then rerecorded in early 1960 by Chubby Checker, likely with Joe Macho on electric bass (who years later would play on Bob Dylan's "Like a Rolling Stone"). Checker's single was released in June 1960 on Parkway Records, a new label run by Bernie Lowe, and became one of the decade's biggest hits.

Having been adopted in fits and starts, by the early sixties the electric bass was a far more common sight in American popular music. This shift was due, in part, to the groundwork laid by the rock 'n' roll bassists discussed in this chapter. But it would take more than a small handful of players to solidify the instrument's position. Instead, it required both a critical mass of musicians to adopt the electric bass and, ultimately, for new, distinctive sounds to be developed for it.

Born in Chicago

As detailed in the previous chapter, the first musicians to play the electric bass were largely drawn to its practical advantages: it was easy to transport, easy to play, and its amplification made it easy to hear. But after they adopted it, the electric bass also had an undeniable impact on the sound of their music. This cycle repeated throughout the fifties, as more and more musicians began to play the instrument. Although, in retrospect, it is tempting to treat these developments as a unified national trend, that is not how musicians experienced it at the time. Instead, for most, the electric bass's growing popularity was primarily driven by the sense of competition and camaraderie that existed within their own individual music scenes. It is therefore in some ways more useful to conceive of the instrument's initial acceptance as a series of simultaneous yet overlapping local phenomena.

This interlude details how the electric bass came to be accepted within one particularly influential musical community: the Chicago electric blues scene. Once it was introduced within this highly competitive, tight-knit environment, the electric bass quickly became so prevalent that within less than four years every major blues band in town featured one, both live and on their recordings. Through this process, the Chicago blues scene became likely the first Black musical culture to fully embrace the instrument. Moreover, this shift in local music-making practices would have far-reaching, global effects: not only did these new electric bassists fundamentally alter the sound of the electric blues, but they also contributed to the development of sixties rhythm & blues and the cultivation of new, white audiences for the electric blues itself. Their work, in turn, would directly influence the soul, rock, blues rock, and psychedelic styles that would come to dominate popular music in the middle to late sixties.

The Chicago Electric Blues, Chess Records, and Willie Dixon

The electric blues scene in Chicago was an outgrowth of the Second Great Migration. Coinciding with the start of World War II, millions of African Americans left the South seeking better jobs and new opportunities in the large industrial cities of the North. Chicago became one of the most common destinations, second only to New York. By the end of the forties, the city's Black population had nearly doubled in size—growing from 277,731 in 1940 to 492,265 in 1950 (with approximately 55 percent of that increase coming directly from migration).[1] Earlier in the decade, Chicago's Black music scene had been dominated by postwar rhythm & blues styles, with local musicians emulating the jump blues of Louis Jordan or the urbane West Coast electric guitar sounds of T-Bone Walker. But the scene shifted as the city's newly migrated population instead came to favor performers like Muddy Waters, who adapted the older rural blues style of the Mississippi Delta to fit the electric-guitar-centered aesthetic prevalent in Chicago nightclubs at the time. As Elijah Wald explains, "Compared to the West Coast artists, [Waters's] sound was clearly archaic. . . . Nonetheless, for a lot of transplanted Mississippians his electrified version of the Delta style was a perfect combination of old and new."[2] This hybridized form of electric blues quickly became popular among the city's Black adult audiences, and by the early fifties it was the leading style in the scene. At the same time, thanks to Chicago-based independent labels, Chicago electric blues recordings were also becoming hits on the national rhythm & blues charts.

Initially, for live performances, most Chicago electric blues bands did not include bass players. However, in the recording studio—where the bass's absence would've been more noticeable—it was upright bassists, such as Willie Dixon (1915–1992), who would accompany the musicians. Born in Mississippi, Dixon started playing bass shortly after he relocated to Chicago in 1936, and by the mid-forties, he had already established his reputation as a performer and recording artist. With the Chicago electric blues style growing in popularity, Dixon was quick to adapt. In 1948, he started playing bass on blues sessions for Aristocrat Records, a local independent label owned and operated by Leonard Chess that specialized in music for the Black market; two years later, Leonard brought his brother Phil into the company, and they renamed the label Chess Records.[3] Having worked with Dixon on multiple sessions, Leonard and Phil Chess both recognized his skills as a musician, songwriter, arranger, talent scout, and producer, and so in 1953 they hired him as a full-time employee. As part of his duties, Dixon became Chess Records' in-house bassist, adding the sound of his upright to the company's bevy of adult-oriented electric blues hits, including Muddy Waters's "I'm Your Hoochie Coochie Man" (1954), "Just Make Love to Me" (1954), "I'm Ready" (1954), and "Mannish Boy" (1955); Little Walter's "My Babe" (1955); Howlin' Wolf's "Smokestack Lightning" (1956); and more. At the same time, Dixon also appeared on Chess's more youth-oriented, rhythm & blues/rock 'n' roll-oriented releases, such as the Moonglows' No. 1 hit "Sincerely" (1954) and nearly all of Chuck Berry's and Bo Diddley's early hits.

As a session bassist, Dixon embraced his role as an accompanist, playing lines that filled out a recording without drawing too much attention. Describing his approach in the studio, guitarist Jimmy Rogers recalled, "It wasn't hard at all to work with Dixon because he would never really stay in the way. He knows how to lay in the background. An upright bass is not very loud anyway and in the studio he wasn't really coming through to interfere with our sound."[4] But while Dixon's subtle approach served to ground Chess's releases throughout the fifties, his bass lines were still studio inventions. They represented a particular musical aesthetic that the Chess brothers wanted for their records, rather than one that represented the actual sounds of Chicago's nightclubs. As the fifties wore on, many of the younger musicians in the scene instead wanted their records to better match their live performances, which were now increasingly featuring the distinctive sound of the electric bass.

The First Electric Bassists in Chicago

At the heart of the Chicago electric blues style were electric guitarists who played their instruments through loud, overdriven amplifiers.[5] Yet, despite their appreciation of volume and amplification, Chicago electric blues musicians were somewhat slow to adopt the electric bass. As Robert Palmer notes, the instrument was only introduced into the scene in the late fifties, as part of a generational divide between musicians associated with Chicago's South and West Sides.[6] Rather than following Muddy Waters's old-fashioned, Delta-inspired model, young West Side guitarists like Otis Rush, Magic Sam, and Buddy Guy instead emulated B.B. King's more modern (and, at the time, far more commercially successful) style. Musically, the West Side groups also incorporated contemporary trends in rhythm & blues, including the styles popularized by current Chess hitmakers Chuck Berry and Bo Diddley. Their eventual embrace of the electric bass was thus part of a wider effort to update the sound of the electric blues for a new, younger audience.

By most accounts, the city's first electric bassist was Willie D. Warren (1924–2000), an Arkansas native who had moved to Chicago in the early fifties. From about 1956 to 1958, Warren worked with Otis Rush's band, where he developed a style of playing in which he would mimic the sound of a bass by detuning his electric guitar and only playing on its lower strings. According to Rush, this ramshackle "guitar bass" method became highly influential:

> I took Willie D. Warren and had him tune his strings down. I kept listening to the sound, and I said, "I'm gonna stick with this guy." I went and bought a better amp for him, okay? That made the guitar sound a little more stronger and deep. And then everybody from every direction came to see what we was doin'. Muddy Waters, the [Howlin'] Wolf, you name 'em—they was comin' by to see how we was getting the sound. After they learned what was happenin', they didn't ask who or where it came from. They found it, and *gone.* That's how it went all over Chicago.[7]

In the highly competitive Chicago blues scene, Warren's innovation proved to be a lucrative advantage: live audiences could hear and feel a bass line that could compete with the volume of the amplified electric guitars. As it had with other styles, the incorporation of electric bass made the music louder and better for dancing. Drummer Fred Below, Warren's bandmate, described its impact:

> When I got with Otis Rush we had the first band in the city of Chicago to use electric bass. And this guy Willie he come in and played that bass . . . and when this guy came in and played that rundown guitar sound like a bass. Oh, man, that turned the blues medium just around a little bit. Because before he came on the scene everybody was using two guitars and no bass. Then we got two saxophone players. . . . Then we had a big sound.[8]

Below's implication is that, in Chicago, the bigger sound, the better the band. And, given the city's surplus of guitarists, any of whom could potentially make the lateral move to electric bass, it is not surprising that even the older South Side bandleaders were quick to follow suit.

But Warren's story begs the question: Why didn't he play an actual four-string electric bass? Although no definitive answer appears to survive, it is likely that he simply did not have access to one. For example, when electric bassist Andrew "A. W." Stephenson auditioned for Muddy Waters's live band in 1958, he followed Warren's detuned guitar model. After he got the gig, he recalled, "I had to order an electric bass from Fender, and it took me six months before I could get it."[9] In other words, even though instrument manufacturers were ostensibly selling electric basses, that did not mean that they were easy to get. Stephenson's account, in fact, implies both that local instrument retailers didn't carry Fender Precision Basses *and* that there was a backlog for them at the factory.

Scarcity was not the only issue. Around the time that Stephenson joined Waters's band, guitarist Dave Myers (1926–2001), known for his work with the Aces, got his first electric bass through an endorsement deal with Fender.[10] As he recalled,

> I never was able to buy [an electric bass], but I just happened to have been in the right place at the right time. A guy that knew me owned [the Chicago Music Company at Eighteenth and Halsted] . . . So this [Fender representative] come in with five Precision Basses. This young fella called me up and so I came up and take a look. That thing was *terrible*. Long neck, like that. Had the big strings on it, and I was thinking about my corns [calluses]. I was scared of that. Shit, that thing looked odd to me.[11]

Like other musicians in the electric bass's early years, Myers was initially skeptical of this strange-looking new instrument. To make matters worse, when he took it home, he ran into a much bigger problem: "I just hooked it up to the amplifier and hit the strings and all the speakers shot out. And I had to play that night. I was mad, boy. I turned around and got another amplifier, and it blew that one too. . . . That bass blew out five amplifiers for me."[12] After voicing his complaints to Fender, the company eventually sent him a brand-new, third-generation Fender Bassman, which featured four 10-inch speakers and 40 watts of power. "That amplifier brought it really out," he stated. "It brought it out to where it was four times louder than the acoustic [bass]. The sound that come out of that was amazing to me. With that amplifier, I run everybody in this city that play acoustic out one by one."[13] Myer's first steady work as an electric bassist came when he joined Earl Hooker's touring band, and he soon discovered that his new instrument elicited enthusiastic responses from audiences. As he explained, "We'd start on one tune, and they'd have to stop us from playing so the people could settle down. They would all be standing up on their chairs and going wild. That's when I knew I really had something going with that Fender Bass."[14] These frenzied reactions convinced Myers that he had been right to switch instruments, and while he did not stay with Hooker for very long, these formative experiences helped establish him as an in-demand gigging blues bassist.

Although the early electric bassists in Chicago had found it difficult to acquire reliable equipment, once they were able to harness the power of a fully functioning instrument and amplifier, the results were undeniable: audiences absolutely loved it.

Jack Myers, Reggie Boyd Sr., and Jerome Arnold

Fueled by the approval of local audiences and bandleaders, Chicago blues musicians quickly came to embrace the electric bass as a live instrument. Moreover, at a time when most rock 'n' roll bands continued to privilege the upright for recording sessions, these musicians were also among the first to regularly use the electric bass in the studio. The careers of three in particular—Jack Myers (1937–2011), Reggie Boyd Sr. (1931–2010), and Jerome Arnold (b. 1936)—demonstrate how the increasing acceptance of the electric bass coincided with and contributed to consequential shifts in the sound and culture of the Chicago electric blues scene.

Jack Myers's playing epitomized the new bass-driven sound of the city's Black blues clubs.[15] Having moved with his family from Memphis to Chicago at the age of four, he started out as a guitarist before switching to electric bass. His professional career as a bassist began in September 1959, when he briefly joined Otis Rush's band.[16] Shortly thereafter, he replaced Dave Myers (reportedly his second cousin) in Earl Hooker's band and then spent a year apprenticing with Hooker, before he was lured away by Buddy Guy.[17] According to Guy,

> When the Fender bass first came along, I remember seeing this kid Jack Myers play it with Earl Hooker's band. . . . Hooker actually owned the bass, so the only time that boy could play, he had to work with Earl Hooker. But I found out that Willie Dixon had a Fender bass that he'd pawned at a place on 47th and State. So I told that boy, "If you wanna play with me, I'll go get that Fender out of pawn from Dixon." And I gave it to Jack, 'cause he was a good little bass player.[18]

Now in possession of one of the few electric basses in Chicago, Myers joined Guy's live band and found that his style complimented Guy's modern West Side, single-string soloing technique, as his prominent bass lines gave the music such a strong harmonic foundation that Guy was freed from having to play chords. When Chess offered Guy his own record deal in 1960, he brought Myers with him into the studio, and Myers subsequently appeared on nearly all of Guy's recordings for Chess, including "First Time I Met the Blues" (1960) and "Stone Crazy" (1962).

Ultimately, Guy was never fully satisfied with his Chess recordings, as Leonard Chess infamously forced him to fit the label's more conservative electric blues aesthetic. But while Chess may have made Guy tone down his recorded performances, he appears to have had no problems with Myers playing electric bass. In fact, many of Guy's records for Chess ended up foregrounding both Myers's assertive style and the distinctive sound of his Fender Precision Bass—so much so that, according to Guy, "You can hear him on a couple of my records where it sounds like he was soloing. The horn players would say he was playing too much, but at the end of the bar he would come out on top, and they'd all bust out laughing."[19] Working with Guy, Myers also recorded at Chess as a sideman, accompanying artists such as Sonny Boy Williamson II, Little Walter, and Koko Taylor (he played electric bass on Taylor's hit 1966 version of "Wang Dang Doodle").

Myers's most significant recordings, however, were with Junior Wells, most notably Wells's landmark debut album *Hoodoo Man Blues* (1965). Released on Bob Koester's Delmark Records, *Hoodoo Man Blues* is now considered one of the greatest blues albums of the sixties, and its success was due, in part, to the unprecedented creative control that Koester afforded Wells.[20] Contrary to the practices at Chess, Koester agreed to let Wells handpick his musicians (Jack Myers on electric bass, Buddy Guy on electric guitar, and Billy Warren on drums), choose his own material, and extend beyond the standard three-minute single format. The result was a twelve-track LP that came as close to recreating the diverse sounds of the city's blues clubs as any album to date. It included original songs alongside James Brown–inspired funk, modernized versions of blues classics, an uptempo cover of "Hound Dog," and more. Reflecting the electric bass's now-established position within the Chicago electric blues scene, the sounds of Myers's Precision Bass and Bassman amplifier are prominently featured in the mix, providing both a dynamic contrast to Guy's guitar playing and a solid foundation that anchors the entire ensemble.

Reggie Boyd Sr. likewise developed his own innovative approach to the electric bass while working as a session musician for Chess.[21] Originally from Jackson, Tennessee, Boyd's family relocated to the South Side of Chicago when he was in elementary school. He then started playing guitar in the late forties, drawing inspiration from the music of Louis Jordan and Nat King Cole. He joined the Army after graduating from high school, where he was exposed to bebop and joined the Special Services swing band. After his stint was over, he returned to Chicago and used the GI Bill to enroll in a local music school, where he studied classical music theory, sight-reading, and arranging. With electric blues coming to dominate the city's live music scene in the early fifties, Boyd adapted to prevailing trends and found regular work as a gigging sideman. He also became an in-demand guitar instructor and eventually taught multiple generations of musicians (among his students were Otis Rush, Louis Myers, Howlin' Wolf, Syl Johnson, and Fenton Robinson).[22] Though he never became as well known as some of his pupils, his technical and theoretical knowledge were legendary across Chicago, and he was widely regarded as a musician's musician. As Robert Lockwood Jr. described him, "He can play his ass off! None of the guys he taught didn't really do nothin' with it like they should have done. He taught a lot of peoples . . . but none of 'em ever made it up close to him. . . . He was too far away from everybody."[23]

Boyd's transition to the electric bass came out of his recording work for local Chicago studios, a career move that Willie Dixon helped facilitate. For example, Dixon first hired Boyd to accompany an Otis Rush session for Cobra Records in 1957 and, two years later, brought him in to play lead guitar for a Jimmy Rogers session at Chess, where Boyd deployed his considerable technical abilities on Rogers's "Rock This House" (1959). In an effort to pick up more recording gigs, Boyd acquired a Fender Precision Bass and adapted his skill set once again, this time to contemporary rhythm & blues styles.[24] His first session as an electric bassist was at Chess, where Dixon paired him with the Vibrations to record a new novelty dance number, "The Watusi" (1960). As Boyd recalled the session, "I was playing bass with a different style, like a guitar. I was using fingerings, and I played it fast, because I wasn't a real bass player. So [Leonard] Chess had this idea; he said, 'Blow the bass up.' It was the first time they ever blew the bass up. The bass was a background instrument prior to that."[25] Although Chess may have enforced a relatively narrow aesthetic for his label's blues releases, when it came to recording other styles of Black popular music, he was far more open to experimentation.

For "The Watusi," Chess decided to artificially boost the sound of Boyd's bass, an unconventional move that sonically situated the electric bass as the song's primary rhythmic driver. His instincts paid off, as Boyd's prominent bass line helped establish a new Black dance craze.[26]

The success of "The Watusi" also convinced Chess to bring Boyd back for future sessions, which is how, in January 1961, he became the first electric bassist to record with Chuck Berry.[27] Of the three songs that Boyd recorded with Berry, "I'm Talking About You" epitomizes his hard-driving approach.[28] For almost the entire song, Boyd plays a relentless, picked bass line that clocks in at around three hundred beats per minute, and when the rest of the band drops out on the final two bars of each verse and chorus, Boyd simply powers through. (Berry was reportedly so impressed with his playing that he offered to employ Boyd full time, but Boyd turned him down.)[29]

Chess continued to hire Boyd as an electric bassist on and off through the mid-sixties. In 1961, he played on Etta James's rhythm & blues hits "Something's Got a Hold on Me" (1962) and "Next Door to the Blues" (1962), and in 1965, he also cut a few album tracks with Buddy Guy. But, in the end, Boyd never really thought of himself as an electric bassist. It was just something he did on the side to earn a little extra money. Nonetheless, he deserves credit for establishing a new bass-centric aesthetic at Chess and for his distinctive style, which anticipated the virtuosic approaches that later session bassists would develop throughout the sixties.

Jerome Arnold's career, by contrast, ultimately highlighted white audiences' increasing fascination with the electric blues style. Born and raised in Chicago, Jerome was the younger brother of singer/harmonica player/guitarist Billy Boy Arnold. As Billy Boy recalled,

> By about 1958 [Jerome] started getting' interested in music. He saw Syl Johnson's brother Mack play bass, and he said, "I think I can play that." So he went and got himself [a Fender Precision Bass], and Jerome started playin' with Byther Smith and some smaller, unknown bands. He didn't sing, but he learned the bass real fast. He decided he wanted to get into music, and he was dedicated.[30]

Arnold, like the other bassists discussed in this interlude, initially made his living as a gigging musician in the city's electric blues scene, moving from band to band, including short stints with his brother, Otis Rush, Muddy Waters, and Little Walter. By the early sixties, he had landed a steady gig playing in Howlin' Wolf's band, and starting in September

1962, he also accompanied Wolf on sessions at Chess, making him the first electric bassist to record with the singer. With Wolf, Arnold's electric bass style is most clearly audible on "Three Hundred Pounds of Joy" (1963) and in his insistent rhythmic playing on "Tail Dragger" (1964).

In late 1963, Arnold began working with a local white harmonica player and singer named Paul Butterfield. A Chicago native from a middle-class family, Butterfield had developed an interest in the electric blues after visiting South Side nightclubs while he was in high school. In his late teen years, he taught himself to play amplified harmonica in the style of Little Walter and began to regularly sit in with many of the top Black bands in the city. When Butterfield was offered a residency at Big John's, a folk club on the North Side frequented by white college students, he sought out a Black rhythm section to accompany him, hiring Jerome Arnold and drummer Sam Lay away from Howlin' Wolf's band with the promise of better pay. As Lay recalled, "We was looking at the money part of it. . . . We had a guaranteed four nights a week in one place. . . . And the money was, like, 20 bucks a night, man—that was a lot of money back then . . . Working with Wolf we was getting, like, $12.50 a night, and we were working just on the weekends."[31] Although Arnold and Lay benefited financially from this new arrangement, Butterfield's ability to offer these higher wages was inherently tied to the entrenched racial segregation in Chicago.[32] White clubs paid substantially better than the Black clubs, and although Butterfield may have employed an integrated band and eventually brought in even more Black South Side musicians, he would not have been offered the initial residency if he himself had been Black. As Wald explains,

> The white players [in the Butterfield Band] had paid some dues on the Black club scene, but also had access to audiences their Black peers couldn't reach—specifically all the white kids who wanted to enjoy the South Side sound but did not feel comfortable in ghetto bars . . . [B]y attracting a new audience these artists opened up opportunities for their Black peers, but the fact remained that competent white novices could get jobs that expert Black veterans could not.[33]

Grounded by Arnold's steady bass playing, the Paul Butterfield Blues Band became a top draw and built a new, local white audience for the Chicago electric blues.

In 1964, the Butterfield Band signed to Elektra Records after producer Paul Rothchild scouted them playing at Big John's. Unlike Chess,

Figure 19. Jerome Arnold with the Butterfield Blues Band at the 1965 Newport Folk Festival. (Source: *Festival*, dir. Murray Lerner, 1967.)

which was still attempting to sell its product to mainstream Black listeners, Elektra was a New York–based indie label that specifically aimed their releases at a niche white folk revival audience. The connection between the Butterfield Band and the folk revival was further solidified when they were asked to perform at the 1965 Newport Folk Festival (Figure 19), where they became the first band to introduce the Chicago electric blues style to Newport audiences. Additionally, at the festival, Arnold and other members of the Butterfield Band accompanied Bob Dylan's infamous "going electric" set.[34]

Even though the Butterfield Band was the first electric blues act on the Elektra roster, the company decided to simply market them the same way they marketed their acoustic folksingers. Thus, the group's first official release—an early version of "Born in Chicago"—was included on an Elektra budget compilation LP titled *Folksong '65* alongside recordings by the likes of Judy Collins, Tom Paxton, and Phil Ochs. Aided by the buzz that came with the Butterfield Band's role in the Dylan/Newport controversy, the LP became an unexpected hit, reportedly selling sixty thousand copies in its first month.[35] The band's national reputation was finally established with the release of *The Paul Butterfield Blues Band* LP in October 1965, which reached No. 123 on the *Billboard* albums chart. On it, Arnold sticks to short, repeated electric bass riffs. His playing is foundational, laying down a steady, yet clearly audible, groove that locks in with the drums and provides a harmonic scaffolding for the soloists to build upon. This straightforward approach essentially defined Arnold's style, and he used it again to great effect on the band's second LP, *East-West* (1966)—which made it to No. 65 on the albums chart. Arnold parted ways with the Butterfield Band in 1967. In an interview two years later, he succinctly summarized his experience with Butterfield, stating, "I was with the band four years, and in that time gathered in some bread."[36]

Between their first two LPs and their live tours, the Butterfield Band amassed an impressive following of devoted fans, most notably in San Francisco, where they came to be associated with psychedelic bands like Jefferson Airplane and the Grateful Dead (their success also prompted Elektra to sign other blues rock bands, such as the Doors, the Stooges, and MC5). The Butterfield Band therefore has come to represent a significant shift in the history of the Chicago electric blues, marking the music's adoption by white underground rock and folk fans.

Conclusion

If, in 1958, electric basses were nearly unobtainable in Chicago, by the early sixties, they were considered indispensable components of the city's electric blues bands. In fact, for recording work, upright basses had become so passé that, by 1962, Willie Dixon had largely given up playing on sessions altogether.[37] Although he still participated in sessions as a producer and songwriter, his role as an accompanist had now been taken over by an ever-growing roster of local blues electric bassists, which—in addition to A. W. Stephenson, Dave Myers, Jack Myers, and Jerome Arnold—also included Mack Thompson and Odell Campbell, who both played on Magic Sam's Cobra-era recordings; Earnest Johnson, who played on Muddy Waters's "You Need Love" (1962); Milton Rector, who played on Sonny Boy Williamson II's "Help Me" (1963); and Andrew "Blueblood" McMahon, who replaced Arnold in Howlin' Wolf's band and played on "Killing Floor" (1965).

Despite their best efforts to modernize the sound of the Chicago electric blues, the style's national popularity continued to wane among Black audiences, and by the mid-sixties, the same musicians were now more likely to find support among the white folk revival than the Black musical mainstream. Whereas the Chicago electric blues's initial mixture of rural and urban styles had appealed to the tastes of the Second Great Migration generation, their children instead preferred newer rhythm

& blues styles, such as soul. These new tastes were as much political as they were musical. As Wald notes, "The soul era was a time of burgeoning Black pride, and if life was hard in the ghettos of urban America, young African Americans still had no interest in being reminded of the Southern cotton fields."[38] Some electric bassists, such as Reggie Boyd Sr., were initially able to capitalize on these changing trends, but they too were soon replaced by a younger generation of musicians who specialized in the new styles.[39]

Coming out of the local Chicago electric blues scene, the bassists discussed in this interlude encapsulate significant developments in popular music, even if their commercial successes were somewhat limited. First, these musicians fundamentally altered the sound of the electric blues, ushering in a new aesthetic in which audiences would now come to expect a loud, prominent low end that could both support and drive the music. Second, by collectively popularizing the electric bass within the local Chicago electric blues scene, these musicians played a key role in promoting the instrument's wider acceptance within Black musical styles. Lastly, they would have a large, if unexpected, impact on the next generation of white rock musicians. As detailed later in this book, even before the advent of psychedelia, their recordings were being embraced by young British groups like the Beatles and the Rolling Stones, who drew on their inspiration to craft some of the most widely celebrated and commercially successful pop music of all time.

FOUR | The Picked Instrument

Reinventing the Sound of the Electric Bass

The most distinctive electric bass recording of the early sixties was also *Billboard*'s best-performing single of 1963. Recorded at Norman Petty's studio in Clovis, New Mexico—the same studio where Buddy Holly recorded his hits—Jimmy Gilmer and the Fireballs' "Sugar Shack" was unconventional by design. It foregrounded a catchy keyboard hook played on a Hammond Solovox and it featured not one, but *two* electric basses: bassist Stan Lark played a standard bass line on his Rickenbacker 4001, while guitarist George Tomsco used a six-string Danelectro Longhorn bass guitar to supply the song's distinctive, growling lead.[1] Lark specifically remembers choosing the Rickenbacker for its "snappier" bass timbre, and Tomsco recalls that Petty was fascinated with the Longhorn's peculiar sound and insisted they use it on the song.[2] In the end, Petty was right. The combined effect was pure novelty, and it worked: starting first as a regional radio hit, "Sugar Shack" climbed to the top of the *Billboard* Hot 100, where it spent five weeks at No. 1 (more than any other single that year). Although later critics have tended to belittle the gimmicky recordings of the early sixties, "Sugar Shack" encapsulated a significant moment in popular music history: it was the culmination of an experimental pop tradition in which producers and musicians found commercial success by foregrounding new and distinctive sounds on their recordings.

This chapter chronicles the prehistory of songs like "Sugar Shack," revealing how studio experiments in the late fifties and early sixties produced some of the first popular recordings to showcase the electric bass's unique timbral possibilities. Operating in different musical genres, bassists such as Buddy Wheeler, Guybo Smith, Ladi Geisler, and Harold Bradley collaborated with producers to develop innovative ways of playing and recording their instruments, notably by emphasizing the use of a plectrum (or "pick," as it is better known today). Building on the work of Albin J. Zak III and Travis D. Stimeling, I discuss the different contexts that fueled these timbral experiments and detail how each of the distinctive picked timbres these musicians created came to act as sonic trademarks for the artists they recorded with, including instrumental rock pioneer Duane Eddy, rockabilly singer Eddie Cochran, easy-listening bandleader Bert Kaempfert, and Nashville Sound icons Brenda Lee and Patsy Cline. These novel sounds, I argue, not only helped craft hit records, but ultimately fostered a new low-end aesthetic in American popular music, one that valued prominent, clearly audible bass lines.

Thumbs, Fingers, and Picks

The way that electric bassists physically strike the strings of their instruments has a significant impact on their sound. In the fifties, there were three predominant approaches that bassists could choose from: playing with their thumb, playing with their index finger, or playing with a pick.[3] Each has its own advantages, and today many bassists switch between these techniques, selecting the one most appropriate for a given song. For example, because thumbs are soft, fleshy, and have a large surface area, they give the bass a warm, thick tone. Bassists like Monk Montgomery combined this approach with their Precision Bass's factory-standard foam mute to create a close timbral approximation of an upright bass. Index fingers have less surface area and therefore tend to produce a rounder tone; also, because we use our index fingers more than our thumbs, this added dexterity means that bassists who play with their index fingers—as Shifty Henry and J. W. Brown did—can usually play faster and with a stronger attack. Playing with a pick, usually made of out celluloid, produces a markedly distinct timbre, one that is much sharper and tends to add a percussive effect. As discussed previously, Elvis Presley's, Bobby Lee Jones's, and Reggie Boyd's use of picks are what makes their bass playing stand out in their recordings. These playing styles are then further emphasized (or de-emphasized) based on the settings of the musician's amplifier, not to mention how producers and engineers manipulate the sound of their instruments during the production and postproduction processes.

Although each of these techniques produces a different sound, bassists in the fifties tended to select their approach for practical, rather than musical reasons. Most simply chose what felt natural for them given their prior experience. Upright bassists, then, tended to be thumb or index finger players, while guitarists (like Presley, Jones, and Boyd) were often more comfortable playing with picks. This split has led to a curious authenticity debate among modern electric bassists, who sometimes view picked playing as a sign that the musician is playing "like a guitarist" and therefore not a "real" bassist. Yet, part of what helped the electric bass become so widespread in popular music was its inherent adaptability: the instrument was flexible enough that musicians from a variety of backgrounds could play it using a variety of techniques. And, in the late fifties, the instrument was so new that there simply wasn't any established "right" or "wrong" ways to do it. Moreover, as I argue in this chapter, it was bassists who used picks that were the first to sonically separate the electric bass from the upright.

Novelty Records and Musical Branding

In *I Don't Sound Like Nobody: Remaking Music in 1950s America*, Albin J. Zak III analyzes how fifties pop "recordists" (songwriters, arrangers, engineers, and producers) working for independent labels deliberately crafted unique-sounding records.[4] Unable to compete with major labels' crisp, high-fidelity recordings, indie recordists fundamentally reconceived the recording process by expanding their role beyond simply reproducing live performances. In essence, they embraced the musical and technological possibilities of the studio itself to create new sounds that could only exist on recordings. This fundamental reconceptualization would eventually become the de facto aesthetic of pop production, but in the short term it also manifested in hundreds of hit records that were designed to sonically stand apart from their contemporaries (including, for instance, Sam Philips's recordings with Elvis Presley and Norman Petty's recordings with both Buddy Holly and the Fireballs).

This emphasis on crafting new and distinctive sounds necessitated creative experimentation within the studio. As Zak argues:

> Pop records made the freest, boldest, and for many the most tasteless but ultimately most creative uses of technology, for their only purpose was to make an immediate impact. If their gimmicks wore thin and success proved fleeting, it mattered little once the money had been made. Yet in their preoccupation with commercial success lay also their aesthetic liberation. Despite a lowly mandate of attention-

grabbing sensationalism, postswing recordists and producers worked the interface between music and gadgetry with an inventive, often visionary mind-set.[5]

As more and more of these records became hits, the pop marketplace was increasingly inundated with novelty records, which in turn incentivized recordists to further expand their sonic palette. Timbre therefore became one of the most important ingredients, as producers sought sonic originality by collaborating with musicians to elicit (and manipulate) new sounds from their instruments. This process is most evident in recordings that feature exaggerated, gimmicky effects (such as "Sugar Shack"), but many other producers in this era were conducting similar, if perhaps more subtle, experiments. Significantly, these producers encouraged electric bass players to step beyond the traditional limitations placed on their instruments to finally explore what it might sound like if they were no longer required to approximate the timbre of an upright. In response, these musicians decided to play their electric basses with picks, an approach that gave their bass sounds an added clarity and presence.

Each of the picked electric bass timbres discussed in this chapter became an essential component of specific hit records. Through the popularity of these records, audiences also came to hear these particular timbres as a characteristic component of specific artists' musical styles. And once these connections had been established, many producers deliberately sought to replicate these sounds on those artists' future releases. Timbre was thus also a key marketing tool in the late fifties and early sixties, a practice that Travis D. Stimeling analyzes within the context of country record production practices.[6] As they argue, "Nashville's producers and session musicians were aware that radio listeners and record buyers expected brand consistency from their favorite recording artists," and they therefore turned to a form of musical branding "to distinguish individual recording artists from one another while simultaneously balancing consistency and variety to attract radio listeners and record buyers to their product."[7] This practice, however, was not limited solely to country music. In this era, multiple teams of producers and musicians crafted unique musical brands for the artists they worked with. Working across a wide spectrum of popular music, the four teams discussed in this chapter each invented new bass sounds in an attempt to craft records that were both timbrally distinctive and commercially appealing.

Buddy Wheeler, Lee Hazelwood, and the "Click Bass" Sound

As discussed in Chapter 3, by 1957, multiple rock 'n' roll bands were incorporating the electric bass on stage and, to a lesser extent, in the studio. When it came to recording, however, the electric bass was almost always used as a direct sonic replacement for the upright, and its potentially distinctive timbral characteristics were therefore minimized. This situation changed in 1958, when bassist Buddy Wheeler (ca. 1932–2012) and producer Lee Hazelwood (1929–2007) collaborated to create the "click bass" sound that became a hallmark of guitarist Duane Eddy's records. Adding a markedly percussive feel to Eddy's hit rock 'n' roll instrumentals, Wheeler's picked bass lines provided a solid rhythmic drive that accentuated Eddy's floating guitar melodies. For Hazelwood, this "click" also gave these records a distinctive "cowboy" flavor that he felt perfectly matched Eddy's signature twangy tone.[8] Experienced together on record, these two elements would come to represent Eddy's sonic trademark. Yet this sound came together in stages, developing piecemeal through multiple collaborative experiments in the studio.

Originally a steel guitar player, Buddy Wheeler got his start working as a freelance musician in support of traveling country acts, including Hank Williams and Hank Penny, and as a teenager, he played mandolin in a country duo with his brother around the Washington, DC area. Notably, on July 31, 1948, he performed as part of a country showcase at DC's Constitution Hall organized by future Country Music Association cofounder Connie B. Gay. Featuring Eddy Arnold, Johnnie & Jack, and a then-unknown Kitty Wells, the showcase became the first country concert ever broadcast on network television.[9] By the mid-fifties, Wheeler was living and working in Phoenix, Arizona, playing gigs at country bars and on local television, where he occasionally supported a young Marty Robbins.[10] Through the Phoenix music scene, Wheeler came to know guitarists Al Casey and Duane Eddy, who in turn introduced him to a local DJ named Lee Hazelwood.[11]

In 1955, Hazelwood began to supplement his radio work by recording local talent out of Floyd Ramsey's Ramsey Recorders, using Al Casey's Arizona Hayriders as his in-house backing band. Two years later, Hazelwood relocated to Los Angeles, where he entered into a partnership with Lester Sill, an experienced rhythm & blues record label executive who was then managing the Coasters.[12] Looking to cheaply expand their roster of rock 'n' roll singles, Hazelwood and Sill traveled back to Phoenix, where they eventually recorded Duane Eddy's first instrumental, "Movin' n' Groovin,'" for just ninety dollars.[13] Sill then used his music industry connections to persuade Harry Finfer to release the single on Jamie Records, a Philadelphia-based label co-owned by Dick Clark.[14] At that time, Clark's syndicated television show, *American Bandstand*, had made him the most influential rock 'n' roll tastemaker in the country, a power that he was more than willing to wield for recordings in which he had a direct financial interest. In the end, "Movin'" ended up being only a minor hit, but the release solidified the partnership between Hazelwood, Sill, Eddy, Finfer, and Clark. All they needed now was a sound unique enough to capture the attention of the teen market.

Hazelwood and Eddy were determined to crack the Top 40. To do so, they set out to craft a new, distinctive sound that would be exclusive to Eddy's records. They began with two new pieces of equipment. First, in an attempt to make their recordings sound bigger, Hazelwood and Ramsey procured a makeshift echo chamber for the studio.[15] As Hazelwood recalled, they spent $200 on a cast iron grain tank, placed it in the studio parking lot, and equipped it with "a four-dollar mike at one end and a sixty-cent speaker at the other."[16] Second, Eddy acquired a new amplifier: a Magnatone that had been custom-modified by Buddy Wheeler. Reworking its circuitry, Wheeler had boosted the amp to run 100 watts of power through a single, 15-inch speaker and a tweeter, making it more powerful than any commercially available guitar amplifier at that time.[17] Combining this with a DeArmond Tremolo unit, Eddy eventually discovered the distinctive "twang" that would come to define his guitar tone. With these pieces in place, they were ready to make Eddy's next record.

In March 1958, Hazelwood and Eddy reentered Ramsey Recorders with members of Al Casey's band to record two songs, "Stalkin'" and "Rebel Rouser." Susan Schmidt-Horning describes their approach:

> Along with a group of dedicated local session musicians (including one woman, [rhythm guitarist] Corki Casey), Eddy and Hazelwood consciously sought to *shape* a distinctive sound within the confines of the recording studio. Like Sam Phillips, Lee Hazelwood went for a total effect, but it was an effect generated by the electric guitar as centerpiece.[18]

Nowhere is this guitar-centric approach more evident than on "Rebel Rouser." For this recording, Hazelwood augmented the studio's new echo chamber and Eddy's loud, twangy amplifier with an equally expansive rhythm section. He had planned for this in advance, hiring two rhythm guitarists and two bassists for the session. But here, again, he was not about to pass up a chance for novelty. Rather than hiring two upright players, Hazelwood decided to use one upright bass and one electric— with the upright performing its standard, foundational duty, and the electric providing timbral contrast. At Al Casey's recommendation, Hazelwood brought in Buddy Wheeler to play electric bass, although he had no experience playing the instrument. As Wheeler remembered,

> The electric bass was new and Al told Lee "well Buddy can do that" and I had never touched one. I played steel guitar for Lee before on a few sessions. Al had Jody Reynolds's bass with him in his car. He showed me the basics a couple of days before the session—we didn't even know what songs were going to be recorded. I was working very hard and my fingers were too short.[19]

Despite Wheeler's inexperience, he brought something unique with him: his amplifier. Just as he had done for Eddy, Wheeler had modi- fied his own Magnatone amp (this one featuring *two* 15-inch speakers) to produce a powerful, clean tone with lots of headroom. Drawing on his background playing guitar and mandolin, Wheeler also played the elec- tric bass with a pick, which—when fed through this modified amplifier— created a distinctive, percussive "clicking" sound. This click bass timbre is obviously indebted to the slap style that was then popular among coun- try upright players, but it is clear within the context of the recording that Wheeler is not playing an upright, as the deep, powerful sound of his picked electric bass carries through in each note and accentuates the song's rhythm. And, ultimately, it was the record's full effect that really mattered: Eddy's twangy lead guitar, supported by Wheeler's prominent bass line and the rest of the band, was run through an echo chamber and then overdubbed with saxophone, hand claps, and background vocals. By the standards of the day, "Rebel Rouser" sounded absolutely colossal.

The single, however, came very close to not becoming a hit. When Jamie Records first issued "Rebel Rouser" in May 1958, it was actu- ally intended to be the B-side, as both Hazelwood and Dick Clark had thought that "Stalkin'" was a better single. Fortunately for all involved, Clark eventually gave the flip side a try. As Eddy explained,

> Dick Clark was doing a record hop, and he'd underestimated how many records to bring. About a half hour to go, he'd played every-

thing, including "Stalkin'," which you couldn't really dance to. So he started turning records over. When he played "Rebel Rouser," the kids came up and said, "Play that again." He ended up playing it three or four times. That got it on *Bandstand*, and then the radio stations started playing it.[20]

With Clark's backing, "Rebel Rouser" became a smash, eventually climbing to No. 6 on the Hot 100. Unlike "Movin'," "Rebel" oozes novelty—it was a rock 'n' roll instrumental with a country flair. Nothing on the radio in 1958 sounded quite like it. Better still, its prominent, "click" bass line meant that you could dance to it.

What had begun as an experiment in the studio to produce novel-sounding records soon became Duane Eddy's musical brand. It was a sound that his audience came to expect from his subsequent recordings, and the rhythmic drive supplied by Wheeler's click bass was one of its defining features. Over the next few years, Eddy would have a string of Top 40 hit instrumentals undergirded by Wheeler's picked bass lines. Perhaps most tellingly, Wheeler's role was considered so essential to Eddy's sound that the bassist was continually contracted to play on his recording sessions well after he stopped touring with Eddy's live band.

Guybo Smith and Eddie Cochran

Eddie Cochran's rockabilly classic "Summertime Blues" entered the *Billboard* Hot 100 the same week that "Rebel Rouser" peaked on the chart. Like Eddy, Cochran's recording foregrounded the distinctive sound of a picked electric bass, played by Connie "Guybo" Smith (1939–2023). Yet, while the percussive timbres of Wheeler's and Smith's basses are very similar, the latter bassist's contributions are even more apparent, as his bass is not only louder in the mix but is situated within a much thinner musical texture. At the time of their release, Cochran's "Summertime Blues" and its follow-up, "C'Mon Everybody," featured the most prominent electric bass sounds yet put on record.

Smith and Cochran met in junior high in 1951.[21] Back then, Smith was playing upright bass in the school band, while also learning mandolin and steel guitar. He and Cochran became fast friends, and in 1953 they formed a group called the Melodie Boys. After meeting Hank Cochran (no relation to Eddie), they all teamed up to form the Cochran Brothers, with Smith on upright bass. Together the group recorded a series of country singles for Ekko records in the mid-fifties, and although none became hits, these sessions allowed Cochran and Smith to build their confidence in the studio, a skill set they further expanded by recording demos for American Music at Gold Star's Studio B in Los Angeles.

With the newfound popularity of rock 'n' roll, Eddie decided to pursue a more rockabilly-infused sound and embarked on a solo career in 1956. That summer he achieved two important career milestones: he released his first single, "Skinny Jim," on Crest Records, and he landed a short appearance in the movie *The Girl Can't Help It* (1956), where he mimed along to his recording of "Twenty Flight Rock." Both recordings prominently featured the sound of Smith's upright, slap bass style—a style that Gold Star's cofounder Stan Ross described as "Guybo's trademark."[22] On the basis of these performances, Cochran secured a recording contract with Liberty Records, and Smith came with him. Describing their working relationship, biographer Rob Finnis writes that "Smith developed a telepathic musical rapport with Cochran and went on to play on virtually all of his recordings until late 1958."[23]

After Cochran's first Liberty single became a hit in early 1957, he and Smith went on tour, performing alongside acts like Chuck Berry and the Everly Brothers. They were soon dividing their time between the road and the studio, where they continued to experiment. In September 1957, they returned to Gold Star to work on a song called "Ah, Pretty Girl," and on January 12, 1958, they recorded "Pretty Girl" (a different song) at Liberty Custom Recorders in Hollywood (they eventually scrapped the former, re-recording it in April, and Liberty released the latter as the B-side to "Teresa").[24] For both recordings, Smith decided to play electric bass. Although his bass timbre is not particularly distinct on either song, these sessions allowed him to try out the Fender Precision Bass and Bassman amplifier that he would come to use on his future sessions with Cochran, including Cochran's two most recognizable hits.

Featuring Smith on electric bass, Cochran on vocals and guitar, and Earl Palmer on drums, "Summertime Blues" was recorded at Gold Star in May 1958 and released the following month.[25] As had long been the norm, Cochran not only played on his own session, he also produced it. For this session, he and Smith decided to try out a new percussive electric bass timbre, one that might have a similar propulsive drive to Smith's signature upright, slap bass style. Ultimately, this new sound was the result of three key decisions: first, Smith removed the Precision Bass's bridge cover (which housed its rubber mute); second, he turned up his amplifier; and third, he played his bass with a pick.[26] Using a pick, and a thick one at that, Smith developed a forceful attack that gave his bass a clear, powerful tone, and without the mute to deaden the strings, his bass has noticeably greater sustain. For example, the bass line to "Summertime Blues" is actually quite similar to Presley's bass line on "Baby I Don't Care," with Smith opening the song by hammering on his electric bass from a D# to an E (a "menacing bass line" that Julie Mundy and Darrel Higham argue "sets the tone of the song").[27] Unlike Presley's recording, however, the bass never recedes into the background. Rather, by loosening the usual restrictions placed on bass amplification in the studio, Smith's trebly bass line rings out loud and clear throughout, providing a foundation on which Cochran could build his interlocking, overdubbed parts. By modifying the electric bass away from its factory-designed setup, Smith and Cochran crafted their own innovative electric bass timbre, one that would become a key part of Cochran's signature musical brand.

The sound of Smith's electric bass playing, and the sound of his pick specifically, are even more audible on Cochran's follow-up single, "C'Mon Everybody," which features a nearly identical bass line. Recorded at Gold Star in October 1958, "Everybody" has a much faster tempo (by about twenty beats per minute). Smith's loud, forceful playing at this speed makes the sound of his electric bass even more conspicuous, as the microphones capture not only the notes emanating from his amplifier but also the clicking sound that his thick pick makes as he strikes the strings. Mixed louder than the drums, Smith's sustaining, picked bass line drives the record's up-tempo rhythmic feel while simultaneously adding to it an overall sense of sonic novelty.

In 1959, Guybo Smith stopped touring and settled down with his wife Marilyn. Cochran tragically died in England the following year after sustaining injuries from a car crash.[28] Today, "Summertime Blues" and "C'Mon Everybody" are remembered as the core of their recorded output. Both songs were hits in their time: "Summertime" climbed to No. 8 on the *Billboard* Hot 100 and "C'Mon" reached a respectable No. 35; in the UK, "C'Mon" was the bigger hit, peaking at No. 6 on the singles chart, while "Summertime" only made it to No. 18. They also remained in circulation decades after their release thanks to covers by subsequent musicians.[29] The enduring appeal of these two songs is in many ways inseparable from the distinctive electric bass timbre that Smith and Cochran developed together.

Ladi Geisler, Bert Kaempfert, and the *Knackbass* Sound

At the same time that Buddy Wheeler and Guybo Smith were adding their own percussive electric bass sounds to rock 'n' roll records, German session musician Ladi Geisler was experimenting with his own version of a picked bass timbre. His goals, however, were markedly different from his American contemporaries': whereas Wheeler and Smith had been using the electric bass to add a sense of rhythmic drive, Geisler instead sought to emphasize *pitch*, making his bass lines sound clearer on record than had been previously possible. To accomplish this feat, he had to overcome not only the constraints of the recording studio, but those of his instrument as well.

Born in Prague, Miloslav Ladislav "Ladi" Geisler (1927–2011) learned to play the violin as a boy.[30] He became a German in 1938, after Hitler annexed the Sudetenland, and at the age of fifteen, he was conscripted into the Nazi Air Force. After being injured while stationed at the Eastern Front, Geisler was captured by the British and sent to a prisoner-of-war camp in Denmark. There he acquired an acoustic guitar that he taught himself to play. Drawing on informal electrical engineering training he had received from his father, Geisler also began experimenting with electric guitar technology, eventually designing a pickup for his acoustic guitar and building his own amplifier.

After World War II, Geisler relocated to Hamburg to work as a professional musician. As an important shipping port, Hamburg had long been home to a thriving entertainment culture, and with the British helping to rebuild, music and nightlife quickly returned to the city. Once Germany was officially divided into two states in 1949, Julia Sneeringer notes, "Hamburg became [West Germany's] largest city and media capital," and its increasing economic recovery throughout the fifties expanded the city's attraction as a tourist destination.[31] Geisler flourished within Hamburg's music scene and was quickly recognized as one of the most versatile guitarists in the city. By the mid-fifties, this recognition had opened up further performance opportunities for him on Norddeutsche Rundfunk (North German Radio), a key launching pad for German musicians in this era. As Klaus Nathaus explains:

> Radio was of primary importance for the [West German] music industry from the late 1940s to the early 1960s, not only because it maintained recording studios and employed musicians on which record companies depended. In the early post-war years, record firms bought master tapes produced in broadcasting studios or commissioned recordings conducted by producers, engineers and musicians who were employed with the broadcasters and did recording sessions as an increasingly lucrative side job.[32]

Geisler's career followed this exact trajectory: he augmented his radio and nightclub performances with session work for Germany's expanding record industry, including for Polydor Records, which operated its own Studio Rahlstedt in Hamburg. Through his work with Polydor, Geisler began the career-defining collaboration with the German composer and bandleader Bert Kaempfert (1923–1980) that would lead him to adopt the electric bass.

Geisler's switch to electric bass was born out of an attempt to overcome the technical limitations of Polydor's recording process. Before the widespread adoption of magnetic tape-recording, recording studios like Studio Rahlstedt recorded directly to acetate disc. This process worked by having a band perform live into a series of microphones set up around the studio. Their signals were then sent through a mixing board, which in turn sent a single, mixed signal through to the acetate machine that carved the recording directly onto disc. Robust bass frequencies tended to make the carving arm on acetate machines jump out of its grooves and were thus severely restricted. This process consequently produced recordings on which the sound of the bass was muffled, if not completely inaudible. As a potential workaround, Kaempfert originally decided to have Geisler double the upright bass with his guitar, thereby increasing the prominence of a recording's bass line without necessarily increasing its volume. As Geisler recalled,

> At first I tried to emphasize the bass with a detuned guitar. But the strings were a bit dull and slack, even though it was quite a good effect. Then I got a brochure with an announcement that Gibson, the US company, was making an electric bass. Of course, I ordered it straight away. Unfortunately, the thing had such a dark, queasy sound, that you couldn't get this effect with it. The bass had to be made clearer and easier to hear. [Kaempfert] advised me to increase the highs and take out the lows—which should come from the double bass. . . . So I built a little [pickup] that I could use to lighten the bass and played with a pick, a style in which striking the strings creates a distinctive, sonic *knackendes* [ripping] attack. That was something that became characteristic of Kaempfert's music.[33]

In order to better blend with the upright bass he was doubling, Geisler augmented his picked bass style by muting the strings with the palm of his right hand. He further honed this style through his collaborations with Kaempfert; as he explained:

In the very beginning, I actually played in unison with the double bass. As a guitarist, it was too boring for me, and [Kaempfert] noticed that he could give me a little more "meat" because I was always throwing in some filler notes and embellishments to my parts. . . . After that happened, he told me that I should work even more on this effect. While playing, he would often look over at me and say, "Ladi, komm, lass mal knacken!" ["Ladi, come on, let it rip!"]. So naturally that is how this sound came to be known as *knackbass*.[34]

Now playing a modified first-generation Gibson EB-1, Geisler became known for this characteristic *knackbass* tone, which Kaempfert would repeatedly use as a sonic signature of his recordings.

In 1960, Bert Kaempfert and His Orchestra recorded the bandleader's easy-listening arrangement of "Wonderland by Night," a slow, sentimental instrumental. The recording is essentially an extended showpiece for trumpeter Charly Tabor, but Geisler's *knackbass* is also featured prominently in the mix. Unlike the "clicking" rock- and country-influenced styles discussed earlier in this chapter, Geisler's muted, picked timbre does not add a percussive layer to the music. Rather, it is designed so that each clearly articulated note cuts through the larger orchestral texture, offering a strong harmonic foundation (one, in this instance, that was perfect for slow dancing).

All told, "Wonderland" had the makings of a hit, but there was one remaining obstacle: Polydor was not interested in releasing it. Obviously disappointed, Kaempfert set out to get the record released in the United States. Drawing on all of his music industry connections, he eventually got the record into the hands of Decca producer Milt Gabler, who immediately recognized its potential, signed Kaempfert to an exclusive contract, and released the song as a single in August 1960. Starting with airplay on local radio stations across the South, "Wonderland" grew into a massive hit. Bolstered by Geisler's *knackbass*, it eventually became the first German recording to reach No. 1 on the *Billboard* Hot 100. By February, the single had achieved gold status for selling more than a million units, and by the end of the year, *Cash Box*'s annual disc jockey poll had named Kaempfert's group the "Most Promising Up and Coming Orchestra."[35] After its proven success, Polydor acquiesced and released the single in Germany, where it also reached the Top 10. "Wonderland" kick-started Kaempfert's career as a bandleader and solidified Geisler's *knackbass* as a signature component of his sound. What had begun as an attempt to solve a practical limitation had led to a creative innovation, one that made his records stand out in the marketplace.

The success of "Wonderland" also highlights the inherent diversity of the US pop charts in 1961: the week that it reached No. 1, Kaempfert's easy-listening single beat out both Elvis Presley's "Are You Lonesome Tonight" and the Shirelles' "Will You Still Love Me Tomorrow." Although popular music histories have repeatedly overemphasized music targeted to young people, it is important to recognize that adult-oriented, easy-listening styles continued to have a wide fan base even well into the rock 'n' roll era. It is also worth noting that these two genres also had more in common than is traditionally acknowledged. For instance, a few months after "Wonderland at Night" was released in the United States, Elvis Presley starred in the film *G.I. Blues* (1960), in which he performed "Wooden Heart," a traditional German folksong that Kaempfert had arranged; likewise, Kaempfert also produced the Beatles' very first commercial recordings, for which they reportedly borrowed some of Geisler's amplifiers.

Harold Bradley, Owen Bradley, and the Rise of "Tic-Tac" Bass

The most far-reaching of these new picked bass timbres was the "tic-tac" style that appeared on hundreds of country hits. The American equivalent of Geisler's *knackbass*, tic-tac bass became a key component of the "Nashville Sound."[36] The musician most responsible for popularizing the tic-tac bass sound was guitarist Harold Bradley (1926–2019), who developed the technique while working on sessions with his older brother, producer Owen Bradley (1915–1998). Together, the Bradleys crafted some of the most successful music to come out of Nashville in the sixties.

Born and raised in Nashville, Harold Bradley started playing guitar at the age of twelve, and his first apprenticeship in country music came during the summer of 1943, when he was hired to play electric guitar in Ernest Tubb's Texas Troubadours.[37] As part of the war effort, he was drafted into the Navy the following year and served as a radioman while stationed in Hawaii. After being honorably discharged, he returned to Nashville, where he resumed his work as a professional musician and used the GI Bill to pursue a music degree at George Peabody College. At that time, Peabody did not offer a degree in guitar, so Bradley spent three years studying upright bass, a skill set that he would later draw on when he began playing electric bass. In the meantime, he became a regular at the Grand Ole Opry, where he supported country acts like Eddy Arnold and Bradley Kincaid. His accumulated experience within various styles of country music allowed him to naturally transition into session work, where he adapted his guitar playing to whatever was needed for a particular recording.

Owen Bradley, by contrast, was a full ten years older than his younger brother, and by the time Harold was first learning his instrument, Owen was already a respected multi-instrumentalist, arranger, and bandleader. In 1940, he had been hired as an arranger and musician for Nashville's famed WSM radio station (home of the Opry) and by 1948 had worked his way up to Musical Director. In addition to his radio job and managing his own dance band, Owen also branched out into the world of record-making, first as a session musician, contractor, and A&R man, and then as a producer himself. Owen and Harold Bradley then decided to open a series of small film and recording studios, including one located in the Hillsboro Village neighborhood of Nashville where Kitty Wells, Red Foley, and Pat Boone all recorded. In the mid-fifties, as behind-the-scenes developments instigated a substantial restructuring of Nashville's music industry, Owen's many years of experience positioned him to become one of the leading forces in country music.

The first of these developments came when WSM President Jack DeWitt issued an ultimatum to his employees, forcing them to choose between working for the station or pursuing their side businesses.[38] This demand had the greatest impact on the day-to-day operations of Castle Studio, Nashville's primary recording venue, most of whose employees were in some way connected to WSM. Taking DeWitt seriously, they erred on the side of their steady radio paychecks and abandoned their outside commitments; Castle folded shortly thereafter. Paul Cohen, head of Decca Records's country division, then approached Owen to see if he might relocate to Dallas to work for another established studio. Seizing the opportunity, Owen instead convinced Cohen that he and Harold had the requisite experience to build a brand-new studio in Nashville that could meet Decca's needs. Cohen agreed and guaranteed the Bradleys a minimum of one hundred sessions per year.

In 1955, the brothers opened the new Bradley Film & Recording Studio in the basement of a house at 804 Sixteenth Avenue South—making it the first studio built on what is today known as "Music Row." Despite its confined space and relatively primitive equipment, the studio still produced multiple hits, including Ray Price's "Crazy Arms" (1956),

Gene Vincent's "Be-Bop-a-Lula" (1956), Marty Robbins's "Singing the Blues" (1956), the Johnny Burnette Trio's "The Train Kept a-Rollin'" (1956), Sonny James's "Young Love" (1956), and Ferlin Husky's "Gone" (1957).[39] The Bradleys expanded their operation sometime around 1958, erecting a large Quonset hut in the back of the property to accommodate a second, larger studio, which soon became their primary recording space. When Paul Cohen left Decca's country division in April 1958 to head up the company's subsidiary label, Coral Records, Owen Bradley was named as his replacement, a move that solidified his pride of place within Nashville's recording industry and provided him even more license to experiment with the sound of country music.

With his newfound creative freedom, Owen Bradley became a principal architect of what has come to be known as the "Nashville Sound," a new style of country music that drew on the production practices of easy listening, including classical-influenced string arrangements, layered background vocals, and an increased emphasis on clean electric guitar timbres.[40] Simultaneously, Owen also de-emphasized some of country music's established sonic markers, most notably the sound of steel guitar and fiddles. The ultimate effect was a rich, warm sound that fit comfortably alongside other adult-oriented styles of the time. Yet rather than being a single, standardized style, Travis Stimeling convincingly demonstrates that there were in fact multiple "Nashville Sounds":

> Concerns about the changing musical aesthetics of country music in the Nashville Sound era have exaggerated the similarities between mainstream popular music of the 1950s and 1960s and Nashville country music productions, as well as the apparent homogenizing forces that pop crossover aspirations had on the genre. . . . Although numerous recordings do, indeed, support such assertions, a broader examination of country music recordings made in Nashville during the 1950s and 1960s reveals a remarkable heterogeneity of musical style that complicates—and, in many cases, undermines—this narrative of homogeneity.[41]

Stimeling therefore suggests that it is more productive to hear Nashville Sound–era productions as a series of related, but ultimately distinct musical brands designed around particular artists. The most significant element in maintaining brand consistency for these artists, they argue, was the stable coterie of session musicians—known as the Nashville A-Team—that played on most of these recordings. It was these musicians who ultimately normalized the electric bass's presence in Nashville studios.

Owen Bradley preferred to use the same musicians for each of his sessions. Among these were upright bassist Bob Moore (1932–2021) and guitarists Grady Martin (1929–2001), Hank Garland (1930–2004), and his younger brother Harold. Having forged their musical relationship over the course of many sessions, Owen and his musicians developed into a tight working unit that could quickly and easily adapt to the needs of the various country singers with which they recorded. One of his key production philosophies was that the musicians should avoid playing in the same register as the singer, thereby avoiding any sense of competition between the vocals and the instruments. In principle, this effect spotlighted the singer's lyrics and melody, placing them within a supportive musical cushion of lush orchestration. In practice, however, adhering to this convention was frequently challenging, especially for the three guitarists. For instance, if all three played in the same position on their instruments, the resulting recording would sound muddy and indistinct; yet, being barred from performing in the singer's range also meant they had limited options. In such a situation, at least one of the guitarists was bound to conflict with the other two, and as Harold Bradley recalled, "No one wanted anyone to have to lay out, so we were all trying to solve the problem."[42] One early attempt at a solution came from Hank Garland, who restrung his guitar so that the lower four strings sounded an octave higher (known today as "Nashville Tuning"). Following a similar logic, they came to another potential workaround: make one guitar sound *lower*.

According to Harold Bradley, the foundation for the tic-tac style came around 1958, when Garland showed up at the studio with an odd and cheap-looking black six-string bass guitar. Intrigued, Bradley went to Strouble's Music Store the next day and purchased a bronze one for himself.[43] Both instruments were Danelectro UB-2s.[44] They were the brainchild of Danelectro founder Nathan Daniel (1912–1994), who, like Leo Fender, was an engineer rather than a musician.[45] Daniel had started off building amplifiers for Epiphone in the thirties, before founding his own company in New Jersey in 1947, where he developed lucrative partnerships with both Montgomery Ward and Sears, Roebuck, and Company. In 1954, he began producing his own solid-body electric guitars at the urging of Joe Fisher, Sears's musical instrument buyer. As Fisher recalled,

Nat Daniel . . . introduced the affordable solid body electric guitar in the early fifties. . . . Nat was an innovator who understood the princi-

ple of "rigid control of expense," an example of which was his innovative and inexpensive guitar magnetic pickups used in electric guitars.
He made them from surplus lipstick tubes, bought from a cosmetics
manufacturer. He inserted the electronics in the tubes and produced
the lowest cost guitar pickup in the industry.[46]

Daniel's design philosophy stood in stark contrast to most other guitar
manufacturers of the era. Instead of producing slick, high-end guitars, he
was intent on producing relatively playable instruments that could be sold
at the cheapest price point possible. The single-pickup UB-1 and double-
pickup UB-2 were Daniel's first attempts to translate this philosophy into
the bass market. Affordably priced at $135 (cheaper than either a Fender
or a Kay), the UB-2 (Figure 20) resembled the company's solid-body electric guitars: it was constructed out of inexpensive pine and Masonite, it
featured two of their "lipstick" pickups, and it was awkwardly screwed
together. In fact, as was common practice for most budget bass manufacturers, Danelectro created the UB-2 by simply adding a longer bass neck to
their standard electric guitar body (this gave the instrument an awkward
30-inch scale length, which negatively affected its intonation).[47] It was by
all accounts a crude instrument, and it would have been an unlikely tool
for a professional session musician had it not had two unique advantages:
it played like an electric guitar but it sounded a full octave lower. Despite
being, in Harold Bradley's words, a "piece of junk," the UB-2 thus fit
within the three-guitar texture that had become commonplace at Bradley
Studios by freeing one guitarist to easily play in a lower register.[48]

Although Garland, Martin, and Harold Bradley all experimented
with the UB-2, it was Bradley who was most responsible for developing
the tic-tac style. Paralleling Ladi Geisler's work with Bert Kaempfert,
Harold stumbled across the style while experimenting in the studio. To
combat the instrument's aforementioned intonation problems, which
made it clash dissonantly against the sound of the upright bass, Harold
decided to mute the instrument with the palm of his right hand. When
played with a pick, this new muted timbre produced a distinctive sound.
As Harold later recalled, "We had the bass guitar, which Owen really
loved. . . . The acoustic bass didn't record evenly. Some of the notes
would drop out and so, naturally, it would drop out on radio. So the six-
string bass, when I'd mute it with my hand, it gives you a click and a note,
and that note would come out on the radio as a kind of bass. So it reinforced whatever the bass was doing."[49] Just as it had for Geisler, Harold's
tic-tac style reinforced a recording's bass frequencies and therefore
added sonic clarity to its low end, which in turn made Owen's records

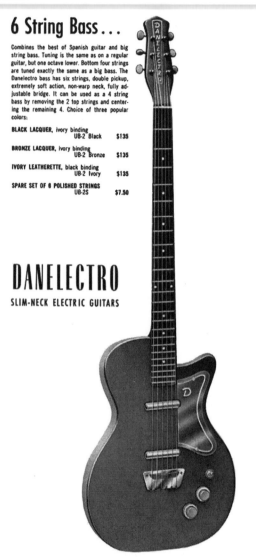

6 String Bass...

Combines the best of Spanish guitar and big string bass. Tuning is the same as on a regular guitar, but one octave lower. Bottom four strings are tuned exactly the same as a big bass. The Danelectro bass has six strings, double pickup, extremely soft action, non-warp neck, fully adjustable bridge. It can be used as a 4 string bass by removing the 2 top strings and centering the remaining 4. Choice of three popular colors:

BLACK LACQUER, ivory binding
                    UB-2 Black $135

BRONZE LACQUER, ivory binding
                    UB-2 Bronze $135

IVORY LEATHERETTE, black binding
                    UB-2 Ivory $135

SPARE SET OF 6 POLISHED STRINGS
                    UB-2S $7.50

DANELECTRO
SLIM-NECK ELECTRIC GUITARS

Figure 20. The Danelectro UB-2 six-string bass guitar. (Source: 1956 Danelectro catalog.)

sound fuller when played over the radio. Like Geisler, Harold also chose not to double Bob Moore's upright bass lines exactly, but instead found ways to compliment them. Describing how he and Moore coordinated their parts, Bradley recalled,

> He's [alternating between a] tonic and fifth, and then he'd play a run. He did bum-bum-bum-bum, and so while we were working it

out, I'd made note of where he's doing the lead-ins, and then I made sure I was playing [the] tonic and fifth. And then I'd play in-between notes, some notes that just kind of keep the record a little more lively. . . . I had more leeway to play, not exactly fills, but lead-ins than the [upright] bass, because if you did that on the big bass, it sounds like a cannon going off over there.[50]

Together, Harold Bradley and the Nashville A-Team established tic-tac bass as a regular feature of Owen's productions and fashioned it into a key sonic signifier of Decca's country pop artists, most notably Brenda Lee and Patsy Cline.

Brenda Lee (b. 1944) was barely over the age of twelve when she first began recording at Bradley Studios. She first came to the attention of mainstream audiences in the mid-fifties with rockabilly-infused tracks like "One Step at a Time" (1957) and "Dynamite" (1957), but by the early sixties, Owen Bradley was instead encouraging her to record ballads that could be marketed directly to pop audiences. On March 28, 1960, fifteen-year-old Lee, Owen Bradley, and the Nashville A-Team went into the studio to record "I'm Sorry" (1960). Harold Bradley's tic-tac bass is an indispensable feature of this recording. Working in tandem with Bob Moore's upright bass line, Harold breaks up the monotony of the song's pulse and slow rate of harmonic change by rhythmically varying his bass line in a loose call-and-response pattern with Lee's vocals.[51] The distinctive sound of Harold Bradley's tic-tac bass is ubiquitous throughout the song; louder than the other members of the rhythm section combined, its muted, picked timbre is prominently situated in the mix, placed nearly on equal footing with the background vocals. "I'm Sorry" became Lee's first No. 1 hit and its production style established the template for her musical brand throughout the sixties. Drawing on its basic components—including Harold's tic-tac bass—Lee and Owen Bradley would revisit this style again and again on a string of Top 10 hits over the next few years, including "I Want to Be Wanted" (1960), "Emotions" (1960), and "Fool #1" (1961).

"I'm Sorry" also encapsulated the complexities and contradictions of the popular music marketplace in the early sixties. Even though it was recorded in Nashville by the head of Decca's country division with a musical style that would soon come to dominate country radio, "I'm Sorry" was exclusively marketed as mainstream pop. Decca specifically chose not to release the single to country radio stations, and it never appeared on *Billboard*'s country chart. Yet Harold Bradley's contributions to Lee's recordings provide a useful reminder that there is not always a direct correlation between musical style and genre, and that the music industry's conception of an artist's work can sometimes entirely disregard its cultural context.

Having established the commercial viability of the Nashville Sound, Owen Bradley decided to adapt it to another singer he had been working with, Patsy Cline (1932–1963). Through her work with Bill Peer, Cline's career had grown slowly over the course of the fifties. In 1953, she became a regular attraction on Connie B. Gay's syndicated radio (and later television) program *Town and Country Time*, and in 1954, she secured a recording contract with 4 Star Records. Rather than release Cline's records directly, 4 Star's president, Bill McCall, instead leased them to Decca and its subsidiary Coral. In keeping with this partnership, McCall hired Owen Bradley to producer her sessions at Bradley Studios but maintained strict control over the material she recorded. During the 4 Star years, Cline and Bradley recorded seventeen singles and nine EPs, of which "Walkin' After Midnight" (1957) was the only hit. When her contract finally lapsed in September 1960, Bradley cut out the middleman and signed Cline directly to Decca, where he would have more freedom to experiment with the sound of her records.

Even though her previous recordings had featured the same musicians, the same producer, and were recorded in the same studio, there is a clear change in the stylistic direction of Cline's records after leaving the 4 Star label. Following his success with Brenda Lee and others, Owen Bradley encouraged Cline to record more ballads, which he then set within a variation of the Nashville Sound formula. This is apparent even from her first Decca session, which took place on November 16, 1960, and produced "I Fall to Pieces" (1961), Cline's first country hit in nearly four years. Featuring a shuffle feel with a relaxed tempo, smooth background singing from the Jordanaires, and a call-and-response guitar line played by Hank Garland, Cline's voice sits within a musical texture that highlights her expressive power. As Joli Jensen describes the session, "For the first time [for Cline], more melodic and emotional material was being matched with a relaxed, expressive, personal voice."[52] Harold Bradley's tic-tac bass is audible on "I Fall to Pieces," but his contributions are even more prominent on Cline's follow-up single, "Crazy" (1961).

Written by Willie Nelson, "Crazy" would become Cline's signature song, due in large part to the song's distinctive tic-tac bass line. The recording process, however, was particularly arduous. The first "Crazy" session came on August 21, 1961, when Cline, Owen Bradley, and members of the Nashville A-Team assembled to work on the song at Bradley Studios. At the time, Cline was still recovering from a near-fatal car accident, and despite her best efforts, she wasn't able to record a suitable vocal. When it became clear that Cline's injuries were impeding her performance, Owen Bradley uncharacteristically decided to dedicate an entire four-hour session (including an hour of overtime) to perfecting the song's backing track. Just as with "Pieces," Owen crafted a musical cushion that would spotlight Cline's vocals, which she would overdub a few days later. On the recording, Harold Bradley is foregrounded in the mix, with his tic-tac bass situated as an essential component of the arrangement, and as in "I'm Sorry," his wandering bass adds variety to the recording and serves as an ideal counterpoint to Cline's vocals. His ascending sixteenth-note fills at the end of nearly every bar, in particular, provide a sense of tension and anticipation that perfectly prepares the listener for the melancholy emotional effect that Cline unleashes with each line—an especially notable feat given that the bass and vocal tracks were recorded independently of each other.

Unlike Brenda Lee's recordings, "I Fall to Pieces" and "Crazy" were marketed as country songs with crossover appeal, and they eventually placed on both the country and mainstream pop charts. "Pieces" spent fifty-four weeks on the *Billboard* Hot Country & Western Sides, where it eventually reached No. 1, and it climbed all the way to No. 12 on the Hot 100. "Crazy" spent twenty-one weeks on the country chart, reaching the No. 2 position, and made it to No. 9 on the Hot 100. These songs are now considered country standards, and their continued popularity has far outlasted Cline's tragic death in 1963. Today, Cline is regularly regarded as one of the greatest country singers of all time. Yet her success was also facilitated by Owen Bradley's productions, including the sound of Harold Bradley's distinctive tic-tac bass. Collectively, they used the components of the Nashville Sound to craft an individual sonic identity for Cline, one that gave her recordings widespread commercial appeal.

Although the tic-tac bass sound is most remembered as a signifier of a sixties pop-country aesthetic, it was also heard within other musical contexts, whether listeners actively recognized it or not. For instance, while Elvis Presley's early popularity was met with mixed reactions by the country music establishment, after the singer moved from the Sun label to RCA, he recorded much of his mid-fifties rock 'n' roll at Nashville's RCA Studios. On these recordings he was accompanied by many of the same members of the Nashville A-Team that would accompany Patsy Cline, including the Jordanaires, upright bassist Bob Moore, drummer Buddy

Harman, and pianist Floyd Cramer. Likewise, Hank Garland played a version of tic-tac bass on some of these sessions, appearing on hits such as Elvis Presley's "Stuck on You" (1960), "Fame and Fortune" (1960), and "(Marie's the Name) His Latest Flame" (1961).[53] Additionally, for many today, the most recognizable recording to feature the tic-tac bass is likely Brenda Lee's Christmas classic "Rockin' Around the Christmas Tree," which was originally released in 1958 but only became a hit after the success of "I'm Sorry." In its original context, Bradley's tic-tac bass served to reinforce Lee's particular musical brand. For modern listeners, even if they are unaware of this history, it continues to give the recording a particularly distinctive sound.

Conclusion

The electric bass timbres discussed in this chapter appear to have been developed independently of each other, though they had much in common. They were all part of a new producer-led pop aesthetic that focused intently on crafting the overall sound of records. As part of that aesthetic, these producers all closely collaborated with their bassists to craft distinctive bass timbres that could add a layer of sonic novelty to their recordings. For Buddy Wheeler, Guybo Smith, Ladi Geisler, Harold Bradley, and George Tomsco, the new timbres they each developed were all built on their use of a pick, which at that time was still a relatively uncommon approach to electric bass playing. And though each musician had his own specific, individual goals, the net effect of their bass lines was often the same: they supplied an unprecedented audibility to the low end. In so doing, they also found creative ways to overcome the technological limitations of both the recording studio and consumer audio equipment. Perhaps most significantly, once their recordings became hits, each musician's unique bass timbre became part of a signature musical brand for the artists with which they recorded.

Spread across the spectrum of popular music, these were the first hit recordings to demonstrate the electric bass's individual character as an instrument. By stepping outside of the bass's traditional role of simply supporting the internal function of the music, these musicians fostered a noteworthy shift in popular tastes toward recordings that foregrounded clearly audible bass lines. Going forward, audiences would now expect to hear a more prominent low end, and this expectation would ultimately lead producers to further spotlight the sound of the electric bass.

FIVE | The Amateur Instrument

The Teenage Garage Band Revolution

In 1958, friends Don Wilson and Bob Bogle walked into a pawnshop looking to buy their first electric guitars. Both men were amateur musicians; they spent their days working traveling construction jobs and their nights playing acoustic guitars for fun. Having recently formed a rock 'n' roll band, they knew they would need louder instruments if they were going to successfully perform at local parties and dances. They eventually settled on two solid-body electric guitars, a Harmony and a Kay, each of which they purchased for ten dollars. Shortly after, the duo started to gain traction as a band—winning local talent contests, playing nightclubs, and preparing to put out a record—and they began to look for a drummer and a bassist to round out their lineup. They found the latter in Nole "Nokie" Edwards (1935–2018), a hotshot guitarist who had been making the rounds playing local country bars. Edwards had recently purchased a third-generation Fender Precision Bass from a pawnshop for $125 and therefore met their only requirement for a bassist: he owned his own instrument. In 1960, this group released a single that slowly grew from a regional hit into a national one, eventually spending 18 weeks on the *Billboard* Hot 100, peaking at No. 2—sandwiched between Elvis Presley at No. 1 and Chubby Checker's new hit, "The Twist," at No. 3. That song was "Walk, Don't Run" and this group was the Ventures, the preeminent American instrumental rock 'n' roll band of the sixties.[1]

Featuring guitarists Wilson and Bogle, guitarist-turned-bassist Edwards, and drummer Skip Moore, the Ventures' version of "Walk, Don't Run" was recorded on March 22, 1960. They had first heard the song, an instrumental by jazz guitarist Johnny Smith, on Chet Atkins's

1957 album *Hi-Fi in Focus*. Atkins's version featured his signature quick finger-picking style, a technique that proved too difficult for either Wilson or Bogle to imitate. As Wilson recalled,

> Chet's version was a complicated semi-jazz thing that he played finger-style. We tried playing along with it, but we couldn't even come close. It was far too advanced for us, but for some reason we kept going back to it. In about three months we had it completely rearranged into a rock style that we were satisfied with. We didn't think it was a big deal or anything, but after adding the number to our repertoire, we noticed a new excitement from our audience. Each time we played in public, we were swamped with requests to play "Walk, Don't Run," sometimes up to five or six times![2]

The simplification that Wilson describes is readily apparent in the band's recording. Following in the footsteps of Duane Eddy, the Ventures decided to create a simplified arrangement of "Walk, Don't Run" in the new rock 'n' roll style, in essence taking Atkins's complicated solo guitar arrangement and dividing it into three more manageable parts: rhythm guitar, bass line, and lead guitar.

According to *Guitar Player* contributor Dan Forte, songs like "Walk, Don't Run" "made the Ventures probably the most influential combo of the early sixties, particularly with aspiring guitar players—influential because their spare instrumentation and simple arrangements made just about any four kids believe they could save their money, get some drums and guitars, and start their own rock and roll band."[3] Jas Obrecht has similarly hailed the Ventures' debut LP as "the album that launched a thousand bands."[4] And Peter Stuart Kohman has even gone as far as to say that the Ventures' visual image (Figure 21) signaled the demise of the upright bass in popular music: "The group's first two album covers really drove the message home with full-color photos of the Fender-wielding band. . . . The cover of the second Ventures album . . . is the classic turn-of-the-decade band shot and Nokie Edwards's maple neck Precision Bass serves notice to teenage rockers everywhere that the [upright] is on the way out!"[5] Although these statements may be hyperbolic, their sentiments reflect an important shift in the history of American popular music: beginning around 1958, there was a rapid increase in the number of amateur electric guitar- and electric bass-centric rock 'n' roll bands. The Ventures, however, were not the instigators of this new garage band movement as much as they were a microcosm of it. By 1960, there were

Figure 21. Nokie Edwards (second from right) and his third-generation Precision Bass on the cover of the Ventures' second LP. (Source: *The Ventures*, Dolton Records, 1961.)

hundreds, if not thousands, of other amateur rock 'n' roll bands that had independently formed across the United States. And, like the Ventures, many of them came to specialize in playing instrumentals.

As discussed in the previous chapters, the electric bass had little mainstream exposure in American music prior to 1957. Up until this time, electric bassists largely had been professional or semiprofessional musicians who switched from upright bass to electric for practical reasons. But the instrument was ultimately popularized by a very different group of musicians: middle-class, teenage amateurs—many of whom were originally guitarists. A handful of these musicians found commercial success, but for most, their loftiest goals were to play at parties and local dances. Rather than seek fame or fortune, most simply made music for fun in their spare time. This chapter explores the material conditions that fueled this amateur culture, demonstrating how this generation of would-be rock 'n' roll musicians instigated a new, unprecedented demand for electric instruments and, in so doing, ultimately normalized the electric bass.

Rock 'n' Roll ('n' Race 'n' Class)

In his book *Time Passages*, George Lipsitz provides perhaps the most persuasive account of rock 'n' roll's social origins. As he argues, early rock 'n' roll was an outgrowth of the increasing racial integration of the American working classes. However, as is often the case, what began as a working-class cultural expression was quickly appropriated by the white middle class:

> Because rock-and-roll music developed in highly concentrated urban markets, it became accessible to the middle class in a way that had not been true of blues and country music. The radio stations and record stores that specialized in rock and roll reached audiences previously unaware of working-class cultures. Young whites especially requested music by Black artists as well as the blues/country fusions evident in "rockabilly" performances. . . . That generation of teenagers occupied a pivotal position in U.S. history. As the first generation of young people with money of their own to spend without necessarily having to work, they had the freedom to reject the values of their parents and to seek out cultural alternatives. Raised in times of unprecedented consumer affluence, they found more meaning and value in working-class culture than in the signs and symbols of their own emerging middle class.[6]

As rock 'n' roll became increasingly suburban and middle class throughout the fifties, it also became increasingly "whitewashed," moving further and further away from the genre's Black and working-class roots. According to Lipsitz,

> Despite [an] enduring working-class urban presence . . . popular music between 1959 and 1964 became whiter, blander and less working-class each year. It took the stimulus of the "British Invasion," spearheaded by the Beatles and Rolling Stones, to restore the viability and profitability of the record industry—by reviving the very same American

urban, working-class sounds that had been gradually purged from American popular music over the previous five years.[7]

Lipsitz's nuanced account provides a much-needed window into the complex class and racial tensions at the heart of early rock 'n' roll. But the overall trajectory of his narrative should be familiar from nearly any rock history book: early rock 'n' roll, wrought from previous Black musics, became a mainstream phenomenon in the mid-fifties and was then increasingly diluted by less-than-authentic white performers until it was eventually resuscitated by the Beatles. This story is not necessarily inaccurate. Rock 'n' roll was a deliberate synthesis of earlier popular styles, and it did become "safer" toward the end of the fifties as its major rebellious forces disappeared; it is also difficult to overstate the impact of the Beatles on American popular music. The problem with this narrative, however, is that it overlooks the significant developments of those intervening years. The era between Elvis and the Beatles has been presented as "bleak," as a "lull," and a time when "rock 'n' roll faltered."[8] Yet this was the time of Motown, of James Brown and Sam Cooke, of the Crystals and the Chiffons. It was also the time of the first generation of teenage rock 'n' roll garage bands.

If scholars have overlooked the first wave of amateur rock 'n' roll musicians, it is because its subjects—presumably (but certainly not entirely) white, male, middle-class teenagers—embody a perceived "blandness" that is incongruous with the genre's standard racially charged depictions as rebellious, sexual, and dangerous. But, as Lipsitz describes, this specific group of teenagers had privileges that were unavailable to rock's previous, working-class generation: they were socially and economically liberated to be "amateur" musicians in the original sense of the word, making music for their own gratification. As beneficiaries of America's postwar economic boom, most amateur musicians in the late fifties were free from the responsibility of supporting their families, and they had the time, energy, and, most importantly, disposable income to invest in this music. Using their own incomes or allowances, these teenagers began acquiring electric guitars and basses at a startling rate, and in so doing, they transformed rock 'n' roll into a middle-class leisure activity. Their venue was not the recording studio, most did not achieve national acclaim. Many of them never played outside their hometowns; many never even played outside their own basements and garages. From a modern vantage point, the privileges they benefited from in their day-to-day lives may make them seem like less interesting historical agents.

Yet, ironically, those very privileges are what allowed their contributions to be so significant.

From the Electric Guitar to the Electric Bass

The history of the electric bass is inextricable from the history of the solid-body electric guitar. As detailed previously, early electric basses were explicitly designed for guitarists, and one of the instrument's early proposed selling points was how easy it was for guitarists to master (recall the 1953 Kay ad promising, "Now, any guitarist can learn to play bass almost overnight"). While this marketing strategy proved unsuccessful in popularizing the electric bass among upright players, it was the perfect sentiment for the millions of amateur rock 'n' roll guitarists that existed in the late fifties.

The American Music Conference (AMC)—a musical instrument industry-supported nonprofit designed to research and promote amateur music-making—estimated that in 1955, 2.6 million Americans played guitar.[9] By 1960, that number had nearly doubled to 4.45 million, and by 1964, an estimated 7 million amateurs played guitar—of which 30 percent were female.[10] According to industry insiders, this drastic increase in amateur guitarists was the result of a new, burgeoning teenage market. In his 1956 review of the state of the industry, AMC president Jack Feddersen wrote, "The year 1956 may be remembered as one of the most important in the history of the music industry. For during this year it became apparent that the healthy growth of the past few years has not been just a temporary flurry; that the basis for greater demand for music is solid and widespread; and that the future almost certainly will be even better."[11] An oncoming teenage population boom, he claimed, secured the industry's bright future:

> The trend of population, alone, is almost ideal for the future of this industry. In 10 years there will be a 40 percent increase in the number of youngsters between 10 and 17 years old. Even if our present rate of attracting these children is maintained, and if prices stay at 1956 levels, this would make 1965 retail volume $610,000,000. Yet there is every reason to believe that this prospect is too conservative. There is a strong rising tide of demand for our product—the fun and benefits of making music. The Gilbert Youth Research Organization found that the number of teenagers who had taken up music as a hobby doubled between 1951 and 1956—becoming the most popular hobby

for this age bracket. All signs are that efforts to interest youngsters in music will continue to be successful, so that by 1965 the percentage we reach will be substantially greater.

Feddersen was right—his figure was too conservative. In 1965, AMC actually estimated musical instruments sales to be $768,300,000.[12] These dramatic sales figures were the result of nearly a decade of successful targeted marketing geared toward increasing the number of amateur teenage musicians. This newfound amateur culture, in turn, was essential to the popularization of the electric bass.

Even by the time the Ventures had formed in 1958, there was already an incredible and unprecedented surplus of amateur guitarists. Since the solid-body electric guitar was the cheapest and most accessible rock instrument at this time (a brand-new one could run as low as $40) most amateur rock 'n' roll musicians learned to play guitar first. However, once these musicians formed a group, there was often a problem with the division of labor: traditionally, one guitarist played rhythm while another played lead; a third guitarist was either going to get in the way or be redundant—unless, of course, they switched to the electric bass. This lateral move became increasingly common in this period, and the list of bassists who started out as guitarists includes such luminaries as Donald "Duck" Dunn, Bill Wyman, Paul McCartney, Noel Redding, and many more. In the case of the Ventures, this situation actually played out *twice*. Wilson and Bogle—two guitarists—brought in Edwards—a third guitarist—to play electric bass; eventually, Edwards switched to lead guitar duties and Bogle became the group's bass player.

The Expanding Electric Bass Market

When the Fender Precision Bass was first introduced in 1951, it retailed for $200, a hefty price tag that would have placed it outside the reach of most amateurs. Even the Kay Electronic Bass was still prohibitively priced at $150. Yet as the musical instrument industry started to actively court a teenage market, the range of prices expanded radically. As illustrated in Table 1, by 1961 a high-end electric bass could run as much as $310 (not including an amplifier or accessories), while a low-end model could cost as little as $79.95 (still a little more than $800 in today's money). Although still costly, this range of prices meant that, by the end of the fifties, there were electric basses on the market tailored to the musical and financial needs of amateur and professional musicians alike. The

Table 1. A selection of electric basses on the US
market between 1959-1963 with retail prices compiled
from various manufacturer price lists.

Brand	Model	MSRP
Silvertone	1444	$79.95
Danelectro	3412 ("Shorthorn Bass")	$85
Harmony	H-22	$95
Danelectro	4423 ("Longhorn Bass")	$150
Kay	K5965	$150
Kay	K5970J ("Jazz Special")	$195
Gibson	EB-0	$210
Fender	Precision Bass	$229.50
Gibson	EB-1	$235
Fender	Jazz Bass	$279.50
Rickenbacker	4000	$279.50
Gibson	EB-2	$282.50
Epiphone	Rivoli	$300
Gibson	EB-3	$310
Mosrite	Mark X ("Ventures Bass")	$310

growing diversification of the electric bass market is most apparent in
three new instruments: the Fender Jazz Bass, the Danelectro Shorthorn
Bass, and the Silvertone 1444.

Fender first introduced the Jazz Bass (originally marketed as the
"Deluxe Bass") in March 1960 to meet an increasing demand for electric
basses. According to Don Randall, "We were always market driven. . . .
After establishing the fact that bass guitars would sell and that people
wanted them, then the next thing was to make a prettier one, a more
elaborate one. We wanted an upscale model to put on the market."[13]
As Leo Fender himself later described it: "Well, it's like a car you know:
You come out with the standard model, then you have a deluxe model,
a Cadillac version. It had a narrower neck and the offset waist; it was
fancier."[14] Retailing at $279.50 (around $2,800 today), the Jazz Bass cost
a full $50 more than a Precision Bass and was one of the more expensive
electric basses on the market. It was dubbed the "Jazz" Bass both because
of the company's ongoing association of the instrument with professional
jazz musicians and because Leo Fender had incorrectly assumed that jazz
musicians would favor the instrument's thinner neck and punchier midrange. As demonstrated by Fender's initial ad campaign (Figure 22), the
Jazz Bass was marketed as a superior product for a professional musician:
it touts new features, such as its "micro-adjustable bridge" ("for perfect
string intonation"), its new dual pickups (which "provide instant string
response and full tone during string vibration"), and it's reduced scale
(which is "more slender than most any guitar" and "facilitates rapid play-

Figure 22. Ad for the new Fender Jazz Bass. (Source: *Down Beat*, January 19, 1961.)

ing technique of the most difficult musical passages").[15] Regardless of who actually purchased it, the Jazz Bass was intended for experienced musicians interested in professional equipment.

At the same time that Fender was producing the Cadillac of basses, manufacturers such as Danelectro had found success marketing lower-end "budget" instruments. As described in the previous chapter, Danelectro's Nathan Daniel was intent on producing the cheapest instruments possible. Accordingly, the primary demographic for his instruments were beginners—young people just starting to make music themselves. By 1958, Danelectro began marketing multiple four-string electric basses, including the 3412 Shorthorn and 4423 Longhorn Basses, which were named for their distinctive body shapes. Like the UB-2, these instruments were both constructed out of inexpensive pine and Masonite, featured lipstick pickups, and had a short 30-inch scale length with only fifteen frets. They were cut-rate instruments, to be sure, but their small size and lightweight construction also made them ideal for small hands and small bodies.

Combined with its relatively inexpensive $85 price point, the Shorthorn Bass was a hit among the new generation of young electric bass players in the late fifties, especially those riding the wave of instrumental rock 'n' roll.[16] For instance, Johnny and the Hurricanes had a Top 10 hit in 1959 with their instrumental "Red River Rock." That same year, the back cover of their first LP showed bassist Lionel "Butch" Mattice (1939–2006) playing a Danelectro Shorthorn Bass. Their story, as detailed on the album's liner notes, was typical for the time:

> Johnny and the Hurricanes—teen-agers all—hail from the Toledo, Ohio area. . . . The quintet of lads got together first as pals in school, partly drawn to each other by their mutual interests in music. Along the way, they decided to pool their talents and organized a dance band of their own. Soon, through playing for high school and regional teen-age hops, they built up a demand for their services and found themselves playing regular engagements. . . . Once out of high school, the lads decided to try their luck at a professional music-making career.[17]

As with many teens in this era, Mattice's formative experiences as a rock musician were inherently tied to his ability to procure affordable equipment, a process that had been made much easier by the introduction of the Danelectro Shorthorn. And even though it was a budget bass, it was still good enough for him to form his first band, build a local reputation, and, eventually, even record a hit single.

Young women also participated in this era's teenage rock bands, although they have rarely been spotlighted in guitar histories. Take, for example, the Chantels. Formed by five high school friends from the Bronx, the Chantels were led by lead singer Arlene Smith (b. 1941), who was then just sixteen years old. They were discovered by singer Richard Barrett, who helped them secure a deal with End Records. In late 1957, the group released their second single, "Maybe," which became a Top 20 pop hit. Combining their all-girl vocal harmony with a strong lead performance from Smith, "Maybe" established the template for the so-called "girl groups" of the early sixties. As Jacqueline Warwick notes,

The voices of the Chantels were an exciting sound in 1958. . . . Their choirgirl diction and the focused, ringing timbres of their upper vocal registers were novel, resembling in some ways the sweet-voiced sounds of urban black teenage boys singing doo wop, and in other ways the barbershop aesthetics of white, mid-Western women like the Chordettes, and even the polished recordings of white, adult starlet/ pop singers such as Debbie Reynolds or Patti Page. . . . Ultimately, the Chantels' music could not be categorized with any other style of the day, and their success spawned many imitators and precipitated a new genre in popular music.[18]

In support of "Maybe," the group performed on many of the era's rock 'n' roll package tours, performing alongside the likes of Chuck Berry, Fats Domino, and the Teenagers. In their live appearances, Barrett was careful to emphasize the girls' youth and innocence, presenting them in conservative, frilly dresses. But he also understood the appeal of a gimmick. So, in 1958, he outfitted them with their own musical instruments. As bandmember Renée Minus White recalled,

Richie introduced us to playing musical instruments. At the time, there were no other girl groups on the road playing instruments. . . . I played the drums, Lois played the piano, Sonia and Jackie each played guitar, and Arlene played the bass. We were self-contained and definitely ahead of our time, and it made us more marketable.[19]

Promotional photos from this era clearly show Arlene Smith playing a Danelectro Shorthorn Bass (Figure 23), perhaps because it fit Smith's smaller frame, or maybe because it was simply the cheapest option. In early 1959, just months before Smith left the band, the Chantels even went into the studio and recorded their own rock 'n' roll instrumental, "Peruvian Wedding Song," which went unreleased until 1987.[20]

At the same time that Nathan Daniel was selling guitars under his own Danelectro brand name, he was also supplying his instruments to Sears, Roebuck, and Company, which rebranded them under their Silvertone label. Unlike Fender Basses, which could only be purchased from a local musical instrument dealer or from the factory directly, Silvertone guitars and basses were available exclusively through the Sears mail-order catalog and department store—which, by 1965, was the world's largest retailer. The first four-string Silvertone electric bass, the 1444 (Figure

Figure 23. The Chantels, ca. 1958, featuring Arlene Smith (far left) on a Danelectro Shorthorn Bass. (Source: *The Chantels: The Complete Singles & Albums*, Acrobat, 2022.)

Figure 24. Ad for the Silvertone 1444. (Source: Sears, *1965 Fall/Winter Catalog*.)

24), appeared in the 1959 Sears Fall/Winter Catalog. Modestly priced at $79.95 cash or "$8 down, $8 monthly," the 1444 remained the most inexpensive electric bass on the American market until it was discontinued in 1966 (by which time the financing option had fallen to $0 down and only $5 per month).[21]

The surviving ads for the Silvertone 1444 tell us much about the instrument's target consumer. First and foremost, they were middle class. Although the 1444 was cheaper than most basses on the market, its $79.95 price tag (not to mention its accompanying $99.95 amplifier) still meant that the instrument was intended for a relatively affluent buyer. Second, and more importantly, the intended consumers were obviously not professional musicians. Instead, they were beginners who had at least some familiarity with the guitar. For example, starting in the 1960 Sears Fall/Winter catalog, the ad copy for the 1444 described the instrument as an "Electric Bass [that] plays like a guitar"; by the 1964 Fall/Winter catalog, the connection to the guitar was made even more explicit, as it stated that the 1444 "fingers easily like a guitar" and that its "guitar-spaced frets plus low-set strings assure easy, fast action playing."[22]

Although the 1444 ostensibly sold well, fewer concrete examples survive of musicians playing it. This likely stems from their status as beginner instruments. They met the needs of local amateur rock bands that were just starting out, but a bassist who decided to get more serious about making music would almost always seek out a higher-quality instrument eventually. This was the case for Bob "Mole" Schmidt Jr., a bassist from Fairmont, West Virginia.[23] As Mole explained to me, he got his first bass, a Silvertone 1444, in 1962, at the age of fourteen. His mother cosigned for it, so that he could pay for it in installments using money he was earning from mowing lawns. He soon joined a group called Gary and the Royals, who built their reputation playing dances at the teen venues in town. By 1964, they had become successful locally and rebranded themselves simply as the Royals. As part of this success, Mole upgraded to a nicer, more expensive Fender Jazz Bass. While they never had a national hit, the Royals played together locally in north central West Virginia well into the mid-eighties.

Whereas in the early and middle fifties electric basses were primarily advertised to professional musicians and were prohibitively expensive, the Danelectro Shorthorn Bass and the Silvertone 1444 catered to an emergent market of aspiring electric bassists seeking affordable equipment. The latter's appearance in the Sears catalog fundamentally expanded access to amateur rock 'n' roll music-making to millions of homes across North America. As was the case with Nokie Edwards and the Ventures, the sole qualification for becoming a bassist was now simply having enough money (or credit) to buy your own instrument.[24]

Teenage Economics

Not only were electric basses in the 1950s becoming cheaper and easier to get a hold of, the American middle-class teenagers that were buying them also had greater financial independence than ever before in history. For instance, a 1956 survey published by *Scholastic Magazine*'s Institute of Student Opinion reported that American teenagers represented a combined income of $7 billion (an increase of 23 percent from 1953) and that the "average" teenager earned approximately $10.55 per week.[25] A 1958 study conducted by the pioneering youth-marketing agency Gilbert Youth Research Organization—the same organization Jack Feddersen cited in 1956—elaborated on these trends, breaking them down by age group and gender; it claimed that American teenagers now represented a combined income of $9.5 billion and that "the weekly average [income] for a boy is $4.16 at thirteen, $8.26 at sixteen, and $16.65 at eighteen; a girl averages two or three dollars less."[26] If this information is reliable, it would mean that Sears's financing option ("$8 down, $8 monthly") would have been well within the reach of most middle-class teenagers. Moreover, it meant that in the year after the Ventures formed, it would only have taken a little over a month for the average American middle-class high school senior to save up enough money to buy a brand-new, entry-level electric bass outright.

We do not have specific data on electric bass sales, but overall guitar sales figures corroborate the increasing impact of teenage amateur musicians in this era. According to data collected from the Guitar and Accessory Manufacturer Association and the US Tariff Commission, in 1958, annual guitar sales reached an all-time high of 305,000 units; by 1963, the year before the Beatles "invaded" America, this figure had more than doubled to 700,000 units (see Figure 25).

In reality, these numbers were probably much higher, if we take into account secondhand sales, which are not included in the aforementioned figures. For instance, in 1964, the AMC claimed that "the demand for guitars currently exceeds the supply. *Used guitars in good condition often are worth more than new guitars*," and in 1967, it blamed a dip in guitar sales on market saturation and the availability of used equipment:

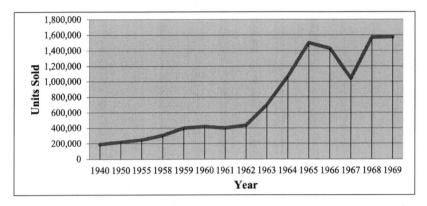

Figure 25. National guitar sales, 1940–1969. (Source: *1970 Review of the Music Industry and Amateur Music Participation*. American Music Conference. Chicago: American Music Conference, 1970.)

"More than 5,600,000 [guitars] have been purchased during the past four years, which is believed to be part of the reason for the lower sales figures for 1967. There are many good used instruments on the market, a result of young people trading up in quality after learning to play on beginner-type instruments."[27]

Although we have few surviving records of their inventories or pricing, secondhand venues, like pawnshops, also played a crucial role in the development of amateur rock 'n' roll music-making in the late fifties because they sold used equipment well below retail price. Here again the Ventures function as a microcosm: Don Wilson and Bob Bogle formed the band with two electric guitars purchased from a pawnshop for a meager $10, and Nokie Edwards likewise purchased his 1957 Fender Precision Bass from a pawnshop for $125 (which was still $100 cheaper than retail). Even though they all eventually upgraded to newer equipment, their early pawnshop guitars allowed them to affordably get started in rock 'n' roll. Just like millions of other aspiring musicians, the Ventures' first steps into rock 'n' roll were intrinsically tied to this increasing availability of affordable equipment.

Electric Bass Pedagogy

The electric bass's rapidly expanding popularity among amateur musicians can also be traced through the increasing number of "Teach

Yourself to Play Bass" method books published in the fifties and sixties. As far as I am aware, the earliest known guide to electric bass playing is *Bert Gardner's Complete Course for Electric Bass*. Published in 1957, the book was endorsed by Fender and was intended to complement the company's second-generation Precision Basses. In his preface, Gardner forcefully states, "Most available instruction books for bass are out-dated, hard to understand, limited in their content, padded with useless filler material and CANNOT BE APPLIED TO THE NEW ELECTRIC BASS."[28] Despite this bold proclamation, however, Gardner's text is actually quite sparse. He provides no information on technique whatsoever, and although he states that "no previous knowledge of music [is] necessary," he includes no explanation of rhythm or music theory and he takes for granted that students are familiar with musical terminology.[29] Although Gardner strongly recommends that bassists learn to read traditional notation, the book teaches you to play bass solely by realizing chord symbols based on movable patterns. With its discussion of how to realize major sixth, dominant seventh, augmented, and diminished chords, as well as its discussion of "Linking Seventh Chords to Avoid Monotony," this method book is designed by and large to teach someone how to construct smooth walking bass lines from lead sheets. These assumptions clearly tie it to the jazz dance band tradition, which makes sense given that Fender endorsed the book and that the company believed those musicians to be the primary demographic for their instrument.

By contrast, *Smith's Modern Electric Bass Guitar Method*, by Anthony J. Manfredi and Joseph M. Estella, from 1959, avoids any mention of the dance band tradition altogether and instead offers a more generic type of pedagogy.[30] And, unlike Gardner's method, *Smith's* is obviously directed at the youth market. This is evident even from the cover, which features a black lightning bolt on a gold background (the word "electric" is also stylized as if bursting with electric current). Here is how Manfredi and Estella describe their target audience: "This modern course . . . should be a boon to the self-taught player, as well as those who enjoy the advantages of a teacher."[31] Showing a clear bias toward guitar players, they explain that the first several pages of the book "are written to show the comparison of the Bass Guitar notes to the Regular Guitar notes," which they tellingly claim "will be helpful to the players who are already familiar with the Regular Guitar."[32] Also contrary to Gardner, Manfredi and Estella don't seem to have a clear conception of what type of music the electric bass would be used for and instead take a catchall approach. This is most evident in the book's choice of material: it teaches how to play the melodies to waltzes, polkas, children's songs, western songs, folk songs, and more. The closest it comes to relevant popular styles are in a final few "boogie woogie" examples, including the tellingly titled "The Teen-Age Party."[33]

Both Gardner's and Manfredi and Estella's books attest to the electric bass's unsettled role in popular music at the time. Even in the early sixties, there was a definite lack of models for aspiring amateurs, and electric bass pedagogy was still an open field. No single method for playing or learning the instrument had come to dominate. These books were thus trying to fill a void by establishing themselves as the primary method for learning the instrument. Just as the electric bass's musical role would become increasingly codified moving into the mid-sixties, its pedagogy likewise would soon come to be dominated by two competing approaches exemplified in two popular texts: the Mel Bay method books written by Roger Filiberto—which promoted a traditional form of musical literacy—and the *Play Guitar with . . .* series of LPs produced by Dolton Records—which promoted a semi-notated "play-by-ear" approach.

Mel Bay Presents the Electric Bass, Volume 1, written by Roger Filiberto, originally sold for two dollars and has been in print continuously since 1963. To date, it is likely the best-selling electric bass method book of all time (it reportedly had sold one million copies by 1979 and nearly two million by the late nineties).[34] These dramatic sales figures were partially the result of Bay's extensive distribution network—which included eighty distributors and reached every continent except Antarctica.[35] But looking at its actual content, it's also easy to see why it was such a success. The book begins with a short foreword from Bay himself, in which he writes, "This book is the answer to many requests for a thorough and carefully graded approach to the electric bass. This instrument has attained great heights with only a limited amount of instructional material available. We highly recommend this book to anyone desirous of playing the electric bass as a musician."[36] This last clause is key: this book doesn't just teach you to play the bass, but to play the bass *as a musician*, in other words, as someone who understands the fundamentals of music theory and, more importantly, as someone who can read traditional musical notation.

Filiberto begins by teaching the "rudiments of music," including how to read from a staff, how pitch and rhythm are notated, how time signatures work, and so on. He then slowly teaches you the instrument string by string, followed by scales and position work. Unlike *Smith's* method, when it reaches actual tunes, the choice of material is diverse yet coherent. For instance, the first three examples are, in order, a nuanced walking bass pattern for the folk song "Careless Love," a 4/4 "Western Folk Song" pattern, and a 3/4 pattern to the mariachi tune "Cielito Lindo."[37]

Filiberto then teaches typical root-fifth bass patterns, shuffles, eight-bar blues, and twelve-bar blues, as well as how to construct smooth walking bass lines with varied rhythms. One of the book's final examples is "Rock and Roll—Rhythm and Blues—Boogie Patterns," a modified eight-bar blues whose title suggests that it encompasses nearly all popular styles.[38] Although it was still aimed at amateurs, *Mel Bay Presents the Electric Bass, Volume 1* provides a comprehensive introduction to the instrument, teaching the reader how to construct bass lines in a wide variety of styles. The book's content, in conjunction with its dramatic sales figures, not only represented a dramatic step forward from earlier method books, but also reflected the massive increase in the number of amateur electric bassists in the sixties, an increase that is further demonstrated by one of Bay's biggest competitors: the *Play Guitar with . . .* series produced by Dolton Records.

If Bay's method emphasized "completeness" and becoming a "real" musician, the *Play Guitar with . . .* series took the opposite approach: it didn't strive for breadth, it didn't teach traditional notation, and it wasn't a book. Instead, these were LPs that claimed to teach an immersive "new, simple play-by-ear way to play the guitar."[39] The first album in the series, 1965's *Play Guitar with the Ventures*, taught the "lead, bass, and rhythm guitar" lines to four of the Ventures' songs, including "Walk, Don't Run." And, at least in the short term, this series was even more successful than Mel Bay's book: in a likely first for a "play-along" album, *Play Guitar with the Ventures* actually cracked the *Billboard* album chart in August 1965 and stayed there for thirteen weeks, peaking at No. 96. The record also reportedly sold ninety-three thousand copies in its first eleven months and, cumulatively, the seven records in the series (released between 1965 and 1967) are estimated to have sold over six hundred thousand copies.[40]

The *Play Guitar with . . .* series was the brainchild of appliance salesman Wilbur M. Savidge, a man who had always wanted to play lead guitar but felt inhibited by not knowing music theory or how to read traditional notation. Savidge came up with the idea for the series while taking guitar lessons at a local music store. As he described it,

> [My teacher] George [Mamlakis] would run through a song, getting me on the right track, and I would go home that evening and try to recall what he had shown me. . . . I just could not remember what George had told me, and could not recall the note pattern. . . . [George] had a remedy for my problem. . . . He and his fellow teachers at the music store were using a diagram system whereby numbers representing finger placement of the notes on the guitar neck were

shown, and the playing sequence of the numbers were placed below each diagram. . . . This worked, if you knew the song. . . . [But] the diagram did not, and could not show time values. You had to know the song.[41]

After noticing a lack of available method books for learning rock guitar, Savidge decided to create his own guitar pedagogy system. Dubbed "Guitar Phonics," his system borrowed his teacher's diagram method but added an aural component: isolated and full-band recordings of all parts. This way, the student could learn bass or guitar by simply playing along with a guided record.

The Guitar Phonics system works by breaking a song into sections. Every section is given its own diagram of the guitar fretboard (Figure 26).[42] Then specific frets are assigned numerical values (1, 2, 3, 4, etc.), and those numbers are written under the diagram, indicating the order in which you play them. This is used in conjunction with the record, which teaches each part individually both at "slow speed" and "normal speed" before playing the whole song with various parts omitted so that the student can play along.[43] For those familiar with modern guitar tablature, Savidge's numbering is not particularly intuitive, and the entire system seems unnecessarily complicated. Yet the point of the system was to teach students to play by ear, not to codify a new form of musical notation. The diagrams were a supplement to the records, but the records always remained the most important part.

When it comes specifically to the electric bass, the *Play Guitar with . . .* series had something none of the previous methods provided: interesting real-world examples set in an actual musical context. As Paul Harris and others have noted, "It can be excruciatingly boring to play [the electric bass] by oneself."[44] Its primary function as an accompaniment instrument usually requires that it hold down the fort while the best parts are given to someone else. This is what can make playing through most method books so dull—you just hear your own supporting line. However, by the time Dolton Records released 1966's *Play Electric Bass with the Ventures* (aka *Play Guitar with the Ventures Volume 4*), students not only had a full band to play along with, they also got to play fun bass lines, as it teaches you to play bass to arrangements of Ritchie Valens's "La Bamba," the Supremes' "I Hear a Symphony," the Toys' "A Lover's Concerto," Jr. Walker & the All Stars' "Shotgun," James Brown's "Papa's Got a Brand New Bag," and the Ventures' own version of "Red River Rock."[45] These bass lines are not only entertaining, they are also a far cry from the rote lines and blues patterns of the previous method books.

WALK, DON'T RUN

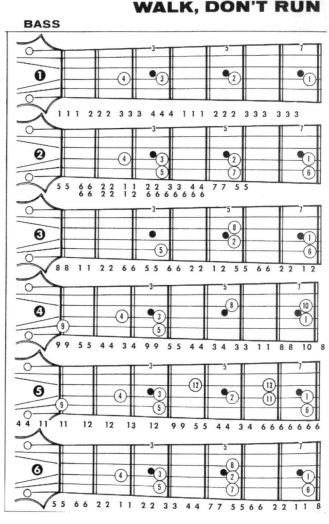

Figure 26. Guitar Phonics notation for the bass line to "Walk, Don't Run." (Source: *Play Guitar with the Ventures*, Dolton Records, 1965.)

Play Electric Bass with the Ventures thus epitomizes a newfound electric bass aesthetic in which bass lines were nuanced, propulsive, and worthy of equal attention in the music.

Unlike the *Mel Bay* series, which taught you to be a "musician," *The Play Guitar with . . .* series let you vicariously inhabit an actual rock 'n' roll band. By letting amateur musicians play some of the biggest hits of the day, the series showed that they too could learn to play guitar or bass without the hurdles of music theory or traditional notation. That the entire system was convoluted only makes the aforementioned sales figures all the more dramatic. These records appealed directly and deeply to a substantial generation of teenage musicians desperate for a path into music-making that was both immediate and fulfilling.

Conclusion

In 1964, the Ventures rerecorded "Walk, Don't Run" in a more contemporary rock style. Now featuring Bogle on bass and Edwards on lead guitar, the only real divergence from their original version is the timbre of Wilson's reverb-drenched rhythm guitar, which emulated the new sounds of surf rockers like Dick Dale and the Del-Tones. (Today the Ventures are often erroneously labeled as a surf band, but they had no real connection to surf music or surf culture—they were just always on the lookout to capitalize on the latest craze.) "Walk, Don't Run '64," as it was called, peaked at No. 8 on the *Billboard* Hot 100, making it one of the last times the group would reach the top of the US charts.[46]

Although the Ventures continued to enjoy success throughout the 1960s, supported by an amateur guitar culture that they had helped expand and a newfound international fan base (especially in East Asia), much had changed by 1964.[47] The sights and sound of American popular music had shifted as new styles had come to the fore—doo-wop, girl groups, surf rock, Motown, and more. Even the amateurs had found mainstream success, as a wave of American garage rockers topped the charts: The Kingsmen's "Louie Louie" and the Trashmen's "Surfin' Bird" both cracked the Top 10 in 1963, the Rivieras' "California Sun" did the same in 1964, and Paul Revere and the Raiders had a slew of hits starting in 1965.

After the Beatles' famous performance on the Ed Sullivan show in February 1964, a second boom of amateur rock 'n' roll culture spread across America, and the musical instrument industry was happy to exploit the moment. In May 1964, *The Music Trades*—an industry publication—ran a feature story specifically explaining "How to Promote with the Beatles."[48] Ads for Vox, the musical instrument company the Beatles officially endorsed, drive this point home: in October 1964, Vox ran an ad in *The Music Trades* that stated, "The Beatles have made a lot of money with Vox. Now: so can you." It continued:

> Now you can cash in on the money making momentum created by the Beatles. Now you can sell the Vox guitar, amplifiers and accessories. They're available on national distribution for the first time. But

they've already been presold for you by the Beatles. And the Animals and the Dave Clark Five and the Rolling Stones and a host of other big names. That's why selling the Vox line is easier than letting your hair grow long.[49]

The most explicit pitch came in June 1965, with a Vox ad featuring a photo of the Dave Clark Five. After listing a litany of bands that use Vox equipment, it simply read:

The top groups rely on vox.
The top groups pre-sell vox with every appearance.
vox: the sound of money.[50]

Today, garage rock is most often portrayed as an American reaction to the British Invasion. But although the Beatles certainly brought this culture to new heights, the garage rock revolution had been developing locally for years. When it came to the normalization of the electric bass—thanks to this grassroots movement of mostly unknown amateur musicians—that shift had already taken place. In the short time between 1957 and 1964, the electric bass had transitioned from being seen as a poor substitute for the traditional upright to becoming such a common sight that its presence was now simply taken for granted.

Critics, scholars, and historians have regularly dismissed this era of rock 'n' roll. But it was nonetheless significant, especially when it came to fostering a vibrant movement of young amateur musicians. To discount these amateurs is to hold to a version of history that is forever told from the top down, with only the most famous musicians receiving attention and credit. But not all historical developments can be explained that way. Most notably, the electric guitar's overtaking of the saxophone as rock's lead instrument and the electric bass's overtaking of the upright as its de facto low-end instrument were not caused by any single individual. Rather, they were the result of both musical and cultural shifts brought about by a critical mass of amateurs who purchased these instruments, played them, and ultimately made them indispensable. Through their collective actions, these mostly unknown young men and women standardized the instrumentation and format of the modern rock band and, in so doing, were responsible for a massive shift in the look, feel, and sound of American popular music.

The Electric Bass in England

The Ventures' "Walk, Don't Run" entered the *Billboard* Hot 100 on July 18, 1960. Less than two weeks later, on July 27, a different rock instrumental began climbing the UK charts. Written by Jerry Lordan, the Shadows' "Apache" remained on the British Singles Chart for twenty weeks, spending five of those at No. 1.[1] It would be the first in a string of fifteen Top 10 hits for the band throughout the sixties. Like "Walk, Don't Run," the song's success came from the band's accessible, four-part rock 'n' roll style: guitarist Hank Marvin plays a simple, echo-drenched lead line, while Bruce Welch's rhythm guitar and Tony Meehan's drums provide the song's exoticist groove; underneath it all, Jet Harris's electric bass drives the song forward, providing a melodic counterpoint to the lead guitar. The total effect was infectious, and "Apache" solidified the Shadows' position as the most influential British rock 'n' roll band of the pre-Beatles era.

   The electric bass's early history in Europe paralleled prior developments in America. However, the instrument's rise to prominence there is essentially a different story—one comprised of different markets, different instruments, different musicians, and different musical contexts. In this interlude, I detail how two German-based musical instrument companies, Framus and Höfner, came to produce the first commercially available electric basses in England. I then trace how these companies' instruments made their way into Britain's burgeoning skiffle and rock 'n' roll scenes via bassists Shirley Douglas of the Chas McDevitt Group, Brian Gregg of Johnny Kidd and the Pirates, and Jet Harris of the Shadows. The electric bass's initial popularity in England therefore

resulted from the complicated intersection of global politics, technological innovation, and emerging British youth cultures. Moreover, Douglas,
Gregg, and Harris each established models of electric bass playing that
would influence the next wave of British rock bassists, who in turn further expanded the instrument's reach.

The American Guitar Embargo

Throughout the fifties, it was nearly impossible to find a Precision Bass in
England. In fact, musicians wouldn't have been able to find any Fender
guitar, nor any Kay or Gibson, nor nearly any other American-made
musical instruments. As guitar historian Tony Bacon explains,

> Following the end of World War II, the British Board of Trade con-
> trolled imports to try to improve the UK's balance of payments. . . .
> The government's main objective was to secure what they saw as
> necessary savings in the UK's overseas spending, in order to reduce
> the growing dollar deficit. The broader restrictions of the early
> '50s applied primarily to food and drink imports, but among the
> restricted manufactured goods were musical items, namely gramo-
> phone records, harmonicas and their parts, musical boxes and their
> movements, stringed instruments (including guitars), wind instru-
> ments (not including organs), and some organ parts.[2]

Active from late 1951 through mid-1959, this trade embargo, in effect,
cut off British musicians from many key innovations occurring in the
American guitar market, including the advent of the modern electric
bass guitar.[3] Yet, just as in the United States, the increasing popularity
of new, guitar-centric musical styles in England fostered a huge demand
for guitars among teenage amateurs. This demand would be met via an
influx of instruments imported from Germany, Japan, Czechoslovakia,
and elsewhere. As a result, electric basses were not commercially available in England until the mid-fifties, when retailers began importing
German-made Framus and Höfner basses.

Höfner and Framus

In 1887, Karl Höfner established a violin-making company in Schönbach,
a city in the ethnically German Sudetenland region of the Austro-
Hungarian Empire that had been home to musical instrument manufacturing since the late seventeenth century.[4] Höfner's business expanded

over the following decades—even as the Sudetenland was reconstituted as part of Czechoslovakia after World War I—and he eventually brought in his sons, Josef and Walter, to help run the company. By the mid-thirties, Höfner employed over 325 workers and produced a variety of string instruments, including violins, cellos, upright basses, and acoustic guitars. According to guitar historian Christian Hoyer, "Höfner was so successful . . . that, by the beginning of the Second World War, . . . it had become the most important producer and exporter of stringed instruments, not only in Schönbach, but in the whole of Central Europe."[5] However, in 1938, under pressure from the British and French, the Czechoslovak government ceded the Sudetenland to the Nazis, and Josef and Walter were eventually conscripted into the German army.

As in America, World War II dramatically curtailed musical instrument manufacturing, and Höfner's staff was diminished to less than fifty workers. In the aftermath of the war, the Czechoslovak government regained control of the Sudetenland and seized the property of its German-speaking population, including Höfner's company, which was subsequently taken over by the state. At the time, anti-German resentment was at an all-time high, and the Czechoslovak government initiated an ethnic-cleansing campaign that forced the ethnically German residents of Schönbach to either leave or face execution.[6] With their lives and livelihoods in jeopardy, Schönbach luthier Fred Wilfer convinced the nearby Bavarian government to resettle the city's soon-to-be-displaced craftsmen across the border in the Franconia region of Germany. There, in the rural town of Möhrendorf, Wilfer established his own company in 1946, Fränkische Musikinstrumentenerzeugung (Franconian Musical Instrument Production)—which was shortened simply to "Framus."

Walter Höfner came to work for Framus soon thereafter and was put in charge of the company's guitar department. Josef and Karl joined Walter in Möhrendorf in 1948, and the following year they left Framus to help reestablish their family's company. Seeking better accommodations and workspaces, both Framus and Höfner eventually relocated a few miles west to Bubenreuth, where they used refugee loans from the West German government to build state-of-the-art musical instrument-manufacturing facilities. Thanks to England's ongoing embargo against American instruments, both companies established lucrative partnerships with British distributors to import their acoustic and electric guitars. Throughout the fifties, nearly 70 percent of all Höfner's guitars were exported outside of West Germany, and by the end of the sixties, Framus had become the largest guitar manufacturer in all of Europe.[7]

At the 1956 Frankfurt Music Trade Fair, Framus introduced its first line of electric basses: the Star Bass (Model 5/149), a short-scale, thinline hollow-body electric bass with a single pickup, and the Star Bass Deluxe (Model 5/150), a two-pickup version (see Figure 27).[8] At the same event, Höfner introduced the 500/1 Violin Bass, which was distinct from its American counterparts both in design and in purpose. According to the company's official history of the 500/1,

> It seems that Walter's intention was to produce a bass guitar that would be appealing to players of the upright bass . . . who no longer wanted to carry such a big heavy instrument around to play in beat and jazz groups. He also designed the bass so that the construction method would be familiar to the workers at Höfner who had been making violins for decades. So we got a bass that has the style and shape not unlike a classical stringed instrument and built in much the same way, hollow bodied, arched topped and a set in neck.[9]

Framus's vision, by contrast, was much more clearly aligned with Fender's:

> Fred Wilfer's concern was the creation of an instrument that, because of its smaller scale, could easily be played by any guitarist and which possessed the technical features of a guitar. This was—partially due to the dearth of excellent bassists—constantly the subject of complaints brought forward to Fred Wilfer by several dance orchestras. The Star Bass worked to counter that. . . . Framus advertised its new product with the slogan: "Every guitarist—is also a bassist."[10]

Just as with the Precision Bass, Star Basses were designed so that guitarists could easily double on bass, and its eventual success proved there was a European demand for an electric bass. The instrument became a bestseller in West Germany and then, through London-based distributors Dallas and Besson, in England.[11] Höfner likewise supplied basses to England through its own UK distributor, Selmer. Selmer, however, considered the 500/1 Violin Bass too unconventional and declined to import the instrument; instead, it chose to import the newer 500/5 bass (later known as the President Bass), which was a more traditional-looking variation of one of the company's hollow-body guitars.

The British Skiffle Craze

The Lonnie Donegan Skiffle Group released its version of the American folk song "Rock Island Line" in 1955. Driven by a simple three-chord

Figure 27. 1963 ad for the Framus Star Bass and Star Bass Deluxe. (Source: *Dallas London Catalog*, 1963.)

structure, an up-tempo rhythm, and Donegan's memorable vocal performance, the song became a hit in January of the following year and in so doing singlehandedly ushered in the British skiffle craze. Skiffle, an outgrowth of England's trad jazz scene, was an Anglicized revival of old American blues and folk songs. Revitalizing this material for a new audience of British teenagers, skiffle's catchy rhythms and memorable melodies garnered it commercial success, while its easily imitable style led to a wave of amateur music-making across the UK and a corresponding boom in guitar sales.[12]

The earliest British electric bassists all came out of the skiffle scene, and they almost exclusively played Framus Star Basses. For example, the first musician in the scene to own a Star Bass in England was likely Don Wilson, who started playing one in early 1957 while performing with Dickie Bishop and the Sidekicks. As he recalls, the instrument was immediately met with both intrigue and suspicion:

After breaking the neck of my stand-up bass, I visited Lew Davis's music shop in Charing Cross Road . . . and I emerged with a Framus bass and a 12-watt amplifier, which was considered to be quite adequate for the task. It was one of only three [electric basses] in Britain and was a talking point wherever we went—even though some of the purist skifflers thought it was heresy.[13]

In March 1957, at the height of the skiffle craze, Dickie Bishop and the Sidekicks released their signature tune, "No Other Baby," possibly featuring Wilson's Star Bass. Yet while the Sidekicks may have been the first to upset skiffle's acoustic status quo, the oncoming ascendance of rock 'n' roll pushed other bands to follow in their footsteps. In an attempt to modernize, many skiffle musicians soon began to not only perform more contemporary material, but also to adopt amplified electric instruments.

Shirley Douglas

Irish singer/guitarist Shirley Douglas (1939–2013) got her big break at the end of 1957, when she joined the Chas McDevitt Skiffle Group—one of the country's most prominent skiffle outfits. The group had scored a No. 5 hit just a few months earlier with their version of "Freight Train," yet the unexpected departure of singer Nancy Whiskey had left them without a female vocalist. Douglas joined as a replacement and shortly thereafter the group began incorporating more American rock 'n' roll songs into their act. McDevitt justified this change in a January 1958 *NME* article that explicitly asked the question, "Is [skiffle] dying?"

> My singer, Shirley Douglas, has been singing [recent] things like "My Special Angel" and "With All My Heart," in addition to the established skiffle favourites. The group now do songs like "That'll Be the Day" and "Wake Up, Little Susie" in the skiffle idiom. You see skiffle is just a style of playing, and almost any form of music can be played in the style—within reason.[14]

By the end of the year, Douglas had also taken up the electric bass.

She had first encountered the instrument in the summer of 1958, when the Chas McDevitt Group went on tour with the Treniers and the Hedley Ward Trio as a last-minute replacement for Jerry Lee Lewis, whose place on the tour had been canceled after his marriage to his thirteen-year-old cousin had been exposed by the British press. Witnessing the Treniers perform onstage each night, Douglas and McDevitt were captivated by the band's electric bassist, Jimmy Johnson, and decided that

Figure 28. Promo-
tional photo of
Shirley Douglas
(right) and Chas
McDevitt. Note
that once the
American guitar
embargo was
lifted, Douglas
switched to
playing a Fender
Precision Bass.
(Source: Columbia
Records UK, ca.
1960.)

they should incorporate the instrument into their own group. According
to British guitar historian Mo Foster,

> This was the first time that the Chas McDevitt Group had ever seen
> [an electric bass], and it prompted them to invest in the only one
> available to them at the time, a Framus. At the time no one in Chas'
> group had a clue how to play the communal bass, but Shirley Douglas

became the bass player by default because she was the only member who could both sing and play at the same time.[15]

Playing an imported Framus Star Bass with one of the country's leading skiffle bands, Douglas thus became one of England's pioneering electric bassists. She began using it in the group's live act—and eventually on their studio recordings (Figure 28)—where it served as a further break with the group's skiffle roots. Compare, for example, "Across the Bridge" from November 1957, Douglas's first recording with the group, to "Sad Little Girl," a B-side released in October 1959; the former's acoustic guitars, upright bass, and washboard rhythm stand in stark contrast to the latter's prominent electric bass line, tenor saxophone, and tremolo electric guitar.[16]

Brian Gregg

As a teenager, Brian Gregg (b. 1939) spent his days working at an HMV record shop and his nights frequenting local skiffle venues in London. His preferred hangout was the basement of the 2i's coffee bar, an influential Soho music venue that would later be described as the "Birthplace of British Rock 'n' Roll." After a serendipitous encounter with members of the skiffle group Les Hobeaux at his day job, Gregg helped the band secure an audition with 2i's owner Paul Lincoln, during which he sat in on a tea-chest bass that had been left at the venue.[17] After Les Hobeaux secured a residency at the 2i's, Gregg became the group's permanent bass player—eventually switching to an upright. In the summer of 1957, the band embarked on a national tour alongside Terry Dene and filmed a brief cameo in Dene's star-vehicle *The Golden Disc* (1958). By 1958, they had also secured a contract with EMI and released three singles on the HMV label.

Gregg first came across the electric bass in 1956, witnessing it in the film *The Girl Can't Help It* and then, in person, during Lionel Hampton's fall tour of England.[18] Shortly thereafter, he saw a newly imported Höfner 500/5 in the window of Selmer's music shop and jumped at the opportunity.[19] This new instrument, however, did not jibe with Les Hobeaux's skiffle style, and Gregg soon left the band intent on pursuing rock 'n' roll.

At the time, bass players were hard to come by, and Gregg found that he and his electric bass were in demand among England's top rock acts. He first joined Colin Hicks & the Cabin Boys, embarking on one of Italy's first rock 'n' roll package tours in May 1958, followed by a brief stint backing up Tommy Steele, Hicks's more famous older brother. By April 1959, Gregg had become part of the latest iteration of Terry Dene & the Dene Aces, along with drummer Clem Cattini.[20] At the behest of British rock impresario Larry Parnes, Gregg and Cattini then became the core rhythm section of the Beat Boys, a touring group that supported Parnes's stable of artists on his "Big Beat Show" package tours. As Gregg recalled, "One after the other, they would jump out on stage . . . all looking the same, silhouetted in the spotlight, in their sparkly jackets. 'Which one's this?' Clem would shout. 'I think it's Dickie [Pride],' I would shout back. Most of the time, it was an endless blur of Elvis Presley and Little Richard songs."[21] Financial disputes brought their relationship with Parnes to an end, and by early 1960, Gregg and Cattini had joined a new band, Johnny Kidd and the Pirates.

On May 13, 1960, Johnny Kidd and the Pirates recorded their magnum opus, "Shakin' All Over" at EMI's Abbey Road Studios. The song had been written at one o'clock in the morning of the session, while Gregg, Kidd, and guitarist Alan Caddy were killing time at Chas McDevitt's Freight Train coffee bar. According to Gregg,

> As we were sat waiting at the Freight Train, I said we should use the time to write a song before the session tomorrow. After all, we only had to write a simple rock 'n' roll tune and we three were all experienced in playing that, after years on the road. We had no thoughts of writing anything lasting or technical, just a B-side, something that would bring us in some more cash. In 1960 you would be paid the same amount of royalties for writing the B-side as you would the A-side so we didn't have to try and be clever, just do something acceptable. . . . We all kind of looked at each other not knowing where to begin. I said, "Look Johnny—I've got a bass run that I like which might be a good start." I didn't have my bass guitar with me, so I sang it to him. "It goes DUM-DUM, DUM-DUM, DUM-DUM, DUM-DUM," tapping out the timing at the same time . . . The words came really quickly, in fact we were all laughing, thinking how amateurish and corny they were because Jerry Lee Lewis had "Whole Lotta Shakin'" a few years before and the old style Rock 'n' Roll terminology was on the way out, so the word Shakin' was quite suspect but we couldn't think of anything to put in its place.[22]

Having figured out the song's basic elements, the band reconvened at the studio a few hours later to put it down on tape, and the track was recorded in a single take (with a few overdubs). On the session, Gregg played a Framus Star Bass run through a custom amplifier. Placed prominently in the final mix, his electric bass has a rich, full tone that anchors the band's power trio format. As he later described his style,

> It was thought that the bass was the instrument you only "missed hearing" if it stopped playing. Well I had other ideas about that and made it an instrument with a purpose. . . . Also, I played with my thumb, which gave a much deeper resonance than using a plectrum. This worked perfectly—playing very closely with the drummer in a three-piece music set up—to create some "guts."[23]

Instead of relegating it to a B-side, EMI released "Shakin'" as a single in June, and it spent nineteen weeks on the British Singles Chart, climbing all the way to No. 1.

In 1962, Gregg, Cattini, and Caddy all quit the Pirates. Cattini and Caddy went on to join the instrumental rock band the Tornados, and their recording of "Telstar" (1962) reached No. 1 in both the United Kingdom and the United States. Gregg joined them soon after, replacing original electric bassist Heinz Burt—another early Framus Star Bass adopter.

Jet Harris

Terence "Jet" Harris (1939–2011) started out playing upright bass in London jazz clubs. When the skiffle craze hit, he had a job working behind the counter at the 2i's, and after work he would sit in with other bands playing in the 2i's basement.[24] This led to his first professional gig as part of Terry Dene & the Dene Aces, followed by a brief stint with the Vipers skiffle group, which led to his first commercial recording (a slowed-down version of Eddie Cochran's "Summertime Blues" released on Parlophone).[25]

Harris decided to pick up an electric bass at the prompting of drummer Tony Crombie, whose band, Tony Crombie and His Rock 'n' Roll Rockets, were England's first homegrown rock 'n' roll act. Formed in 1956, the Rockets were self-consciously styled on Bill Haley and His Comets and Freddie Bell and the Bellboys, both of whom Crombie had seen in the film *Rock Around the Clock.*[26] Describing his decision to move from jazz into rock 'n' roll, Crombie recalled,

It was money. I had been a long time in the business and I hadn't earned anything so far [laughs]. I went to see that movie *Rock Around the Clock* at the London Pavilion. And it was a pretty tedious film, but then when Bill Haley's band went on and did . . . that rock 'n' roll number "Rock Around the Clock" . . . suddenly the theater was full of stamping people. And I thought to myself, something's going to happen with this music. And I immediately contacted my agent, Kruger, and I said I've just been to see this film and this thing's got a big opportunity here. Let's get a band together and go out on the road with a rock 'n' roll band. . . . We got an immediate tour of the Moss Empires, top of the bill. And we were away. Publicity and coverage was absolutely tremendous. And we had a very, very successful twelve to eighteen months topping the bill with this rock 'n' roll show.[27]

Crombie asked Harris to join the Rockets for a tour in 1958, but he suggested that Harris switch to electric bass, an instrument that he—like Brian Gregg—had seen at one of Lionel Hampton's UK performances in late 1956. As Harris later explained:

I was playing double bass around the modern jazz clubs with a Willesden-based jazz trio called the Delinquents . . . [which] led me to being invited to join Tony Crombie's Rockets backing [singer] Wee Willie Harris. To me Tony was the guvnor—he was *the* jazz man for me. One day he asked me, "Have you seen this new invention?" I said, "No, what is it?" "It's a new type of bass only it's shaped like an electric guitar." So I became the proud owner of the first bass guitar in the country. There I was on stage every night with this thing around my neck.[28]

Jet Harris wasn't technically the first electric bassist in England, but he was one of the earliest—and over the next two years he would certainly become the most famous.

Harris's first electric bass was a Besson Aristone, which he purchased from Macari's Musical Instruments (another of the music shops on Charing Cross Road).[29] Despite the name, the instrument was actually a Framus Star Bass Deluxe—just as Sears had rebranded Danelectro basses into Silvertones, Besson had imported Framus guitars from Germany and rebranded them for the British market. Harris then joined the Rockets and quickly found that he liked the attention that his new bass brought:

"People used to come down to the 2i's to see this bloke playing this new instrument, you know, because they'd never seen one."[30] Combined with his signature bleached-blonde hair, this added novelty value translated into better job offers, and during a late 1958 tour, Harris's career took a decided lead forward when he joined the Drifters, the backing band for teen sensation Cliff Richard.

At the time Harris joined the band, Richard was riding a wave of success from his first single, "Move It," which had peaked at No. 2 in October 1958. At just eighteen years old, Richard's good looks and musical talent had made him a national rock 'n' roll icon; yet his original backing band was falling apart just as he was becoming a star. As a series of replacements, Richard eventually formed the Drifters out of four regulars from the 2i's: Hank B. Marvin on lead guitar, Bruce Welch on rhythm guitar, Jet Harris on electric bass, and Tony Meehan on drums. Their first gig with this lineup came in January 1959, when they backed Richard for a performance at the Manchester Free Trade Hall. That same month, producer Norrie Paramor secured the Drifters a separate recording contract with Columbia UK (an EMI subsidiary), and thereafter the group split their time between touring and recording with Richard and recording their own material.

Harris's electric bass played a substantial role on Richard's recordings. Take, for instance, the single "Living Doll," released in July 1959. The song opens with a short, memorable electric bass solo, and throughout the rest of the song, his Besson Aristone is placed prominently in the mix (louder in the verses than both the rhythm and lead guitar). But while "Living Doll" quickly shot up to the top of the charts, the same could not be said about the Drifters' early releases. Their first single, the Buddy Holly-esque "Feelin' Fine," flopped when it was released in February 1959, and their follow-up single, "Jet Black," similarly failed to chart. Despite its lack of mainstream success, however, "Jet Black" marked the group's debut as an instrumental band and thus established the formula that they would follow for the next decade.[31] One benefit of this turn toward instrumentals was that the Drifters were no longer in direct competition with Richard's material. In fact, Richard even encouraged the group to include some of their instrumentals in his stage show and his LPs. His debut album, *Cliff* (1959)—an in-studio recreation of the his live show, complete with screaming fans—featured early versions of three Drifters instrumentals, including "Jet Black."[32] By mid-1959, however, the band had run into a new problem: they had received an injunction from the American doo-wop group the Drifters, forcing them

Figure 29. Jet Harris (center) and the Shadows performing with their new Fender guitars. (Source: *The Young Ones*, dir. Sidney J. Furie, 1961.)

to cease and desist from using the group's name or else face legal conse-quences.[33] At Harris's suggestion, the group changed their name to the Shadows.

After "Apache" was released in July 1960, the Shadows became the most famous rock band in England—the 1960 *NME* Reader's Poll listed them as the No. 1 "British Small Group" and named "Apache" the "Best British Disc of the Year."[34] The group was given a further boost in vis-ibility via a number of British rock 'n' roll teenpics, where they appeared backing Richard, who was quickly becoming a bankable movie star. The most notable of these were *Expresso Bongo* (1959) and *The Young Ones* (1961), the latter of which featured a choreographed sequence where the Shadows performed "The Savage," another exoticist instrumental. Aside from the music, two important components of this performance are notable: First, the band executes an extended choreographed dance sequence (what would come to be known as "The Shadows' Walk"), which Welch and Marvin had modeled on the Treniers, who they had also seen perform on that aforementioned 1958 UK tour.[35] Second, the band members are all playing matching red Fender guitars (Figure 29). As the trade embargo had just been lifted, the group had rushed to pro-cure American equipment, and Harris had switched to playing a Fender Precision Bass.

The Shadows remained in the top spot of the "British Small Group" category for the 1961 *NME* Reader's Poll—this time by a whopping 34,545 votes.[36] Yet for Harris, the cracks were beginning to show. Faced with mounting tensions inside the band due to his escalating issues with alcohol, Harris quit the Shadows in April 1962 to pursue a solo career. The next month, *NME* contributor Derek Johnson laid out the risks of this move, stating, "Much depends on the success of [Harris's] first solo record, which was [recorded] in the Decca studios last Saturday and which will be rush-released in a week or so. And from what I hear, the disc is going to make a few people sit up and take notice."[37] That disc, a go-go version of the Latin standard "Besame Mucho," did make people take notice—perhaps simply because it sounded so unusual.

For "Besame Mucho," Harris switched instruments yet again, abandoning his Precision Bass in favor of a brand-new Fender Bass VI. Introduced in 1961 as Fender's answer to the Danelectro UB-2, the Bass VI was a six-string, short-scale electric bass that was constructed like a traditional electric guitar but tuned down an octave.[38] These idiosyncratic features allowed Harris to more easily execute lead lines while still playing in the bass's lower range. As a subsequent *NME* feature described it: "For 'Besame Mucho,' Jet uses an unusual instrument—a six string bass guitar, which Decca claims has never been heard on any other British-made disc. . . . The throbbing, driving instrumental hits an all-time low in bass notes . . . which sends musicians into delirious fits."[39]

"Besame Mucho" managed to crack the British Top 40, spending seven weeks on the Singles Chart and peaking at No. 22. While this paled in comparison to the Shadows' ongoing chart success, Harris's solo career only further solidified his reputation as the most popular electric bassist in England. This much is demonstrated by the 1962 *NME* Reader's Poll, in which Harris dominated the "Solo Instrumentalist" category—not only coming at No. 1, but also beating Shadows lead guitarist Hank B. Marvin (listed as No. 4) by a total of 14,346 votes.[40] This level of recognition was unprecedented for an electric bassist, British or otherwise. Harris reached the apex of his career a few short months later, when his third single, another Jerry Lordan instrumental titled "Diamonds," made it to No. 1 in February 1963.[41]

Conclusion

In 1960, Shirley Douglas released *Shirley Douglas' Easy Guide to Rhythm & Blues for Bass-Guitar*, one of the first electric bass method books available in the UK.[42] In the introduction, she explicitly traced the newfound popularity of the electric bass back through skiffle:

> In its infancy, skiffle favoured the use of the [wash]tub-bass. . . . The guitar however was the instrument of the moment. Some groups found themselves with three or four guitarists and no bass player. They soon realized that the essential rhythm was lacking. The tub-bass produced merely dull thwack and the cumbersome double-bass was often too ponderous, and a little too difficult to pick up over night. Many young guitarists adapted their newfound knowledge to the bass-guitar, it is to these that this [book] will prove invaluable.[43]

Like the *Mel Bay Electric Bass Method,* Douglas's *Easy Guide* starts by teaching traditional musical literacy and then demonstrates how to play in a variety of different pop contexts, including Fats Domino-style walking bass lines, Duane Eddy-style riffs, Leadbelly-style boogie patterns, Bo Diddley-style rhumba patterns, Howlin' Wolf-style blues, and more. In total, the book functions as a primer on most popular bass styles of the early sixties and demonstrates how quickly electric bass playing had become ingrained within UK popular music.

The electric bass's early history in England was fundamentally distinct from its American origins. Popularized via an influx of inexpensive basses imported from Germany, it was played by musicians in the London skiffle scene before being adopted by the first generation of UK rock 'n' rollers. In their wake, the electric bass became an increasingly common sight in the early sixties, as new groups of amateurs started creating their own versions of electric-guitar-driven rock music. By 1964, with the barriers between the American and British rock 'n' roll scenes eroding, bands like the Beatles, the Rolling Stones, and the Who further expanded the role of the electric bass—in part, bringing the formative models established by pioneers such as Shirley Douglas, Brian Gregg, and Jet Harris to the forefront of popular music on both sides of the Atlantic.

PART III

New Sounds, New Roles

SIX | The Studio Instrument

Session Musicians and Stylistic Innovations

In January 1965, Brian Wilson announced that he would stop touring with the Beach Boys and instead dedicate himself to recording new music for the group as a full-time producer and songwriter. The following month, on February 24, he entered Western Recorders in Hollywood to work on the group's next single, "Help Me, Rhonda." The Beach Boys had already recorded a complete version of the song a few weeks prior, but facing intense pressure from their label—and to justify Wilson's new, behind-the-scenes-only focus—the band reconvened in the studio to create an even more radio-friendly version.[1] Ultimately, though, the responsibility for giving life to this new arrangement fell to the group of professional session musicians who had been contracted to play on the recording. They were the ones who eventually supplied the "better feel" that Wilson thought the song needed.[2] Perhaps the most significant addition to the arrangement was Carol Kaye's electric bass line, which is prominently featured in the final mix. Written by Wilson (himself an electric bassist), it starts with an elaborate countermelody in the verses before transitioning into lightly embellished, quarter-note lines in the prechoruses and choruses that reinforce the song's sense of stability and forward momentum.

Though Kaye's contributions would help turn "Rhonda" into the Beach Boys' second No. 1 hit, she does not remember the session fondly: "Brian made me angry on that session as he kept us playing extra-long."[3] According to Kaye, "We were all blowing our chops, the take must have been ten minutes long and my fingers started to bleed from the grinding hard part."[4] With the action on her Precision Bass set high, Kaye had to

dig into her thick electric bass strings to get a good clean sound; combined with the repetition of the song's quick, contrapuntal riff, Kaye was
left to injure herself as Wilson obliviously forced the band to keep running through the arrangement over and over again. As she left the session, Kaye carried out a small act of defiance. "I gave him the [middle]
finger," she recalled. "Guess he was shocked, but he was careful after that
not to work us to death."[5]

"Help Me, Rhonda" encapsulates some of the complexities of session work in this era. For many labels, session musicians were a crucial
part of the recording process. Yet, even in the intimate social space of
the recording studio, producers sometimes had to be reminded that the
musicians were, in fact, human beings. And despite their apparent value,
most session musicians in the sixties were rarely, if ever, credited on the
singles or albums on which they appeared.

This chapter chronicles how session electric bassists became established within the most prominent recording scenes in the United States.
Coming at a time when producers and engineers were increasingly spot-
lighting the sound of the bass in their overall mixes, these musicians ultimately developed their own distinctive styles, and although their names
were largely unknown to the public, their performances fueled the commercial success of hundreds of hit recordings throughout the sixties and
beyond.[6] Taking a broad approach that examines the Los Angeles, Detroit,
Memphis, Muscle Shoals, and New York recording scenes, this chapter
has three goals: First, given the various ways that these scenes functioned
as workplaces, it provides a general account of how each operated and
the expectations placed on its session musicians. Second, it recounts the
careers of the earliest electric bassists in each city and highlights the later
stylistic innovations of key players. And, lastly, it address the day-to-day
challenges each of these musicians faced within their respective recording scenes. Ultimately, this chapter reaffirms the significant impact that
session bassists had, both on the history of the electric bass and on popular music as a whole, while still acknowledging the contradictions and
complexities that often accompanied their work.

Demystifying the Job of the Session Musician

Session musicians have been a consistent feature of the American music
industry since nearly the beginning of recording.[7] As James P. Kraft demonstrates, advances in phonograph, film, and radio technology during
the thirties resulted in a loss of jobs for local musicians around the coun-

try; at the same time, these forces created a demand for a new professional class of musicians in major media centers.[8] These musicians were tasked with performing on radio broadcasts, on commercial recordings, and on film soundtracks—all of which would then be exported across the country. By the fifties, session players were a standard component of the music industry, being regularly employed at dozens of studios across the United States (including J&M Studio in New Orleans and Bradley Studios in Nashville). For both major and independent labels, employing session musicians became a reliable method to continually produce new product while still maximizing their return on investment.

Session work was a particularly difficult and highly specialized form of creative labor. Generally speaking, session musicians had to be reliable, experienced professionals who were adept at playing their instruments and were willing and able to collaborate. Perhaps most crucially, they also needed to know how to craft parts that would sound good on a record. Given labels' insistence on investing as little capital as possible, session musicians were also required to work well under pressure and be able to record multiple songs per session (in the sixties, the industry standard was four songs in three hours). In addition to their musical ability, session musicians had to learn how to navigate the unspoken etiquette of the recording studio, an especially important skill since they represented the lowest rung of the studio's social hierarchy. Each of these skills allowed session musicians to craft commercial-grade recordings quickly and efficiently, yet these were only the minimum requirements.[9] Although temperament, interpersonal skills, and industry connections all influenced which musicians were brought in for a session, the most significant factor in their perceived value was their ability to regularly contribute distinctive musical ideas that could improve a recording—"that extra thing," as Isabel Campelo describes it.[10] When it comes to the history of the electric bass, this fundamental characteristic—the expectation that session bassists would provide unique, compelling bass lines—was the primary driver of stylistic innovation throughout the sixties. To maintain their positions in the competitive, high-stakes recording scenes in which they worked, many session bassists developed their own distinctive approaches to playing their instruments, which, in turn, further expanded the bass's role in popular music.

Since session musicians consistently provided memorable contributions to hundreds of hit records, it is not an exaggeration to say that they were essential workers within the music industry. But, in the sixties and seventies, session musicians' creative labor was (and is still) categorized as "work for hire," meaning that they relinquished any claim to copyright and instead transferred ownership of whatever they played to the label that hired them. In exchange, the musicians were either paid an agreed-upon one-time fee per session or were compensated as regularly salaried employees. At the time, the unequal nature of this financial relationship was a lesser concern for most first-call players, who were relatively well-paid and could count on plenty of work. Musicians working in scenes with a strong Musicians' Union presence also received some additional forms of compensation for their labor—such as through "reuse" fees or from the Phonograph Record Manufacturers' Special Payments Fund, a trust for recording musicians into which the major labels agreed to pay a very small percentage of their profits.[11] Yet, when a recording they played on became commercially successful, session musicians didn't receive traditional royalties, regardless of how many copies it sold. Hence the inherent complexity of session work: these musicians were expected to provide a unique, valuable contribution to a recording, but if their contributions successfully helped make that recording a hit, they were largely barred from sharing in its potentially multi-million-dollar profits.[12]

Furthermore, because professional session musicians helped craft some of the greatest music of the sixties and seventies, it is tempting to romanticize their profession. Back then, however, session musicians were simply treated as small cogs in the larger record-making machine. No matter how skilled or innovative they might have been, they were all considered replaceable. As Charles Hughes convincingly demonstrates, a more accurate historical account of session musicians in this era requires that—as the music industry did—we primarily conceive of them as "workers" and recording studios as "working environments."[13] In fairness to each of the bassists discussed in this chapter, it is therefore important to acknowledge and celebrate their accomplishments without overlooking the sometimes grim realities of their occupation.

Los Angeles and the Wrecking Crew

Los Angeles became a major media center in the thirties, thanks to its direct ties to the film, radio, and television industries.[14] Its position as the West Coast pole of the commercial music industry was further solidified in the postwar years as multiple record labels established LA as their home base, and it flourished as a recording scene throughout the sixties thanks to the many prominent studios operating within its city limits.

Some of these were owned by major labels—Columbia, RCA, Decca, and Capitol, for example, all had their own dedicated LA studios—but many more were independent operations that leased the use of their space and equipment on an ad hoc basis—these included Gold Star Recording Studios, the United Recording Company, Western Recorders, and Sunset Sound Recorders. Since vast amounts of music were recorded in LA, its session musicians could be contracted to play on nearly anything and were thus expected to be proficient across a wide variety of musical styles. They were also expected to adapt to the needs of any given session, which could range from simply executing a prewritten arrangement, to improvising their own part from scratch, or something in between.

The LA recording scene, as in Nashville and New York, was heavily regulated by the Musicians' Union. Falling under the purview of AFM Local 47, LA session musicians were independent contractors who were free to record for any studio or label. Union regulations also standardized the format for recording sessions, dictating that they would be three hours long, with extra wages paid for overtime and late-night sessions. Although it is difficult to trace concretely, it seems that standard union scale in LA was around $40 per session in the late fifties, which then increased to around $80 by the mid-sixties.[15] In a practice that was mostly unique to LA, top-tier players were also able to ask for double or even triple scale per session. This meant that first-call session musicians in LA were likely the highest paid in the nation and, adjusting for inflation, could potentially have earned more than $500,000 per year in today's money.

The electric bass was introduced into the LA scene in the late fifties as part of a wider generational shift. The older session players, who were accustomed to performing sophisticated musical arrangements, were openly hostile to rock 'n' roll and other contemporary youth-oriented styles, believing that such simple, repetitive music was unworthy of their efforts. Their dismissals opened up opportunities for a new generation of musicians who did not let musical snobbery stop them from earning a paycheck. This generation of LA session musicians has come to be known as the "Wrecking Crew," a nickname popularized by drummer Hal Blaine. As he explained, "The established studio musicians always wore their blue blazers and neckties and always cleaned their ashtrays after a date. We were the new guys [*sic*], and we dressed as we lived—in Levi's and T-shirts. We were informal and spontaneous, and a lot of the old hands thought we were wrecking the music industry."[16] More of a loose collective than a cohesive band, the Wrecking Crew included as many as four hundred session musicians, of which approximately fifty to one hundred were considered top-tier players.[17]

The first Wrecking Crew musician to regularly play electric bass was Ray Pohlman (1930–1990). Born in Iowa, Pohlman started off learning piano and trombone.[18] As a teenager, he and his family relocated to LA, where he took up the guitar at the age of seventeen. He then built up his chops apprenticing within the local jazz scene and, in the mid-fifties, began supplementing his income from live performance by working as a second-string session player. Around 1957, anticipating changing trends in the music industry, Pohlman acquired a third-generation Fender Precision Bass, which he played with his thumb. As was the case with many session bassists, Pohlman's early adoption of the instrument proved to be a key advantage, as he quickly became the go-to electric bassist in the LA recording scene, a position that became increasingly lucrative as producers began to regularly feature the instrument on their recordings. Summing up his work as a session musician, Pohlman recalled,

> I was playing a lot of electric bass then, because I knew where the notes were and what they should be. A lot of the rock and roll guys liked my ideas. A lot of people don't know that the early Beach Boys records and Jan & Dean and all that Phil Spector stuff from the sixties were made largely by jazz musicians. As long as it was within their context, they liked what we did.[19]

As the earliest electric bassist in the LA scene, Pohlman was a pioneer, yet he remains less well known than his later Wrecking Crew contemporaries, likely because his electric bass style privileged simple lines designed to fit an early rock 'n' roll aesthetic. Nevertheless, his electric bass playing can be heard on numerous hit songs, which—as was customary in LA—traversed multiple musical genres: Pohlman played bass on recordings by Sam Cooke, the Ronettes, the Righteous Brothers, Jan & Dean, the Beach Boys, and more. One of his most prominent bass lines comes from Dean Martin's "Everybody Loves Somebody" (1964), which knocked the Beatles' "Hard Day's Night" off the top of the pop charts. From late 1964 through early 1966, Pohlman also served as the musical director for ABC's hit rock 'n' roll television show *Shindig!*, which marked the end of his reign as LA's No. 1 electric bassist.[20] His position at the top of the call sheet was subsequently ceded to bassists Lyle Ritz (1930–2017) and Larry Knechtel (1940–2009).

An upright bassist and jazz ukulelist, Ritz's entry into the LA recording scene came through rock 'n' roll demos. Unlike traditional sessions, which were highly regulated, demo sessions were usually conducted off the books, with the musicians paid under the table and the "official" understanding being that this material would not be commercially released. However, many labels flouted this arrangement and simply used demo sessions to cheaply finance their recordings. The musicians, for their part, were more than happy to record demos on the side— especially since they wouldn't have to take any money out for taxes or the union pension fund. Many also accepted lower-paying demo work as a way of proving their skills.[21] Ritz, for instance, recalls that he only became an established session player after the success of the Cascade's "Rhythm of the Rain" (1962), a rock 'n' roll demo that he played upright on that became a No. 1 hit.[22] Although these unregulated sessions were a common occurrence, if the union discovered that its members had performed on a commercially released demo (especially a successful one), it would often fine both the record company and the musicians themselves; such was the case for Sonny & Cher's "I Got You Babe" (1965), on which Ritz played his 1959 Fender Precision bass.[23]

Larry Knechtel was primarily known as a keyboard player, but he also played electric bass on multiple hit records in the middle to late sixties. A Los Angeles native with perfect pitch, Knechtel's first big break came as a member of Duane Eddy's touring band, where he took over the position once held by Buddy Wheeler. Knechtel settled back in LA in the early sixties and began working on sessions in 1963, including playing keyboards on *A Christmas Gift for You from Philles Records*. Over the next few years, he supplemented his session work by playing electric bass, and he was even hired by Pohlman to be the house bassist for *Shindig!*'s studio band. Knechtel later went on to play electric bass on recordings by the Byrds, Simon & Garfunkel, the Doors, Elvis Presley, and Frank Sinatra.

Although each of these early Wrecking Crew bassists played on significant hit records, they all fundamentally treated the electric bass as a straightforward accompaniment instrument. By the mid-sixties, however, the cutthroat nature of the LA recording scene had given rise to more inventive electric bass styles. Contrary to their predecessors, both Carol Kaye (b. 1935) and Joe Osborn (1937–2018) used picks, an approach that gave their playing an added clarity and ultimately elevated the sound of their electric basses.

Carol Kaye was the first of the LA session musicians to expand the conventions of electric bass playing. Originally a jazz guitarist, she broke into the LA recording scene around 1957 and then worked as a session guitarist for the next six years, notably playing rhythm guitar on Ritchie Valens's "Donna" (1958) and "La Bamba" (1958), as well as the Righteous Brothers' "You've Lost That Lovin' Feelin" (1964). She picked up an electric bass around 1963, after she was conscripted to play the instrument on a session after the contracted bassist failed to appear. Enjoying its simplicity (and bored with playing repetitive rhythm guitar parts), Kaye purchased a Fender Precision Bass and decided to make it her primary instrument. Drawing on her prior experience as a guitarist, Kaye played her bass through a Fender Super Reverb guitar amplifier and accentuated its sound by playing with a hard pick and strong attack. She also modified her instrument to produce a cleaner sound. As she explained, "[Fender Precision Basses] had that awful rubber muting that also wore unevenly, making you sound terrible. . . . What I did with the early 1960s Fenders was take the bridge cover off, tape my felt mute on top of the strings where they exited the bridge, and replaced the bridge cover."[24] In total, Kaye's approach produced a distinctive bass timbre that had volume, depth, and clarity, especially in the instruments lowest register, and she quickly rose through the ranks to become a top-call session bassist. Today she is most remembered for her work with the Beach Boys, playing electric bass on "Help Me, Rhonda" (1965), "California Girls" (1965), "Sloop John B" (1965), and "Wouldn't It Be Nice" (1965). Yet, like Pohlman and other LA session musicians, Kaye was proficient across multiple styles and recorded with musicians as diverse as Frank Zappa and the Mothers of Invention, Glen Campbell, and Quincy Jones. As the go-to bassist for Motown's lesser-known West Coast recording operations, she also appeared on Martha and the Vandellas' "I'm Ready for Love" (1966) and the Supremes' "Love Is Here and Now You're Gone" (1967) and "In and Out of Love" (1967), as well as dozens of album cuts.[25] Notably, around 1966, Kaye switched to using a 30-watt Versatone Pan-O-Flex Model 133 bass amp, which featured a "bi-amplification" design in which two circuits were used to individually power the high and low frequencies—giving the sound of her bass even more clarity and drive.

As was the case with all LA session musicians, the amount that Kaye could personally embellish her bass lines varied widely from session to session. For this reason, the biggest hits she played on were not necessarily her most personal or interesting bass lines. Instead, it was on deeper cuts like Brenda Holloway's "You've Made Me So Very Happy" (1967), Mel Tormé's "Games People Play" (1969), and Ray Charles's "Feel So Bad" (1971) that she was given much more leeway to craft her own parts. Overall, when given the opportunity, Kaye tended to treat the bass as a song's primary rhythmic driver, a feat she accomplished thanks to the speed and clarity that came from her picked playing. On up-tempo songs, she was known for playing fast, syncopated grooves, interspersed with quick fills. Take, for example, the two contrasting sections of Joe Cocker's "Feelin' Alright" (1968): entering at the first chorus, Kaye starts by repeating a hard-driving rhythmic groove in the bass's lower register; she then contrasts this in the subsequent verses by playing a syncopated two-bar figure with elaborate flurries of sixteenth notes.[26] By contrast, on slower songs—such as Barbra Streisand's "The Way We Were" (1973)—Kaye plays in a far more melodic style, adding in slides and scalar walking passages that cut through the background orchestra and accentuate the song's turbulent depiction of lost love. As Kaye explained, "You have to invent lines that fit that tune, that music. It could be very simple lines, it could be kind of complicated lines."[27] Revealingly, she added, "I was always accused of overinventing, playing more notes than necessary. So I had to be careful."[28] Though her preferred unencumbered style wasn't considered appropriate for every session, Kaye's bass lines—even when purposefully subdued—demonstrated a nuanced emphasis on groove and timbre that far outshone her LA predecessors.

While Kaye was most known for her hard-driving low end, Joe Osborn was known for his more laid-back approach. Born in Louisiana, Osborn got his start playing guitar in the Shreveport rhythm & blues scene. He switched to a Fender Precision Bass in 1959 while accompanying country singer Bob Luman, and like Kaye, he developed his personal approach to the instrument by adapting his prior skill set as a guitar player and modifying the instrument itself. As he recalled, "I was a guitarist who knew nothing about bass, which is why I used a pick—but the instrument felt comfortable. I immediately removed the bridge cover with the foam mute, because I didn't like the way it muffled the strings, and I turned the treble on the amp way up."[29] Through his hometown connections, Osborn was hired to replace bassist James Kirkland in Ricky Nelson's backing band, and he subsequently appeared on Nelson's biggest hit single, "Travelin' Man" backed with "Hello Mary Lou" (1961).[30] The bright, clear bass timbre audible on "Travelin' Man" would go on to become a hallmark of Osborn's electric bass style. It also served as his introduction to the LA recording scene. As he explained,

When I got out to LA with Ricky Nelson and began working on records and publishing demos, people would say, "Wow, we can hear the bass all of a sudden." All the notes came out clearly, and I had no idea why. Eventually, I realized that my bass, played with the pick, had its own frequency space. Instead of competing with the kick drum at the very bottom, there was more of a blend . . . there was an attitude about it, a certain tone that you couldn't lose.[31]

Thanks to an endorsement deal between Nelson and Fender, Osborn received one of the first Fender Jazz Basses, and he found that its slimmer neck better suited his short fingers. Pairing it with a Fender Concert guitar amp, this instrument became his primary workhorse.[32]

When Nelson disbanded his group in 1964, Osborn became a full-time LA session bassist, eventually playing on an estimated minimum two hundred Top 40 hits.[33] Among these were songs by the Mamas and the Papas, the Association, Glen Campbell, the Partridge Family, the Carpenters, and many, many more. As was typical for a LA session musician, his style varied based on the needs of each recording, but overall, Osborn was inherently a groove player. The clearest representation of his approach—and likely his most famous bass line—comes from the 5th Dimension's No. 1 hit "Aquarius / Let the Sunshine In (The Flesh Failures)" (1969), a medley adapted from the musical *Hair*. For the first half of the recording, Osborn locks in rhythmically with drummer Hal Blaine, mostly outlining the root and fifth of each chord. Then, as the recording transitions into the second song in the medley, Osborn lets loose. Suddenly, on top of his original groove-based approach, he adds in increasingly elaborate melodic flourishes—slides, hammer-ons, rapid fills—all of which build in intensity until the song fades out. It is an impressive feat, and like Kaye's work, is far more technically challenging than anything attempted by the first generation of Wrecking Crew bassists.

Although Kaye and Osborn had slightly different styles, both developed approaches that broke with convention and, in so doing, became highly influential. In 2001, Osborn was asked about how his bass style changed popular music; describing Kaye's style as much as his own, he stated, "It let bass players, and in turn everyone else, know that it was okay for the bass to be heard."[34]

Kaye and Osborn are rightfully remembered as the scene's most innovative electric bass players, yet the immense size and scope of the LA recording scene meant there were many other musicians who also played electric bass on sessions in the sixties—including René Hall (1912–1988), Arthur G. Wright (1927–2015), Bob West, and Jerry Scheff (b. 1941). Hall, who was known more for his work as a rhythm & blues guitarist and arranger, specialized in playing a Danelectro six-string bass, which he used on Richie Valens's "La Bamba" (1958) and Chan Romero's "The Hippy Hippy Shake" (1959). Wright, who also specialized as a rhythm & blues guitarist, played bass on most of Motown's LA sessions before Kaye switched instruments. West also played on some West Coast Motown dates and worked on album tracks for the Monkees; his electric bass playing is featured on recordings such as Sonny & Cher's "The Beat Goes On" (1967).[35] Jerry Scheff had a long career as an electric bassist: working as an LA session player, he contributed to the Association's "Along Comes Mary" (1966) and the Doors' *LA Woman* album (1971); most notably, he was a part of Elvis Presley's TCB Band, accompanying the singer's return to live performances in the late sixties.

Each of these bassists' careers flourished within the confines of LA recording studios, yet these studios were also complex social spaces. As mentioned previously, session musicians occupied the lowest rung of the studio's social hierarchy, and in a scene with so many musicians constantly competing for steady work, LA session players were especially incentivized to put up with mistreatment, lest they get branded as "difficult" and therefore stop getting called. As described in Kaye's earlier anecdote about "Help Me, Rhonda," producers sometimes treated session musicians more like machines than people. The musicians were also expected to endorse their own anonymity. For if the record companies' lack of explicit credit for session musicians was a problem by itself, in the case of bands like the Monkees and the Association, this omission took on the added dimension of intentional deception, as it led audiences to assume that the band's members were the ones that played on their records. In interviews, Joe Osborn repeatedly described a memorable moment in the studio when the members of the Association turned to the musicians and said, "Please don't tell anyone you guys are doing all our records."[36] However, even if it was not unique for the time, the scene's biggest problem was likely its rampant culture of sexism and misogyny. For instance, producer Phil Spector's abusive behavior toward his then-girlfriend Ronnie Bennett (lead singer of the Ronettes) was not only common knowledge at the time but was also carried out in the physical space of the recording studio. For example, in her memoir she describes the following violent aftermath of one of Spector's jealous rages:

> There wasn't a soul in the studio, but all the music stands had been knocked over, and there were pieces of broken glass everywhere. A long, thin ribbon of recording tape stretched the length of the room

like a streamer of shiny brown confetti, and our feet made a squishing sound when we walked on spots where the carpet was still wet from soaking up an entire pot of coffee—or what had *been* an entire pot of coffee before Phil threw it across the room.[37]

As a "genius" record producer, Spector's behavior and its later escalation were accepted within the LA recording scene so long as he was generating revenue. Furthermore, though Spector's actions were perhaps the most egregious, smaller sexist offenses were also commonplace in LA studios. Kaye, one of the only female members of the Wrecking Crew, has spoken publicly about being called a "dumb cunt" by a fellow session musician and about witnessing men groping other women in the studio.[38] Although she usually softens these recollections by presenting them as jokes, these stories highlight how—in spite of her value as a top-call session bassist—even she was not always exempt from sexual harassment.[39]

Motown and the Funk Brothers

While Los Angeles's recording scene was the largest, both in terms of size and scope, smaller regional scenes were also able to effectively compete in the pop marketplace. In the sixties, the most significant of these scenes coalesced in Detroit, fueled by the astonishing success of Berry Gordy Jr.'s Motown Records. Following wider music industry practices, Motown used local session musicians to churn out hundreds of catchy, chart-topping singles with remarkable efficiency, eventually making it the most successful independent label in popular music history.

By the time Motown's crossover rhythm & blues style became a dominant force in the American music industry in 1964, the company was relying upon a stable coterie of Detroit session musicians who have come to be known as the Funk Brothers. Like the musicians in the Wrecking Crew, the Funk Brothers were expected to quickly generate material that had widespread commercial appeal. With limited direction, these musicians were able to improvise intricate arrangements that sounded good on record and gave the label a distinctive sonic identity—what is commonly referred to as "the Motown Sound."[40]

The most important of the Funk Brothers was electric bassist James Jamerson (1936–1983), whose inventive musicality and idiosyncratic technique led him to craft the propulsive bass lines that were a key component of the Motown Sound. Born in South Carolina, Jamerson moved

Figure 30. James Jamerson (right) and Marvin Gaye, performing live in 1972. (Source: *Save the Children*, dir. Stan Lathan, 1973.)

to Detroit in 1954. He started playing upright while in high school and soon built an impressive reputation playing in local blues and jazz clubs. He then began to augment his income as a live performer with session work in Detroit's various recording studios, and shortly after Motown was officially established in 1959, he became the company's first-call session bassist.[41] In 1961, Jamerson switched to playing a Fender Precision Bass and Ampeg B-15 amplifier while on tour supporting Jackie Wilson, and after that bass was stolen, he purchased the stock 1962 Precision Bass that would be his main instrument for the rest of his life (Figure 30).[42] The Funk Brothers then slowly came together as a unit over the course of the early sixties, as Motown began to prioritize working with key players, including both Jamerson and drummer Benny "Papa Zita" Benjamin. In fact, Jamerson was considered so indispensable to the company that he was one of the first musicians it put on exclusive retainer.[43]

What made Jamerson so important to Motown was his ability to craft memorable bass lines. Describing a typical session, he recalled,

[Producing/songwriting team] Holland-Dozier-Holland would give me the chord sheet, but they couldn't write for me. When they did, it didn't sound right. They'd let me go on and ad lib. I created, man.

When they gave me that chord sheet, I'd look at it, but then start doing what I felt and what I thought would fit. All the musicians did. All of them made hits. . . . I'd hear the melody line from the lyrics and I'd build the bass line around that. I always tried to support the melody. I had to. I'd make it repetitious, but also add things to it. . . . It was repetitious, but had to be funky and have emotion.[44]

Like other session musicians, Jamerson was expected to develop bass parts that supported each individual recording. But he went far above and beyond that role by inventing his own approach to the instrument, developing a unique style that would go on to be widely influential, especially among his contemporaries. In terms of technique, he often played in the instrument's first and lowest position, he incorporated open strings into his bass lines (regardless of key), he kept the action of his instrument set high, he favored flatwound strings, he continued to use the Precision's factory-installed rubber mute, and he plucked the strings solely using the index finger of his right hand. Musically, his style was informed by his experiences playing upright bass in small jazz combos, where he had cultivated the sophisticated approach to melody, rhythm, and harmony that he would repeatedly bring to his Motown bass lines, employing off-beat syncopations to emphasize groove and feel, adding dissonant chromatic notes for color, and phrasing distinctive counter-melodies that served as a secondary hook for each song.

Jamerson's electric bass style was also inherently indebted to Motown's production practices. For example, while session bassists like Carol Kaye were occasionally given the freedom to experiment, more often they were expected to play relatively subdued bass lines. Motown, by contrast, gave Jamerson an unprecedented amount of creative freedom, with Gordy and his producers allowing Jamerson to regularly stretch out beyond the conventional parameters of a pop song. In this era, Detroit was also home to world-class engineers who were developing new and innovative recording technologies, many of which would find their way into the Motown studio. One such engineer was Ed Wolfrum, who invented some of the first stand-alone direct input (DI) boxes while working for local radio station WEXL.[45] Wolfrum's invention—affectionally known as the "wolfbox"—made it so that instruments like electric guitars and electric basses could be recorded by sending their signal directly from the instrument through the DI box to a recording console, thereby bypassing the use of an amplifier and microphone. Wolfrum claims to have sold early versions of his DI boxes to all of Detroit's major studios, including Motown.[46] Whatever its origin, in the early sixties, chief engineer Mike McClain expanded Motown's DI capabilities and adapted the technology into the studio's recording console. During recording sessions, Motown's engineers would feed Jamerson's bass through this brand-new DI technology, a process that gave an added presence and clarity to his recorded bass sound, especially in its lower register. This process likewise allowed the engineers to artificially boost his bass signal in the overall mix, making it sound more prominent than the other instruments. When combined, these techniques meant that Jamerson's bass often had an overdriven and slightly distorted timbre. Furthermore, as Andrew Flory points out, "After late 1964, Motown's [new] eight-track apparatus recorded bass performances on a separate track, which allowed for further enhancement and placement in final mixes."[47] Thus, while Jamerson's talents and abilities were undeniable, his celebrated position in the Motown Sound was also a studio creation, one facilitated by his collaborations with the company's producers and engineers.

Overall, Jamerson's electric bass style is best illustrated within the actual context of recordings. To take just two examples, both the Supremes' "You Can't Hurry Love" (1966) and Stevie Wonder's rendition of "For Once in My Life" (1968) highlight different aspects of Jamerson's playing. In "You Can't Hurry Love," Jamerson's bass kicks off the song, loudly situated in the mix. The bass line itself is straightforward, with Jamerson mostly outlining the song's harmonic framework by playing the root note of each successive chord. However, even with this stripped-down approach, many of the key components of Jamerson's style are audible, especially his characteristically overdriven bass timbre, his emphasis on rhythmic feel, and his use of subtle variation. By contrast, on "For Once in My Life," Jamerson pulls out all the stops, crafting a complex, syncopated sixteenth-note groove. He also constantly varies his playing throughout, never repeating the same phrase twice. And, despite both his virtuosic performance and its presence in the final mix, Jamerson never fails to compliment the vocals, adjusting his rhythmic and harmonic activity to support Wonder's melody while still driving the song's forward momentum. Working with artists such as Smokey Robinson and the Miracles, Marvin Gaye, Stevie Wonder, the Temptations, the Supremes, the Four Tops, Martha and the Vandellas, and many more, Jamerson appeared on hundreds of Motown hits throughout the sixties.

Jamerson's style was such an essential component of the Motown Sound that when the company eventually hired other electric bassists for its Detroit operations, they were all expected to emulate it. One of these bassists was Tony Newton (b. 1948). Born and raised in Detroit, Newton started out playing saxophone and was gigging regularly by the time he was in junior high. As he explained to me, he became interested in the electric bass in 1963 while working with a local rock 'n' roll band, and he first acquired a cheap Epiphone Newport that he quickly traded for a Fender Precision Bass.[48] Not long after, Newton found steady work playing on the local blues circuit, supporting acts such as John Lee Hooker, T-Bone Walker, and Little Walter. He became involved with Motown at the age of sixteen, after being scouted by producer Hank Cosby, and was put on a $250 per week salary to be the touring bassist for Smokey Robinson and the Miracles.[49] In order to replicate the Motown bass sound in a live setting, Newton boosted his volume by playing through an Ampeg B-15 amplifier with an added extension speaker—a trick he had learned from Jamerson himself.[50] His first recording work for Motown came in early 1965. As he recalled,

> Holland-Dozier-Holland, the illustrious Motown writing and producing team, were going into the studio to record some new songs using some innovative production skills. One of these included using two bass guitars simultaneously. And who would know? They wanted me to play alongside Jamerson. . . . Jamerson welcomed me with open arms and some great playing ideas. He said . . . "Just keep that groove and don't stop for anything! Keep it steady and in the pocket!"[51]

According to Newton, Jamerson improvised both of their parts in the studio and told him what to play, which was often a straight-ahead groove-oriented bass line in the instrument's upper register that freed Jamerson to play more intricate, melodic lines in the lower register.[52] Surviving Musicians' Union contracts document that Newton and Jamerson played together on multiple Holland-Dozier-Holland productions in this era, including the Supremes' "Stop! In the Name of Love" (1965) and "Love Is Like an Itching in My Heart" (1966), Martha and the Vandellas' "Nowhere to Run" (1965), and the Four Tops' "Reach Out I'll Be There" (1966).[53]

Although Newton continued to intermittently record for Motown, he was principally a touring bassist, recreating Jamerson's bass lines live onstage each night. In 1965, he played electric bass on the ill-fated Tamla-Motown UK Tour, supporting Martha and the Vandellas, the Miracles, Stevie Wonder, and the Supremes.[54] And while he primarily worked with the Miracles, in the sixties he also briefly toured with the Four Tops, the

Temptations, and Marvin Gaye. When pay disputes led Holland-Dozier-Holland to leave Motown in 1968 and form Invictus Records, Newton joined them, working both as a session bassist and as part of the group 8th Day. He went on to have an extensive recording career in the seventies, recording with Mavis Staples, the Mamas and the Papas, Aretha Franklin, Donny Osmond, and more.

Whereas Newton's primary role was to replace Jamerson on the road, later Motown electric bassist Bob Babbitt (1937–2012) was tasked with replacing him in the studio.[55] A Pittsburgh native, Babbitt took classical bass lessons as a teenager and split his time performing in local youth orchestras and nightclubs. He moved to Detroit around 1959, and the following year he traded in his upright for a Fender Jazz Bass. Soon thereafter, he became the bass player for the Royaltones, an instrumental rock band with whom he had his first hit, "Flamingo Express" (1960). His career as a professional studio musician began in the early sixties when the Royaltones were hired to play on sessions for various local musicians, most notably Del Shannon. Through his work with Shannon, Babbitt came to record at Ed Wingate's Golden World Studios, a state-of-the-art studio that was then Motown's main competitor in Detroit.[56] Babbitt was persuaded to switch to a Fender Precision Bass around 1964 by a producer who convinced him that Precisions were better suited for rhythm & blues.[57] With it, he played on hundreds of sessions at Golden World, and in 1967, after Motown purchased Golden World and turned it into its secondary studio, Babbitt was brought into the company to fill in for Jamerson on an as-needed basis.

At Motown, Babbitt was expected to perform in Jamerson's bass style, which he learned by listening to records, seeing Jamerson perform live around town, and through informal discussions he had with Jamerson when the two occasionally socialized. Following Jamerson's model, Babbitt's Motown bass lines tend to feature a strong sense of groove, distinctive melodic phrasing, the use of open strings, chromaticism, and elaborate embellishments (he even added part of a household sponge under his strings to mimic Jamerson's muted bass timbre). Babbitt may have tended to lay out a bit more than Jamerson and play higher on the neck, but their styles were ultimately so similar that it is difficult to tell the difference between them from the recordings alone.[58] However, it is clear that by the end of the sixties, when Jamerson's alcoholism was affecting his ability to show up on time and adequately perform, Babbitt was increasingly being called in to replace him. Babbitt's most notable work for Motown therefore came in the early seventies, when he played on hits by Edwin Starr, the Temptations, Stevie Wonder, and Marvin Gaye. After Motown relocated to Los Angeles, Babbitt moved to New York City to continue his career as a session musician, eventually recording with artists such as Gladys Knight & the Pips, Jim Croce, Alice Cooper, the Spinners, Elton John, and more.

All told, Motown's relationship with the Funk Brothers was complicated. As Nelson George explains,

> Berry [Gordy] knew the worth of his Detroit musicians. . . . However, that didn't mean he paid them top dollar until he had to, and it didn't mean he felt they should be stars. *None* of Motown's albums carried the musicians' credits until the seventies. The musicians were *never* cited by name in interviews with artists, producers, or executives during the sixties.[59]

On the one hand, throughout most of the sixties, the Motown studio was in nearly constant use, and for the regular session players, there was more than enough work to go around. And by the end of the decade, first-call Funk Brothers like Jamerson were earning the equivalent of at least six-figure salaries today, maybe more. On the other hand, Motown—like the rest of the music industry—treated their session musicians' labor as "work for hire" and therefore barred them from sharing in the multi-million-dollar profits they had helped the company earn. As Jamerson later recalled, "We were doing more of the job than we thought we were doing and we didn't get any songwriting credit . . . they felt that as long as you got paid your name didn't have to be on the record."[60] Furthermore, the company treated each individual member of the band as replaceable—even Jamerson—and unlike the Wrecking Crew musicians, the Funk Brothers were signed to exclusive contracts that heavily favored the company's interests, prohibiting the musicians from taking on outside recording gigs or for leaving the company to seek more lucrative employment. For instance, in 1970, British guitarist Jeff Beck reportedly asked Bob Babbitt to join his band and try session work in London, but Motown refused to let him go.[61] The company, however, did not repay this enforced exclusivity with any sense of loyalty, as it relocated to Los Angeles in 1972 and left most of the Funk Brothers behind in Detroit. Jamerson, like some of the others, moved to LA to continue working for the company, but he and Motown formally parted ways in 1973, and his career flagged as he was unable to become fully established in the LA recording scene.

Motown's music has continued to be celebrated in the decades since it was first released. Yet, as Nelson George notes, for many years the Funk Brothers were excluded from company narratives and were therefore unable to capitalize on their own legacies. This exclusion was most glaringly displayed in the 1983 TV retrospective *Motown 25: Yesterday, Tomorrow, Forever.* Even though it included an entire segment asking, "What was the Motown Sound?," the Funk Brothers were not mentioned once in a broadcast that lasted more than two hours. In fact, they weren't even allowed to watch the taping (when Jamerson unexpectedly showed up to the celebration, he was initially let in backstage but left after his guest was denied admittance to the auditorium).[62] Within six months of the *Motown 25* special, Jamerson had died in total obscurity. Thanks largely to the 2002 documentary *Standing in the Shadows of Motown,* Jamerson is now posthumously celebrated for his innovative electric bass style, and the Funk Brothers are now rightfully credited as key figures in Motown history.[63] While this film represented an important corrective to the historical record, its success was inherently bittersweet, as the musicians had to wait over three decades for their recognition. By the time Motown released *Hitsville: The Making of Motown* (2019), a documentary commemorating the company's sixtieth anniversary, it was now openly crediting the Funk Brothers.[64] But by then, too much time had passed. Only two Funk Brothers (Jack Ashford and Tony Newton) were still living, and neither was included in the film.

Memphis, Stax Records, and Booker T. and the MG's

In the mid-sixties, no other independent label in America could rival Motown's share of the mainstream pop market. Most indies thus stuck to the established formula of concentrating on smaller markets while deliberately keeping production costs to a bare minimum. Such was the case with Stax Records in Memphis. Rather than following Motown's assembly-line process, Stax instead specialized in stripped-down, groove-oriented Southern soul music geared specifically for the rhythm & blues market. This business model became widely emulated within the city's recording scene and was so lucrative that, in 1967, music produced in the city was estimated to have grossed $20 million in retail sales (of which Stax was responsible for more than half).[65] Even though Stax and Motown operated quite differently, they had at least one important commonality: their success was contingent on the use of local session musicians.

The foundations for Stax came in 1957, when Memphis fiddler Jim

Stewart opened his own independent record label, Satellite Records. With financial backing from his sister, Estelle Axton, Stewart purchased a one-track Ampex recording console and began making records, assisted by guitarist/producer Chips Moman. By 1960, Satellite Records was in need of a permanent location and, at Moman's urging, Stewart moved the company into a defunct movie theater in one of Memphis's poor Black communities. He then transformed the theater into a recording studio and turned the former concession area into a neighborhood record store. The first single produced in this new studio was "Cause I Love You" (1960), a rhythm & blues record by renowned Memphis DJ Rufus Thomas and his daughter Carla. For the session, Stewart hired local Black musicians, including sixteen-year-old Booker T. Jones on baritone sax and Wilbur Steinberg on upright bass; he reportedly paid them fifteen dollars to record both sides, less than one-third union scale.[66] Upon its release, "Cause I Love You" became a regional hit, and its success marked a sea change for the company. Prior to Rufus and Carla, Satellite had primarily specialized in country and pop, but shortly afterward Stewart decided to focus instead on the rhythm & blues market—a move that was aided by the studio's location within a Black community.[67] Eventually, "Cause I Love You" also came to the attention of Jerry Wexler at Atlantic Records, a New York–based label that had spent the last decade as a leader in the rhythm & blues field.[68] Impressed, Wexler made a deal with Stewart to license the recording for national distribution on Atlantic's subsidiary label, Atco Records, which paved the way for a more comprehensive distribution deal between Satellite and Atlantic. Musically, "Cause I Love You" also established the stripped-down, rhythm-heavy template that the company would come to follow on its future releases—what the company's marketing materials would later describe as "the Memphis Sound." Two electric bassists would soon come to define that sound: Wilbur's younger brother Lewie Steinberg (1933–2016) and Donald "Duck" Dunn (1941–2012).

Born into a family with long-standing ties to the Memphis music scene, Lewie Steinberg started out playing trumpet in his junior high marching band.[69] He then briefly switched to upright, before finally settling on a first-generation Fender Precision Bass. Steinberg was an established gigging musician by the end of his teen years and, after serving a brief stint in the Army, he became one of a handful of electric bassists in the Memphis scene. As a Black musician working in a highly segregated city, Steinberg faced constant indignities. Gigs paid so little that to eke out a living he was forced to work seven days a week in clubs where Black musicians were treated as subhuman. He recalled that

> you had to go straight to the bandstands through the back door. Wasn't anytime when you go through the front door. That was a no-no. Even while you're playing there, if you want to take an intermission you had two places to go: either the kitchen or outdoors. Take your choice. Snow on the ground. It didn't make any difference, rain, whatever.[70]

Over the course of the fifties, Memphis clubs transitioned from jazz to rhythm & blues, and Steinberg found steady work in Bill Harvey's band, among others, which he supplemented by occasionally playing on recording sessions.

Steineberg's introduction to Satellite Records came in 1961, when saxophonist Gil Caple convinced him to step in as a last-minute replacement and play electric bass on an instrumental called "Last Night."[71] Cowritten by Moman, the song had been developed with a local all-white teenage rhythm & blues band that went by the name the Royal Spades. ("The name's racist overtones," Robert Gordon notes, "smacks of teens believing they're getting away with something.")[72] Among the band's members were guitarist Steve Cropper, electric bassist Duck Dunn, and tenor saxophonist Charles "Packy" Axton—son of Satellite's Estelle Axton. Unconvinced of the band's abilities, Moman also hired local Black session musicians to play on the record, including Floyd Newman, Caple, and eventually Lewie Steinberg. Even though Memphis's live music scene remained strictly segregated, the city's recording studios were less regulated spaces where Black and white musicians could work side by side. According to Steinberg, "That's what made Stax. See, we integrated Stax down there. . . . But we couldn't go and play on the same *bandstand* together! No. We couldn't do that. We'd get together inside the studio and cut up and do everything we want to, but you couldn't play on that bandstand. . . . That was a cardinal sin."[73] Satellite released "Last Night" in June 1961—with the band's name listed as the less problematic "Mar-Keys"—and the record quickly became a hit, reaching No. 3 on the *Billboard* Hot 100, No. 2 on the Rhythm & Blues Chart. Despite the potential promise of its integrated session, however, the Black and white musicians did not equally reap the benefits of this success. As Steinberg recalled, "I got paid fifteen dollars for that. I didn't get no writer's royalties. . . . I didn't get nothing out of that."[74] Additionally, when the company decided to send the Mar-Keys on tour to capitalize on the single, all of the Black musicians who had played on the session were replaced.[75]

Unbeknownst to Stewart, there was already an independent label in California that had been operating as Satellite Records. Rather than pay to buy out that company, he decided to simply change the name of his own, rebranding it as Stax Records (a portmanteau of Stewart and Axton). At the same time, Stewart began to regularly hire Steinberg as an electric bassist, culminating in a fateful session in early 1962. The session was initially intended to record material for country singer Billy Lee Riley, but it quickly fell apart. Not willing to lose even a modest financial investment, Stewart instead tasked the assembled band of session musicians—Lewie Steinberg on bass, Steve Cropper on guitar, Booker T. Jones on Hammond organ, and Al Jackson Jr. on drums—to record some instrumentals. For the second number they recorded, the musicians improvised a twelve-bar blues based on a riff that Jones had been trying out live on stage. After some minor adjustments to the arrangement, the song was recorded in just a few takes. In need of a title, Steinberg suggested they call the song "Funky Onions," which was softened to "Green Onions," in order to be less provocative. Attributed to Booker T. and the MG's, "Green Onions" was released first on Volt, Stax's subsidiary label, but Stewart eventually rereleased the song on the Stax label in September 1962 and, with national distribution from Atlantic, it reached No. 3 on the Hot 100 and No. 1 on the Rhythm & Blues Chart. The recording also effectively solidified the Memphis Sound, as Charles Hughes explains: "Generally funkier and grittier than most northern offerings, the Memphis Sound echoed its roots in the blues and gospel of southern tradition and offered an accurate reflection of its origins in the city's club scene. The success of 'Green Onions' and other Stax recordings established this approach as a commercially viable and creatively exciting alternative."[76] Most importantly, its success convinced Stewart to use these four musicians as Stax's house band from then on. Steinberg thus spent the next two years as part of Booker T. and the MG's, playing on the majority of Stax's releases.

Steinberg's electric bass style was indebted to his years spent as a professional musician in Memphis's jazz and rhythm & blues clubs, especially his formative experiences as an upright bassist. Musically, he was known for his laid-back approach, utilizing walking bass lines to outline a song's harmony and rhythm. He also preferred to play in the bass's lowest position, purposefully limiting himself to the instrument's first five frets. As he explained, "Everything that I want to play, I can get with them five fingers, down in that lower register. That's *all* bass. . . . You ain't going to get no lower."[77] By emphasizing this low end, Steinberg's bass lines provided a strong, supportive foundation. On "Last Night," for example, he outlines each chord of the song's twelve-bar blues form with the same simple walking bass pattern, working in unison with the piano to provide a sense of stability and continuity. Most famously, on "Green Onions," he plays another repetitive walking bass pattern, at times working in unison with Cropper's guitar and Jones's left hand. Acting as the song's musical bedrock, he creates a solid groove for the other musical lines to interact with. In both examples, Steinberg's bass lines are simple yet powerful. They provide forward momentum, they clearly outline the harmonic changes, and they fill out the sonic space of the recording. However, while Steinberg's walking bass style fit well within a fifties rhythm & blues aesthetic, by the early sixties, it was quickly becoming old-fashioned. Thanks to James Jamerson and others, the airwaves were now filled with more elaborate electric bass styles that emphasized syncopated grooves and hooky countermelodies. For modern listeners, walking bass lines—like the upright bass itself—were now beginning to sound like the music of the previous generation.

The MG's' sound changed after Duck Dunn was brought in to replace Steinberg. Dunn had been born and raised in Memphis, and he and Steve Cropper had been friends since the sixth grade. Obsessed with the music of Bill Doggett, Chuck Berry, and B.B. King, Dunn attempted to learn guitar in high school, but quickly realized that bass suited him better. He thus procured a Kay K-162 Electronic Bass sometime around 1958, which he played through a Silvertone amplifier. Within a year, he had convinced his brother to cosign for a 1958 Fender Precision Bass, which became his main instrument. As he was starting out, he took lessons with Larry Brown, a Black bassist whom Dunn regularly saw perform at the Plantation Inn, one of the many Memphis clubs in which Black musicians performed to an all-white clientele. From Brown, Dunn learned the basics of the bass, including how to craft walking bass lines and how to play in contemporary rhythm & blues styles. He further honed his skills working with Cropper, playing covers with the Royal Spades on dance gigs across Memphis. Although Dunn had missed the recording session that produced "Last Night," he reclaimed his bass chair shortly after its release and went on tour promoting the single with the Mar-Keys. After he returned to Memphis in August 1962, he made ends meet by working three jobs: during the day, he worked as a distributor for King Records;

he would occasionally record at Stax when Steinberg wasn't available; and he would play in local Memphis clubs until the early morning hours. Dunn even ended up replacing Larry Brown in Ben Branch's band, becoming the lone white member of Branch's otherwise Black outfit—a move that, Hughes documents, was protested both by the local chapter of the Musicians' Union and by the Memphis police.[78]

In the early sixties, Chips Moman was Jim Stewart's second-in-command at Stax, and Moman preferred to work with Steinberg. But after Stewart and Moman had a falling out in 1964, Cropper was chosen to take his place, and Cropper increasingly preferred to record with his childhood friend. After an incident in Knoxville where Steinberg was arrested for drunk driving before an MG's show, Cropper began lobbying hard for Dunn to join the band.[79] But Dunn's initial entrance into the MG's was controversial. In 1965, while Jones was away at college, Cropper recorded "Boot-Leg," an instrumental featuring Dunn that Stax released as the latest MG's single. Here is how Jones recalled the incident in his memoir:

> How can you be the leader of a band, one that's named after you, that records without your knowledge? What's the message? What does it say to you? The seed was planted. They didn't need me. . . . "Boot-Leg" was already recorded and released under the name Booker T. & the MGs without my prior knowledge or consent. . . . Duck Dunn was the bass player on "Boot-Leg." There was no denying Duck's playing was more urgent, more demanding, if just as sensitive as Lewie's. And Lewie persisted in being difficult outside the studio. . . . On the other hand, the choice of changing bass players had been made in my absence, without consulting me. At best, I could continue, lick my wound, keep my mouth shut, finish school, and see what my future held. At worst, if I raised objections, I might bring about an early truncation of the life of Booker T. & the MGs.[80]

Confronted with his own powerlessness, Jones kept his reservations to himself, and Dunn transitioned from intermittently recording at Stax to becoming the studio's default electric bassist.

Stax's unique record-making formula was firmly in place by the time Dunn officially joined the MG's. Contrary to nearly every other recording scene, Stax's music was constructed in the studio itself. As had been the case with "Green Onions," each recording was crafted through extended jams, with the singers, songwriters, and musicians collectively writing the song through a trial-and-error process. For other studios—especially in recording scenes with a strong union presence—this process would have been far too costly and time-consuming. Yet Stewart was able to cut costs simply by operating his studio outside of union regulations. In the company's early years, he treated each recording as a "demo," reportedly paying the musicians a flat rate of fifteen dollars per session, regardless of how long the session ran; if the recording was commercially released, he would go back and retroactively increase the musicians' pay to the union rate for a single session. By 1965, after Otis Redding's records had turned Stax into a profitable operation, Stewart put the MG's on a $125 per week salary, and in return expected them to work full-time as session musicians.[81] This was a low rate, relative to what other session musicians were earning in major markets, but it was still a good wage compared to their other prospects as musicians in Memphis (Dunn, for one, was overjoyed to be able to quit his day job and concentrate on playing bass).

Stax's recording process also influenced the sound of the label's releases, which tended to have simple arrangements that emphasized groove, rhythm, and repetition—characteristics that would become synonymous with the Memphis Sound. For Jerry Wexler, this process made Stax's singles sound fresh and spontaneous, an effect that was seemingly all the more significant because of the MG's' status as an integrated Southern soul band. Enamored by the Memphis Sound, Wexler further expanded the relationship between Stax and Atlantic by bringing acts down from New York to record with the MG's. Dunn therefore spent the next few years recording a string of rhythm & blues hits for artists on both the Stax and Atlantic rosters, including Eddie Floyd, Otis Redding, Wilson Pickett, and Sam & Dave. Though he and the MG's were primarily a studio band, they also toured occasionally, including a notable 1967 Stax/Volt European tour and a set supporting Redding at that year's Monterey International Pop Festival.

Steinberg and Dunn had far more in common than is usually acknowledged. First, they both used Fender Precision Basses with flatwound strings, which they played with their fingers, and they both recorded through Stax's in-house Ampeg B-15 amplifier (which Stewart had set to emphasize higher, brighter frequencies). Both also took laidback approaches and are best understood as groove players. As Dunn described it, "I just try to think about not overdoing it. I try to do things the simplest way I know how, and I think more about the groove than the notes. I'm a feel player, so it doesn't take a lot of notes for me to get there—and after you find the groove, anything will work."[82] Dunn and

Steinberg also tended to prefer bass riffs that they could repeat for most of a song (compare "Green Onions" to "Hip-Hug Her," for example). The primary difference between them was that Steinberg favored walking bass lines and the instrument's lower register, whereas Dunn preferred to construct grooves in the middle of the neck that incorporated more space and syncopation.

Dunn's bass lines were also inherently born out of his relationship with drummer Al Jackson Jr., who he often credited with reining in his playing. Describing their relationship, Dunn recalled, "I just stuck with him; we locked down, but we never hitched, and that's what gave us a lot of room in the groove."[83] A classic example of their hand-in-glove approach is Otis Redding's "Respect" (1965). The intro and choruses feature Dunn playing an insistent quarter-note pulse that matches the relentless pounding of Jackson's drumming. On the verses, Dunn switches to a freer line in the middle of the neck, locking in with Jackson on the downbeat of each measure before playing varying eighth-note fills that dance around the drums. He transitions to the bass's lower register for the bridge, returns to his earlier patterns in the subsequent chorus-verse-chorus, and then adds a brand-new bass line for the song's outro vamp. By contrast, on Wilson Pickett's "In the Midnight Hour," Dunn demonstrates his musical restraint, sticking to a midtempo one-bar bass riff that locks in with the feel of Jackson's backbeat drum pattern.[84] In the end, the dual hallmarks of Dunn's bass style were subtlety and simplicity (although, as he explained to Rob Bowman, "It's simplicity, [but] simple can be complicated").[85] And though his technical approach may be less virtuosic than some other sessions bassists in this era, Dunn's style was nonetheless innovative and influential. He proved that simple-yet-distinctive electric bass lines are sometimes all that was needed to get the job done, and for young bassists—especially those who might be intimidated by Motown bass lines—his work at Stax provided an accessible model to emulate.

As with Motown, Stax's relationship with its session musicians was complicated. Unlike the Wrecking Crew or the Funk Brothers, the MG's did get to have their own career as a stand-alone band. They were also credited by name on their own records (only) and even had a band photo included on their 1968 LP *Doin' Our Thing* (Figure 31). They also had an unprecedented amount of creative input in the studio, and by 1966, were even collectively sharing in a small percentage of Stax's profits.[86] These benefits, however, were largely outweighed by the negative aspects of the company's business practices. First and foremost, the musi-

Figure 31. Duck Dunn (top left) with Booker T. and the MG's. (Source: *Doin' Our Thing*, Stax, 1968.)

cians were financially exploited by Stewart. For years, he paid them less than union scale, and even after they were put on salary, the MG's were among the lowest-paid session musicians of the era. To make matters worse, Stewart insisted that Stax artists sign over their publishing rights to him, and he therefore cut the MG's off from earning additional revenue as songwriters, both for their own releases and for the songs they cowrote with others (Cropper, it turns out, had his own financial stake in Stax's publishing, thanks to his position as Stewart's right-hand man). But the biggest problem at Stax was its not-so-subtle racial favoritism. As Hughes explains, while the MG's and the great music they created have come to stand as a symbol for Southern racial equality, this depiction is largely a myth.[87] Lewie Steinberg had been unceremoniously fired and was thereafter written out of Stax's history, and Booker T. Jones felt pow-erless in his own band. At best, in the mid-sixties, Stax bucked prevail-ing norms by hiring both Black and white musicians; at worst, it was an enterprise whose profits were inherently based on exploiting the creative labor of disenfranchised Black workers.

After Dr. Martin Luther King Jr. was assassinated in Memphis in 1968, Stax's Black employees began to confront these racial inequalities head-on, which came as an uncomfortable shock to some within the company and ultimately signaled the beginning of the end for the MG's. Jones left Stax altogether in 1969, and Dunn was called to play on fewer and fewer sessions.[88] Looking back decades later, Cropper would later blame Dr. King himself for having enflamed these racial tensions, telling an interviewer,

> You know, Memphis was a refuge for Black people, it really was. Blacks were Blacks, and whites were whites, and everybody was cool. We all loved each other. The Black people were perfectly happy with what was going on. I don't think anywhere in the universe was as racially cool as Memphis was until Martin Luther King showed up. That just set it off for the world, basically. What a shame. There must be something political about that. Let's go to the one place in the South where everybody is getting along and blow that fuse. That's the only way I can see it.[89]

If nothing else, the unreflective naivete of Cropper's statement reveals that, even though the MG's brought white and Black musicians together in the segregated South, this close working relationship did not ulti-mately foster the cross-racial empathy that such collaborations might have promised.

FAME and the Muscle Shoals Rhythm Section

Not long after Stax was founded in Memphis, an even smaller record-ing scene was developing in northwest Alabama. Like Stax, the studios there would also come to specialize in Southern soul, similarly construct-ing groove-based rhythm & blues hits via extended improvisations in the studio. Yet whereas Stax prided itself—however problematically—on its integrated house band, throughout the sixties nearly all the session musi-cians in the Alabama scene would be white. These musicians were also willing to work even longer hours for well-below union wages, making the scene especially attractive to music industry executives interested in maximizing their profits. And thanks in part to the distinctive electric bass styles that would come to be associated with it, the scene also produced some of the biggest hits of the sixties and seventies.

The first session bassist in the scene was Norbert Putnam (b. 1942). A Florence native, he started playing music at the age of fifteen after some high school classmates conscripted him (and his father's upright bass) into their Elvis-inspired rockabilly band. A year later he formed an all-white rhythm & blues band, Mark V, and graduated from performing at local sock hops to touring the college fraternity circuit, earning twenty-five dollars a night playing James Brown, Ray Charles, and Bobby "Blue" Bland covers.[90] He first encountered the electric bass while attending concerts by national rock 'n' roll and rhythm & blues artists, such as Hank Ballard and the Midnighters, whose tours brought them through Alabama in the late fifties. As he explained to me, he was impressed by the instrument's volume ("You could hear it!" he enthusiastically recalls).[91] After that, he decided to send away for a 1958 Fender Precision Bass and Bassman amplifier, which his parents helped him finance. When Tom Stafford opened SPAR (Stafford Publishing and Recording) Music in Florence in 1959, Mark V became the studio's unofficial house band, playing on demo recordings after school in exchange for free movie passes and swigs of misappropriated cough syrup.[92] As a teenager who had only played in amateur bands, Putnam lacked the years of professional experience that were usually a prerequisite for session work; however, SPAR was far from a professional operation. Instead, it became a training ground where Putnam and his cohort could develop their skills. As he explained: "With each new demo recording, our playing became tighter and more proficient. We were learning to create original parts on brand new songs, something that was much more difficult than simply imitating the parts created on someone else's record."[93]

The area's recording scene officially coalesced in the early sixties, stimulated by the success of FAME (Florence Alabama Music Enterprises) Studios. Opened in nearby Muscle Shoals in 1961, FAME was owned and operated by self-taught producer Rick Hall (1932–2018), who had previously played electric bass in a group called the Fairlaines. Given Putnam's experience recording demos for SPAR, Hall hired him as FAME's first in-house bassist. Even though Hall, Putnam, and nearly all the other Shoals session musicians were white, FAME came to specialize in Southern soul, often building their music around (and, as Hughes emphasizes, profiting off) Black vocalists.[94] Putnam's first taste of success came with Arthur Alexander's "You Better Move On" (1961), a FAME-produced soul hit that reached No. 24 on the *Billboard* Hot 100; this was followed by two Top 10 rhythm & blues hits, the Tams' "What Kind of Fool (Do You Think I Am)" (1964) and Jimmy Hughes's "Steal Away" (1964).[95] In the studio, Putnam recorded through an Ampeg B-15, and, like Duck Dunn, he tended to emphasize clarity and simplicity, usually performing variations on bass patterns that he had learned by listening to hit records.

Compared to the other scenes discussed in this chapter, the success of the northwest Alabama recording scene might appear to be an unlikely development, especially given its remote location, the substandard equipment used in its studios, and its general lack of experienced personnel. However, one significant feature of the scene helped it to flourish: there was almost no Musicians' Union oversight. This meant that Hall, for example, could cut costs dramatically by paying his young musicians just five dollars per hour (or approximately one-quarter union scale). FAME's business model was thus predicated on taking advantage of inexperienced local musicians who, like Putnam, were unfamiliar with standard regulations concerning pay rates and contract hours. After FAME started producing hit records in the early sixties, Putnam recalled that union representatives from Nashville flew down in a private plane and took him and the other musicians to Birmingham, where the representatives paid their dues so that they could join the union. Hall was then forced to create backdated contracts for his commercially released recordings and pay the musicians (and the union) the standard rate.[96] Yet this victory was short-lived. To circumvent these new union regulations, Hall simply required that his musicians sign for a standard three-hour session at union scale regardless of how many hours they worked, which allowed him to continue paying basically the same rate he always had. By this point, Putnam and the others recognized that they were being taken advantage of, but they also felt that their skill sets were not yet at the level required to compete in one of the other major recording scenes. They thus accepted the trade-off that they would bide their time making $10,000 per year at FAME (which, Chris Reali notes, was still "a high standard of living when compared to most Americans in the early 1960s") until they had built up their chops enough to be competitive as session musicians.[97]

By the end of 1964, the members of the first FAME house band finally felt as if they were experienced enough to break into Nashville's more highly regulated recording scene, and so they left in early 1965. Putnam later remembered that Hall tried to dissuade him from going, saying, "Putt, you'll never make it up there. You'll be running back home with your tail between your legs before two months are out."[98] This proved not to be the case, and Putnam recalled that even though he spent his first few years in Nashville playing on demo recordings (which, in that particular scene, paid half union scale), he still made around $50,000 his first year there.[99] After he eventually broke into the Nashville scene, Putnam became a top-call session bassist as part of the third-generation Nashville A-Team.[100] Conforming to the expectations of Nashville in that era, Putnam most often recorded on upright—such as on the Vogues' "Five O'Clock World" (1965) and Bobby Goldsboro's "Honey" (1968)— and would even fill in for bassist Bob Moore to record alongside Harold Bradley playing tic-tac bass. But he also played electric when a session called for a more rock- or rhythm & blues-oriented style, such as Tony Joe White's "Polk Salad Annie" (1969) and Elvis Presley's 1970 "Nashville Marathon" sessions, which produced hits such as "I've Lost You" (1970) and "You Don't Have to Say You Love Me" (1970). In the early seventies, Putnam transitioned into a lucrative career as a studio owner and an in-demand record producer, eventually producing hits by Joan Baez, Jimmy Buffett, and Dan Fogelberg.

In response to Putnam's departure, Hall recruited other local electric bass players to replace him at FAME. The first was Albert "Junior" Lowe (b. 1940), who had taken over Hall's position in the Fairlanes. In 1966, working at a nearby studio, Lowe played upright bass on Percy Sledge's "When a Man Loves a Woman," which Hall then helped acquire national distribution through Jerry Wexler at Atlantic Records. After its release, "When a Man Loves a Woman" became a million-selling single and the first No. 1 pop hit recorded in the Shoals. Having learned from Putnam's sudden departure, Hall also started cultivating a second local bassist, David Hood (b. 1943), who at that point had only been playing electric bass for a few years. As Hood explained to *Guitar Player:* "I had a guitar by the time I was 18, but the guys I wanted to form a band with had a guitar player and needed a bass, so I bought one. But I always liked supportive playing. . . . So I liked the bass once I started playing it. I thought, 'This is really easy.' I started making money immediately—without really knowing how to play it."[101] Playing a Fender Jazz Bass, Hood and his band, the Mystics, likewise cut their teeth playing rhythm & blues on the fraternity circuit, and after the Mystics recorded some demos at FAME, Hall started to occasionally bring Hood in to play on sessions, first as a trombonist and then as an electric bassist. Hood, like Putnam, learned how to be a session musician on the job, trying to come up with new bass lines that sounded like the other bassists he heard on records.[102] As he described his approach,

> I tried to play what [other bass players] were doing. After I started doing session work, I started getting serious about it. Playing in a band, there's a lot of noise going on and they don't hear a mistake—it goes by so quick. Once you get into a studio, that changes, so I really started to learn how to play. I would get records that Duck Dunn played on or [James] Jamerson from Motown. They were the very top bass players to me at the time. I would really try to copy what they were doing, or learn *how* they were doing it more than just copy it note-for-note.[103]

Hood developed his recording chops over the next few years, eventually becoming the main bassist of FAME's second-generation house band. In the intervening years, however, it would be two outsiders, Tommy Cogbill and Jerry Jemmott, who would come to be most associated with the "Muscle Shoals Sound."[104]

By 1966, ongoing disagreements between Jerry Wexler and Jim Stewart were beginning to sour the relationship between Atlantic and Stax, and the success of "When a Man Loves a Woman" had suggested to Wexler that Rick Hall's FAME Studios might serve as a suitable replacement. So, just as Percy Sledge's single was reaching the top of the charts, Wexler took Wilson Pickett down to the Shoals to record some new material. Not quite confident in the Shoals band's abilities, Wexler hedged his bets by hiring Chips Moman to drive down from Memphis to play on the Pickett sessions. He also asked Moman to recommend other musicians for the session, which is how Moman's friend and collaborator Tommy Cogbill (1932–1982) first came to record at FAME.[105] A musical jack-of-all-trades, Cogbill had played steel guitar in Memphis country bands as a teenager before picking up guitar and upright bass. Like Carol Kaye and James Jamerson, he refined his musical approach playing in local jazz clubs, honing his speed, dexterity, and sense of groove. He started playing electric bass sometime around early 1966 while doing session work at Moman's American Studios in Memphis—though when he and Moman arrived for that Pickett session in May 1966, everyone assumed that Cogbill would be playing rhythm guitar. That changed after the musicians ran into problems while trying to record a cover of "Land of 1,000 Dances." As Wexler recalled, "Pickett was in great voice—that wasn't the problem. It was Junior Lowe, the bass player, who wasn't locking on the groove. Chips Moman let me know that Junior was basically a guitarist, not a bassist, and we'd do better with Tommy Cogbill. The switch was magical; Tommy tore it up."[106] The final track stands as an early demonstration of Cogbill's electric bass prowess. He begins by supplying a rush of forward momentum into the first verse with a rapid-fire eighth-note bass line, then settles into a more relaxed groove for the first verse and instrumental breaks, drops out entirely in the choruses, and finally supercharges the end of the song with a syncopated bass fill leading into the second and final verse.

With Cogbill's bass driving it, "Land of 1,000 Dances" became Pickett's third No. 1 rhythm & blues hit and his most successful crossover single, reaching No. 6 on the Hot 100. Its success prompted Wexler to bring Cogbill back for Pickett's subsequent FAME sessions, which led to more Top 10 rhythm & blues hits, including "Mustang Sally" (1966) and "Funky Broadway" (1967). Notably, not only did these hits help popularize Muscle Shoals as a recording center, they also led to the first public acknowledgment of the Shoals session musicians: the back covers of Pickett's Atlantic LPs *The Wicked Pickett* (1966) and *The Sound of Wilson Pickett* (1967) both featured a list of recording personnel, crediting each musician by name. This meant that, even though the Muscle Shoals session musicians had played on fewer hits than the Wrecking Crew, the Funk Brothers, or Booker T. and the MG's, they were the first to be explicitly and regularly credited for their work as sidemen.

Cogbill's success with Pickett persuaded Wexler to also call him in to play on Aretha Franklin's first session for Atlantic, which took place at FAME on January 24, 1967, and produced her first major soul hit, "I Never Loved a Man (The Way I Loved You)" (1967). That session, however, infamously revealed the fraught racial tensions that lay just beneath the surface of FAME's working environment. As Hughes explains,

During the downtime, [freelance trumpeter] Ken Laxton and [Franklin's manager/husband] Ted White began poking fun at each other. The exchange was initially good-natured, but both men's jibes became increasingly unfriendly. "A redneck patronizing a Black man is dangerous camaraderie," Wexler observed, and it was made even more dangerous by the whiskey that made its way around the room. The words between White and Laxton soon turned racial, leading

to a heated argument and ultimately a physical confrontation . . .
[T]he maelstrom continued back at the motel where the out-of-
towners were staying. Here, in a misguided attempt to defuse the
tension, Hall produced more whiskey and attempted to salvage his
disintegrating session. . . . Now it was Hall who got into it with White,
and the two men wound up screaming racial epithets at each other.[107]

Both incidents led Franklin to refuse to record at FAME or work with
Hall ever again, though neither she nor White seemed to blame any
of the session musicians besides Laxton. In the interest of keeping his
hit-making formula, Wexler brokered a compromise in which he would
instead fly the core Shoals musicians to New York to play on her future
sessions at Atlantic Studios. Thus, between January 1967 and April 1968,
Cogbill appeared on six more of Franklin's hits, including "Respect"
(1967), "(You Make Me Feel Like) A Natural Woman" (1967), and
"Chain of Fools" (1967). And starting with Franklin's second Atlantic LP
Aretha Arrives (1967), her albums also began explicitly crediting Cogbill
and the Shoals session musicians.

Musically, Cogbill's bass playing falls somewhere between Duck
Dunn's straightforward repetitive grooves and James Jamerson's ultra-
busy, jazz-influenced style. Take, for example, the main two-bar bass line
of Pickett's "Funky Broadway," which alternates back and forth between
a rapid, syncopated sixteenth-note passage and a more stable ascending eighth-note groove. Cogbill utilizes a similar approach on Franklin's
cover of "Respect" (although at a slower tempo), eschewing Dunn's original part to instead craft a line that Ed Friedland describes as "a classic
example of his use of rhythmic push-pull/tension-release."[108] In terms
of technique and timbre, Cogbill played bass with his index and middle fingers and was known to dip them in Vaseline to help facilitate his
smooth playing and muted sound.[109] And while he favored stock Fender
Precision Basses with built-in mutes and flatwood strings (he owned and
used a 1965 model), he was also known to simply play whatever instrument happened to be at hand. At American Studios, as part of a house
band now known as the Memphis Boys, he played Moman's '59 Precision
Bass on hits such as Elvis Presley's "In the Ghetto" (1969) and, most
famously, Dusty Springfield's "Son of a Preacher Man" (1969).[110]

After Cogbill, the next session bassist to be associated with the Muscle
Shoals Sound was Jerry Jemmott (b. 1946), although he only recorded
in the Shoals a handful of times. Born and raised in the Bronx, Jemmott
started taking classical bass lessons in junior high and landed his first

professional gig at the age of twelve. He then played in jazz big bands and other small combos around the New York area throughout his high school years, but found that he disliked the elitist attitudes he encountered among young players in the scene. As he recalled, "The cats playing jazz were very much into themselves. . . . That really turned me off. Now, I'd been going on some jobs where there would be two bands—an acoustic one playing jazz and an electric one playing dance music. It seemed to me that the people playing electric bass were playing music for *people*, not just for themselves."[111] He decided to take up the electric bass in 1964, first purchasing a cheap Zim Gar bass (a rebranded Japanese Teisco import) and Epiphone amplifier before ultimately upgrading to the more professional setup of a Fender Jazz Bass and Ampeg B-15. Reflecting back on his early experiences playing the electric bass, he recalled, "[That's when] I really fell in love with rhythm and blues . . . Junior Walker, New Orleans groups, all the Motown stuff—I discovered James Jamerson at that point. That was my inspiration. I learned one Jamerson line and that was it—I've probably been playing it ever since."[112] His big break came in 1967 when he embarked on a national tour with King Curtis's band, the Kingpins, with whom he also recorded a Top 10 rhythm & blues instrumental rendition of Bobbie Gentry's "Ode to Billie Joe" (1967).

Having grown up in New York surrounded by professional musicians, Jemmott had long dreamed of becoming a full-time session musician.[113] By 1967, he had played bass on a few recordings—including Erma Franklin's rhythm & blues hit "Piece of My Heart" (1967)—but was still finding it difficult to come by steady work in the New York recording scene. That finally changed in January 1968, after King Curtis recommended him as a last-minute replacement for a Wilson Pickett session at Atlantic Studios. As he recalls the session, "I took care of business. I took it *out*. I followed the chart until I saw a place where I could put a little something in. I put it in, and they *loved* it. That was it. After that, they started asking me for work, and my studio career was happening."[114] Having proven his musical bona fides, Jemmott suddenly found himself being regularly called to play on Atlantic sessions. Such was the case on April 15, 1968, when Jerry Wexler called him in to be an alternate bassist for the next Aretha Franklin session. As was now custom, Wexler had also flown in the Shoals musicians—including Tommy Cogbill—to be Franklin's backing band, creating a potentially uncomfortable situation for Jemmott, both as an outsider and as the only Black man in the band. As Jemmott explained to me, while he does not recall any overt racial tensions between him and the Shoals musicians, he does remember how uneasy he felt having to sit there and simply observe the session:

> That was a totally new experience to me. But [the session] wasn't happening. I was surprised they couldn't hear what I was hearing. That kind of flipped me out. I felt bad for [Franklin] that they couldn't hear what was needed to propel the music. I was in pain, because from the downbeat, I knew exactly what it was supposed to be . . . and I had to sit there suffering as they took shots at it. It took five hours [to record "Think"], three hours of rehearsing and an hour lunch break. At the top of the of two o'clock session, Jerry [Wexler] said, "Go in there and see what you can do."[115]

With Jemmott's contributions, "Think" (1968) became Franklin's sixth No. 1 rhythm & blues hit. Looking back on the session, he remembers Cogbill fondly, noting that, with his prior string of hits, "[Cogbill] could've kept playing bass after the riddle of 'Think' was solved; but he didn't. Instead, he insisted that I play bass while he played guitar. Like all great session musicians, he put the song before himself, and his decision allowed magic to happen."[116] Thereafter, Jemmott took over bass duties from Cogbill on Franklin's sessions and, like the Shoals musicians before him, began to be explicitly credited on Franklin's LPs, starting with *Aretha Now* (1968). Additionally, on the greatest hits compilation *Aretha's Gold* (1969), pictures of each session musician were prominently featured on the back of the LP (Figure 32)—a rare honor in a profession where anonymity was the norm.

Given Jemmott's established working relationship with the Shoals musicians, Wexler also decided to fly him down to record at FAME. When I asked him if it felt strange for him to record in Alabama as a Black man, he replied,

> It was strange, in a sense. But you follow the music. So, it was just another gig. Hopping on a plane this time and, you know, going to a place that's known for a lot of discrimination. But in the recording industry, everything is insulated. Nobody wants to mess around. You want to take care of business. In the studio everybody's on their best behavior. You don't know what's in their mind. You don't know what's behind that smiling face . . . Sometimes you can smell something, but you deal with it. You do your thing, and you move ahead.[117]

Figure 32. Photos of Jerry Jemmott (left) and Tommy Cogbill (right) recording with Aretha Franklin. (Source: *Aretha's Gold*, Atlantic, 1969.)

Jemmott ultimately describes his experience recording in the Shoals positively. But he does recall disapproving of how the other musicians were treated. As he told Reali, "I found out that the musicians down there would work all day for one session . . . [T]hey could work on a song for twelve hours and they would get paid for one session. I got down there, and I was making double, triple of what they were making. We did four sessions a day. So I got paid for four sessions."[118]

Just as Putnam had, this new generation of Shoals musicians eventually came to recognize they were being taken advantage of, but they also knew that there was not much they could do about it. They were all considered expendable, a lesson that Jemmott himself would soon learn. In mid-1969, Wexler contracted Jemmott for three days of Aretha Franklin sessions but canceled them at the very last minute. The bassist nevertheless held Wexler to his contract and insisted that he be paid for the sessions; after that, Jemmott told me, "He never hired me again."[119] In the end, it all came down to the money. Regardless of his track record of hits or Wexler's avowed appreciation for Black musicians, when Jemmott stood up for himself and asked for the money he was rightfully owed, he was immediately replaced. To add insult to injury, when Franklin's *This Girl's in Love with You* album was released in 1970, Jemmott's name had been excised from the credits entirely—despite the fact that the photos appearing on the back of the *Aretha's Gold* LP were taken during the session in which he recorded three songs for the album, including Franklin's hit version of "The Weight."

Like Carol Kaye, Jemmott was a chameleon, able to adapt to any type of session, though his contributions to the Muscle Shoals Sound were often distinct from Cogbill's. For example, on "Respect," Cogbill's tension-and-release bass line gives the song a syncopated groove that acts as its own distinct rhythmic layer in the music; by contrast, on a song like "Think," Jemmott takes two separate approaches, first reinforcing the rhythm and melodic arc of Franklin's vocal melody in the verses and then switching to a subdivided eighth-note line in the choruses that adds tension and forward momentum. Reflecting back on that performance, Jemmott recalled that his playing was informed by his background as a jazz musician, specifically the interactive way he structured his bass line around Franklin's voice.[120] In further contrast to Cogbill's short-term, tension-and-release style, on Pickett's "Hey Jude," Jemmott develops his bass performance over the course of the entire recording. He starts by laying back in the first verse before transitioning into the relaxed, syncopated eighth-note groove that undergirds most of the song. At its climax, underneath the horns, guitar solo, and Pickett's shouts, Jemmott lets loose with a flurry of sixteenth notes, building momentum by rhythmically subdividing and varying his original bass line. He then settles back into his earlier groove as the song ebbs and comes to a close.

Though Jemmott primarily recorded in New York, his brief appearances in Muscle Shoals left a lasting impact, especially on David Hood, who was also on-hand to play bass during the *Hey Jude* sessions. As Hood recalled,

> On the first Pickett session I played on, they brought Jerry Jemmott, who was an accomplished bass player, down from New York. And so I'm sitting here with my dumb self, and Jerry Jemmott's just ripping it up over there. And I'm thinking, "Gosh, what am I even doing here?" So it was scary. And, of course, the best songs on that session were the ones he played on. "Hey Jude" and all that stuff. Though there were some songs that I played on as well. The hits were all the ones that he played

on. It was intimidating, but it was a learning experience, and I guess, at least as far as I'm concerned, I hung in there, and learned from what was going on, to come back the next time, and the next time.[121]

Though Cogbill and Jemmott were the Shoals's biggest hitmakers in the 1966–69 era, at that same time Hood had been building his own studio chops as part of FAME's second-generation house band, the Muscle Shoals Rhythm Section (or as they are sometimes known today, thanks to Lynyrd Skynyrd, the Swampers).[122] For example, in 1967, Hood performed on a series of Shoals recording sessions that became the basis of Etta James's *Tell Mama* album (1968), which contained both the hit title track and the rhythm & blues classic "I'd Rather Go Blind." And after Wexler severed ties with Jemmott, Hood was brought in to play bass in Franklin's session band, recording hits like "Eleanor Rigby" (1969) and "Call Me" (1970), as well as contributing to *Spirit in the Dark* (1970).

In April 1969, Hood and other members of the Muscles Shoals Rhythm Section officially split from Rick Hall and FAME. With financial backing from Wexler and Atlantic, they opened their own recording studio, Muscle Shoals Sound Studios (MSSS), in nearby Sheffield, Alabama.[123] Here again the Shoals musicians were pioneers among their contemporaries: by owning the means of record production, they were finally able to legitimately earn union scale (although, following Hall's model, they initially undercharged for their own sessions). More importantly, they found new ways to share in the profits of their labor. In addition to their union scale as session musicians, they earned money by renting the studio to artists and by producing their sessions. They also opened their own in-house publishing company, Muscle Shoals Sound Publishing, which provided the musicians another revenue stream. Over the next few years, Hood would play bass on dozens of hits recorded at MSSS, including songs by the Staples Singers and Paul Simon.

Though Hood had witnessed both Cogbill and Jemmott play bass at FAME, his personal approach gravitated much more to the Duck Dunn school, crafting simpler, repetitive bass riffs that anchored a song without pulling focus from the vocals. As he described his style:

I'm not a real technical player . . . so I'm more comfortable playing less. Having a good sound and playing in tune and in time is *much* more important than chops. You're not playing for yourself or for other bass players—you're playing to make a song come out. It's not brain surgery. It's all about entertainment. If you're not pleasing someone you're wasting your time.[124]

Hood's playing demonstrates how a stripped-down, song-centric bass line can still be quite effective. Take, for example, Etta James's "Tell Mama." His opening bass riff explores the instrument's midrange through a simple variation on an ascending F-major scale repeated eight times. In the verse, Hood plays a moving root-fifth pattern, with added fills that lock in with the horns. By the time that opening riff returns in the chorus, listeners are already primed to hear it as a stable home base and thereby are freed to revel in the call-and-response between James's vocals and the horns. With the next verse, the cycle repeats again, and the rest of the song simply alternates between these two contrasting sections. On the Staple Singers' "I'll Take You There," Hood plays a bass line he lifted from the classic 1969 reggae instrumental "Liquidator" (which featured Aston "Family Man" Barrett on electric bass).[125] Prominently placed in the final mix, Hood plays the same lightly syncopated two-bar groove for nearly the entire song, providing a stable foundation both for Mavis Staples's vocals and for the various interweaving instrumental solos. Approximately one minute and fifty seconds into the song, Hood breaks from his riff to play his own melodic eight-bar solo, before jumping right back into his repeating groove. This approach—providing a strong, stable, and supportive structure for the other musicians—became Hood's calling card, and he used it to great effect throughout the seventies. Most lucratively, Hood would appear on Bob Seger's classic rock hits "Mainstreet" (1977) and "Old Time Rock & Roll" (1979), both of which were controlled by MSS Publishing.

In the sixties, as Hughes demonstrates, the northwest Alabama recording scene was plagued by many of the same underlying racial tensions as Stax in Memphis, which were only mitigated by how rarely Black session musicians participated in it.[126] For the white Shoals musicians, Reali likewise documents that they were chronically underpaid for their services. Unlike LA, the northwest Alabama scene lacked the strong union support necessary to enforce its regulations, and FAME's session musicians were among the lowest paid in the industry, even if they were the first to be regularly credited for their work. These circumstances changed thanks to the success of Muscle Shoals Sound Studio. Owned and operated by the musicians themselves, MSSS challenged the long-held music industry belief that session musicians were not entitled to share in any future profits. It is unfortunate that this model never became more widespread, as many of the most popular session musicians in the sixties eventually fell on hard times as they were replaced by the next generations of studio players. Although the members of the Muscle Shoals Rhythm Section were underpaid for many years, they were ultimately saved from a similar fate, thanks to the financial stake they eventually held in the music that they recorded.

New York: The "Lost" Scene

In the sixties, the two poles of the US music industry were LA and New York. Both were the base of operations for multiple record labels, both were home to dozens of top-tier recording studios, and both were tightly regulated by their local chapters of the Musicians' Union. They also had important geographic ties to other culture industries: LA was connected to film and television, New York was connected to Broadway and the advertising industry. Yet, while New York rivaled LA in size, scope, and significance, its recording scene and its many session musicians remain glaringly absent from most popular music histories.[127] This omission is the result of multiple, overlapping factors. Paradoxically, the sheer breadth of musical activity that took place in New York makes it difficult to distill into a single, coherent narrative. Furthermore, as Andrew Mall points out, popular music scholars often display an inherent bias in favor of smaller independent labels, an "indie prejudice" that has problematically dismissed "the study of major labels and musical mainstreams."[128] This prejudice is why, for instance, small recording scenes such as those surrounding Stax in Memphis or FAME in Muscle Shoals have been far more thoroughly documented than the larger New York scene, even though the latter was not only responsible for many more hit records but (through Atlantic) was also the necessary conduit through which both Stax and FAME achieved national distribution. Most significantly, the New York recording scene is particularly difficult to mythologize. There were simply so many session players in New York that there was never really a "core" group of musicians whose stories could be simplified into a convenient fiction like the "Wrecking Crew." Without a collective name that could be easily marketed to the public, many of the New York players have continued to languish in obscurity, despite their immense impact on popular music.

The New York scene's closest equivalent to the Wrecking Crew or the Funk Brothers was King Curtis's band, which acted as a formative training ground for many notable session players.[129] Originally inspired by

Louis Jordan, King Curtis (1934–1971) was part of a long line of Texas-based tenor saxophonists. He first left Fort Worth around 1952 to briefly join Lionel Hampton's band, and by 1954 he was living and working in New York City as a professional musician. Curtis became part of the New York recording scene a few years later and, thanks to his contributions to the Coasters' "Yakety Yak" (1958), he solidified his position as a first-call session saxophonist. Working in New York studios, he played on hits in a wide variety of musical styles, including doo-wop, girl group, and Brill Building pop. He even had his own instrumental hits, such as 1962's "Soul Twist." In addition to his career as a session musician and contractor, Curtis was known for his popular live band, which was consistently considered one of the best in New York.

Nearly all of the earliest electric bass players in the New York recording scene worked with King Curtis at some point, as demonstrated by surviving session records. For instance, prior to appearing on Simon & Garfunkel's "The Sounds of Silence," Bob Bushnell had played electric bass on Curtis's solo single "The Birth of the Blues" backed with "Jest Smoochin'" (1958); together, he and Curtis also appeared on Bobby Lewis's No. 1 pop hit "Tossin' & Turnin'" (1961) and Solomon Burke's Top 20 rhythm & blues hit "I'm Hanging Up My Heart for You" (1962).[130] Likewise, electric bassist Jimmy Tyrell started recording with Curtis in 1964, appearing on album cuts for Curtis's *Soul Serenade* LP (1964) and later on Solomon Burke's "Keep Looking" (1966).[131] Bassist Jimmy Lewis (1918–2000), who had played in the Count Basie Orchestra in the fifties, also became a long-standing member of Curtis's band. He appeared on upright on "The Birth of the Blues" and "Soul Twist," and eventually switched to playing electric bass in Curtis's live band, which worked as both a stand-alone group and as a backing band for touring artists such as Sam Cooke and Otis Redding. As would become common for Curtis's musicians, Lewis left the band after he had become established as a studio player in New York and could therefore no longer afford to leave town to tour. He went on to have a long career as a session musician, playing both upright and electric bass; most famously, he played electric bass on the Original Off-Broadway Cast Recording of *Hair* (1967), as well as on the later Original Broadway Cast Recording (1968).[132]

Similar to the developments in LA, the early electric bass players in the New York recording scene tended toward more simple or straightforward performance styles. Yet thanks to the session bassists working in other recording scenes, by the mid-sixties, new, more elaborate electric bass styles had become commonplace in popular music. Following these trends, it would be the next generation of musicians to come through Curtis's band that would similarly popularize more sophisticated electric bass styles in New York. The first of these was bassist Chuck Rainey (b. 1940).

Born and raised in Ohio, Rainey grew up in a musical family and spent time learning multiple instruments, including piano, snare drum, trumpet, and baritone horn. Looking back on his childhood, Rainey told me that he only remembered encountering the electric bass twice: at age fourteen, he snuck out of the house to see a Hank Ballard and the Midnighters show, and a few years later he experienced the Flamingos' energetic performance of "Jump Children" (featuring electric bassist Zeke Carey) in the 1958 rock 'n' roll teenpic *Go, Johnny, Go*.[133] As he recalls, he was impressed with the instrument's clarity, which seemed capable of matching the volume and presence of the gospel organ bass players that he was accustomed to hearing. Rainey picked up the guitar in the Army Reserve and by the early sixties was the third guitarist in a local rhythm & blues band. To better fit the music, he decided to try out a Fender Precision Bass and Bassman amplifier, which his parents helped him purchase for $375.[134] As he recalled, "I loved it as soon as I got my hands on it. I was almost reborn. Where I came from, in Ohio, it was all upright and organ basses, so when I got the instrument, I was the only guy in town that had it. Everyone seemed to like what I played; [my] popularity just started spreading."[135] With his reputation growing, Rainey worked as a freelance musician and started landing better gigs. His first big break came after he was hired for saxophonist Big Jay McNeely's band, which was then playing white jazz clubs in Cleveland. He then joined saxophonist Sil Austin's touring band, which brought him to New York around 1962.

While there were more electric bass players in New York, Rainey found that older musicians in the scene still looked down on his instrument:

> When I got to New York, it was another kind of trip. In the early '60s, the jazz musicians didn't really accept the electric bass. The only people in jazz that accepted it were leaders, because they were always looking for gimmicks, trying to get over with different things. . . . At first I had a tremendous ego about my playing. I had sort of a chip on my shoulder about the older cats, the older bass players especially, who talked negatively about the instrument, not so much putting me down, but putting the *instrument* down.[136]

Figure 33. Chuck Rainey in the studio, ca. 1963. (Photo courtesy of Chuck Rainey.)

Rainey spent the next year or so establishing himself in the New York scene, playing pickup gigs in Top 40 bands. Through this process, he began to develop his own approach to the electric bass, which expanded as he discovered James Jamerson's music. As he recalled, "In terms of me playing bass, Jamerson gave me the keys to get into the house. In those days, I had to play a lot of Top 40 music, which meant a lot of Motown—and every time I had to learn one of James's lines, it would kick me in the butt and open my eyes a little wider. That really motivated me to study and evaluate what could be done with the instrument."[137] In 1964, after short stints touring with Etta James and others, Rainey joined King Curtis's band and spent the next three years working constantly (including a notable stint opening for the Beatles on their 1965 US tour).

After Curtis changed bands in 1967 (bringing in Jerry Jemmott on electric bass), Rainey decided to pursue full-time session work as a way to make ends meet, and he soon found that his former bandleader's reputation helped him get his foot in the door. As he explained to me,

> If you played with King Curtis for any amount of time, you were on the radar, because everybody that he hired could play. . . . Everybody in his bands were just excellent musicians. Also, everybody knew that if you worked for King Curtis, you understood the professional side of things. You would be on time, you would play in tune . . . [To be in Curtis's band] you [also] had to be able to understand and play all kinds of music, because that's what he did.[138]

Like many other session musicians, Rainey switched to using an Ampeg B-15 (or, occasionally, a B-12) and cut his teeth recording demos. Within a year he had become the first-call electric bassist in New York, earning union scale playing three or more sessions per day, five days a week. In the late sixties and early seventies, he appeared on recordings by the Coasters, the O'Jays, Ben E. King, Solomon Burke, the Rascals, Roberta Flack, Donny Hathaway, Louis Armstrong, and Quincy Jones, as well as on hundreds of jazz LPs. After King Curtis became Aretha Franklin's music director, he hired Rainey to take over the bass spot in her recording band, and Rainey would go on to appear on many of her early seventies hits, including "Bridge Over Troubled Water" (1970), "Spanish Harlem" (1971), and "Rock Steady" (1971). He also joined Franklin's touring group for a short time and appeared on her best-selling live gospel album *Amazing Grace* (1972). In the early seventies, Rainey relocated to LA. As he explained to Dan Forte in 1976, "When I moved to Los Angeles, my income almost doubled. Scale is $100 now for three hours. For people like me, Larry Carlton, Wilton Felder—the guys people really want to use for name's sake, to help sell the record—they'll give double or triple scale in LA because they have the budget."[139] Through his work for recording sessions and television, as well as his various residual payments from the Musician's Union, Rainey estimates that he was earning around $80,000 a year in LA (the equivalent of around $500,000 today).

Just as in LA, New York session musicians could be called to play in a wide variety of musical styles and were therefore expected to be versatile. To meet these requirements while still forging his own musical identity, Rainey developed a unique approach to the electric bass based on speed and virtuosic technical facility. His quick-playing style came from his idiosyncratic index finger plucking technique. Keeping the finger straight, then moving its tip back and forth across the strings, Rainey was able to consistently play rapid subdivided passages even at fast tempos. He combined this with a left-hand technique that emphasized groove and rhythm. As he told me, "A lot of people think that I play a lot of notes, but I don't. I play a lot of rhythm on the few notes I do play."[140] A good example of his style can be heard on Aretha Franklin's "Every Natural Thing" (1974), which has a quarter-note pulse of around 130 beats per minute. In the verses, Rainey takes an approach somewhere between James Jamerson and Tommy Cogbill, creating a push-and-pull effect by constantly varying a syncopated two-bar bass line. Situated at the eighth-note level, this line provides the song a quick propulsive groove. But then, at the chorus, Rainey explodes, playing an even more rapid, synco-pated double-time line at the sixteenth-note level. Matching his previous description, his chorus bass line sticks to mostly emphasizing a few notes (roots and octaves) played with unprecedented speed and dexterity. He then returns to the opening line and this cycle repeats again. In conjunc-tion with his speed, Rainey also expanded the standard conventions of electric bass by incorporating ghost notes (unfretted rhythmic notes) and slides—such as in the opening of Franklin's "Rock Steady"—as well as double stops (playing two strings at the same time)—such as on Steely Dan's "Josie" (1978).

Unlike some of the other session bassists discussed in this chapter, Rainey has no regrets about how he was compensated as a session musi-cian. Although he admits that he was at times mistreated within the music industry, he is quick to point out that he knew what he was sign-ing up for. As he explained in 1997, "I've never listened back to any of the hits I played on and thought, I should have gotten a piece of that or been paid more, because I wasn't there under those circumstances. I'm a sideman—that's my role—and I'm usually paid very well for it."[141]

The size of the New York recording scene meant that there was a need for multiple session electric bassists, and just as in LA, the competi-tive nature of session work ensured that there would always be a high-quality pool of players available. By the early seventies, other electric bassists had also become top-tier players in the New York scene, such as Gordon Edwards—who played on John Lennon's *Mind Games* (1973) and Van McCoy's "The Hustle" (1975)—and Willie Weeks—who played on the Rolling Stones' "It's Only Rock 'n Roll" (1974) and David Bowie's "Young Americans" (1975).

As in LA, the strong Musicians' Union presence in New York meant that many of its session musicians were spared from the more egregious exploitation found in smaller scenes across the country. Jemmott and Rainey, for instance, both believe that they were properly paid for their labor, and both dismissed my questions about any potential racial tensions in the scene. Perhaps the real problem when discussing the New York recording scene is just how little information survives about it. Despite being one of the most vibrant and important centers for popular music in the country, its internal operations remain underexplored. Hopefully, future critics and scholars will continue to reconstruct its history and shed further light on what it was like to work as a New York session musician, both the good and the bad.

Conclusion

The landscape of session work varied widely from scene to scene. New York and LA, the biggest scenes, were the most competitive and required the most diverse skill set. Yet, thanks to strong union support, they also paid the best, allowing their top-tier session musicians to earn sizable livings freelancing for multiple companies. During Motown's time in Detroit, the Funk Brothers could likewise count on steady work, as long as they signed exclusive contracts, and, although they earned less than musicians in New York or LA, they still took home large salaries. At Stax in the mid-sixties, Booker T. and the MG's earned half of what the Funk Brothers were paid, making them among the lowest-paid session musicians in the country. However, unlike the Funk Brothers, the MG's were also able to build their own careers as performers and were even eventually given a small cut of Stax's profits. At FAME, session musicians were likewise paid relatively low wages, but they were the first to be consistently credited for their work. And after leaving FAME, the Muscle Shoals Rhythm Section also became the only collective of session musicians to buy their own studio and develop a strong financial stake in the music they recorded.

Looking back decades later, it is easy to romanticize session musicians and the studios in which they recorded, and recently a whole slate of documentary films has brought their stories to wider audiences.[142] This recognition is certainly important, but too often it has failed to adequately address the complexities of their profession. The reality is that most session musicians were low-level employees who were regularly subjected to various forms of mistreatment. To keep their jobs, they often had to become complicit in their own exploitation, which for some even included putting up with sexism and racism from their employers and colleagues. Although it may be uncomfortable to embrace such a clear-eyed view of history, it is necessary if we are to come to terms with the role session musicians have played within the music industry.

Acknowledging these bassists' struggles, however, does not diminish the significance of their accomplishments. Through their work on thousands of records throughout the sixties, session musicians firmly established the electric bass as an essential component of modern popular music. The most original—James Jamerson, Carol Kaye, Joe Osborn, Duck Dunn, Tommy Cogbill, Jerry Jemmott, David Hood, and Chuck Rainey—also developed unique approaches that fundamentally expanded the conventions of bass playing. Their new sounds and new techniques would go on to impact generations of musicians and listeners, and they ultimately paved the way for even further innovations. Most of their names may still be unknown to the public, but the music these bassists created continues to shape the sound of popular music, even today.

SEVEN | The Default Instrument

British Bassists and Mid-Sixties Rock

On February 9, 1964, the Beatles appeared on *The Ed Sullivan Show* for the first time, performing songs such as "I Saw Her Standing There" and "I Want to Hold Your Hand." Watched by an estimated seventy-three million viewers—or approximately 40 percent of the entire US population—the broadcast transformed the Beatles into the biggest band in the world. On May 26, 1965, the Rolling Stones appeared on *Shindig!* In between performances of "Little Red Rooster" and their still-yet-to-be-released next single "(I Can't Get No) Satisfaction," the band helped introduce Chicago blues legend Howlin' Wolf and enthusiastically sat at his feet as he sang. On September 17, 1967, the Who appeared on *The Smothers Brothers Comedy Hour*, where they performed "I Can See for Miles" and "My Generation." Their set had a literally explosive ending, as the band destroyed their equipment and drummer Keith Moon set off an overloaded pyrotechnic device. Although the Beatles, the Stones, and the Who have long been canonized as pioneers of sixties rock, they are still often viewed through the same lens that American audiences watched each of these televised performances: as part of a cohesive influx of rock bands from England, regularly described by the press as the "British Invasion." This framing, however, is an oversimplification, one that overlooks significant differences between these bands and the contexts from which they emerged.

This chapter explores the careers and bass styles of the Beatles' Paul McCartney, the Rolling Stones' Bill Wyman, and the Who's John Entwistle. All three came of age in the aftermath of World War II and were part of a generation of British youth fascinated with American popular music. Drawn to its perceived rebelliousness, these Brits embraced American musical styles, particularly African American styles, as part of their own identities. Yet, since they only had limited access to this music and its creators, their understanding of it was largely based on their own imagined fantasies. Though often problematic, these fantasies nonetheless creatively fueled young British musicians, many of whom evolved from imitating American records to writing and performing their own material—a process that Andrew Kellett succinctly describes as "adoption, emulation, creativity."[1] McCartney, Wyman, and Entwistle all followed this trajectory, but through this process they each came to develop radically different approaches to the electric bass. Building on the work of Jack Hamilton, Andy Babiuk, and others, I demonstrate how their individual innovations resulted from a complex mix of factors, including their musical interests and personal temperament, their conceptions of American culture, their access to musical equipment, the expectations of their audiences, and their relationships with their collaborators. Ultimately, while all three bassists forged separate musical paths, their commercial success, first in England and then America, represented the final step in the electric bass's journey to becoming popular music's default low-end instrument.

Rethinking the British Invasion Myth

In *Just Around Midnight: Rock and Roll and the Racial Imagination,* Jack Hamilton persuasively argues against what he calls "the British Invasion myth," the common narrative that, in the sixties, "rock and roll was on the verge of dying until the Beatles 'invaded,' along with their countrymen, and heroically rescued the music from the very Americans who had created it and then neglected it."[2] Even if this explanation of popular music history is not wholly inaccurate, Hamilton argues that it has four fundamental problems: First, it "contains a deeply American bias" that places "America at the center" and depicts "the 'invaders' . . . as irreducibly alien."[3] Second, it presents the British Invasion as an immediate, overnight success, rather than a sustained effort built slowly over time. Third, it problematically subsumes all British bands under one catchall category, regardless of their contrasting backgrounds or musical styles, ignoring difference "in favor of false unity."[4] Lastly, by implying that it was a geographically isolated phenomenon, it obscures "how profoundly transatlantic the aesthetics of the British Invasion were, and specifically how creatively dependent these bands were on African American artists."[5] Following Hamilton, this chapter specifically situates the Beatles, the Rolling Stones, and the Who within the contrasting British musical subcultures that they inhabited in the mid-sixties and shows how those subcultures ultimately shaped the different styles of each of their bassists.

Paul McCartney and the Beatles: From Merseybeat to *Sgt. Pepper*

The Beatles' global popularity was the single most significant cultural development of the middle to late sixties, so much so that it is difficult to fully convey the immensity of their impact. Over the course of their short career, they had seventeen No. 1 hits in the UK and twenty in the US. Millions and millions of young people bought their records, and their commercial success was so vast and unprecedented that it fundamentally altered the direction of both the British and American music industries. While there were multiple factors that contributed to their popularity—sustained attention from the media, savvy marketing, their charming and irreverent public personae, and so on—their music was always at the heart of their appeal.

To this day, music historians continue to obsess over the trajectory and significance of the Beatles' career. Relatively few, however, have specifically explored Paul McCartney's development as a bass player. This section thus analyzes the wider cultural, social, and technological factors that shaped McCartney's bass playing across the Beatles' recorded output. In particular, it chronicles how McCartney's fascination with contemporary American popular music led him to develop his own melodic bass style, as well as some of the inherent complexities of his cultural borrowing.

McCartney (b. 1942) was born and raised in Liverpool, a major port city in the north of England. Like many postwar British youth, he was drawn to American popular music during his teen years, in part due to its subversive reputation. By the mid-fifties, American rock 'n' roll had been adopted by a subset of disenfranchised, working-class British teenagers known as Teddy Boys, whose violent antics were covered extensively in the national press.[6] Among these, notably, were a series of riots that broke out after UK screenings of the films *Blackboard Jungle* (1955) and *Rock Around the Clock* (1956), which, Dick Bradley notes, firmly fixed the association between rock 'n' roll and juvenile delinquency in the British cultural imaginary.[7] In addition to the music's perceived foreignness and its disreputability, its cultural cachet among British youth was further enhanced by its relative inaccessibility, as state-sponsored BBC radio (the only broadcaster in the UK at that time) initially refused to play it and the records themselves were not always readily available.[8] To be a British fan of American rock 'n' roll in the fifties thus entailed some small effort. For example, to hear the music on the radio, McCartney had to tune in to broadcasts from faraway Radio Luxembourg; to see it performed "live," he had to watch imported films, such as *The Girl Can't Help It*, or attend a concert by whatever American act happened to be touring England; and to have his own records, he had to save what money he could come by, and even then, he was limited by the small and scattershot selection offered by local retailers.

In England, the popularization of American rock 'n' roll also coincided with the rise of skiffle, which, as previously discussed, spurred thousands of young Brits to become amateur musicians. The combined impact of skiffle and rock 'n' roll was especially potent in Liverpool, where it would eventually influence the formation of numerous local bands. As a young man, McCartney was drawn to both traditions: he decided to start playing guitar after seeing skiffle legend Lonnie Donegan in concert in late 1956 but quickly transitioned to learning rock 'n' roll songs by Little Richard, Gene Vincent, and Eddie Cochran. In July 1957, he met John Lennon at a local school dance where Lennon's skiffle band, the Quarrymen, were playing. Bonded by their love of American music, as well as their mutual aspirations to be songwriter-performers, Lennon asked McCartney to join the Quarrymen. By early 1960, the group included McCartney and Lennon, as well as George Harrison on lead guitar and Stu Sutcliffe on electric bass, and they had changed the band's name to "the Beatles" (a reference to Buddy Holly's Crickets). In May 1960, a local Liverpool venue owner named Allan Williams became the Beatles' first manager, and he used his connections to arrange for the group to take on an extended residency in Hamburg, West Germany. Adding drummer Pete Best at the very last minute, the Beatles played forty-eight consecutive days in Hamburg starting on August 17, 1960. Each of the five band members were paid thirty deutsche marks (or, at that time, the equivalent of £2.50) per day, in exchange for performing for four and a half hours on weekdays and six hours on weekends. This residency proved to be a crucial apprenticeship for the band, as to play for so long each night, they had to develop both an extensive repertoire of cover songs and a compelling onstage presence. Notably, the Beatles' early sets predominantly comprised covers of American popular music, which, Dave Laing demonstrates, included everything from show tunes to rock 'n' roll, rhythm & blues, girl group, and pop songs.[9]

McCartney begrudgingly took over electric bass duties after Sutcliffe quit the band in late 1960. Initially, he borrowed Sutcliffe's bulky Höfner 500/5 Bass, but since McCartney was left-handed, he was forced to play it upside down. Starting in April 1961, the Beatles returned to Hamburg for a three-month residency, and at some point during this trip, McCartney visited a local Steinway retailer to seek out a more suitable instrument. He famously settled on a Höfner 500/1 Violin Bass, which at the time were not yet commercially available in England. The Violin Bass appealed to McCartney for a number of reasons: its distinctive, symmetrical design seemed easy to adapt for a left-handed player; its lightweight, hollow-body construction made it comfortable to wear onstage for long periods of time; its thin neck, low action, and short, 30-inch scale length made it easy for him to adapt his prior skill set as a guitarist; and, most importantly, it was inexpensively priced at 287 deutsche marks (equal, in 1961, to approximately £25 or $70, about the price of a Danelectro bass in the United States).[10] McCartney was likely even further convinced after the salesman explained that he could custom-order a left-handed version from the factory. The instrument therefore met McCartney's practical needs as a gigging musician and had a retail price that he could afford. Yet, as was the case with most budget basses, Violin Basses were low-quality instruments. They were extremely fragile and had terrible intonation issues (the lowest notes on the instrument were often muddy and indistinct, while the upper frets were so inaccurately placed that it was impossible to play in tune in the instrument's higher register). Despite these issues, the Violin Bass became McCartney's primary instrument, and he immediately incorporated it into the Beatles' live shows in Hamburg. Not long after, in late June 1961, Bert Kaempfert hired McCartney and the Beatles to act as Tony Sheridan's backing band on some sessions for Polydor. These sessions produced multiple recordings, including rock versions of "My Bonnie Lies Over the Ocean" and "When the Saints Go Marching In," as well as a Shadows-inspired instrumental "Cry for a Shadow." All three recordings capture how quickly McCartney took to playing the bass and the warm, thuddy tone that his Höfner produced.

The Beatles arrived back in Liverpool on July 2, 1961. Less than one week later, Bill Harry published the first issue of *Mersey Beat*, a biweekly magazine dedicated to the local Liverpool music scene. Harry's magazine gave wider visibility to the more than three hundred young bands currently active in the city, many of whom, like the Beatles, were centered around electric guitars, electric bass, and drums and performed songs that emphasized catchy melodies, vocal harmonies, and a strong sense of rhythm. Thanks to the magazine's success, these bands became known as "Merseybeat" or "beat" groups. It was also through *Mersey Beat* that a local record retailer named Brian Epstein first heard about the Beatles, and after some local fans came to his shop looking for a copy of the "My Bonnie" single, Epstein decided to go see the band at the Cavern Club. He was impressed by their performance and set out to become their manager, a position he contractually solidified in January 1962. Possessing a keen eye for public relations, Epstein remolded the Beatles to fit within preexisting British pop traditions. To market the group and their brand of rock 'n' roll to a wider audience, he had them abandon the leather-clad tough guy look that they had picked up in Hamburg and instead presented them as professional entertainers, complete with matching stage outfits. Removing any association with juvenile delinquency (outside of their shaggy haircuts), Epstein combined this new image with the boy's youthful, working-class charm, their showmanship as live performers, and their catchy American-influenced music, thereby rebranding the Beatles as a wholesome, respectable band with widespread appeal.

Epstein spent most of 1962 trying to get the Beatles a record deal with a British label. In January, the band auditioned for Dick Rowe, head of A&R at Decca, who infamously passed on the group but allowed Epstein to keep the recordings of the band's audition. Using these demos, Epstein eventually secured an audition in early June at Abbey Road Studios with George Martin of Parlophone, a small EMI subsidiary that at the time was known mostly for comedy and novelty records. By all accounts, the audition went terribly, due in part to the band's substandard equipment. McCartney, for example, was then playing his bass through a large, homemade bass amplifier known as the "Coffin," which produced a large sound that was useful for live performances in local clubs but was not suitable for the more controlled environment of the studio. As EMI engineer Norman Smith recalled: "I got nothing out of The Beatles' equipment except for a load of noise, hum and goodness-knows-what. Paul's was about the worst."[11] Despite these issues, Martin decided to take a chance on the group, and brought them back in September (with new drummer Ringo Starr) to record their first single, an original song they'd written called "Love Me Do." While it was a modest hit, their commercial breakthrough came in January 1963 with the release of their second single, "Please Please Me," which ushered in the era of Beatlemania. By the end of the year, the Beatles had become the most famous pop act in the UK, with multiple successful national tours, four No. 1 hit singles, and two No. 1 albums.

For the Beatles' early Parlophone recordings, McCartney took a functional approach to the bass, playing in a style that reflected the many practical restrictions put upon him in the studio. First and foremost, he was constrained by the equipment that was available to him. As previously mentioned, his Höfner Violin Bass suffered from intonation problems, which confined him to playing in the middle and lower positions of the instrument's neck. EMI's technicians also insisted he play through a better-quality bass amplifier. At first, they simply assembled their own makeshift amp in the studio, but by 1963, Vox had developed dedicated bass amplifiers for the UK market. These then became a part of McCartney's default recording setup, although they too were not always reliable.[12] At the time, the Beatles were still primarily a gigging band, and McCartney was further constrained by the practical expectation that he would need to reproduce the band's recorded material live. He likewise recognized that his role as a singer was more important than his role as a bassist and therefore deliberately limited himself to bass lines that would best allow him to sing and play at the same time. Also, for most of their recorded career, the Beatles recorded on a four-track tape machine, and it was standard practice for McCartney and Starr to record their parts together, both to create a basic rhythm track for each song and to save space on the tape. Similarly, the band was expected to work quickly to record as much material as possible (they famously had to record the bulk of their first LP in just a single day). The combined effect of all these limitations was that, on the Beatles' earliest recordings, McCartney's bass lines were often technically simple and buried in the final mix.

Musically, McCartney's approach to bass playing reflected the aesthetic sensibilities he and the Beatles had developed through years of performing covers of American popular music. American styles, especially those from Black traditions, had a formative impact on McCartney, and he drew heavily on them as he began to write his own bass lines. He acknowledged as much in an interview with *Beat Instrumental* from October 1964:

> Most of the [bass] figures that I have used on our records are not new. I am certain that I have picked up many of them from listening to American R 'n B discs . . . One thing I would like to say about learning an instrument . . . is that you SHOULD STEAL various bits and pieces

from other guitarists and bassists. O.K., so you know they belong to other people—so what! Does it really matter?[13]

Such a statement demonstrates a young artist's naivete toward intellectual property and undoubtedly opens the Beatles to charges of cultural appropriation; but, by owning up to his own theft, he was also, in a way, attempting to pay tribute to his American influences. Later in the same interview, he is even more explicit, stating, "Here's one example of a bit I pinched from someone: I used the bass riff from 'Talkin' About You' by Chuck Berry in 'I Saw Her Standing There.' I played exactly the same notes as [his bassist] did and it fitted our number perfectly."[14] The bass line to "I Saw Her Standing There" (1963) is likely the most distinctive of any song on the Beatles' first LPs, yet as McCartney readily admits, it rips off Reggie Boyd's bass riff from "I'm Talking About You" (1961). McCartney's disregard for the ethical, compensatory, or racial implications of this "pinching" was typical of young, British rock musicians. For them, American popular music represented a romantic fantasy in which American culture, especially African American culture, was glamorous, cool, and distinctly non-British (not to mention freely available to copy and emulate). As McCartney's comment makes clear, however, such a conception was inherently predicated on an unspoken distance from the realities of these recordings—a distance that had little room for someone like Boyd, a Black man in Chicago trying to scrape together a living playing bass for $25 a session. Yet it was also this fantasy, problematic or not, that allowed the Beatles and their contemporaries to embrace American music as part of their own identities, and ultimately it was what spurred them to develop their own musical innovations.

After the Beatles' February 9, 1964, performance on *The Ed Sullivan Show*, Beatlemania spread across the United States and their music became a global phenomenon. They then spent the next eighteen months establishing themselves as successful pop songwriters and performers.[15] At the same time, they set out to further hone their skills as recording artists, which for McCartney included expanding his approach as a bass player. A key catalyst in this expansion was McCartney's acquisition of a left-handed Rickenbacker 4001S electric bass, which Rickenbacker President F. C. Hall personally gave to him in August 1965.[16] Contrary to his Höfner, the 4001S was a professional-grade instrument and one of the most expensive electric basses then on the market. It was built using high-quality materials, it featured a through-body neck design that increased sustain, and it had a strong bass response, meaning that the

"The 'Fiddle Bass' Sound is GREAT"
–says PAUL

When Paul McCartney says the Hofner Violin Bass is just Great, you bet it's worth havin'! That's why SELMER take every one the manufacturer can produce and rush them out to the dealers.

Make a bee line for your nearest Selmer stockist now and see this masterpiece . . . easily the most popular and widely used bass guitar today. Has double-pole, double-coil NOVA-SONIC pick-ups and flick-action switches for instant tone change. Only 55 Guineas. Rich felt-lined Case, 8 Guineas.

Send NOW for free Guitar Brochure

NAME
ADDRESS
                                    Hofner Guitars/NME 14/8
114 CHARING CROSS ROAD, LONDON, W.C.2.

Selmer

Figure 34. Selmer ad in the August 14, 1964, issue of *New Musical Express* featuring Paul McCartney and his Höfner Violin Bass. (Image courtesy of the Rock and Roll Hall of Fame and Museum.)

instrument produced a clearer attack, both in the low-end and midrange. McCartney took an immediate liking to the instrument and decided to use it on the *Rubber Soul* recording sessions in October and November 1965, though he would continue to play his Violin Bass onstage, as by then it had become both his visual trademark and, through an endorsement deal with the instrument's distributor, an additional source of revenue (Figure 34).[17] Unencumbered by the Höfner's limitations, McCartney was finally able to exploit the full potential of an electric bass, and he crafted his own unique punchy bass timbre by feeding his picked Rickenbacker bass through the studio's new Fender Bassman amplifier.

On *Rubber Soul*, McCartney continued to take direct inspiration from American bassists, although he had graduated from simply copying their bass lines to adopting various elements of their individual styles. As a careful student of contemporary popular music, he was well aware of his competition, especially the innovative styles being developed by American session musicians. In the verses of "Drive My Car," for example, McCartney plays a rhythmic bass figure that is clearly adapted from Duck Dunn's bass riff on Otis Redding's "Respect" (George Harrison later took credit for the bass line and admitted to the borrowing, telling *Crawdaddy* in 1977, "On 'Drive My Car' I just played the line, which is really a lick off 'Respect,' you know, the Otis Redding version . . . and I played that line on guitar and Paul laid that with me on bass").[18] Although it is less overt, on the rhythm & blues-inflected "The Word," McCartney similarly invokes Dunn's style by playing a repetitive, syncopated riff that then switches to a stable quarter-note pulse in the subsequent section. For "You Won't See Me," McCartney adopts a freer approach that incorporates arpeggiations, passing tones, and syncopated rhythms. He himself later described the song as "very Motown-flavoured," explaining, "It's got a James Jamerson feel. He was the Motown bass player, he was fabulous, the guy who did all those great melodic bass lines."[19] As Hamilton notes, Jamerson's style profoundly influenced McCartney's bass playing on *Rubber Soul*, especially on the track "Nowhere Man."[20] As he had in earlier eras, McCartney constructed his own bass lines by drawing heavily on American models. To keep up with the times, he had needed to adopt both a new bass and new, more contemporary ways of playing it. Yet, through this process of emulation, he was also developing his individual style as a bassist.

It was during the *Rubber Soul* sessions that McCartney also first experimented with overdubbing his bass lines.[21] Originally, this was simply a practical consideration, as McCartney sometimes played a different instrument on the backing track and therefore had to fill in his bass parts later. The overdubbing process, however, allowed McCartney to be more thoughtful with his bass playing because it let him hear a more finalized version of a song's arrangement before adding his bass to it. This thoughtfulness, for example, can be heard in the opening to "Michelle," on which McCartney improvises a contrasting melodic passage in the bass's upper register that complements the chromatic descent in his prerecorded acoustic guitar part. Although he only overdubbed his bass lines on three songs from *Rubber Soul* ("Michelle," "Think for Yourself," and "The Word"), this process would become more common for later

Beatles recordings, especially once the band began to spend more time in the studio refining the sound of their records.[22]

In April 1966, the Beatles returned to EMI to work on material for their next LP, *Revolver* (1966). On these sessions, the band deliberately embraced more experimental production methods, working with EMI's engineers to develop new technologies and studio techniques that might give their music a distinctive, innovative edge. One particular challenge the engineers wanted to tackle was how to improve the sound of the bass on the Beatles' records. Although McCartney's bass playing had been far more audible on *Rubber Soul* than on the band's previous releases, its presence in the final mixes had still been suppressed by EMI, who remained concerned that robust bass frequencies might cause phonograph needles to jump. By 1966, however, this was an outdated recording philosophy, and the Beatles had repeatedly complained that the bass sound on their records paled in comparison to what they were hearing on American releases. EMI's engineers thus set out to copy this more prominent American bass sound, but like McCartney, their only experience with it came through the records themselves. Lacking any direct knowledge about the production practices in American studios, their attempts at recreating this sound instead led them to develop an independent, experimental solution. As balance engineer Geoff Emerick recalled,

> [Paul McCartney] and I would often get together in the mastering room to listen intently to the low end of some new import he had gotten from the States, most often a Motown track. . . . The bass sounds we were getting were decent . . . but still not as good as what we were hearing on those American records. . . . It occurred to me that since microphones are in fact simply loudspeakers wired in reverse . . . why not try using a loudspeaker as a microphone? . . . To my delight, the idea of using a speaker as a microphone seemed to work pretty well. Even though it didn't deliver a lot of signal and was kind of muffled, I was able to achieve a good bass sound by placing it up against the grille of a bass amplifier, speaker to speaker, and then routing the signal through a complicated setup of compressors and filters. . . . [T]his was pretty way out, even by Beatles standards.[23]

Envisioned by Emerick, and realized by technical engineer Ken Townsend, McCartney used this setup to record his bass lines for both sides of the Beatles' next single, "Paperback Writer" backed with "Rain"

(1966). For "Paperback Writer," McCartney again employs the Stax/ Duck Dunn formula (albeit at a faster tempo), playing a push-and-pull riff in the bass's middle register. For the latter song, Hamilton notes,

> The bass on "Rain" is the song's most active melodic instrument, providing a similar sort of galloping, driving low end heard on a track like [Martha and the Vandella's] "Nowhere to Run." As opposed to simply being an unobtrusive half of the rhythm section, McCartney's bass is an intricate and active force in the song itself. The musical content of McCartney's bass line is also remarkably Jamersonian, full of leaps and tumbles between octaves and bubbling chromaticisms. Rhythmically, McCartney's bass line is a whirl of sixteenth-note syncopations and anticipations of the one and three, nimbly sliding and ricocheting off Starr's drum track, nestled behind Lennon's vocal and the churning layers of guitars.[24]

On both recordings, McCartney's picked playing gives an added emphasis to each note and the compression and filtering applied to the sound captured by Emerick's reverse-loudspeaker-mic gives the bass an added sense of presence.

By defying the conventional wisdom of how a bass could and should be recorded, Emerick, Townsend, and McCartney had collaborated to create a unique electric bass timbre, one with a clear attack and a strong low-end response. But although they had captured this sound on tape, the recordings still had to be mastered for home audio equipment. As luck would have it, EMI's research lab had recently developed a new device known as Automatic Transient Overload Control (ATOC), which both enabled records to be mixed at a louder level and simultaneously curbed any errant bass frequencies that might cause a phonograph needle to jump.[25] Mastered with the assistance of ATOC, the commercially released versions of "Paperback Writer" and "Rain" maintained the integrity of McCartney's prominent bass lines and, for the first time on a Beatles record, allowed the bass to occupy a commanding position in the final mix. As it had on *Rubber Soul*, McCartney's desire to rival the bass-heavy sounds of the American records he loved had led him to further develop his own individual approach as an electric bassist.

In the wake of a disastrous August 1966 tour, the Beatles decided to abandon live performances altogether and instead concentrate solely on studio recording. They therefore no longer needed to make music that could be recreated live, and with no strict budget or deadlines, the band was empowered to spend more time building on the experimental studio techniques they had developed during the *Revolver* sessions. Commencing in late November 1966, the Beatles' recording sessions for *Sgt. Pepper's Lonely Hearts Club Band* (1967) were spread over nearly five months, during which McCartney invested a significant amount of time into his bass playing. Most notably, during these sessions, McCartney elected to overdub his bass parts after his bandmates had gone home. Free from distractions or other responsibilities, McCartney was able to construct melodic, intricately woven bass lines and, working with Emerick into the early morning hours, he would record take after take until he had played them perfectly. As Emerick recalls, these cloistered late-night overdub sessions likewise allowed him and second engineer Richard Lush to develop yet another method for recording McCartney's bass:

> It was Paul's desire for perfection that enabled me to finally come up with a recording technique that yielded the ultra-smooth bass sound he and I had been pursuing for years. The key was that we would move his bass amp out of the baffles and into the center of the studio; I would then place a microphone about six feet away. With the studio empty, you could actually hear a little bit of the ambience of the room around the bass, which really helped; it gave the sound a certain roundness and put it in its own space. The sound we crafted effectively transformed the bass from a supporting rhythm instrument into a lead instrument.[26]

By using a tube condenser mic to record McCartney's amplified Rickenbacker and then adding some light compression, Emerick had finally landed on what he later described as "the ultimate bass sound."[27]

McCartney's bass playing on the *Sgt. Pepper* sessions represented the culmination of years of musical growth, cross-cultural borrowing, collaboration, and studio experimentation. Positioned as a key focal point of nearly every track on the album, McCartney mixes and matches his earlier bass styles to suit each song. For example, on the single "Penny Lane" (1967), one of the first songs recorded during the sessions, he opens with a long descending walking bass line that begins in his Rickenbacker's upper register and spans two octaves; at the chorus, he gives the song a sense of stability by moving into the bass's lower register. Echoing his own earlier walking style on songs like "All My Loving" (1963), as well as Carol Kaye's recent playing on the Beach Boys' *Pet*

Sounds, McCartney uses his foregrounded bass line to give the recording a sense of contrast and forward motion. On "With a Little Help from My Friends," he instead focuses on developing his bass lines, playing an increasingly ornamented variation of his initial bass line on each subsequent verse. Perhaps the best encapsulation of his fully fledged bass style can be heard on "Getting Better," as he combines a massive leaping figure in the verses with a melodic bass line in the choruses that he again varies each time; furthermore, throughout the song, McCartney is extremely thoughtful about his note choices, as he crafts interesting and compelling bass lines by eschewing traditional root notes in favor of other chord tones or notes that are outside the chord altogether.[28] Describing this approach, McCartney later recalled,

> *Sgt. Pepper* ended up being my strongest thing on bass, the independent melodies. . . . On "Lucy in the Sky with Diamonds," for example, you could easily have had root notes, it would be like "Louie Louie" or something. Whereas I was playing an independent melody through it, a little tune through the chords that doesn't exist anywhere else, and that became my thing. It's only really a way of getting from C to F or whatever, but you get there in an interesting way.[29]

By dedicating his efforts to writing thoughtful, independent bass melodies, McCartney ultimately developed his own individual bass style, one that was indebted to his American influences but was no longer confined to simply imitating them. And although he continued to develop it throughout the remaining years of the Beatles' career—exemplified, most notably, by his melodic line on "Something" (1969) and his iconic bass riff on "Come Together" (1969)—as he acknowledges, the *Sgt. Pepper* sessions stand as the pinnacle of his bass playing.

In the mid-sixties, the Beatles established electric-guitar-based rock as the most commercially significant form of popular music. Their success and their musical innovations, both of which were built on their initial American influences, opened new doors for their immediate contemporaries and paved the way for subsequent generations of rock musicians. Following the Beatles' model as a self-contained band, many of the groups that became popular in their wake likewise elected to write and record their own material, a shift that greatly diminished the need for professional songwriters and session musicians. Most significantly for bass history, it was Paul McCartney who was perhaps most responsible for establishing the electric bass as rock's default low-end instrument. Although the instrument's popularity had been steadily increasing throughout the late fifties and early sixties, McCartney had something that previous bassists did not: visibility. Unlike the various American session bassists he emulated, he was, by 1964, one of the best-known musicians in the world. Even if it took him many years to develop his own approach to playing the instrument, his mere embrace of the electric bass played an outsized role in solidifying its position within the popular consciousness.

Bill Wyman, the Rolling Stones, and British R&B

The Rolling Stones were one of the first groups to capitalize on the British music industry's attempts to replicate the Beatles' success. Though the bands had much in common, the Stones ultimately found their own commercial niche by adopting a deliberately anti-Beatles image, depicting themselves as dangerous, overtly sexual "bad boys." Yet even before this image had firmly taken hold, British critics and fans had already come to understand the Beatles and Stones as emanating from separate traditions: whereas the Beatles' northern, beat style grew out of their eclectic embrace of a wide variety of American popular musics, the Stones more narrowly derived their style from the electric blues (or "R&B," as it came to be known in England). The Stones' fascination with American culture thus took on an even more overtly racialized dimension, as they consciously sought to recreate and embody the Blackness that they heard in the recordings of performers such as Muddy Waters, Howlin' Wolf, Bo Diddley, and Chuck Berry.

Bassist Bill Wyman's restrained approach was an essential element of the Stones' initial R&B sound. Unlike many other famous bass players, Wyman wholly embraced his supportive role as part of the rhythm section. He valued simplicity and precision above all else, and he was content to remain in the background, where he could serve the music and support his bandmates. The most distinctive component of his style was his pioneering use of a fretless electric bass, through which he attempted to emulate the upright bass sounds of American blues records. This section details Wyman's development as an electric bassist, the Stones' formation and early growth within the British R&B scene, and the complex racialized fantasies that animated both.

Wyman was born in 1936 to working-class parents from South London. Like many young Brits raised in the postwar years, he grew up listening to Radio Luxembourg, through which he developed an early interest in American popular music. Given his age, he was conscripted into the Royal Air Force in 1955 and stationed in Germany, where he first heard country and early rock 'n' roll through American Forces Network radio.[30] After being exposed to skiffle, he purchased an acoustic guitar and formed an amateur skiffle band with some of his squadmates. He returned from the service in 1958 to find the rock 'n' roll craze sweeping the UK, and within the span of a few months, he saw Chuck Berry perform in the film *Rock, Rock, Rock* (1958) and attended one of the few concerts Jerry Lee Lewis performed before he was kicked off his UK tour. In 1960, Wyman purchased his first electric guitar and formed a band called the Cliftons, which performed covers of American rock 'n' roll and soul songs for local dances. He was inspired to switch to electric bass after attending a gig by the Barron Knights in July 1961. As he recalled, "The sound of their bass guitar hit me straight in the balls. Staggered by its impact and the foundation it gave the sound, I realized immediately what was missing in the Cliftons. From that moment, I wanted to play the bass."[31] Though Wyman was initially drawn to the electric bass's presence and audibility, he also found the role of the bass player appealing: "It suited my personality. At twenty-four, I didn't see myself as an 'up-front' musician, singing or playing at the head of a band. I was always more attuned to the overall sound, the need for internal dynamics and *precision*. I'm an orderly person; bass playing suits my outlook."[32]

Once he had made up his mind to switch instruments, however, Wyman quickly found out that most electric basses were prohibitively expensive: "Fender had introduced the electric bass in 1951; by 1961, a new one [in England] cost around £200 ($560), and we only got £6 ($17) to £10 ($28) a night for playing. One day [Cliftons drummer] Tony Chapman said he knew a man with an old bass guitar to sell: all he wanted was £8 ($22.50). It was a battered old thing, but we pooled together and bought it."[33] As it turned out, that bass was a Dallas Tuxedo, a low-quality instrument that—with a retail price of around £25—was likely the cheapest electric bass then available in the UK.[34] To bring it up to a playable condition, Wyman decided to fully overhaul the instrument, and he asked friends to help him cut away its solid mahogany body, rewire its electronics, and add a second pickup (to accommodate his small frame and hands, Wyman also developed a technique, similar to Sonny Jay, in which he played his electric bass in an almost vertical position). Most importantly, he removed the instrument's frets, which were simply glued-on pieces of metal wire. As he explained to Andy Babiuk and Greg Prevost, "The frets were all worn and rattley on the strings, so I pulled them all out, meaning to replace them later . . . But when I played it [without the frets], it sounded like an upright bass. It was perfect!"[35] Having accidentally stumbled onto this distinctive bass timbre, he found that he liked the way it sounded and thus decided not to replace the frets. In so doing, Wyman became the first electric bassist of note to play a fretless instrument.

In December 1962, Wyman auditioned to play bass in a newly formed group called the Rolling Stones. For the audition, he brought his secondary bass, a Vox Phantom, a homemade bass amplifier, and an extra Vox AC30 amplifier.[36] But it soon became apparent that this was not necessarily a natural fit. The straitlaced Wyman was significantly older than the other band members, he had short hair, and he was married, all of which made him stand apart from the rest of the band and their bohemian lifestyle. More importantly, while they were impressed by his spare AC30, the band was dismissive of his fondness for white rock 'n' rollers like Jerry Lee Lewis and Eddie Cochran; he recalled them saying something to the effect of "We're a blues band, we're not a rock 'n' roll band. We don't play that shit."[37] This declaration confounded Wyman, who up to that point had not heard many blues records.

He was not alone in his ignorance. For if there were minor obstacles that impeded postwar British youth from accessing American rock 'n' roll, accessing R&B was far more of a challenge. In early sixties England, R&B was an extremely niche market. Only a small handful of contemporary blues releases were commercially available, and most had to be purchased from specialist record shops.[38] Older releases were even more difficult to find; often the only way to hear them was to import the records directly from the United States, a process that was expensive and, prior to 1959, often illegal.[39] Despite (or more accurately, because of) these difficulties, a small but fervent R&B fandom developed in London, initially as part of the city's thriving trad jazz scene. Like many young Brits, these fans were fascinated with the non-Britishness of American popular music, but as hipsters, they also prided themselves for being cultural outsiders with elite, discerning tastes. They were therefore drawn more to obscure blues records by African American artists, which according to Roberta Freund Schwartz, they could ultimately appropriate "as a signifier to define and reflect their sense of otherness."[40] Importantly, Andrew Kellett explains, "Britain 'got the blues' not through any sustained, direct contact with African Americans or American society but instead, indirectly and sporadically, through blues texts and artifacts that had been separated from their immediate sociocultural contexts."[41]

This separation, in fact, allowed British fans to identify with R&B even more strongly, as their general lack of knowledge about the blues made it easy for them to project their own values, beliefs, and racial fantasies onto the music. For example, because R&B records were not commercially successful in England, many British fans believed the music was *intended* to be anti-commercial. Even more troublingly, their idolization of African American musicians was derived from primitivist tropes that associated Blackness with poverty, authenticity, danger, and a naturally virile hyper-masculinity. As Hamilton notes, "British blues had a relationship with Black music that was deeply reverent but also fetishistic, the music's content often inseparable from its perceived danger and subversive liminality."[42]

Having been steeped in the music and rhetoric of the London R&B scene, the founding members of the Rolling Stones had developed into diehard blues purists. Even though Wyman was not, they decided to look past their initial misgivings and let him join the band, in part because they were impressed with the sound of his fretless bass, which he had brought to his second rehearsal with the group.[43] Their first task then was to give Wyman a crash course in what they considered to be "real" R&B. Describing this formative moment in the band's history, guitarist Keith Richards recalled:

> We went for a Chicago blues sound, as close as we could get it—two guitars, bass and drums and a piano—and sat around and listened to every Chess record ever made. . . . We'd all grown up with everything else that everybody had grown up with, rock and roll, but we focused on that. And as long as we were all together, we could pretend to be Black men. . . . And we didn't want to make money. We despised money, despised cleanliness, we just wanted to be Black motherfuckers. Fortunately we got plucked out of that. But that was the school; that's where the band was born.[44]

These first encounters with R&B left a lasting impression on Wyman, who began to strongly identify with the music himself. As he explained in the foreword to his own blues history book, "I was born in Southeast London just prior to the outbreak of WWII. Although my father worked, we were far from well-off; life was a struggle. Years later, I found that many Black musicians grew up in the Southern states of the US in difficult circumstances, something of a shared experience."[45] He goes on to acknowledge that he did not "share the experience of segregation and the problems of being treated as a second-class citizen" but concludes by saying, "When I was 11 years old I experienced one small instance of being on the 'outside.' I did well on my exams and was sent to a school where my cockney accent and my background made me different. . . . I didn't like it."[46] Richards's and Wyman's accounts testify to the complex racial fantasies that the Stones projected onto American blues records. On the one hand, invoking their own sense of class struggle and cultural alienation, they heard the music of presumably poor, working-class Black men as representing a sort of "shared experience." On the other, they were also clearly drawn to the subversive status of Blackness and used R&B as a type of minstrel mask through which they could act out their own imagined assumptions about what it was like to be "Black motherfuckers." The Stones thus subscribed to fundamental misconceptions about the music, most notably the belief that blues records represented "pure," unmediated expressions of Black experiences.[47]

In May 1963, just a few months after Wyman had officially joined the band, the Stones signed with a new manager, Andrew Loog Oldham, who had briefly worked with Brian Epstein to promote the Beatles. One of his first tasks was to have the band record a single that he could then shop around to British labels; they ultimately decided on "Come On," a Chuck Berry song that had yet to be released in the UK. With it, Oldham secured the band a recording contract with Dick Rowe at Decca. Still miffed about missing out on signing the Beatles, Rowe was desperate not to pass up another opportunity and decided to sign the Stones to an unusually favorable deal, which included a generous royalty rate, ownership of their own masters, and the freedom to record at whatever studios they wanted. Decca, however, decided to provide almost no media support for the band, leaving it to Oldham to drum up publicity. At first, he attempted to market the Stones similarly to the Beatles, but after the band fought back against this image, he changed course and decided to present them as a more dangerous, sexually charged alternative. This conception of the band entered the public consciousness after the success of their second single, "I Wanna Be Your Man" (1963)—which, ironically, had been written by Lennon and McCartney. As Oldham recalled,

I was promoting the idea that the Rolling Stones were "the group parents loved to hate," based on my belief that pop idols fall into one of two categories—ones you wished to share with your parents and ones you did not. The Beatles were accepted and acceptable, they were the benchmark and had set the level of competition. The Stones came to be portrayed as dangerous, dirty and degenerate, and I encouraged my charges to be as nasty as they could wish to be. At last, we had a genuine hit and I leveraged that mileage daily to embed the Stones in the psyche of the British press, like a grain of sand irritates an oyster.[48]

Combined with their growing fan base of teenage girls, the Stones' rebellious, "bad boy" image enflamed the conservative British press, whose condemnations in turn garnered the band even more publicity and young fans. As Hamilton demonstrates, these public condemnations regularly trafficked "in the language and imagery of racial threat" and were thus inextricable from the band's "purported connection to Blackness and racial transgression, both in a musical sense and a more vague, imaginative one."[49]

At the same time that the band was garnering commercial success and public notoriety, Wyman was developing one of the most atypical electric bass styles in England. Its primary component was his fretless Tuxedo bass, which he used on nearly all the Stones' recordings in this era (on the road, he played a Framus Star Bass to keep his fretless safe from damage or theft).[50] As he described his rebuilt Tuxedo, "It was a perfect instrument for playing blues, as it had more of an upright bass sound. I wanted that sound because all those records we covered, like Muddy Waters and Chuck Berry, had an upright bass played by Willie Dixon."[51] Through his careful study of Chess releases, Wyman had come to idolize Dixon and drew on the quasi-"upright" tone of his fretless bass to imitate Dixon's playing. What he did not know was that Dixon's bass lines were inherently studio creations that did not necessarily reflect the sound of the Chicago electric blues. For the Stones, who experienced American R&B primarily through the medium of recording, the timbre of Wyman's amplified Tuxedo bass thus gave their music a desirable sense of sonic authenticity; that authenticity, however, was still fundamentally a projection, one descended from their own inherent separation from the music's original cultural context.

In conjunction with the sound of his fretless bass, Wyman also adopted a deliberately modest, restrained approach to bass playing, which he attributed, in part, to the influence of Duck Dunn. As he explained, "I tried to play with the simplicity of Duck Dunn of Booker T.'s band . . . [H]e was there, he didn't stick out. He didn't get in the way of anybody. He just did the right things in the right spaces. His timing was perfect. That's what I tried to do, right from the very beginning and it worked for me—that's my style."[52] Unlike Paul McCartney, who eventu-

ally developed a more elaborate, melodic approach, Wyman unasham-
edly embraced his role as a member of the rhythm section. As he later
summed up his philosophy of bass playing: "Don't be busy, don't fill it
up. You're not a fucking lead guitarist, you're a bass player. Focus on
what the drummer's doing and play exactly with the drums, so you've
got a strong foundation there that's solid, that everybody else can build
upon."[53] Wyman's conviction that bass lines should be supportive but
not get in the way is clearly audible on the Stones' self-titled debut LP
(1964). For most of the covers, including their versions of Chuck Berry's
"Route 66" and Rufus Thomas' "Walking the Dog," Wyman sticks closely
to the original bass lines, adding rhythmic drive without overpowering
the other instruments. On the Stones' own "Little by Little," Wyman
plays a bit more ostentatiously, but it is still in service to the song's off-
the-cuff, manic energy.

By early 1964, the Stones' first EP and LP had both gone to No. 1 on
the UK charts. This success opened the band up to criticism from R&B
fans and the music press, as it not only contradicted their prior anticommercial stance but also meant that their covers of Black music were now
far outselling the originals. In response, Jagger wrote an infamous article
for *Melody Maker* in March 1964 outlining the band's position. He begins
by addressing the charges that the Stones are posers and sellouts and
instead highlights their insider knowledge:

> I get very brought down when I see a lot of people branding us as
> bandwagon boys, in it for the loot. At the risk of sounding big-headed,
> let me say this: I probably know more about the "real thing," as they
> call it, than the lot of them put together. . . . To the critics, then, who
> think we're a beat group who came up overnight, knowing nothing
> about it, we invite them to examine our record collection. It contains
> things by Jimmy Reed, Elmore James, [John Lee] Hooker, and a stack
> of private tapes by Little Walter. That's a good start.[54]

He then argues that the Stones should actually be *praised* for promoting
the Black musicians they are covering:

> My big point, I think, is that these legendary characters wouldn't mean
> a light, commercially, today, if groups were not going round Britain
> doing their numbers. It's made them all popular again—particularly
> [Chuck] Berry and [Bo] Diddley. We often announce a song saying:
> "This is a so-and-so number." Then the fans come up to us saying that

they've never heard of him. Well, that's at least a few more educated people in the world. If they put the original record out, it wouldn't sell much. But it's likely to spread more if we plug the song, isn't it? Can that be bad?[55]

To their credit, the Stones were forthright about the sources of their material; they also had a deep respect for Black musicians and would ultimately use their fame to reinvigorate the careers of many older blues artists, notably by bringing them on tour as opening acts.[56] Nonetheless, the defensiveness of Jagger's rhetoric highlights the group's inability to reflect on their own racial privilege: they saw themselves as R&B evangelists, rather than commercially successful white pop stars. They wholeheartedly believed that they were supporting Black music and simply could not understand why the critics—or even some of their idols—did not see it that way. For instance, in his memoir, Wyman details multiple chilly encounters between the Stones and Chuck Berry in this era, which left him fundamentally perplexed; as he writes, "Our relationship with the originators of blues and rock 'n' roll music should have been excellent. As genuine lovers of their art, we had substantially helped its recognition. . . . It seemed odd, therefore, that Chuck Berry continued to treat us with such disdain."[57]

In June 1964, the Stones set out on their first tour of the United States. Describing the band's mindset at the time, Wyman explained to *Rave* magazine, "We realised our crusade was well on the way to being won when we were offered an American tour. . . . It seemed that at last we were going to play for the people who really knew our kind of music!"[58] Except, as it turned out, America was not as they had imagined it to be. As in England, the white, teenage audiences they were playing for had very little knowledge of the records they were covering, and since the band had only a few minor hits in the States, the crowds were sparse and disappointing. In a last-ditch effort to rebuild morale, Oldham arranged for the group to spend two days recording at Chess in Chicago, the very studio where so many of their Black heroes recorded.[59] As Wyman recalled,

It was a milestone event for us to be in an American studio, recording on 4-track. We knew the sound we were getting live in clubs and concerts was not what came across on the records we had cut in England. People were not used to that kind of roughness: a really, good funky American feel was what we were after. . . . When we recorded at Chess, [producer] Ron Malo knew exactly what we wanted and got it almost immediately. We felt we were taking part in a little bit of history there.[60]

For the Stones, this trip to Chess was more than just a pilgrimage, it was an attempt to position themselves within the lineage of Black blues traditions. It was also a way to add yet another sense of sonic authenticity to their recordings. For example, on the sessions Wyman played his Framus Star Bass, which he had been using on the road. Contrary to British studio practices, he recorded his bass direct, which gave it a slightly distorted timbre. Although DI bass technology was not available in England at that time, it had become increasingly common in American studios, especially those that specialized in recording Black music, such as Motown and Chess. For the price of a moderate studio rental fee, Wyman and the Stones suddenly had access to the "American" bass sound that Paul McCartney and the engineers at EMI were still having trouble replicating. This sound, in turn, allowed Wyman and the Stones to better imitate the Black records that they were covering, such as the Valentinos' "It's All Over Now" (1964). Released by Sam Cooke's SAR Records just a few weeks prior to the Stones' trip to the United States, the Valentinos' version featured a DI'd electric bass line that, apart from the lead vocals, was the most prominent feature of the recording. For the Stones' version, although Wyman's playing is less rhythmically snappy than the original, the tone that he elicited from his own DI'd bass made this recording the closest any British band had yet come to capturing the sound of a contemporary American R&B record. Yet, "It's All Over Now" also demonstrates the complexities and limitations of the Stones' R&B evangelism. The original version of the song had been only a moderate hit, but the Stones' rendition made it to No. 26 in the United States, and in the UK, it became their first No. 1. Likewise, their cover of Irma Thomas's "Time Is on My Side" (1964), which was also recorded during the Chess sessions, became their first Top 10 US hit and effectively opened the door for the band's future success in America. No matter how much the Stones may have earnestly seen themselves as promoting and celebrating Black music, ultimately, they were still the ones who reaped the lion's share of the attention and profits.

The peak of the Stones' status as R&B torchbearers came in November 1964, with the release of their fifth UK single, "Little Red Rooster," a slow Chicago electric blues number with implicitly sexual lyrics. Written by Willie Dixon and originally recorded by Howlin' Wolf in 1961, the song fit the Stones' self-professed status as outsiders. As Richards recalled,

When we put out "Little Red Rooster," a raw Willie Dixon blues with slide guitar and all, it was a daring move. . . . We were getting no-no's from the record company, management, everyone else. But we felt we were on the crest of a wave and we could push it. It was almost in defiance of pop. In our arrogance at the time, we wanted to make a statement. . . . See if you can get that to the top of the charts, motherfucker. . . . Mick and I stood up and said, come on, let's push it. This is what we're fucking about.[61]

The press coverage surrounding the single likewise fed into the Stones' image as rebellious, authentic, and anticommercial. The *Beat Instrumental* review stated, "This disc . . . is going to test the Stones' popularity to its fullest extent, because their version of the number is out-and-out authentic R&B with hardly a trace of commercialism."[62] *Record Mirror* similarly noted that the single "would probably prove uncommercial if tackled by any lesser group" but ultimately praised it for being "more bluesy, more 'coloured' in feel, more way out than anything they've done yet on a single."[63] In *NME*, Derek Johnson was even more explicit in identifying the recording's sonic association with Blackness, noting, "What makes it so *colourful* is the throbbing and pulsating backing—with electronic pulsating gimmicks, a reverberating bass, and a steadily strumming shuffling rhythm."[64] As Johnson describes it, part of what makes the song so sonically "Black" is Wyman's "reverberating" bass line. Though he may not have known it, what Johnson is describing here is the sound produced by Wyman's fretless Dallas Tuxedo, which the bassist consciously used to mimic the timbre of Willie Dixon's upright bass on the original record. Within less than a month of its release, "Rooster" became the band's second No. 1 hit in the UK. In the Stones' biography, this moment is traditionally presented as a triumph over the establishment in which the band found mainstream success without having to compromise their R&B authenticity. More likely, however, the single's success was a result of the Stones now being established pop stars, rather than antiestablishment blues purists. As the press reports noted, there were over two hundred thousand preorders for the single.[65] Thanks to the popularity of the band's previous covers, the Stones had developed an enthusiastic fan base that was willing to support their music, even before they had heard it.

After 1964, the Stones decided to focus more on writing and recording their own material. At its core, this change in direction was financially motivated, as Oldham had explained that they could keep a larger

Figure 35. Framus ad congratulating Bill Wyman for being voted No. 1 "Bass Guitarist" of 1965. Note how he holds the instrument nearly vertically while playing. (Source: *Beat Instrumental*, January 1966.)

share of the profits from their recordings if they didn't have to pay outside songwriters. Despite years of public agonizing from the band regarding their own authenticity, their evolution from blues cover band to self-contained rock band was relatively seamless, as their mainstream fan base had always been pop idol fans, rather than R&B purists. Thus, in 1965, three of the Stones' originals—"The Last Time," "(I Can't Get No) Satisfaction," and "Get Off of My Cloud"—made it to No. 1 on the UK charts, with the latter two also going to No. 1 in the United States. "Satisfaction," now considered the band's most iconic song, captures the Stones in this moment of transition. The song is strongly indebted to the Stax/Southern soul sound of artists such as Otis Redding, and Wyman uses the opportunity to emulate Duck Dunn. Following Dunn's model, Wyman adds a sense of contrast in the intro and choruses by playing an ascending figure on his fretless bass against the descending section of Richards's guitar riff; in the verses, he then switches to a simple rhythmic root-fifth bass pattern that locks in with the drums to provide energy and momentum. With "Satisfaction," the Stones performed and composed in the *style* of the Black artists they admired rather than covering their recordings. In essence, they had found a way to maintain the purported "Blackness" of their music, image, and reputation, without having to materially support Black songwriters such as Willie Dixon or Otis Redding. If "Rooster" had in some ways signaled the British public's acceptance of the Chicago electric blues style, its success was ultimately the beginning of the end for the British R&B boom. By the time "Satisfaction" was released in mid-1965, British popular music had changed so much that, according to Sean Lorre, "the term R&B as it was used in prior years ceased to be a useful genre designation."[66]

Today, Wyman is the least celebrated member of the Rolling Stones. Likewise, his bass style, when it is discussed, tends to be unfavorably compared to Paul McCartney's. But he and McCartney had much in common: as children in postwar England, they grew up fascinated with American culture, they both developed their own bass styles by copying American records, and, as the bassists in two of the most successful bands of the mid-sixties, they both were responsible for solidifying the electric bass within the public consciousness. Musically, they simply took different paths, with Wyman instead demonstrating that electric bassists could play an important role without having to be virtuosos. If modern commentators may have difficulty accepting the value of his simple, restrained bass lines, it is important to note that audiences at the time had no such hangups—this is demonstrated most clearly by a *Beat Instrumental* reader's poll that named Wyman the best bass guitarist of 1965 (see Figure 35).[67] For Wyman, his bass style was an homage to the blues musicians that he and the Stones loved and, to be fair, never stopped promoting. Yet, in the end, this love will forever be complicated both by the problematic misconceptions on which it was based and the radically unequal benefits that the Stones accrued from copying Black music.

John Entwistle and the Who: Rock's First Bass Virtuoso

In his memoir, Who singer Roger Daltrey recalled, "In our world, the Beatles were the first pop band. The Stones were their antithesis. We had to find our own niche, something fresh."[68] As their slightly younger contemporaries, the Who benefited from the doors that the Beatles and

Stones had opened in the British music industry. Yet, as Daltrey acknowledges, those bands' continued success also meant that, if the Who were ever to stand out, they would need to develop their own distinct public persona. The foundations for this persona came through their formative ties to the mod subculture, an outgrowth of the London R&B scene. Drawing on the mod image, the Who built their own fan base through their onstage expressions of masculine aggression and violence, which eventually devolved into the destruction of their own gear at the end of every set—a ritual that John Dougan notes, "made for great publicity and cemented the band's reputation as the most exciting (and potentially dangerous) live act in England."[69]

Bassist John Entwistle was the Who's anchor. Amid the chaos of the band's live performances, he stood calmly off to the side of the stage, filling in the gaps and holding everything together. But his subdued demeanor belied the intensity of his bass playing: loudly and forcefully positioned within the Who's sound, Entwistle augmented the band's hard-driving approach through his own dazzling displays of musicianship. At a time when McCartney and Wyman were still playing relatively simple bass lines, Entwistle was using his immense, virtuosic technical abilities to turn the electric bass into a lead instrument. This section details how he came to develop this style through his early career with the Who, as well as how his approach fundamentally reshaped the sound of the electric bass.

Entwistle (1944–2002) was the only member of the Who to have had formal musical training. Raised in West London, he began taking piano lessons at the age of seven, and by eleven he had expanded to playing trumpet and French horn. As a young teenager, he played in trad jazz bands, including a short-lived group with his schoolmate Pete Townshend called the Confederates. Through these bands, Entwistle had his earliest experiences as an improviser and songwriter. In the late fifties, thanks to the broadcasts he heard on Radio Luxembourg, Entwistle developed a love of American rock 'n' roll, particularly Duane Eddy's twangy guitar instrumentals. He then decided, around 1959, that he would rather play rock 'n' roll and set out to find a more suitable instrument. After a few brief attempts at snare drum, he ultimately settled on the electric bass, which he had recently seen at a local teen dance. Playing bass seemed like a good practical choice, as he recalled, "Everybody I knew played guitar, and everybody needed bass players, and they just weren't about."[70] But there were other factors that piqued his interest as well. First, since Duane Eddy tended to play on the lower strings of his guitar, Entwistle had incorrectly assumed that his hero was a bass player. Second, he was impressed by the instrument's size (he later half-jokingly wrote that he "chose the bass because, bigger than the guitar, it was a much larger phallic symbol").[71] Third, he was impressed by its sound and playability: "Soundwise, I liked the sort of sinister low drone that a lot of bands had at the time. Also, it had only four strings, so I figured it would be easy to play and a good way to get into a rock band, because no one wanted a trumpet player."[72]

Having decided to switch instruments, however, he found, as Wyman had, that he could not actually afford an electric bass:

> I began saving and eventually made a pilgrimage to Harry's music shop in Hammersmith, where I'd bought my latest trumpet. . . . I now informed [Harry] of my new love for the bass guitar. "Well, mate, you've got three alternatives," he said. "There's the Höfner violin bass, fifty quid; a Framus Star bass, at sixty; or a Tuxedo, thirty quid and a piece of shit." I moaned that these were all too expensive for me. "Then there's only one thing you can do, son," Harry said, picking up a little blue box from under the counter. He opened the box and inside was a small, chromed pickup . . . Hanging from it was a short, white lead with a jack plug. "Buy a lump of wood," Harry continued. "I'll fret the fingerboard for you and stick this on—£2 10s! There's a timber yard on the corner. Tell the geezer there it's for a guitar; he's done it before."[73]

Procuring some cheap pieces of wood that the owner of the timber yard cut for him, Entwistle returned to the music shop, where Harry added frets to the instrument, as well as a bridge, tailpiece, pickup, and strings. Though the instrument barely held together, all that mattered was that it (mostly) worked. "I could forgive all its faults," Entwistle recalled. "It was a bass guitar, and mine, all mine."[74] When this first bass ultimately fell apart, he built another out of stolen parts. This process inadvertently instilled in Entwistle a lifelong fascination with bass technology, which led him to constantly experiment with modifying his basses—even the factory-made ones.

With his new homemade bass and a cheap amplifier, Entwistle began to learn rock 'n' roll songs with Townshend, especially the latest offerings from the Shadows. But, as he had anticipated, being one of the few bass players in the local scene soon led to other performance opportunities, such as in the summer of 1961, when guitarist Roger Daltrey persuaded

Entwistle to join his band, the Detours; a few months later, at Entwistle's suggestion, Townshend was also brought into the group. The Detours were a dance band. They primarily covered the hits of the day, including Cliff Richard and the Shadows, Buddy Holly, Roy Orbison, and Del Shannon, but also played some country and trad jazz as well. Sometime in late 1962 or early 1963, the Detours had a formative experience opening for Johnny Kidd and the Pirates. They were so impressed by Kidd's showmanship and the aggressive, menacing music produced by his band that, as Daltrey recalled, the Detours then "became a Pirates clone."[75] Notably, they rearranged their lineup to match Kidd's, with Daltrey on vocals, Entwistle on a new Fender Precision Bass, Doug Sandom on drums, and Townshend as the group's sole guitarist. After the Beatles' breakthrough, the Detours started incorporating more beat material into their sets, but quickly decided to focus instead on R&B.

The Detours' fascination with African American music was complicated and multifaceted, even within the band itself. Daltrey, like the members of the Rolling Stones, identified with the music as representing a sort of shared, working-class experience. For Townshend, who had recently enrolled at Ealing Art College, the primary advantage of R&B was its outsider status and its popularity among his discerning, hip classmates. Though their conception of the music was still problematically racialized, the band's interest in R&B appears to have been more aesthetic than cultural: they were drawn to the music's blustering bravado, its emphatic rhythms, and its distorted guitars, more than an imagined conception of the people who created it. Through their covers of John Lee Hooker, Jimmy Reed, Sonny Boy Williamson, Bo Diddley, Howlin' Wolf, and James Brown, Daltrey recalled, "We were finding ways of expressing our aggression. The phrasing of things, the punch of the chords, more onbeat than swing. Our word for it was drive. Let's drive, we used to say before a gig. . . . I used to feel like we were trying to drive our music through the audience to the back wall."[76] For the Detours, R&B became the vehicle for a new, more aggressive performing style, which in turn allowed them to stand out among the ever-growing roster of young British guitar groups.

1964 was the year when everything changed for the band. In February, they learned that another group was already called the Detours, and so they decided to change their name to the Who. Shortly thereafter, their lineup was solidified when Keith Moon officially became their new drummer. And in May, the band came to the attention of Peter Meaden, a twenty-two-year-old publicist who had briefly helped Andrew Loog

Oldham promote the Stones. Meaden was a "mod," part of a loose British youth subculture that had begun to coalesce in London in the early sixties. The mods prioritized style and attitude above all else, performing a subversive working-class rebelliousness by wearing expensive clothes, driving Italian scooters, taking amphetamines, and getting into fights. Like other young hipsters of the time, the mods were attracted to the music of lesser-known African American artists and therefore became a part of the growing London R&B scene. But mods were not blues purists. Instead, while they could appreciate the Chicago electric blues, they were more interested in contemporary soul styles, such as those heard on Tamla-Motown records (which at that time were still relatively unknown in England). As a tastemaker in the scene, Meaden saw an opportunity for a band to represent mod culture and, after hearing the Who play live, he decided they were the ones to do it. With their consent, Meaden completely rebranded the group. He had them cut their hair, add more Tamla-Motown covers to their setlists, and made them dress in the latest mod fashions (which Entwistle apparently despised). Meaden also had them change their name to the High Numbers, a mod slang term, and arranged for them to record their first single, "Zoot Suit" backed with "I'm the Face," both of which were rip-offs of American R&B songs with new, mod-inspired lyrics.[77] Although the single ultimately flopped, Meaden succeeded in establishing the High Numbers as the preeminent band in the mod scene, giving them both a distinctive image and a zealous fan base. At the end of June 1964, the High Numbers began a residency at the Railway Hotel, where they were eventually discovered by two young filmmakers, Kit Lambert and Chris Stamp, who became the group's new managers. By the fall, the band had changed their name back to the Who, and Lambert and Stamp set out to get them a new record deal.

Even at this point in the Who's career, Entwistle had already developed into a formidable and idiosyncratic bass player. His approach had stemmed from his initial boredom with playing a "background instrument" and his desire to take on a more prominent role in the music.[78] He thus set out to turn the bass into a solo instrument, a move that was facilitated by the Who's sparse instrumentation. As he explained, "The fact that the Who were only two melodic instruments with drums and a singer left a lot of space for me to fill in. I found myself playing bass, rhythm, and lead."[79] Given the freedom to experiment, Entwistle consciously elected not to directly emulate other bassists (with perhaps the exception of James Jamerson) and instead drew on his prior musical experience to forge new techniques: "One day I had a brainstorm: I figured the piano had made my hands supple, the trumpet put speed in my right hand, and the French horn did the same for my left, so why not use all 10 fingers on the bass? I started slowly and eventually built up my speed and endurance."[80] As he was developing his dexterity as a bassist, Entwistle was also acquiring new gear that gave his bass playing an innovative edge. In 1964, he exchanged his Fender Precision Bass for an Epiphone Rivoli that he then exchanged for a Rickenbacker 4001S.[81] That same year he acquired one of the first Marshall amplifiers, a 50-watt bass amp with four 12-inch speakers that made him the loudest member of the band. This provocation caused Townshend to get himself a louder amplifier, which then led to Entwistle getting a second Marshall, and the two continued on and on in an arms race for sonic supremacy. The ultimate effect was that, as John Atkins notes, "the Who used twice as much equipment as was customary and played exceptionally loudly."[82] The extreme volume of Entwistle's bass, especially in the small confines of London clubs, produced a literally deafening sound, one that would've been viscerally felt by his audience. With Townshend beginning to experiment with feedback and destroying his guitars on stage, Entwistle enacted his own sonic assault on the audience, one that kept the music from devolving into complete incoherence while also bolstering the band's expressions of masculine aggression.

Through a recording deal with producer Shel Talmy, the Who recorded their first single, the Townshend-penned "I Can't Explain," in early November 1964. After its release by Brunswick the following month, the song became the band's commercial breakthrough, eventually reaching No. 8 on the UK singles chart. Over the course of 1965, thanks to their televised performances on ITV's *Ready, Steady, Go!* and the BBC's *Top of the Pops*, as well as the heavy airplay of "I Can't Explain" on pirate radio stations, the Who grew from a local London club band to a national sensation.[83] Their popularity was further bolstered by the British music press, which regularly highlighted their violent and destructive stage shows with headlines such as "The Who: A Disturbing Group," "The Who: The Group That Slaughters Their Amplifiers," and "The Who Use Force to Get the Sound They Want!!"[84] At the same time, Entwistle continued to refine his approach to the bass, focusing not just on his technical abilities but on the overall sound of his instrument. As he later recalled,

When I began experimenting, I still had a thuddy, boomy bass sound, but I remember a turning point a few years later. We had our first hit record with the Who, "I Can't Explain," and showed up at a big hall for a concert, only to find the place empty because the promoter had forgotten to promote it. So we decided to make use of the situation by having a rehearsal. I had a Rickenbacker bass and Marshall amps at the time, and after we started playing, our manager came up to me and said, "It's all very well, you playing that fast, but I can't hear the notes you're playing in the back. Why don't you try putting a bit of treble on it?" I'd always been tempted to turn up the treble but didn't dare, because bassists just didn't do that. So I opened up the treble on my amp and bass and started playing like Duane Eddy. That was the turning point.[85]

Combining his speed, dexterity, and volume with this new emphasis on the higher frequency spectrum, Entwistle had discovered the overdriven bass sound that would become his sonic signature. With its added clarity and harmonic richness, he could now hold his own against Moon's manic drumming and Townshend's feedbacking guitar. It subsequently became a key component in the aesthetic of collective chaos that defined the band's music (as Entwistle described it in 1975, "We just play as much as we can. Once the Who gets on stage, everybody starts playing a solo straight away").[86]

By mid-1965, however, the Who were already distancing themselves from mod culture. "We think the mod thing is dying," Townshend explained to *Melody Maker*. "We don't plan to go down with it, which is why we've become individualists."[87] Drawing on his art school training, Townshend instead began to describe his band's music as "pop art," associating it with a style of visual art that celebrated mass media, mainstream popularity, mass production, and youth culture. As part of this shift, the Who abandoned the mod visual style and ironically embraced British nationalist symbols (including the union jack and military regalia). In line with the burgeoning cultural renaissance of "Swinging London," the band adopted an iconoclastic—yet nonetheless distinctly British— posture that Peter Stanfield describes as intentionally "nonconformist, insolent, and disrespectful."[88] In so doing, they rebranded their aggressive performance style as a type of high art *and* as a repudiation of societal complacency, both of which the band enshrined in their fourth single, "My Generation" (1965).

As Townshend described it to the press, "My Generation" was "really pop-art. I wrote it with that intention . . . the lyrics are 'young and rebel-lious.' It's anti middle-age, anti boss-class and anti young marrieds."[89] This sense of youthful rebellion, however, was not simply confined to the song's lyrics, it was also embedded in the sound of the music itself, most notably through the bass. Although Entwistle is prominently featured throughout the entire song, his shining moment comes at the end of the second chorus, when he lets loose with a now-legendary bass solo. Fast and technically challenging, the solo comprises quick-fire rhythmic passages that incorporate bends, slides, hammer-ons, and eighth-note triplets (which he played via three-finger flourishes with his right hand). It is truly a virtuosic feat, one that deliberately broke all the standard conventions of electric bass playing. In other words, it perfectly matched the song's overall attitude of nonconformist defiance.

Yet, the eternal irony of the "My Generation" bass solo is that—despite being perhaps the most recognizable bass solo of all time—Entwistle was disappointed with nearly every aspect of it. For the initial takes of the song, he performed the solo on a newly acquired Danelectro Longhorn Bass, which had a short scale length and thin neck that made it easier to play the quick, elaborate passages he was experimenting with. More importantly, the Longhorn was also one of the few electric basses on the market to feature roundwound strings, which gave the bass a much brighter sound than traditional flatwounds.[90] "They were so thin," he explained, "they sounded just like a piano, an unbelievably clear sound."[91] These strings, however, were prone to breaking, and since they could not be purchased on their own, in order to replace one, Entwistle had to purchase a brand-new instrument. As he recalled, "I went through three [Longhorns] during the recording of 'My Generation.' In the end, they decided to record it again and the last string had busted, and there weren't any more Danelectros in the country. So I went out and I bought a Fender Jazz Bass [Figure 36]. I put the trebliest set of strings I could find on it, which were tapewound LaBella strings. And I played the solo on that."[92] Entwistle was also perpetually frustrated that the Who's records never really captured the rich bass sound that he used on stage, noting, "Most of the time, [producers and engineers] didn't know what to do with the top end of the bass, they were frightened of pushing the bass up too loud in case it clouded the guitar out. So, in the end, they'd be using half of my sound, which wasn't even a good bass sound."[93] For "My Generation," the final indignity came when he was forced to subdue his playing: "I'd play a fast solo, and they'd say, 'Well, that didn't really record very well, can you play something a little simpler?' [The solo on the record] was about the most

Figure 36. John Entwistle and his Fender Jazz Bass pictured on the back of the Who's *My Generation* LP, which was released on December 3, 1965, the same day as the Beatles' *Rubber Soul*. (Source: Brunswick, 1965.)

complicated thing they'd let me put on it."[94] In the end, Entwistle felt that the "My Generation" bass solo was in fact an oversimplification, one that was more of a representation of the constraints placed on him in the studio than of his actual abilities as a bassist.

Although the Who were now becoming known for their original material, they still often emulated Black American music, especially artists associated with Tamla-Motown—whose material they continued to cover in their live sets and on their LPs. Taking inspiration from the Miracles' "The Tracks of My Tears" (1965), Townshend adapted the Motown style for the Who's next single, "Substitute" (1966). Unlike the Rolling Stones, however, Townshend claims to have had a certain self-awareness about what exactly he was doing; describing his demo for the song, he recalled that "I heard in my own voice the tumult of a young man playing a role, uneasily, repackaging Black music from America, relying on gimmicky outfits, and pretending to be wild and free."[95] A similar discomfort is audible within Entwistle's bass line, which he admits was adapted from James Jamerson's playing on the Four Tops' "I Can't Help Myself (Sugar Pie, Honey Bunch)" (1965).[96] In a conscious attempt to avoid sounding "too Motown," Entwistle decided to use a short-scale Gibson EB-3 with roundwound strings and to play with a pick, which together gave his bass sound a distinctive trebly growl.[97] He also added yet another bass solo, although this time he had to sneak it on the record. As he explained,

"Because we were recording and mixing it virtually live, I thought, yeah, this should be a bass solo, so I turned my volume up and they couldn't mix me out."[98] Ultimately, "Substitute" reached No. 5 on the UK pop singles chart, placing the Who, along with the Beatles and Stones before them, within a tradition of postwar British musicians who found commercial success by emulating Black American musical styles. And while Townshend and Entwistle may have felt uneasy about their cultural borrowings, the ultimate effect was the same. In the UK, Tamla-Motown records had only recently begun to break into the mainstream, meaning that that Who's version of the Motown sound ultimately outsold the originals: "The Tracks of My Tears" only made it to No. 9 on the UK pop charts, while "I Can't Help Myself" peaked at No. 23.

If Entwistle had proven that the electric bass was a viable lead instrument, he nonetheless continued to seek out other potential basses and bass timbres. In between his Fender Jazz Bass and Gibson EB-3, he had experimented with a Fender VI and a Mosrite Ventures Mark X, but starting in 1966, he returned to using Fender Precision Basses (including multiple ultrarare "slab" style Precisions) as his default instruments.[99] That same year, he also collaborated with the UK string maker Rotosound to produce a commercial set of roundwound bass strings. As he recalled,

> It was in 1966 and I was looking for that Danelectro sound again. I tried everybody's strings but the E and the A's just didn't work. It was the same with Rotosound but there was something about them that was almost there but not quite. To solve the problem, I got in touch with James How and told him his D and G strings were great, but the E and A didn't vibrate properly. He told me to take my bass along to Rotosound and have some strings made until they got it right. After a couple of hours, we realised that the problem wasn't in the wire winding, but in the core of the string. You could see that the strings vibrated in a big circle and that was wrong; the core needed to be thicker. We also made the overall gauges a bit heavier. . . . Those strings, the RS 66 sets, were the first that vibrated properly other than the Danelectros.[100]

The development of the Rotosound '66 Swing Bass string set represented a pivotal moment in electric bass history. Up to that point, flatwounds had long been the standard string type for electric basses, as most manufacturers still thought that bassists wanted to explicitly mimic the thuddy, quick-decaying timbre of an upright. Rotosound and Entwistle's roundwound strings therefore explicitly defied the conventional wisdom of the day. By treating the electric bass as a stand-alone instrument, the RS66 string set pioneered a new bass sound that was bright and punchy, with noticeably greater clarity and sustain—in short, one that allowed the electric bass to stand out in the music. This, in many ways, is Entwistle's most lasting legacy: after he and others initially popularized them, roundwound bass strings eventually became so accepted that by the eighties they had become the default string type for *all* electric basses. Entwistle's personal quest to develop his own unique electric bass sound, in the end, fundamentally redefined the sound of the instrument as a whole.

Compared to the Beatles and the Stones, it took the Who much longer to find success in the United States. Their first notable stateside appearance was at the Monterey International Pop Festival in June 1967. They followed this with a ten-week North American tour and their aforementioned appearance on *The Smothers Brothers Comedy Hour*. These efforts garnered them their first Top 10 US hit single with "I Can See for Miles" (1967), which appeared on their post–*Sgt. Pepper* concept album *The Who Sell Out* (1967). That same year, Entwistle constructed his own "Frankenstein" bass out of the surviving parts from six smashed basses, and this became his default touring and recording bass for the next four years. The Who's big commercial breakthrough in America came with the release of their rock opera, *Tommy* (1969), after which they had a series of Top 10 LPs, including *Live at Leeds* (1970), *Who's Next* (1971), and *Quadrophenia* (1973).

If, as celebrities, McCartney and Wyman did more to increase the electric bass's public visibility, it was Entwistle that ultimately most shaped the future of bass playing. His constant tinkering inspired a fundamental shift in the sound of the instrument, and his intricate lead lines went on to inspire multiple generations of rock bassists. He also never stopped expanding his technical abilities, and he perpetually experimented with new ideas and new approaches (see, for example, his playing on "Won't Get Fooled Again" or "The Real Me"). Reflecting on his career shortly before his death, Entwistle stated that he "would like to be remembered as someone who helped change the face of bass guitar and being probably the only bass guitarist that hasn't been copyable."[101] Both claims would be difficult to dispute.

Conclusion

The Beatles, the Rolling Stones, and the Who were all raised in the post-war era and were drawn to American popular music, especially African American music, which they subsequently appropriated as the foundation for their innovations. Moreover, through their own success "invading" the United States, they ultimately sold those styles back to American audiences, who ironically began to hear them as British in origin. Despite these similarities, however, their individual styles and values were shaped by their formative years operating within different musical contexts. As Hamilton demonstrates, it is these differences that matter most, as it would be difficult to understand why each band developed as it did without a sense of where exactly they had come from.

If all three bands' cultural origins were complex and at times problematic, their subsequent influence on the shape of bass history is indisputable. In the mid-sixties, the visibility of Paul McCartney and Bill Wyman embedded the electric bass within the public consciousness—so much so that in the wave of amateurism they both inspired, the instrument was understood to be a necessary component of the self-contained rock band. At the same time, by developing new virtuosic approaches to the electric bass, British musicians like John Entwistle (followed shortly by Jack Bruce, John Paul Jones, Chris Squire, and others) fundamentally expanded the bass player's potential role as a soloist. Through their combined efforts, these musicians collectively solidified the electric bass's position as popular music's default low-end instrument.

Ain't It Funky Now

No history of the electric bass would be complete without a discussion of funk. Popularized in the middle to late sixties, funk replaced traditional pop song forms with a new emphasis on complex, interlocking rhythms. Prioritizing danceability above all else, funk both magnified and elevated the rhythm section, pushing it beyond the traditional confines of simply providing support and accompaniment. As part of this aesthetic shift, the electric bass took on a substantial role: it became funk's focal point, the primary driver of the groove.

This interlude chronicles the development of funk bass playing across James Brown's recorded output in the sixties and early seventies. As the music's founding father and star performer, Brown codified funk and, with the help of his various bass players, established it as one of the most culturally significant styles of Black popular music. Building on the work of Allan Slutsky, Chuck Silverman, RJ Smith, and Anne Danielsen, I reconstruct Brown's rotating lineup of bassists and contextualize their individual contributions within the larger trajectory of Brown's career—from his early successes in rhythm & blues, to his crossover appeal at the end of the Civil Rights Movement, and finally to his becoming an outspoken advocate for Black pride. As I demonstrate, the funk bass style evolved across these eras through a series of productive (if thorny) collaborations between Brown and his musicians. In the end, Brown's bassists crafted syncopated, danceable bass lines that played a key role in his continued commercial success, and this success provided a platform through which their approach to bass playing became iconic and influential. The innovations they developed together would, in turn, shape the direction of popular music for decades to come.

Brown's Early Bassists and the Birth of Funk

James Brown's early career was informed by his wide-ranging musical interests. When he was young, he listened to jazz, blues, gospel, rhythm & blues, and mainstream pop, and he was especially captivated by performers like Louis Jordan, who not only played music, but put on a show. As a teenager, he sang in a gospel quartet that accompanied themselves on homemade instruments, with Brown using a washtub bass that he had taught himself to play.[1] In the mid-fifties, like many young Black musicians, Brown transitioned from gospel to rhythm & blues. He joined a vocal group called the Avons, which became the Flames and then eventually (following a suggestion from Little Richard) the Famous Flames.[2] In 1956, the Famous Flames were signed to a subsidiary of Cincinnati-based King Records. For their initial recordings, they used King's in-house session musicians, including upright bassists Clarence Mack, Carl Pruitt, and Edwyn Conley. The group's first touring bassist was Alabama-native Bernard Odum (1932–2004). "When James hired me in 1956, he didn't have a bass player," Odum recalled. "His band at the time was just piano, sax, guitar, and drums. I was the fifth man."[3] As an early adopter of the Fender Precision Bass, Odum added a robust low end that anchored the band's live performances. He became a permanent member of the Flames in 1958, and in December of that year, he recorded his first hit with the group, "I Want You So Bad" (1959), a ballad that peaked at No. 20 on the *Billboard* rhythm & blues Chart. This was followed by other rhythm & blues hits, including "(Do the) Mashed Potatoes" (1960), "Think" (1960), and "Bewildered" (1961).

Following his idols, Brown dedicated himself to putting on the best show possible, which he believed required absolute perfection from his musicians. To prevent them from becoming complacent, he would also regularly bring in new players. In 1960, Brown hired Hubert Perry, formerly of the Four Steps of Rhythm, as his new electric bassist and convinced Odum to switch over to vocals. "I became a Flame for about a year," Odum recalled. "It was kind of an emergency thing. James needed another singer, so I helped out. He always knew I could sing 'cause in the early days . . . I used to play bass and sing background at the same time. Then after I stopped being a Flame, I took off for a year."[4] With Odum's departure, Perry became the group's sole bassist. Today, he is most remembered for his appearance on the *Live at the Apollo* LP (1963), a massive seller that reached No. 2 on the *Billboard* album chart. Featuring pleading ballads, instrumental bridges, and up-tempo dance numbers, *Live at the Apollo* stands as a monument to Brown's early sixties style and captures Perry's tasteful bass playing. It also, however, preserves Brown's notoriously high standards as a bandleader: on "Lost Someone," at approximately five minutes and fifty-seven seconds into the recording, Perry noticeably flubs a turnaround; moments later Brown ad-libs to the crowd, "You know we all make mistakes sometime," subtly acknowledging the error and letting Perry know that his pay would be docked for it.[5] Odum subsequently rejoined the band in early 1963, working alongside Perry. For Brown, having two electric bassists allowed him to keep his music fresh by constantly varying who played on each song. But it was also a power move that made it clear to both musicians that they were expendable. After Perry left in the summer of 1963, he was replaced by bassist Sam Thomas, who went on to appear with Brown and the Famous Flames in *The T.A.M.I. Show* concert film (1964).

The foundations of funk can be traced back to two of Brown's mid-sixties singles: "Out of Sight" (1964) and "Papa's Got a Brand New Bag" (1965). As Brown recalled, "I had discovered that my strength was not in the horns, it was in the rhythm. I was hearing everything, even the guitars, like they were drums. . . . What I'd started on 'Out of Sight' I took all the way on 'Papa's Bag.'"[6] Together, these two songs popularized a new rhythmic approach within rhythm & blues, one that used syncopated, off-beat electric bass lines to drive the groove.[7] As biographer RJ Smith describes it, "The bass was doing things it hadn't done before in pop music and was perhaps the most active part of either song."[8] These bass lines' precise origins, however, are difficult to parse. For instance, both Odum and Thomas were in Brown's band at the time, and sources disagree about which of the two bassists played on these recordings. This issue of authorship is further complicated by Brown's off-the-cuff approach to writing and recording: typically, he began by humming, grunting, or patting out phrases to his musical director, who interpreted and arranged those ideas into basic parts for the musicians; the musicians then put their own spin on their parts, and the whole band adjusted things through trial and error as the final arrangement coalesced in the studio. Whatever their genesis, these bass lines produced compelling, danceable grooves with widespread appeal: "Brand New Bag" became Brown's biggest hit to date, reaching No. 1 on the R&B chart, No. 8 on the mainstream pop chart, and garnering the singer a Grammy Award for Best Rhythm & Blues Recording. Featuring Thomas's replacement, David "Hooks" Williams, on bass, Brown's next proto-funk single, "I Got You (I Feel Good)" (1965) was even more successful, spending three weeks at No. 3 on the pop chart. By the end of 1965, Brown had secured his position as a successful crossover artist whose music appealed to Black and white listeners alike.[9]

But "Brand New Bag" also overlapped with some of the Civil Rights Movement's darkest moments: the song was recorded in February 1965, the same month that Malcolm X had been assassinated and mere weeks before the Selma to Montgomery marches; the Watts Uprising came less than a month after the single's release in July. Although it was not written in direct response to these events, Brown understood "Brand New Bag" as being inseparable from the wider context of Black social and political life. As he later explained, "To me, the song represented so many things at once—the sound of my people, the beat underneath their social contribution, the rise of Black music into the mainstream, the continuing struggles and victories of the Civil Rights Movement, and just about every aspect of the culture that was happening at the time."[10] Funk, at its inception, was thus both a musical and cultural statement, one that deliberately foregrounded Blackness. As Rickey Vincent describes it, Brown's new style "was vivid, urgent, and dignified. It was a scorching expression of the Black man's soul, just when the entire world was listening in anticipation."[11]

Brown inaugurated funk as a stand-alone style with his 1967 No. 1 rhythm & blues hit "Cold Sweat," which definitively features Bernard Odum on electric bass. What set "Cold Sweat" apart from Brown's prior efforts was the way it abandoned traditional musical forms. As Anne Danielsen notes, in "Brand New Bag," "There is still a song, in the sense that something—a melodic line, a chord sequence—is allowed to spread out on top of the rhythmic foundation. The division of labor is clear: the vocal resides on top, guitar takes care of the middle registers, and drums and bass provide rhythmic drive 'down low.'" By contrast, on "Cold Sweat,"

> Only fragments remain. All of the instruments, including vocals, work more or less in the same way, forming small but significant rhythmic gestures that are linked in every direction. The groove has become an intricate fabric of sharp percussive sounds in which one sound brings on the next: the texture of the music has changed from horizontally divided layers of sound to a rhythmic patchwork.[12]

Additionally, the song's extended verses are built on just a single, static chord.[13] Unable to rely on the direction and contrast provided by a standard harmonic progression, the musicians instead generate interest through their use of intricate, interlocking polyrhythms. Together, they emphasize the first downbeat (or "the One") of their two-bar cycles before splintering off into the contrasting rhythmic fragments that Danielsen describes. On "Cold Sweat," Odum's bass line strongly emphasizes the One, conveying a sense of rhythmic and harmonic stability that he then destabilizes through his use of syncopation and dissonance. Prominently positioned in the overall mix, Odum contributes to the groove through this alternation of tension and release. This approach, which he employed again on "I Got the Feelin'" (1968), would become the basic model for all funk bass playing.

Funk's Shifting Racial Politics

Funk's success placed Brown and his band at the vanguard of Black popular culture. Yet this was not an easy position to maintain, especially with a new generation of Black activists entering the political arena. Dissatisfied with the compromises and slow progress of the Civil Rights Movement, many young African Americans began to call instead for Black Power, emphasizing the need for racial pride and self-determination. In the context of this new political landscape, Brown's crossover success seemed out of step with the times, a perception that was further exacerbated by his work with white musicians.

In 1967, Brown discovered an all-white soul band in Cincinnati known as the Cincinnati Kids.[14] Impressed by their musicianship, Brown signed the group to his company, James Brown Productions, and renamed them "the Dapps." By August, he was regularly using them to record new music, both for himself and his associated acts. Brown's first hit with the Dapps came with "I Can't Stand Myself (When You Touch Me)" (1967). For most of the recording, electric bassist Tim Drummond (1940–2015) plays a restrained four-note vamp; but, two minutes and forty-eight seconds in, Brown starts to call him out by name ("Tim / Help me out, Tim / Let me hear you walk a little bit, Tim"), after which Drummond improvises a short funky bass solo. "He was a playing cat," Brown recalled, "good God a'mighty, I never could get enough of Tim."[15] At Brown's request, Drummond left the Dapps and became Brown's touring bassist—making him the first white musician to play in Brown's band.

Drummond's presence on stage didn't sit well with some members of Brown's audience. According to Smith,

> At the Howard Theatre, Brown received a telegram backstage that said, "You got a white man playing with you, a Black man needs a job." In Chicago, word circulated that Drummond better not play. Brown didn't get the message, though, and when a worker at the Regal Theater gestured for his bassist to get off, Brown threatened to cancel the show. [Brown] had been a symbol of Blackness, and just that quick he was taking flack for being insufficiently Black.[16]

Brown continued to employ Drummond despite these criticisms. On April 5, 1968, the day after the assassination of Martin Luther King Jr., Brown famously performed at the Boston Garden; through a last-minute deal with government officials, Brown agreed to televise his concert, a move that temporarily de-escalated the city's racial tensions.[17] Surviving footage shows Drummond standing stage right playing a Vox Cougar Bass.[18] Eleven days later, Drummond went into the studio with Brown and recorded "Licking Stick-Licking Stick," a laid-back funk single that reached No. 2 on the rhythm & blues chart. In June, Brown traveled to Vietnam to perform for the troops but was only allowed to bring a handful of his musicians. As a statement of racial solidarity, he chose to take Drummond. Brown later wrote that "Tim . . . felt that soldiers seeing a white man and a Black man sharing the same stage together was a good thing, and I agreed."[19] While the shows were a success, Drummond contracted hepatitis while overseas and complications with his recovery ultimately forced him to stop touring with Brown a few months later.[20]

Drummond's departure coincided with a significant shift in Brown's music and public persona toward the new politics of Black Power. Drummond was replaced by "Sweet" Charles Sherrell (1943–2023), a Black multi-instrumentalist from Nashville. As a young man, Sherrell had learned to play trombone, trumpet, drums, and a little guitar. He began to make a name for himself in the Nashville rhythm & blues scene in 1966, after returning home from serving in Vietnam. His first big break came the following year, when he found out that a local band called Johnny Jones and the King Kasuals had been hired to support Jackie Wilson and Aretha Franklin on an upcoming R&B package tour. Hearing that they needed a bassist, Sherrell went to a pawnshop and bought his first electric bass, a Kay, for $69. He got the gig, and with the money he earned from the tour, he ultimately upgraded to better equipment, exchanging his used Kay for a brand-new Fender Precision Bass (although, working with Brown, he later switched to playing a Vox Delta IV). Brown and Sherrell met sometime around July 1968. As Sherrell explained, "I was introduced to James Brown by a couple of Nashville acquaintances, including trumpeter Waymon Reed. [Brown had] heard about this guy who plays almost every instrument, and while [he] was in town we met."[21] Brown offered him a job, and after taking some time to consider the offer, Sherrell agreed to join the band. "Funnily enough, with James I originally played drums, not bass," he recalled. "The reason I ended up picking up the bass was because James's bassist at the time, Tim Drummond, became ill. The next thing I remember, I had to go to LA. I got there at 2 a.m. and we immediately drove to the studio to record 'Say It Loud—I'm Black and I'm Proud.' . . . That was the first song I recorded with James, in 1968!"[22]

If "Brand New Bag" and "Cold Sweat" had established funk as a Black-centric musical style, "Say It Loud—I'm Black and I'm Proud" combined that style with explicit declarations of Black pride and self-sufficiency: as Brown sang, "Now we demand a chance to do things for ourselves / We're tired of beating our head against the wall / And working for someone else." Whether by design or not, "Say it Loud" stood as a rebuttal to the naysayers who had criticized Brown for not being Black enough. It also solidified the perception of funk as a musical expression of unapologetic Blackness. As Brown recalled, "The song cost me a lot of my crossover audience. The racial makeup at my concerts was mostly Black after that. I don't regret recording it. . . . It was badly needed at the time."[23]

Musically, by that time, Brown's style of interlocking, cyclic funk was already well established, and Sherrell understood his role in the collaborative process. "Most of the ideas came from James Brown," Sherrell recalled. "He was a good dictator more than a musician. He would make different sounds and we were musically educated enough to turn the sounds he made into music. Myself, the drummers, the guitarist, we [were] like mechanics on a Rolls Royce. . . . Knowing how to make it run smooth."[24] Sherrell's impeccable timing and nuanced approach to syncopation added a newfound rhythmic precision to Brown's late-sixties hits, including "Give It Up or Turnit a Loose" (1969), "I Don't Want Nobody to Give Me Nothing (Open Up the Door, I'll Get It Myself)" (1969), "Mother Popcorn (You Got to Have a Mother for Me)" (1969), "Ain't it Funky Now" (1969), "Funky Drummer" (1970), and "Brother

Rapp" (1970). Looking back, Brown later noted that Sherrell "hasn't gotten the credit as a player that he should have. A lot of the stuff that Bootsy Collins and some other bass players did later . . . Sweets did first."[25] Thanks in part to Sherrell's bass playing, Brown had reestablished himself as a national symbol of Black pride. Nonetheless, he continued to be a difficult man to work for and, after one too many disputes over pay, Sherrell quit the band in January 1970.

Bootsy Collins and Avant-Garde Funk

Two months after Sherrell left, Brown's remaining musicians protested against his leadership and demanded better pay and working conditions. In response, Brown secretly sent his private jet to pick up a group of young Black musicians from Cincinnati that had been working with James Brown Productions. They were then rushed to meet Brown at his next show, although they had no idea what was going on until after they arrived. As their bassist, Bootsy Collins (b. 1951), recalled,

> James asked us to come in the dressing room. We saw our heroes, Maceo [Parker], "Pee Wee" Ellis, Jimmy Nolen, Bernard Odum, Alphonso [Kellum] and [Fred] Wesley, as we were going in, and they weren't looking too cool . . . We thought something was wrong, because they had always welcomed us in the past. All of a sudden, they weren't talking to us. . . . We knew something was up, but we didn't know what. After we started talking to James Brown, that's when we found out that he wanted us to be [his] band. We were like, "Oh." Then it all started making sense.[26]

Even if it made them uneasy, Collins and his bandmates jumped at the opportunity to work with their hero. Brown then unceremoniously fired all the musicians that had revolted and simply walked onstage with this new band and played the set. In the end, this last-minute change in personnel would ultimately push Brown's funk in a new direction.

For Collins, working with Brown was a major turning point in his career. In a single day, he had gone from performing at mostly empty clubs in Cincinnati to playing major venues on an international tour with one of the country's biggest stars (Figure 37). Brown, for his part, rechristened the band "the JB's" and outfitted them with professional equipment, including a brand-new Fender Jazz Bass. Collins's style, however, was quite different from the bassists Brown was used to working with. Unlike Odum, Drummond, or Sherrell, Collins had a distinctive, virtuosic fingerstyle approach inspired by Jimi Hendrix's guitar playing. "Hendrix is the one I was looking at," Collins explained. "I was freaked out about what he was doing, and I thought, Wow—maybe I can do that with the bass."[27] According to Tony Bolden, "Hendrix's artistic break-throughs, Black hippie persona, and penchant for flaunting presumed contradictions provided younger musicians such as Collins with a new model for avant-garde aesthetics," one that represented creative free-dom and "an utter refusal to genuflect to societal norms."[28] However, Collins's embrace of this deliberately nonconformist style initially posed a problem for Brown. As the bassist recalled,

> I thought I was doing something different . . . I [didn't] want to be like . . . other bass players, just holding the foundation down. I wanted [to] play a lot of things. [But Brown would say,] "Son, listen to me now. I'm the Godfather of Soul . . . You got to stop doing all them things and just give me the One." So when I started doing that, he started to like it and I could tell. So I figured, if I could give him this One and play all them other things . . . I think he'll like me. So I started giving him that One that he needed and playing what I felt.[29]

Ultimately, Collins was forced to temper his expansive technique and avant-garde sensibilities to fit within Brown's established funk formula. Nonetheless, even in its reduced form, Collins's looser, more improvisa-tory bass style still radically transformed the sound of Brown's music.

Take, for example, Collins's first hit with Brown: "Get Up (I Feel Like Being Like a) Sex Machine" (1970). Throughout the song, Collins makes sure to hit the One, but he also varies his bass lines constantly, trying out new ideas on nearly every repetition. Operating at a sixteenth-note level, his lines are both fast moving and intricately designed. As Danielsen describes the song's groove: "The combination of [Collins's] soft sound, smooth phrasing, and clearly drawn sixteenths is extraordinary and fits extremely well with [Jabo] Starks's dynamic drumming: the groove is full of small, well-articulated gestures completing one another in a float-ing curtain of smoothly accented straight sixteenths."[30] Collins, in other words, added an unprecedented rhythmic complexity to the song—and through the platform he now had as Brown's bassist, to funk as a whole.

Collins's complex funk bass playing would go on to fuel more of Brown's hits, including "Super Bad" (1970), "Get Up, Get into It, Get Involved" (1970), and "Soul Power" (1971). But his tenure with the band

Figure 37. Bootsy Collins and James Brown Performing in Italy in 1971.
(Source: Video Beat.)

would ultimately be short-lived. After eleven months of near-constant touring, rehearsing, and recording, he quit Brown's band in search of a better outlet for his experimental, avant-garde funk style. As he remembered, "We started to feel like we were kind of trapped. . . . We couldn't dress the way we wanted to dress. We were taking acid and doing all these crazy things of the day, but we were playing with James Brown. . . . It was great . . . but . . . the way the trend was going, we started feeling like we were missing it."[31]

After Collins's departure in early 1971, Brown hired bassist Fred Thomas, a more restrained player who specialized in simply holding down the groove. Thomas then went on to become a fixture in Brown's band, working with him for the next thirty years and playing on multiple hits, including "Hot Pants" (1971), "Make It Funky" (1971), "Get on the Good Foot" (1972), and "The Payback" (1974). At the same time, Brown once again began hiring multiple bass players. "He used to bring in all kinds of guys," Thomas recalled. "Sweet Charles and Jimmy Mack were in and out. I think Bernard Odum even came back a couple of times."[32] With Thomas and the others, Brown's band reverted to a bass style that aligned most closely with his late-sixties hits. Yet, by the end of the seventies, this approach was already old-fashioned. Building on the slap bass technique popularized by Sly & the Family Stone's Larry Graham—as well as Collins's own innovative work with Funkadelic, Parliament, and Bootsy's Rubber Band—subsequent bassists had developed styles that extended funk bass playing well past its mid-sixties origins.

Conclusion

Scientific studies have shown that the tactile sensations of bass-heavy music actively stimulate bodily movement.[33] Robust bass lines, heard by our ears and absorbed through our bodies, simply make us want to dance. Funk was far from the first style to exploit this phenomenon. But, by combining prominent electric bass lines with syncopated grooves, funk established a new and highly influential form of dance music that would go on to inspire countless subsequent styles, including disco, hip-hop, jazz fusion, electronic dance music, and even some forms of rock. The bass-driven grooves that are now nearly ubiquitous in today's popular music can, in many ways, be traced back directly to Brown's bassists. Collaborating with Brown at key moments in his career, Bernard Odum, Sam Thomas, David "Hooks" Williams, Tim Drummond, Sweet Charles Sherrell, Bootsy Collins, and Fred Thomas defined, promoted, and expanded the funk bass style. In so doing, their collective innovations fundamentally redefined the electric bass's role in popular music.

EIGHT | The Lead Instrument

San Francisco and Psychedelia

There is perhaps no better testament to the electric bass's omnipresence in late-sixties rock music than Michael Wadleigh's *Woodstock* (1970), the acclaimed documentary that preserves performances from the 1969 Woodstock Music and Art Fair. Woodstock was a landmark moment in popular music history, and, in part thanks to the success of Wadleigh's film, today it is remembered as both the high point of the counterculture and the most famous of the decade's rock festivals. Notably, throughout the film, there is not a single upright bass in sight. Instead, it is electric bass players who occupy its stages and appear on its soundtrack. And through their volume and their playing styles, these bassists are no longer simply providing support, but instead lay claim to their own featured positions in the music. This chapter focuses on two American bassists who performed at Woodstock: Jefferson Airplane's Jack Casady and Sly and the Family Stone's Larry Graham.

Like the counterculture itself, Jefferson Airplane and Sly and the Family Stone both came out of the San Francisco Bay Area. There, far from the major music centers of the day, hundreds of bands developed and thrived, supported by enthusiastic local audiences that appreciated live music and were open to creative experimentation. As the archetypal hippie band, Jefferson Airplane developed a free-form rock style that allowed bassist Jack Casady to become a skilled melodic improviser. Sly and the Family Stone, by contrast, were initially a dance band that merged the sounds of funk, rock, and Top 40 pop. Working within this hybridized musical space, their bassist, Larry Graham, came to popularize a unique, percussive style, now known as "slap bass." As I argue, thanks to their freedom to explore new sounds, techniques, and technologies, both Casady and Graham respectively developed innovative approaches that treated the electric bass as a featured lead instrument. The different paths they forged, in turn, allowed for electric bassists in the seventies (and beyond) to imagine a more expansive role for themselves, one that was no longer relegated to the background.

San Francisco and the Counterculture

In the forties, the state of California began a plan to construct a series of freeways in San Francisco, including one near the cross streets of Haight and Ashbury. Although years of vigorous protests from residents ultimately forced the state to abolish this plan, the mere threat of freeway construction triggered a mass exodus of homeowners out of formerly affluent neighborhoods. By the early sixties, with property values having plummeted, the Haight and its surrounding areas included many empty, multiroom houses that could be cheaply rented. Seizing the opportunity, a wave of largely white, middle-class young people moved in, and thanks to the area's relative affordability, many were able to dedicate their time and energies to creative pursuits. It was these low rents that would give rise to the hippies and the San Francisco counterculture of the late sixties.

As Nadya Zimmerman demonstrates, the counterculture is often overly romanticized and erroneously depicted as a radical, oppositional political movement.[1] Instead, she argues, the hippies were not unified by any clear set of goals or beliefs, but rather were a pluralistic community loosely based around a shared desire to operate outside the mainstream. Through their emphasis on personal and communal creativity, as well as their self-conscious attempts to be different, the hippies helped foster a vibrant local music scene centered around the city's ballroom venues, such as the Fillmore and the Avalon. Combining music, dancing, light shows, visual art, and hallucinogenics, these ballrooms gave bands a nurturing, supportive space to experiment musically. Together, these bands crafted a loose style of music that came to be known as the "San Francisco Sound," or, when paired with their British counterparts, psychedelia.

Unexpectedly, these band's deliberately eccentric, psychedelic sounds and images ultimately led some of them to find mainstream commercial success. By the mid-sixties, in search of the next "new thing," multiple major labels began to sign San Francisco bands and promote their music nationally. The release of this music coincided with the media's extensive, panic-filled coverage of the hippies and their unabashed drug use, which further publicized the scene. These and other developments allowed the San Francisco bands to reach a wide national audience, and as their music grew in popularity, so too did their formerly avant-garde musical innovations. Of these innovations, perhaps none would be more influential than the belief that electric bassists should take on a more prominent role in the music.

Jack Casady and Jefferson Airplane

Jefferson Airplane was the first band of note to emerge from the San Francisco scene. Thanks to the success of the hit singles "Somebody to Love" and "White Rabbit," support from critics, and the media's extensive coverage of the band, Jefferson Airplane became the first of the American psychedelic bands to become embedded in the public consciousness. Drawing on the band members' eclectic backgrounds, the Airplane's music was a hodgepodge of multiple stylistic influences— pop, classical, folk, rock, rhythm & blues, Indian music, and more. At the heart of their sound was Jack Casady's (b. 1944) inventive approach to electric bass playing, which by the late sixties, encapsulated a new emphasis on improvisation and tonal exploration in rock music.[2]

Casady's development as a musician was shaped by his upbringing in Washington, DC. Through his father, a dentist and electronics hobbyist, Casady was exposed to an extensive collection of jazz and blues records and, as he got older, he frequented local jazz clubs to hear musicians such as Charles Mingus and Scott LaFaro—two bassists that he would later cite as major influences. In his early teen years, he also developed an interest in rhythm & blues and soul music and would regularly go to the Howard Theatre to hear the latest Black pop acts, including Ray Charles, Little Richard, B.B. King, Bo Diddley, and Hank Ballard. He started playing guitar at age twelve, and by fourteen he had formed a rock 'n' roll band called the Triumphs, with Casady on lead guitar and his older brother's friend, Jorma Kaukonen, on rhythm guitar. Using fake IDs, the Triumphs got work in DC dive bars, where they performed Buddy Holly, Elvis Presley, Carl Perkins, and Gene Vincent covers. After Kaukonen left town in the summer of 1959, Casady became a musician-for-hire in the DC nightclub circuit, where he would perform five sets a night, four nights a week for adult audiences.

Casady recalls that, by 1960, most bands in DC included electric bass players, and it was that summer that his friend Danny Gatton (a well-known guitarist in the scene), convinced him to also try out the instrument. As he explained to me,

> [Danny] said, "My bass player is sick. . . . Do you know a bass player?"
> I said, "No, I don't." And he called me back and said, "Jack, I'm stuck
> here. I've got a good gig. It's for six weeks of the summer. Why don't
> you play bass?" I said, "Listen, I've never played bass before." He said,
> "How hard can it be? It's only got four strings!"[3]

Borrowing a Precision Bass from Gatton, Casady spent a week or two learning the instrument, which proved to be just enough time for him to successfully manage the gig.

As a young jazz fan, Casady was well aware of the electric bass's perceived status as a "bastard" instrument, and he specifically recalls reading the critics' condemnations of Monk Montgomery (condemnations that Casady himself dismissed, especially after he heard the Montgomery Brothers perform live).[4] Through his gig with Gatton, Casady discovered not only that he liked the sound of the bass, but also that electric bassists were in much higher demand locally. He therefore decided to switch instruments, procuring his own Fender Bassman amplifier and a first-generation Fender Jazz Bass (which better fit his smaller hands). Yet he soon ran into the problem that had haunted many early electric bassists: the speakers in his amplifier kept blowing out. To solve the issue, he and his father modified the Bassman, taking it apart and building a new, larger cabinet for it—his father's philosophy, he notes, was: "If something doesn't work right, you make it better."[5] As they had with John Entwistle, these sorts of early experiments instilled in Casady the idea that he could and *should* be modifying his gear to meet his creative needs.

Casady recalled that when he first switched instruments, "there weren't a lot of role models of the bass guitar. . . . It was really pretty much open territory."[6] He did, however, remember James Brown's band as a significant formative influence:

> I go and hear James Brown . . . around that period of time where they
> put out *[Live] at the Apollo.* He was at the Howard and I would hear the
> [electric] bassist that would be playing with him. That really changed
> the sound of a lot of the rhythm & blues because that sound was so
> articulate, and of course it was a bass *guitar,* it wasn't a bass *violin.* So,
> therefore, you got different kinds of notes and syncopation, and [the

electric bass] started to play a different role with the drummers than the standup bass [had].[7]

Through his exposure to Brown's music, Casady came to realize that a prominent electric bass line could fundamentally shape the sound of the entire band. Now that he was playing the instrument himself, this lesson served him well, especially as he began to be hired for gospel and rhythm & blues gigs (including a notable stint backing up Little Anthony and the Imperials). These gigs, he told me, "were educational in getting a feeling for a certain kind of music and . . . as a white kid . . . I got exposed to a lot more of the African American music in Washington DC at that time than I [otherwise] would have."[8]

After high school, Casady became a full-time musician, although his progress as a bass player was stymied by his increasing dissatisfaction with having to play covers. Within a few years, he had become so discouraged that he had largely abandoned playing bass and instead was teaching music lessons and taking college classes to avoid military service. His life changed forever when his old bandmate Jorma Kaukonen invited him to play bass in his new group, Jefferson Airplane. With the incentive of a guaranteed income of $50 per week and, more importantly, the promise that they would be writing and performing original material, Casady agreed to join them in San Francisco.

At that point in time, Jefferson Airplane had only been together for a few months.[9] They had initially been formed by singer/guitarist Marty Balin to act as the house band for a new club he was opening called the Matrix. Influenced by the folk-rock boom of mid-1965, Balin sought a diverse set of musicians to join the group, such as singer/guitarist Paul Kantner and singer Signe Toly. Eventually, the group also came to include Kaukonen on lead guitar, Jerry Peloquin on drums, and Bob Harvey on bass. The band's debut coincided with the Matrix's opening on August 13, 1965. An early write-up from the influential jazz critic Ralph J. Gleason triggered a bidding war to sign the band, and a little more than one month after their first gig, Jefferson Airplane were already in LA auditioning for multiple industry executives, including Phil Spector. In the end, they turned down deals with Fantasy, Elektra, and Capitol (then home to both the Beatles and the Beach Boys) to sign with RCA for a $25,000 advance, but not before shaking up their rhythm section, with drummer Skip Spence replacing Peloquin and Casady replacing Harvey.

Jefferson Airplane recorded its first album, *Jefferson Airplane Takes Off*, in LA between late 1965 and March 1966. Prior to the sessions, Casady had bought a new Fender Jazz Bass and, in search of a wider tonal palate, had an extra split pickup from a Precision Bass installed in it close to the neck. With the ability to blend all three pickups, he now had access to more timbral variety than likely any other electric bassist in that era. Yet, as would become a common problem for the San Francisco bands, the Airplane had difficulty capturing their live sound within the more controlled environment of the studio. As he told Gleason a few years later, "I've always had a terrible time trying to get a bass sound on an album. . . . Because of the way I play . . . I play lots of notes, and . . . our music . . . has lots of stuff going on in it . . . [I]t's very hard to get tone and clearness and I just had a terrible time."[10] *Takes Off* was released on August 15, 1966, just ten days after the Beatles' *Revolver*, and while both signaled a turn toward psychedelia in the mainstream, the Airplane's album ultimately flopped. Despite its limited impact nationally, however, *Takes Off* sold quite well within San Francisco, and combined with their many performances within the city's newly repurposed ballrooms—most notably the Fillmore, run by promoter Bill Graham, who also briefly served as the band's manager—Jefferson Airplane solidified their local reputation as San Francisco's preeminent rock band.[11]

The growth of the San Francisco scene coincided with wider attempts to depict rock music as a legitimate art form. These two developments were inherently linked, as critics like Gleason often described the scene—and Jefferson Airplane, in particular—as proof that rock had outgrown its teen-pop origins. Although Casady told me that the band was never invested in these arguments, such depictions nonetheless benefited their career. For example, Jefferson Airplane's reputation as an innovative folk-rock band allowed them early entry into "serious" festivals, such as the 1966 Berkeley Folk Festival and the 1966 Monterey Jazz Festival (where they performed alongside another electric group, the Butterfield Blues Band).[12]

On January 14, 1967, a daylong celebration of the counterculture was held in San Francisco's Golden Gate Park. Known as the "Human Be-In," the event attracted over twenty thousand attendees. As Zimmerman notes, "Like a sit-in, love-in, bed-in (or even laugh-in), organizers asked participants to *be in*, to be present in the moment, to be involved, to be individual now."[13] At the event, former Harvard psychologist Timothy Leary famously encouraged the assembled crowd to "tune in, turn on, drop out," while amateur chemist Owsley "Bear" Stanley (who was also the Grateful Dead's sound engineer) distributed large quantities of his homemade LSD to the attendees. The event also featured musical performances by many of the San Francisco psychedelic bands, including

Jefferson Airplane. Given its size, its pro-drug philosophy, and its deliberate repudiation of mainstream American values, the Be-In was heavily covered by the mainstream media, often with an overtly disdainful tone. For instance, on February 6, *Newsweek* ran a multipage, color photo spread on the event that presented the hippies as earnest, spontaneous, loving joy-seekers while also noting, "In the Haight-Ashbury district, seriously disturbed people and teen-age runaways make up a sizable fringe of the Movement. Equally unsettling is the incipient anti-intellectualism of the hippies—to say nothing of the dangers of drug-taking."[14] Predictably, the media's sensationalized attempts to warn young people about the dangers of hippie culture had the opposite effect: it popularized the image of San Francisco as the seat of hippiedom and enticed even more young people to seek out the city and its apparent delights.

Five days prior to the *Newsweek* article, Jefferson Airplane released its second LP, *Surrealistic Pillow*. The album featured the band's latest additions, singer Grace Slick, who had replaced Toly a few months prior, and drummer Spencer Dryden. When Slick joined the band, she brought with her two songs that she had been performing with her previous group, the Great Society: "Somebody to Love" and "White Rabbit"— both of which were recorded for the new album. Of the two, "Somebody to Love" is more of a straightforward rocker. Built around Slick's distinctive vocal delivery, the song is powered by a driving rhythm section, with Casady performing variations of a two-bar riff through each verse. His playing is quick and intricate, incorporating hammer-ons, chromatic passing notes, and rhythmic syncopation. In the choruses, he switches to a countermelody that plays off the song's hook before briefly adding in some triple stops (chords played on three strings simultaneously). Overall, it is an impressive bass line, one that highlights how much Casady's style had evolved since the band's first album. As he recalled,

> I wanted to put an aggressive bass line in there in order to move that song, to compete with [Paul Kantner's] twelve-string guitar but also to match up with what Grace was doing with her vocal. So I was playing to Grace . . . [and] Jorma was playing his lead lines and rhythm in there, so I was able to just roll those notes around. I'd start in the low end and just move up through the range of the bass guitar and then come back down for the hooks.[15]

"Somebody to Love" undeniably encapsulates the hard-driving sound of San Francisco psychedelia. Yet, by itself, Casady's bass line also appears indebted to the performance strategies popularized by mid-sixties funk and soul bassists. James Jamerson, for example, often added chromatic passing tones to his Motown bass lines; Duck Dunn similarly emphasized the push-and-pull, tension-and-release approach that Casady uses to differentiate the song's verses and choruses; and Casady's two-bar riff, with a strong emphasis on the downbeat followed by offbeat rhythmic syncopation, resembles early James Brown-style funk (when I asked him about these potential connections, Casady agreed and noted that his approach to bass playing has always, in some ways, been informed by his formative years playing rhythm & blues in DC).[16] The sound of Casady's bass was also indebted to contemporary LA studio practices; as he explained, "For 'Somebody to Love,' I was using my fingers, but producer Rick Jarrard eventually insisted I use a pick because he needed me to get a 'crisper' sound. He was used to working with Carol Kaye and Joe Osborn and the pick-type tone they got. I vehemently resisted at first, but I finally gave in and used a pick."[17] Similar to "Somebody to Love," on "White Rabbit," Casady plays a two-bar riff centered around the bass's middle register. Rather than R&B, here he draws on the tropes of classical music, specifically the quasi-Spanish rhythmic figures of Maurice Ravel's *Bolero* (1928).[18] "It was a fluke," Casady says. "I just started playing it. I think in rehearsal we started it off, and it just sounded good."[19] In effect, Casady's use of the *Bolero* rhythm, combined with his repeating, chromatic half-step ascents, augments the song's trippy lyrics, giving the recording a hypnotic, hallucinogenic feel. Ultimately, both songs resonated with audiences: "Somebody to Love" made it to No. 5 on the Hot 100, while "White Rabbit" reached No. 8; *Surrealistic Pillow* itself stayed on the album chart for a total of fifty-six weeks, peaking at No. 3. This commercial success solidified Jefferson Airplane's reputation as the cultural ambassadors of the San Francisco rock scene, and of the hippie counterculture more broadly. (For example, on April 4, 1967, Casady hosted Paul McCartney in San Francisco, where the two musicians compared bass styles and went on a tour of the Haight-Ashbury; in exchange, McCartney gave him an acetate of "A Day in the Life," from the Beatles' own psychedelic work-in-progress, *Sgt. Pepper*.)[20]

The summer of 1967—the "Summer of Love"—saw tens of thousands of young people flock to San Francisco to be a part of the hippie movement. Culturally, the largest and most important event of that summer was the Monterey International Pop Festival, a three-day music festival held in mid-June. With "Somebody to Love" having recently cracked the Top 10, Jefferson Airplane were by far the festival's biggest stars, and both their performance and Casady's bass playing were widely praised. According to critic Phil Elwood,

The Airplane is one of the few rock groups to have emerged in the last year who understand that the way to avoid the monotony of a hard two or four beat, running forever, is through syncopation. Their bassist, Jack Casady, sets up a furious undercurrent of runs and stop-time accented riffs which keeps the Airplane's sound always changing no matter how straight the front line or lyric sound.[21]

Monterey Pop also represented a milestone in rock culture, as the festival (and D. A. Pennebaker's popular concert film documenting it) served to introduce the Who, Janis Joplin, Ravi Shankar, and Jimi Hendrix to mainstream American audiences.[22] Its success would also inspire a slate of other, late-sixties rock festivals, including Woodstock.

After the Monterey Pop Festival, British blues rock bands like Cream and the Jimi Hendrix Experience began to regularly perform in San Francisco, and their extended rock improvisations were highly influential on the city's psychedelic scene. But this approach had also been inspired by the atmosphere of the San Francisco ballrooms themselves. As Cream electric bassist Jack Bruce recalled,

> The Fillmore was great in San Francisco, and obviously 1967 was the year to be there, really. . . . [T]his was when we first started doing the extended improvisations in Cream. It was new to the band. Up to this series of gigs, we just played little songs live, very short: three, four, five minute versions of the songs. . . . [W]e were fed up with doing that, and the audience was so great at the Fillmore, they were all so out of it, all sort of laidback, and would say, "Just play!" . . . So we just started playing, jamming as it were, and that turned into what we became known for.[23]

For his part, Casady saw Cream as both a challenge and an inspiration, as he told Gleason: "The Cream set all the rock 'n' roll bands in San Francisco up. Made 'em listen. 'Cause here they were getting a little too much confidence, as far as I was concerned, 'cause this English group came in and just blew them off the stage."[24] In response, he and Kaukonen decided to push Jefferson Airplane to adopt a heavier sound and head in a freer, more improvisatory direction.

This new direction necessitated that Casady further hone his skills as a bassist. As he explained to *Jazz & Pop*, "The way I see it right now . . . I've got to have drive, but I want to get the bass into a range where there's more melody and it's more of a melodic instrument. Along with that I

produce lots of sound effects."[25] Through this focus on melodic improvisation, Casady began to treat the bass as a lead instrument, and borrowing from the electric guitar styles he admired, he also expanded his
tool kit of techniques to include the manipulation of harmonics, feedback, and distortion. This new approach had been facilitated by Casady's
acquisition of new gear. During the recording of the Airplane's third
album, *After Bathing at Baxter's* (1967), Casady discovered the Versatone
Pan-O-Flex Model 133 bass amplifier. As he told me,

> We were recording [in LA] at RCA and we were in the big studio. . . .
> Next door, I think Carol Kaye had left her [bass] setup, and [engineer
> Richie Schmitt] says, "Listen, let me show you something," because
> we were bringing a lot of amplifiers into the studio that were too loud
> to record with. [He says,] "Here's a little amp here that all the engi-
> neers love. And Carol Kaye is recording with that and it just has a
> great recorded sound, and it's not loud." So I found out where to
> purchase one . . . and I brought it into the studio and started playing
> with it.[26]

The Versatone eventually became another tool through which Casady
could expand the tonal possibilities of his instrument. "It had separate
tube amps for the highs and the lows," he recalled. "I plugged in and
played, and it had a warm, round tone. When I turned up the volume
to overdrive it, the amp put out a pleasant, smooth distortion instead of
just breaking up. And when I turned it up all the way, it growled! Best of
all, I was still getting the clean, fundamental lows in addition to the dirty
highs."[27] In late 1967, he also switched to playing a Guild Starfire (Figure
38), an archtop, semihollow electric bass. The Starfire had a warmer,
quasi-upright tone that Casady was looking for, while its smaller scale
length made it easier to move up and down the neck. Like other short-
scale basses, however, it had a less powerful output than his Jazz Bass,
especially in the low end. Following the "make it better" philosophy he
had inherited from his father, Casady had Owsley Stanley custom-modify
the instrument to include top-of-the-line components and stronger mag-
nets in the pickups.[28] As he explained,

> After hearing bands like Cream and the Jimi Hendrix Experience,
> I became interested in overdriving my amp. . . . I noticed that the
> Fender [Jazz Bass] didn't distort well, but when I played overdriven
> chords and moved up the neck on the Guild, it had a sweet sustain

Figure 38. Jack Casady playing his original custom-modified Guild Starfire. (Source: *Woodstock*, dir. Michael Wadleigh, 1970.)

with a lot of interesting overtones. Because it sang so well but lacked in low end, due to its short scale, I found myself playing more melodically and higher on the neck.[29]

This new bass and amplifier fundamentally expanded the possibilities of what Casady could do with his instrument, both sonically and technically—an expansion that consequently allowed him to further develop as a lead player, especially in live settings.

Take, for example, the Jefferson Airplane's *Live at the Fillmore East* album, which was compiled from two live sets played at Bill Graham's New York venue in May 1968.[30] The opening number, "The Ballad of You & Me & Pooneil," had originally been released in August 1967 as the follow-up single to "White Rabbit." The single version, which runs approximatively four and a half minutes, is guitar-heavy psychedelia that foregrounds the sound of Casady's bass in the mix and includes a short Versatone-driven lead line. The *Fillmore East* version, by contrast, is nearly twice as long, radically expanding the song's form to provide more space for improvisation. At approximately two minutes and thirty-seven seconds into the performance, Casady embarks on an extended lead that slowly builds in intensity for almost two full minutes. As on the single, he begins with a clean sound to which he then adds more and more of the Versatone's distinctive, distorted growl. He returns with a second extended bass lead at around five minutes and seventeen seconds, initially working with and against a simultaneous line from Kaukonen. After Kaukonen drops out, Casady takes over yet again, exploring and developing new melodic ideas as he goes.

Casady's Guild-/Versatone-powered bass sound is also captured on the band's studio recordings from this era, most notably on the title track of their fourth album, *Crown of Creation* (1968). More prominently featured in the mix than all the other instruments, Casady drives the song with another growling, overdriven bass line, incorporating, at various points, lead lines, improvised fills, countermelodies, and chordal playing. Compared to the band's earlier material, this song features a much darker, heavier sound, one that the band signaled was intended as a deliberate commentary on the political turmoil of the time (*Jazz & Pop* contributor Patricia Kennealy described it as "apocalypse-rock").[31] Notably, it is Casady's bass, primarily, that supplies the recording's doom-and-gloom feel.

Perhaps the best representation of Casady's late-sixties bass style was the Airplane's live album, *Bless Its Pointed Little Head*, which was compiled from multiple late 1968 performances at the Fillmore West and Fillmore East. As Kaukonen recalled in his memoir, "This album shows the Airplane in absolutely top form. What we had been learning over the last couple of years was blossoming in live performance. The natural boundaries of the studio recording were shattered and we could go anywhere the music decided to take us."[32] Casady likewise described the album to me as capturing "the quintessential Airplane sound."[33] By this point in the band's career, their live setup had also grown exponentially. As Chris Jisi notes, Casady's bass rig, just by itself, now included "Four Fender Showman heads . . . run through four McIntosh 3500 power amps, on top of eight custom-built ported plywood cabinets featuring 15-inch Jensen D140 speakers," with the overdriven sound of his Versatone amp "miked separately and blended in when needed through a volume pedal."[34] The ultimate effect of all this gear was a powerful, loud sound that firmly situated Casady's bass at the center of the music. For example, compare the live version of "Somebody to Love" on *Bless Its Pointed Little Head* to the studio recording from two years prior.[35] Whereas earlier, Casady's bass provided rhythmic drive through a series of variations on a propulsive two-bar riff, now he forcefully dominates the song's sonic texture with a loud, newly improvised line that is only loosely connected to the original. He begins by introducing the bass as the song's dominant lead instrument but eschews the studio recording's rhythm-&-blues-inspired push-and-pull rhythmic feel, replacing it instead with a nearly constant stream of eighth notes. At the chorus, he hews closely to the original's hooky countermelody, but by the second verse, he has instituted yet another rhythmic feel, using elaborate syncopation to play against Dryden's drums. Following their new free-form approach, the band collectively decide to continue playing through the song's verse-chorus cycle again and again, giving Kaukonen and Casady the space to play elaborate parallel lines.

By the late sixties, Casady's perpetual search for new tones and techniques had led him to develop a unique style of improvisatory electric bass playing, one that was extensively celebrated at the time.[36] He was, in fact, so well respected that the *Jazz & Pop* critics' poll named him the best bassist in all of popular music for both 1968 and 1970.[37] While these polls likely say more about the prevailing tastes of rock critics than they do about the actual state of bass playing, they are nonetheless notable because of the paradigm shift they document. Simply put, mainstream audiences had now come to embrace and appreciate the electric bass as more than just supportive accompaniment. Following in Casady's footsteps, many subsequent bassists would also come to embrace the idea that they could (and should) be more strongly featured in the music.

Larry Graham and Sly and the Family Stone

Today, Jefferson Airplane is most often classified as psychedelic (or "acid") rock, while Sly and the Family Stone tend to be classified as funk or psychedelic soul. These categorizations are largely based on racially deterministic conceptions of sound and genre, which treat the Family Stone's funk rhythms, horn section, and Black bandleader as evidence that the group was separate from rock. These classifications have served, to invoke James Gordon Williams's phrase, as a type of enforced "aesthetic segregation," one that has retroactively downplayed Sly and the Family Stone's prominent position within late-sixties rock culture.[38] Likewise, this segregation has obscured the many connections and similarities between the Airplane and Family Stone. For instance, in addition to their geographic proximity as San Francisco bands, both were integrated across gender lines and built on an internal dynamic that valued the individual backgrounds and idiosyncrasies of each bandmember. Musically, each also developed a unique style by embracing an eclectic— albeit somewhat distinct—set of prior influences. Furthermore, they both projected a countercultural visual image and a peace-and-love phi- losophy that tied them to the highly publicized hippie movement.[39] And, at the height of their success, Sly and the Family Stone often performed at the same rock festivals as Jefferson Airplane, including Woodstock, most famously, but also the Palm Beach Music & Art Festival and the Wild West Festival in San Francisco. Their bassists, too, had much in common: drawing on their prior experience as electric guitarists, both Jack Casady and the Family Stone's Larry Graham (b. 1946) developed innovative approaches that treated the electric bass as more than just a supportive instrument.

Graham was born in Beaumont, Texas, but relocated to the San Francisco Bay Area with his family when he was two years old. His par- ents were musicians themselves, and they encouraged him to explore his own musical interests. In seventh grade, he started playing drums in the school orchestra and marching band, and his father later gave him an electric guitar and amplifier. By the time he was fifteen, he was working with his mother, pianist/singer Dell Graham, performing jazz standards in Bay Area nightclubs and lounges. To fill out the sound of their piano-guitar-drum trio, Larry started playing an organ's bass pedals with his feet; as he recalled, "We worked at this club that had an organ that had bass pedals at the bottom, and I learned to play the bass pedals along with the guitar and singing. So, we sounded full now having bot- tom. We got used to that, then the organ broke down."[40] To make up for this sudden lack of low end, Graham decided to switch to playing an electric bass: "I went to Music Unlimited over in San Leandro and I rented a St. George bass *temporarily* until the organ could be repaired. As it turned out the organ could not be repaired so I was stuck on the bass."[41] Shortly thereafter, their drummer also left the group, and so, to compensate, Graham developed a percussive right-hand technique that he refers to as "thumpin' and pluckin'" (more commonly known today as "slap" or "slap and pop"). In essence, he would strike the lower strings with the side of his thumb to mimic the missing bass drum, then snap the higher strings with his index finger to mimic a backbeat snare drum pattern. Within a few short years, this style would revolutionize electric bass playing, but, as Graham recalled, "It [simply] came about out of necessity. I wasn't trying to invent something new. I didn't really think I was, actually . . . I just played it the way it was necessary for me to do."[42]

Moreover, since he really considered himself a guitarist, Graham did not care that he was playing the bass the "wrong" way: "Everybody was playing overhand style—fingers over top of the bass. That's cool, but I wasn't interested in learning the so-called correct way of playing, because I wasn't planning to be a bass player. Since I thought it was a temporary thing, I wasn't tied down to thinking I had to learn to play correctly."[43] Eventually, his mindset changed and after a few years, Graham remembered, "I considered myself a bass player. I was already past any criticism about not doing it the correct way. I was working with my mother, and she loved the way I played—so I didn't need anyone else's approval."[44]

Sometime in late 1966, Sly Stone went to hear Larry Graham and his mother perform at an after-hours San Francisco jazz club known as Relax with Yvonne, located at the intersection of Haight and Ashbury. Stone was, at the time, building a following as a DJ on the Black radio station KSOL while also moonlighting as a producer for the local indie label Autumn Records, where he worked with San Francisco rock bands, including the Great Society (Stone, in fact, produced the original version of "Somebody to Love").[45] A multi-instrumentalist with grand ambitions, Stone was on the lookout for local talent and was impressed by Graham's playing, especially his slap style, so much so that he invited him to join a new group he was forming. This band, which would come to be known as Sly and the Family Stone, coalesced around Graham on electric bass, Greg Errico on drums, Cynthia Robinson on trumpet, Freddie Stone on vocals and electric guitar, Jerry Martini on saxophone, and Sly Stone on vocals and organ. Shortly after forming, the group was working on funk-infused arrangements of current Top 40 hits and, by the end of the year, were already developing a following playing in Bay Area suburbs.

Looking back, Graham attributes the Family Stone's success to a variety of factors:

> Sly was a genius of a writer. You also had a group that was racially mixed, male and female, and self-contained. Back then you had a lot of singing groups that were out front, with bands in the back, but we were . . . the band *and* the singing group. [And] I think it was genius on Sly's part to allow each member of the band to be themselves, as opposed to trying to make them play however he wanted to play. He asked me to be in the band because of what he heard. He heard me doing this different way of playing the bass, so if he had tried to change me up to play like him—because he's a bass player too—then that would have made a difference. . . . So Sly letting everybody be

themselves, add that to all the other factors, and I think that that's what made the band successful.[46]

Embracing a hippie philosophy, the members of the Sly and the Family Stone could dress how they wanted to dress, play how they wanted to play. In the end, the group would be known for highlighting the individual talents and personalities of each of its musicians, and at a moment of growing racial tensions in the country, this eclectic, mixed-race, mixed-gender band became, for many, a symbol of the possibilities and joys of integration. As Craig Werner argues,

> No musical group embodies the late sixties better than Sly and the Family Stone. The band brought together the highest aspirations and the underlying chaos of a time defined equally by the Vietnam War and the "Summer of Love," by Black Power and white backlash. Certainly, no musical act presented a more exhilarating image of what America might become.[47]

Yet the Family Stone did not breakthrough overnight. Like Jefferson Airplane, their first album, *A Whole New Thing* (1967), flopped. Released on Epic, a CBS subsidiary, the album captures the band early in their development and previews many of the hallmarks of their later sound. Take, for example, "Trip to Your Heart." Led by Sly's gospel-infused vocal performance, the song features around cyclic funk drumming, call-and-response horn lines, and even—there in the background— Graham thumpin' on a Fender Jazz Bass played through a Bassman amplifier (notably, the song also includes a purposefully disorienting, "freak-out" chorus reminiscent of contemporary psychedelia). Both it and the album represented a unique amalgamation of contemporary pop styles, but, as such, their "whole new thing" was difficult to categorize and therefore dismissed by DJs and industry executives who did not know how to sell it.

If Stone wanted his band to be a success, CBS executives told him, he needed to give them a radio hit. In response, Stone wrote "Dance to the Music" (1967), a catchy three-minute single that literally introduced the band to mainstream pop audiences. Forgoing the James Brown–inspired grooves of their previous album, the recording is built instead around Errico's insistent, easy-to-follow beat, which supplies a foundation for each of the band members to announce themselves to the listener. Here, again, the song is powered by a heavy thumpin' bass line, one that is now even more prominently featured in the mix. But Graham also adds another innovation to the song: an overdubbed fuzz bass. Drawing on his prior experience as a guitarist, Graham was one of the first electric bassists to incorporate stand-alone effects pedals into his sound, including various fuzz pedals (likely, in this case, a Maestro FZ-1) and, later, a CryBaby wah. Like Jack Casady and Paul McCartney, Graham was always interested in exploring new and unique bass timbres, and he used these effects pedals to give his slap playing an added tonal edge. On "Dance to the Music," when it comes time for him to "add some bottom," his distinctive fuzz bass acts as a lead line that dominates the recording's sonic space, allowing him to stand apart from the rest of the band.

"Dance to the Music" became the group's first hit. Released in November 1967, the single spent fifteen weeks on the Hot 100, peaking at No. 8. In the wake of its success, Epic released the band's second album, *Dance to the Music*, to positive reviews the following April. In *Jazz & Pop*, for example, Frank Kofsky wrote that "Sly & The Family Stone is a group that has to be heard—or preferably, seen—to be believed. It is a group which could only have come out of San Francisco: a combination of hard Black & Bean rhythm and blues with Northern California psychedelia."[48] This emphasis on the band's San Francisco origins and stylistic and racial diversity was typical of the time, with many critics expressing a positive-but-slightly-bewildered appreciation of the band's opposition to the prevailing genre logics of the day. Stone, for his part, never seemed to see any of this as particularly unusual; providing the simplest explanation of his band's appeal, he told an interviewer in 1969, "There are black and white members of the group. And there are black and white people and they all like music. So, the result of a black and white group realizing that there are black and white people, that's what happens, you know."[49]

The San Francisco counterculture was, in Greil Marcus's words, "a very white scene," but by 1968, Sly and the Family Stone had found acceptance within it, especially after Bill Graham began to book them for his high-profile rock venues.[50] On May 10, 1968—just one week after the shows that had produced Jefferson Airplane's aforementioned live album—the band famously performed at Graham's Fillmore East in New York on a shared bill with Jimi Hendrix. This was followed by a three-day residency in July at the Fillmore West in San Francisco, where they were placed side by side with Big Brother and the Holding Company and the Jeff Beck Group. And, the following month, they were back at the Fillmore East, with surviving recordings capturing the band's infectious stage show in this era.[51]

By the end of the year, the band had released "Everyday People," the first single off their fourth album, *Stand!* (1969). Issued just a few short months after James Brown's unapologetic turn to Black Power with "Say It Loud—I'm Black and I'm Proud," "Everyday People" instead offered a call for unity and cross-racial understanding, one that was ultimately far more palatable for mainstream white audiences. Musically, like "Dance to the Music," "Everyday People" foregrounded an accessible, easy-to-follow drumbeat that underscored the song's culminating message: "We got to live together." As before, Graham thumps away at the low end, but this time he adopts a far more minimalistic approach, playing just one note throughout the entire song. With its optimistic attitude and simplified groove, "Everyday People" reached No. 1 on both the Hot 100 and the rhythm & blues chart and solidified the band's position at the forefront of late-sixties popular music.

By 1969, the Family Stone had become a fixture on the rock festival circuit. To accommodate these new performance spaces (as well as the larger halls they were headlining), Graham, like Casady, used an increasingly large rig, one that—perhaps even more than the group's records—placed Graham's bass front and center in their sound. For basses, he would use either a Jazz Bass or, occasionally, a Vox Constellation. For amplification, he first replaced his Fender Bassman with four Sunn amps, each of which had two 15-inch speakers; he then replaced these, first with four Fender Showman amps, then ultimately with four solid-state Acoustic 360/361 bass amplifiers. Designed by engineers Harvey Gerst and Russ Allee, the Acoustic 360 head and its 361 speaker cabinet were designed to meet the new challenges that bass players were now facing in the late sixties, especially in live performance. As E. E. Bradman explains,

> The 200-watt, solid-state 360 was perfect for the new breed of bassists, who had been forced to choose between the Fender Dual Showman, which maxed out at 100 watts, and 300-watt Sunn Coliseum amps. The 360 might not have been as loud as the Coliseum, but with its rear-firing horn, 1x18 speaker, proprietary Variamp presets, and distinctive cabinet, it projected all the way to the back of the room with a warmth and a clarity that set it apart from every other [bass] amp.[52]

Launched in 1967, the Acoustic 360/361 was a dependable amp with a clear bass sound and enough volume to stand its own against the volume and intensity of rock guitarists' new Marshall amplifiers.[53] Describing its effect, Graham recalled, "One thing everyone remembered was the floor shaking from the bass. . . . Those Acoustics were right on the money, and they had a built-in fuzztone. When you turned that on, it just rattled your chest."[54] This massive, four-amp Acoustic 360/361 setup notably powered Graham's performance with the Family Stone at Woodstock.

In December 1969, Sly and the Family Stone released "Thank You (Falettinme Be Mice Elf Agin)." Like "Everyday People," "Thank You" would become a No. 1 hit on both the Hot 100 and the R&B chart. But if the earlier song had showcased Graham playing in a deliberately restrained mode, his bass line on "Thank You" was just the opposite. Flashy and ostentatious, the entire recording is constructed around Graham's bass and showcases the unique sound of his thumpin' and pluckin' style far more clearly than any of the band's previous releases.[55] In addition to his right-hand technique, Graham's tone also makes this bass line distinctive. "I used a Dual Showman with a lot of treble and a lot of bass to get that sound," he recalled.[56] Moreover, he strung his Fender Jazz Bass with light-gauge, tapewound strings (Figure 39)—nearly the exact same setup that John Entwistle had used on the Who's "My Generation" just a few years prior.[57] As they had for Entwistle, these tapewound strings gave Graham a bright tone that emphasized the bass's higher frequencies—making the sound of his "pluckin,'" in particular, stand out.

"Thank You" solidified Graham's electric bass as a featured lead instrument in the Family Stone's music. As Rickey Vincent explains,

> Although the chopping, popping, and plucking bass sounds could be heard here and there in earlier works of many bands . . . "Thank You" used the popping bass as the primary melody—a syncopated melodic phrase from the bass, which turned the bass guitar from a background rhythm instrument into the driving force of the song. After "Thank You," both rhythm and melody became the territory of the bass.[58]

Through this and other bass lines, Graham fundamentally shaped the direction of electric bass playing for decades to come. In its wake, thousands of electric bass players would begin to incorporate the slap style, embracing it as one of the few widely accepted ways for bassists to take on a lead role in the music. In this sense, Jimmy Leslie is not exaggerating when he calls Graham's slap bass "arguably the single most innovative

Figure 39. Larry Graham playing a Fender Jazz Bass with tapewound strings. (Source: *The Dick Cavett Show*, July 13, 1970.)

and influential technique in the instrument's history."[59] Reflecting on how far his technique had spread, Graham told an interviewer in 1999, "Well, you can't help but hear it if you're living in the world. It makes me feel good that thumpin' and pluckin' is now part of blues, rock, country—whatever. You could be listening to a blues band, and suddenly the bass player will go off thumpin' and pluckin' when it's his turn to solo. It's not just part of funk anymore; it's the way you play bass."[60]

Conclusion

Fostered by the creative climate of the late-sixties San Francisco music scene, both Jack Casady and Larry Graham developed unique and innovative approaches to electric bass playing. Their bands, in turn, would prove to be highly influential, most notably with Jefferson Airplane helping to lay the foundation for later progressive rock and Sly and the Family Stone inspiring some of the biggest acts in popular music, such as the Jackson 5, Stevie Wonder, Prince, and more.[61] Ultimately, while their styles emphasized different sounds and techniques, Casady and Graham were committed to expanding the electric bass's role in popular music, and, by refusing to adhere to the bass's circumscribed role within the rhythm section, they demonstrated, once and for all, that electric bassists could take center stage.

Conclusion

The Electric Bass and the Adjacent Possible

In his 2010 book, *Where Good Ideas Come From: The Natural History of Innovation*, Steven Johnson notes,

> We have a natural tendency to romanticize breakthrough innova-
> tions, imagining momentous ideas transcending their surroundings,
> a gifted mind somehow seeing over the detritus of old ideas and ossi-
> fied tradition. But ideas are works of bricolage; they're built out of
> that detritus. We take the ideas we've inherited or that we've stumbled
> across, and we jigger them together into some new shape.[1]

Innovations, Johnson argues, are not the expression of pure, limitless
genius, but rather come from human creativity operating within the
material and conceptual constraints that govern any given moment—a
phenomenon he (following biologist Stuart Kauffman) refers to as "the
adjacent possible." As Johnson explains, "The adjacent possible is a kind
of shadow future, hovering on the edges of the present state of things, a
map of all the ways in which the present can reinvent itself. Yet it is not
an infinite space, or a totally open playing field . . . [A]t any moment the
world is capable of extraordinary change, but only *certain* changes can
happen."[2] Under Johnson's model, human beings are constantly inno-
vating (often in parallel with one another), and with each individual
innovation comes an expanded set of adjacent possibilities. Thus, major
advances are actually woven from a complex web of previous innovations, without which such breakthroughs would not be possible.

Johnson's conception of the "adjacent possible" is a useful framework for understanding the electric bass's evolution in popular music. In the thirties, the advent of electrical technology made it possible to amplify musical instruments, which led inventors to create the first electric basses. Though these initial basses were unsuccessful, the idea of an electric bass lingered, and in the early fifties, Leo Fender drew inspiration from these early instruments, as well as from the mariachi bands he saw performing at local Mexican restaurants, to create his own: the Fender Precision Bass. The Precision Bass made it possible for musicians and audiences to hear a clear, loud bass line—one that still plausibly sounded like an upright bass—and its various practical advantages led to it being adopted by professional touring musicians across genres. With the electric bass's newly established track record of success, other musicians began to explore its sonic possibilities in the recording studio, manipulating its sound to fashion new, distinctive timbres that were consciously distinct from the upright. Furthermore, Fender's invention inspired other guitar manufacturers to design and market their own electric basses, which eventually made it possible for young amateur musicians in the late fifties to adopt the instrument en masse. These amateurs, in turn, normalized the electric bass as a legitimate instrument, making it possible for professional session musicians in the early sixties to adopt it and use it to forge their own complex, virtuosic bass styles. These styles radically expanded the electric bass's conceptual and technical possibilities, inspiring other bassists to further hone and expand their own approaches. By the mid-sixties, the electric bass had become the default low-end instrument in most genres. Its parallel, ever-expanding adjacent possibilities then allowed bassists later in the decade to develop their own unique and influential approaches. In the end, this cumulative web of innovations fundamentally transformed the sound of popular music.

Of course, this is just the beginning of the story. In the decades that followed, more electric bassists would continue to explore their own adjacent possibilities. Some, like Suzi Quatro, Leroy Sibbles, Tina Weymouth, Bernard Edwards, Kathy Valentine, Meshell Ndegeocello, Tim Commerford, and Chris Wolstenholme would come to emphasize rhythm and groove. Others, like Chris Squire, John Paul Jones, Geddy Lee, Jaco Pastorius, Stuart Hamm, Esperanza Spalding, and Steve Lawson would instead adopt more melodic, soloistic approaches. And, building on Larry Graham's technique, bassists like Freddie Washington, Louis Johnson, Marcus Miller, Mark King, Flea, Les Claypool, and Victor Wooten all expanded the slap bass style. Although the styles each of these musicians developed would be shaped by different constraints and would perhaps come to mean different things, their work was fundamentally built on the breakthrough efforts of the electric bassists detailed in this book. Without the adjacent possibilities that their predecessors allowed for, those subsequent innovations would literally have been unimaginable.

• • •

There were eighteen years between the first Fender Precision Basses rolling off the assembly line and the release of "Thank You (Falettinme Be Mice Elf Agin)." It took eighteen years, in a sense, for the instrument to come of age, for it to find its rightful place in the world. Musicians, inventors, engineers, producers, promoters, critics, fans, detractors: all of them, famous or not, had a hand in shaping the instrument's early history and development. Ultimately, this book is an attempt to highlight the significance of their contributions—to give credit where credit is due. Thanks to their individual and collective efforts, by 1970, the electric bass was no longer a "bastard instrument."

Notes

Introduction

1. See "The Byrds Top Hot 100 Chart," *Billboard*, June 26, 1965, 1.

2. Dylan briefly acknowledged Wilson's influence in his 1969 interview with *Rolling Stone* editor Jann Wenner. In it, Wenner asked, "There's been some articles on [Tom] Wilson and he says that he's the one that gave you the rock and roll sound . . . and started you doing rock and roll. Is that true?" To which Dylan responded, "Did he say that? Well, if he said it . . . [Laughs] more power to him. [Laughs] He did to a certain extent. That is true. He did. He had a sound in mind." Jann S. Wenner, "The Rolling Stone Interview: Dylan," *Rolling Stone*, November 29, 1969, 25.

3. Don Meehan, "Truth about Simon and Garfunkel Sounds of Silence," *RoughmixDon Meehan*, updated November 30, 2014, https://roughmixdon.com /2014/05/11/simon-garfunkels-s-s-truth/, accessed January 20, 2015.

4. See also Walter Everett, *The Foundations of Rock: From "Blue Suede Shoes" to "Suite Judy Blue Eyes"* (New York: Oxford University Press, 2009), 29–42.

5. For a more specific discussion of how the electric bass is most commonly used in popular music, see my chapter, "The Bass Guitar in Popular Music," in the forthcoming *Cambridge Companion to the Electric Guitar*, edited by Jan-Peter Herbst and Steve Waksman.

6. Lenny Kaye, "Hey, Mr. Bassman," *Fusion*, September 19, 1969.

7. Sting, interview by Vic Garbarini, *Bass Player*, April 1992, 32.

8. Steve Waksman, "Reading the Instrument: An Introduction." *Popular Music and Society* 26, no. 3 (2003): 251–252.

9. Also see Kevin Dawe, "The Cultural Study of Musical Instruments," in *The Cultural Study of Music: A Critical Introduction*, ed. Martin Clayton, Trevor Herbert, and Richard Middleton, 2nd ed (New York: Routledge, 2012), 195–205; and Karen Harvey, "Introduction: Historians, Material Culture, and Materiality," in *History and Material Culture: A Students' Guide to Approaching Alternative Sources*, ed. Karen Harvey, 2nd ed. (New York: Routledge, 2018), 1–26.

10. Steve Waksman, *Instruments of Desire: The Electric Guitar and the Shaping of Musical Experience* (Cambridge: Harvard University Press, 1999).

11. This way of explaining popular music history is further complicated by the fact that genres have never been stable categories, but rather are artificial constructs that are under constant negotiation. See David Brackett, *Categorizing Sound: Genre and Twentieth-Century Popular Music* (Oakland: University of California Press, 2016).

12. Brad Tolinksi and Alan Di Perna, *Play It Loud: An Epic History of the Style, Sound, and Revolution of the Electric Guitar* (New York: Doubleday, 2016), xiv–xv.

13. Also, as Paul Théberge argues, "Musical instruments are not 'completed' at the stage of design and manufacture, but, rather, they are 'made-over' by musicians in the process of making music." Paul Théberge, *Any Sound You Can Imagine: Making Music/Consuming Technology* (Hanover, NH: Wesleyan University Press, 1997), 159–160.

14. For a discussion of embodied cognition and how musicians interact with musical instruments as objects, see Jonathan De Souza, *Music at Hand: Instruments, Bodies, and Cognition* (New York: Oxford University Press, 2017).

15. For more on the power of simple bass lines, see Brian F. Wright, "Transvaluing Adam Clayton: Why the Bass Matters in U2's Music," in *U2 Above, Across, and Beyond: Interdisciplinary Assessments*, ed. Scott Calhoun (Lanham, MD: Lexington Books, 2014), 17–30.

Interlude I

1. For a discussion of how the upright bass came to replace the tuba as the standard low-end instrument in jazz, see Peter Dowdall, *Technology and the Stylistic Evolution of the Jazz Bass* (New York: Routledge, 2018), 12–31.

2. See David Chevan, "The Double Bass as a Solo Instrument in Early Jazz," *Black Perspective in Music* 17, nos. 1–2 (1989): 73–92.

3. Lynn Wheelwright, "Vivi-Tone," unpublished manuscript. Vintage guitar expert Lynn Wheelwright has recently reconstructed a detailed history of the Vivi-Tone Company. My discussion is greatly indebted to his work.

4. According to Wheelwright, contrary to the story told in Julius Bellson's *The Gibson Story* (1973), Loar did not experiment with electric bass technology during his tenure at Gibson. The earliest Gibson electric basses thus date to the late thirties, when the company produced a small run of "Electric Bass Guitars" (four-stringed, five-foot-tall, hollow-body upright acoustic guitars with mounted pickups). However, these instruments were never released commercially.

5. Vivi-Tone, *Electrically Energized Musical Instruments: A Revolutionary Development in the Field of Music*, catalog, 1934, 12–14, personal collection of Lynn Wheelwright.

6. Vivi-Tone, *Electrically Energized Musical Instruments*.

7. Owner Adolph Rickenbacker (née Adolf Rickenbacher) incorporated the company in October 1931 as the "Ro-Pat-In" Corporation (possibly a portmanteau of Elect**Ro-Pat**ent-**In**struments). In surviving catalogs from the early thirties, the company is variously listed as "Richenbacher Electro," "Rickenbacker Electro," and "Electro String Instrument Corporation."

8. Matthew W. Hill, "George Beauchamp and the Rise of the Electric Guitar Up to 1939" (PhD dissertation, University of Edinburgh, 2013), 148–151.

9. "Rickenbacker Electric Bass," *Vintage Guitar*, February 2007, https://www.vintageguitar.com/3399/rickenbacker-electro-bass/

10. Hill, "George Beauchamp," 152–153. Hill also describes another notable Electro String instrument from the 1930s, the Electro Fretted Double Bass, which was an acoustic-electric, fretted upright; see Hill, "George Beauchamp," 154–158.

11. Earlier in the 1930s, Regal had also released their "Bassoguitar," a large acoustic guitar/upright bass hybrid.

12. Both ads are reprinted in Jim Roberts, *How the Fender Bass Changed the World* (San Francisco: Backbeat Books, 2001), 26–27.

13. Tutmarc had also released an upright electric bass the year prior, though it is unclear how many copies were actually produced. An article in the *Seattle Post-Intelligencer* featured a photo of the instrument and noted that "the first electric bass-viol is only four feet tall, instead of six. It could be made a lot smaller, but Tutmarc didn't want to be too revolutionary right off the bat. Bass violinists are a conservative race, and have to be accustomed gradually to the idea, he says." "Pity Him No More—New Type Bull Fiddle Devised," *Seattle Post-Intelligencer*, February 17, 1935, 7.

14. For more on Tutmarc, see "Paul Tutmarc & the Mystery behind Who Invented the Electric Guitar," *Jive Time Records Presents: Northwest Music History*, May 3, 2018, https://jivetimerecords.com/northwest/paula-tutmarc/; and Paul H. "Bud" Tutmarc, "The True Facts on the Invention of the Electric Guitar and Electric Bass," in *The Hawaiian Steel Guitar and Its Great Hawaiian Musicians*, comp. Lorene Ruymar (Anaheim Hills, CA: Centerstream Publications, 1996), 126–127.

15. For more on Lorraine Tutmarc, see Ronald K. Fitten, "Obituary: Lorraine Tutmarc, Lived the Light, the Hope, and the Love of Christ," *Seattle Times*, December 23, 1992, https://archive.seattletimes.com/archive/?date=19921223&slug=1531578

16. See Tim Fletcher, "The First Electric Bass Guitar Player," *Bass Musician*, February 17, 2020, https://bassmusicianmagazine.com/2020/02/the-first-electric-bass-guitar-player/

17. Peter Blecha, "Tutmarc, Paul (1896–1972), and His Audiovox Electric Guitars," HistoryLink.org, http://www.historylink.org/File/7479

18. Tony Bacon and Barry Moorhouse, *The Bass Book: A Complete Illustrated History of Bass Guitars*, 2nd ed. (San Francisco: Backbeat, 2008), 8.

19. Jimmy Mack, "Refutes Claim of First Electric Bass," *Down Beat*, November 1, 1939, 10. The piece he is "refuting" appears on page 19 of the October 1, 1939 issue.

20. "'All-Electric' Bands Cause Big Rivalry in New York," *Down Beat*, October 1, 1939, 6.

21. For another account of Cracraft's and Wagner's orchestras, see S. Gordon Taylor, "The 1940 Sound," *Service*, February 1940, 17–18.

22. Restrictive Measure L-37 was passed on February 17, 1942, followed by Supplementary Limitation Order L-37-a on May 29, 1942. L-37-a was amended and revised several times before being officially revoked on May 10, 1945.

23. Sarah Deters Richardson, "Instruments of War: The Impact of World War

II on the American Musical Instrument Industry" (PhD dissertation, University of South Dakota, 2010).

24. Richardson, "Instruments of War," 164–165.

25. "Hampton Now Has Electric Band," *Metronome*, November 1940, 9; Eddie Beaumonte, "'We'll Starve the Mickey Mouse Bands': Lionel Hampton, for First Time, Reveals Exactly What He Wants," *Down Beat*, November 15, 1940, 4. While Vernon Alley used an electric bass on tour, it is difficult to know which model he played and to what extent he used it. Multiple sources also claim that Hampton utilized Joe Comfort on an unspecified model of electric bass for a September 23, 1946, recording session, which produced the B-Side "Robbins in Your Hair" (Decca 23792). Kévin Jost likewise claims that Hampton utilized an electric bass player on his Victor recording "Jack the Bellboy" backed with "Central Avenue Breakdown" (1940), but I have not been able to independently verify this claim; see Kévin Jost, "La basse électrique: Son histoire, sa facture, son rôle et ses apports à la musique populaire depuis 1960" (MA thesis, Année universitaire, 2007–8), 31.

26. For more on Allen and his deal with Rickenbacker, see Eddy Determeyer, *Rhythm Is Our Business: Jimmie Lunceford and the Harlem Express* (Ann Arbor: University of Michigan Press, 2010), 185.

27. Quoted in Dowdall, *Technology*, 46; originally from Stephen Fratallone, "Super Salesman: Lighthouse All-Stars Founder Howard Rumsey Sold Millions on West Coast Jazz," *Jazz Connection Magazine*, May 2005, archived at http://arch ive.fo/1HCGv

28. Quoted in Steven D. Harris, *The Kenton Kronicles: A Biography of Modern America's Man of Music, Stan Kenton* (Pasadena, CA: Dynaflow Publications, 2003), 16–17.

29. Rex Butters, "Howard Rumsey: The Lighthouse All Star," *All About Jazz*, August 2007, reprinted at https://www.allaboutjazz.com/howard-rumsey-the-lig hthouse-all-star-howard-rumsey-by-rex-butters__3876

30. Marc Myers, "Interview: Howard Rumsey," *JazzWax*, September 2, 2009, https://www.jazzwax.com/2009/09/02/

31. For an overview of subsequent developments in upright electric bass technology specifically, see Kevin Delaney, "The Electric Upright: Common Ground for Bassists," *International Society of Bassists* 19, no. 1 (1993): 48–56.

Chapter 1

1. Waksman, *Instruments of Desire*, 45–46.

2. As media scholars Jeremy Wade Morris and Lisa Gitelman demonstrate, understanding technologies in their moments of newness is crucial to understanding how their eventual meanings are established and solidified. See Jeremy Wade Morris, *Selling Digital Music, Formatting Culture* (Oakland: University of California Press, 2015), and Lisa Gitelman, *Always Already New: Media, History, and the Data of Culture* (Cambridge: MIT Press, 2006).

3. Sales figures and projections taken from Richard R. Smith, *Fender: The Sound Heard 'Round the World* (Milwaukee: Hal Leonard, 2003), 293.

4. Quoted in Joan V. Schroeder, "Patsy in Appleland," *Blue Ridge County*, September–October 1992, 14–17, 41, archived at http://www.oocities.org/ica nseeanangel1961/patsyinappleland.html/

5. For further discussions of women electric bassists, see Mary Ann Clawson, "When Women Play the Bass: Instrument Specialization and Gender Interpretation in Alternative Rock Music," *Gender & Society* 13, no. 2 (April 1999): 193–210; and Tammy L. Kernodle, "Diggin' You Like Those Ol' Soul Records: Meshell Ndegeocello and the Expanding Definition of Funk in Postsoul America," *American Studies* 52, no. 4 (2013): 181–204.

6. There is no evidence to suggest that Fender was familiar with Paul Tutmarc's Audiovox #736 Electronic Bass.

7. Fender's encounters with mariachi bands are briefly detailed in Smith, *Fender*, 103, and Ian S. Port, *The Birth of Loud: Leo Fender, Les Paul, and the Guitar-Pioneering Rivalry That Shaped Rock 'n' Roll* (New York: Scribner, 2019), 91–92.

8. Tom Wheeler, "Leo Fender: An Exclusive GP Interview," *Guitar Player*, May 1978, 116.

9. George Fullerton, *Guitars from George & Leo: How Leo Fender and I Built G&L Guitars* (Milwaukee: Hal Leonard, 2005), 25.

10. The scale length is the distance between the instrument's nut and bridge. These are the two anchoring points for a string.

11. Bacon and Moorhouse, *The Bass Book*, 12–13. Today, 34 inches remains the standard length for "long-scale" bass guitars.

12. Smith, *Fender*, 103.

13. Smith, *Fender*, 105.

14. Smith, *Fender*, 106. While Smith is correct about the flaws in many previous bass amplifiers, it is worth noting (as discussed in Interlude I) that Vivi-Tone was marketing an option for a 30-watt bass amplifier all the way back in 1934.

15. Fender, advertisement, *The Music Trades*, April 1952, 55.

16. The term "ported" refers to the two small circular holes in the back of the cabinet (like a porthole), while "TV-front" refers to the shape of the face of the amplifier, which resembles the shape of early televisions.

17. "Fender Bass and Amplifier Replace Old Style in 1/6 Size," *The Music Trades*, April 1952, 54.

18. Quoted in Forrest White, *Fender: The Inside Story* (San Francisco: BackBeat Books, 1994), 52.

19. Smith, *Fender*, 106.

20. Henry was known to stylize the spelling of his name as "Shifte Henri" (at other times, as Shifté Henré, Shifté Henrí, or Shiftí Henrí). He also occasionally went under the pseudonym "Baron Von Shifte, Esq."

21. For more on the history of the Treniers, see Bill Dahl, liner notes for the Treniers, *Rock*, Bear Family Records, 2010.

22. This clip is preserved on *Dean Martin & Jerry Lewis Collection*, Mill Creek Entertainment, 2018, DVD.

23. A remastered version of the recording can be found on the Treniers, *Rock*. Haley had originally recorded the song in 1952 with his group the Esquire Boys. After developing a rapport with Treniers, he offered to let them record the song. He later rerecorded the song with the Comets in September 1955, and it was this

version that became a hit (reaching No. 23 on the *Billboard* pop chart and No. 4 in UK).

24. In fact, Leo Fender gave the third Precision Bass ever manufactured to a local teenage western swing group, Arlis McMinn and the California Playboys. See Richard R. Smith, "Arlis McMinn and the California Playboys," *Vintage Guitar,* December 2013, https://www.vintageguitar.com/17470/arliss-mcminn -and-the-california-playboys/

25. Neil V. Rosenberg and Charles K. Wolfe, *The Music of Bill Monroe* (Urbana: University of Illinois Press, 2007), 81–82.

26. Quoted in Eddie Stubbs, liner notes to Little Jimmy Dickens, *Country Boy,* Bear Family Records, 1999, 30–31.

27. The other songs recorded during that session were "Wedding Bell Waltz" (the A side of the single that featured "You Don't Have Love at All"), "I'm Gettin' Nowhere Fast," and "Love Must Be Catching." These recordings can all be found on Little Jimmy Dickens, *Country Boy.*

28. The flatwound strings gave the bass a more "dead," i.e., muffled sound, and the mute housed in the bridge cover prevented the plucked strings from sustaining.

29. Little information survives about Jay or his career. Originally from Texas, Thurber Daniel Jay went by the nickname "Sonny" (as he is listed on Louis Jordan's Decca Record Personnel sheets) and sometimes "Sam Guy." He eventually settled in Fresno, California, where he passed away in 1993; see Eric S. LeBlanc and Bob Eagle, *Blues: A Regional Experience* (Santa Barbara, CA: Praeger, 2013), 538.

30. Quoted in John Chilton, *Let the Good Times Roll: The Story of Louis Jordan and His Music* (Ann Arbor: University of Michigan Press, 1994), 182.

31. Pictures of Sonny Jay holding his bass in this manner are reproduced in Peter Grendysa, liner notes to Louis Jordan, *Let the Good Times Roll: The Complete Decca Recordings, 1938–1954,* Louis Jordan, Bear Family Records, 1992, CD.

32. Other songs recorded during this session include "Hog Wash," "Everything That's Made of Wood," "I Want You to Be My Baby," and "You Know It Too." These recordings can be found on *Let the Good Times Roll.*

33. Mark Williams, "Liberace Show, The," in *Encyclopedia of Television,* ed. Horace Newcomb, 2nd ed. (London: Taylor & Francis, 2014), 1356.

34. Reproduced in Smith, *Fender,* 145.

35. This episode can be found on *Liberace TV Classics,* Film Chest, 2013, DVD.

36. This was not the only time the instrument appeared on the show. In a 1956 episode dedicated to "American Composers," Liberace and his band (including Manners on Precision Bass) come out in matching striped jackets and straw hats to play a rendition of Irving Berlin's "Alexander's Ragtime Band." Notably, Manners appears to be playing his bass with a pick.

37. Vincent L. Stephens, *Rocking the Closet: How Little Richard, Johnnie Ray, Liberace, and Johnny Mathis Queered Popular Music* (Urbana: University of Illinois Press, 2019), 155.

38. Smith, *Fender,* 145.

39. Surviving price lists show that Fender's suggested retail price for a Fender Precision jumped from $199.50 in 1955 to $219.50 in 1957; over the same

period, the price of the Bassman amplifier increased even more substantially, from $279.50 in 1955 to $339.50 in 1957.

Interlude II

1. Hull changed the spelling of his name from "Everitt" to "Everett" in the early 1940s.
2. Quoted in Gregg Hopkins and Bill Moore, *Ampeg: The Story Behind the Sound* (Milwaukee: Hal Leonard, 1999), 17.
3. Everette Hull, interviewed by Dorothy Gable, March 12, 1968, Frist Library and Archive of the Country Music Hall of Fame and Museum Oral History Collection, OH325.
4. Hopkins and Moore, *Ampeg*, 21.
5. Quoted in Jonathan Weir, "Amplified Fiddle Leads Way to Big-Time Music Business," *Newark Sunday News*, October 23, 1968, D2–D4.
6. Hopkins and Moore, *Ampeg*, 36.
7. Ampeg, advertisement, *Down Beat*, June 17, 1946, 16.
8. Hull's marketing materials from this era state, "To begin with, [the Ampeg pickup] will give you absolute reproduction. . . . If you have a great bass, it will be greater, and a good beat will become a better beat. In short, it makes for better bass playing and greater satisfaction. . . . The carrying power and undistorted volume throughout the entire range of any bass, made possible by this unit, is something you must experience." Promotional flier, Michael-Hull Electronic Labs, ca. 1946, personal collection of the author.
9. Dowdall, *Technology*, 46.
10. Quoted in Hopkins and Moore, *Ampeg*, 25.
11. Hopkins and Moore, *Ampeg*, 25.
12. Figure cited in Hopkins and Moore, *Ampeg*, 56.

Chapter 2

1. Leonard Feather, "Hamp-lified Fiddle May Lighten Bassists' Burdens," *Down Beat*, July 30, 1952, 22.
2. Feather, "Hamp-lified Fiddle."
3. Roberts, *Fender Bass*, 35; emphasis added. Fabian claims that Hampton met Leo Fender in early 1952, but sources point to this meeting occurring sometime in late 1951. For example, a newspaper article from December 1951 describes a "low pitched bass guitar" in Hampton's touring band; see Clete Wiley, "Lionel Is Cool, Crowd Is Small for Band Show," *Waterloo Daily Courier*, December 13, 1951, 22.
4. Paul Théberge, "'Plugged In': Technology and Popular Music," in *The Cambridge Companion to Pop and Rock*, ed. Simon Frith, Will Straw, and John Street (Cambridge: Cambridge University Press, 2001), 3.
5. See Neil Tesser, "The Electric Guitar and Vibraphone in Jazz: Batteries Not Included," in the *Oxford Companion to Jazz*, ed. Bill Kirchner (Oxford: Oxford University Press, 2000), 642–652.

6. Smith, *Fender*, 107.

7. Martin Kelly, Terry Foster, and Paul Kelly, *The Golden Age of Fender: 1946–1970* (London: Cassell Illustrated, 2010), 66.

8. Monk Montgomery, interview by Maggie Hawthorn, Jazz Oral History Project, 1980 (Rutgers Institute of Jazz Studies, Newark, NJ), 46–47.

9. Quoted in Quincy Jones, *Q: The Autobiography of Quincy Jones* (New York: Doubleday, 2001), 72–73.

10. In his detailed discography of Lionel Hampton's work from this era, Otto Flückiger lists that Montgomery joined Hampton's band circa November 1952 and left in early December 1953; see Otto Flückiger, *Discography of Lionel Hampton and his Orchestra: 1951–1953* (Reinach: Jazz-Publications, 1961), 23–25.

11. Montgomery, interview by Hawthorn, 41–43.

12. Montgomery, interview by Hawthorn, 43.

13. Montgomery, interview by Hawthorn, 44–46.

14. My conception of social stigma is shaped by Erving Goffman's landmark work on the subject; see Erving Goffman, *Stigma: Notes on the Management of Spoiled Identity* (New York: Simon & Schuster, 1963).

15. For a detailed itinerary of this tour, see Mario Schneeberger, "The European Tour of Lionel Hampton and His Orchestra, 1953: Band Routes," *Names and Numbers*, no. 68 (January 2014), reprinted at http://www.jazzdocumentation.ch/mario/lionel-hampton-bandroutes-europe-19531.pdf

16. Quoted in Bacon and Moorhouse, *The Bass Book*, 15–16.

17. Sven Winquist, "Hampton Knocks 'Em Out at Oslo Debut," *Melody Maker*, September 12, 1953, 16; emphasis added.

18. Simon Brehm, "Roligast Hittills—men mycket fin musik också," *Estrad*, October 1953, 4. Translation mine.

19. Jackie Vermont, "Lionel Hampton au Palais du Chaillot," *Jazz Hot*, October 1953, 17. Translation mine.

20. Harry Nicolausson, "Tjo Och Tjim Och Lite Annat: Hampton motsvarade sitt rykte," *Orkester Journalen*, October 1953, 14. Translation mine.

21. Ivor Mairants, "The Electric Bass," *Melody Maker*, November 14, 1953, 13. He published a similarly dismissive follow-up article the following week; see Ivor Mairants, "Instrumental Intelligence," *Melody Maker*, November 21, 1953, 11.

22. The article states that "Jack Seymour . . . *only* uses an amplifier for dances," and that "Johnny Hawksworth . . . is another who uses amplification *only* for dances and concerts." Mairants, "The Electric Bass," 13; emphasis added. It is also worth noting that, by 1965, Mairants had changed his mind enough to write his own "Complete Method for Bass Guitar."

23. Aside from jazz bassist Chubby Jackson, who was featured in Kay's advertising, the most famous musician to use the K-162 was Howlin' Wolf's bassist Andrew "Blueblood" McMahon, who is briefly discussed in Interlude IV.

24. Jim Roberts, *American Basses: An Illustrated History & Player's Guide* (San Francisco: Backbeat Books, 2003), 94.

25. Mike Nevard, "Hampton Band in Britain . . . but Only for 8 Hours," *Melody Maker*, November 28, 1953, 7.

26. Nevard, "Hampton Band in Britain."

27. "Eric in the Evening: Alan Dawson Interview," June 6, 1994, *WGBH Media*

Library & Archives, http://openvault.wgbh.org/catalog/2ae258-eric-in-the-eveni
ng-alan-dawson-interview/, accessed May 2, 2014.

28. Just prior to leaving for Europe, Montgomery had also played on a July 2, 1953, session as part of the Art Farmer Septet. This session would be released by Prestige in 1953 on a 10-inch LP, titled *Work of Art,* and later as a 12-inch LP, *The Art Farmer Septet,* in 1956. Montgomery's performances, especially on tracks like "Work of Art" and "Up in Quincy's Room," clearly demonstrate the Precision Bass's potential sonic presence and clarity in a recorded environment.

29. See Ralph Gleason, liner notes to Lionel Hampton, *Lionel Hampton,* Contemporary C 3502, 1955, LP.

30. Mike Butcher, liner notes to Lionel Hampton, *Lionel Hampton's Paris All Stars,* Vogue L.D.E. 063, 1954, vinyl.

31. Ralph Berton, "Ralph Berton Writes Some More Notes on Lionel Hampton," *Melody Maker,* October 17, 1953, 13.

32. Mike Newman, "Monk Montgomery: The First Man to Record on Bass Guitar," *Guitar Player,* September 1977, 27. While Montgomery often claimed that he arrived at this technique "naturally," it is likely that he adapted this technique from observing his younger brother, guitarist Wes Montgomery, who similarly played with his thumb.

33. These recordings were reissued as Lionel Hampton, *Lionel Hampton's Paris All Stars,* BMG France, 1997, CD.

34. Hugues Panassié, review of Lionel Hampton, *Jazz Time Paris, Bulletin du Hot Club de France,* December 1953, 11–12. Translation mine.

35. Panassié, review of Hampton, 13.

36. In Hampton's band, Montgomery performed a wholly supportive role. According to Mario Schneeberger, of all the recordings that survive from this tour, "All sideman except Monk Montgomery, Alan Dawson, and [singer] Annie Ross can be heard soloing." See Mario Schneeberger, "The European Tour of Lionel Hampton and His Orchestra, 1953: The Recorded Concerts," *Names and Numbers,* no. 64 (January 2013), reprinted at http://www.jazzdocumentation.ch /mario/hamprecords.pdf

37. These recordings were reissued as the Mastersounds, *Introducing The Mastersounds—Water's Edge,* Fresh Sound Records FSR-CD 500, 2008, CD.

38. See Ted Gioia, *West Coast Jazz: Modern Jazz in California, 1945–1960* (Oxford: Oxford University Press, 1992), 112–113.

39. "Down Beat Critics' Poll Results," *Down Beat,* August 6, 1959, 20.

40. Fender, advertisement, *Down Beat,* October 31, 1957, 22–23.

41. Fender, advertisement, *Down Beat,* May 1, 1958, 3.

42. Ralph Gleason, liner notes to the Mastersounds, *Jazz Showcase Introducing The Mastersounds,* World Pacific Records PJM-403, 1957, vinyl; emphasis added.

43. See Brian F. Wright, "Jaco Pastorius, the Electric Bass, and the Struggle for Jazz Credibility," *Journal of Popular Music Studies* 32, no. 3 (September 2020): 121–138.

44. "Bass Lines: Crystal Gazing with a Bonanza of Experts," *Down Beat,* January 27, 1977, 42.

45. Newman, "Monk Montgomery," 26.

46. *Encyclopedia of Jazz,* ed. Leonard Feather (New York: Horizon Press, 1960), s.v. "Montgomery, William Howard (Monk)," 338.

47. Other jazz musicians that adopted the electric bass in the 1950s include Chubby Jackson, who played with Woody Herman; Nappy Lamare, who played with the Riverboat Dandies; Wilburn Green, who played with Sun Ra; Jymie Merritt, who played with Chris Powell (and later, on upright, with the Jazz Messengers); Curtis Ross and Peter Badie, who both later played with Hampton; and Buster Coates, who is largely lost to history but is described in detail in Preston Love, *A Thousand Honey Creeks Later: My Life in Music from Basie to Motown* (Hanover, NH: Wesleyan University Press, 1997).

48. Two notable musicians who claim Montgomery as an influence are Bob Babbitt (discussed further in Chapter 6) and bassist Billy Cox (famous for his work with Jimi Hendrix). As Cox described in an interview with *Bass Player* magazine: "He was incredible for that time on electric bass; I bought everything that Monk Montgomery played on." See Billy Cox, interview by Richard Johnston, *Bass Player*, July 2007, 42.

Interlude III

1. Gary Hartman, *The History of Texas Music* (College Station: Texas A&M University Press, 2008), 2.

2. Bill C. Malone and Tracy E. W. Laird, *Country Music USA*, 50th Anniversary ed. (Austin: University of Texas Press, 2018), 188.

3. Jeffrey J. Lange, *Smile When You Call Me a Hillbilly: Country Music's Struggle for Respectability, 1939–1954* (Athens: University of Georgia Press, 2004), 122.

4. For a wider discussion of Texas dance halls, see Gail Folkins, "Texas Dance Halls: History, Culture, and Community," *Journal of Texas Music History* 6 (2006): 1–9; and Gail Folkins, *Texas Dance Halls: A Two-Step Circuit* (Lubbock: Texas Tech University Press, 2007).

5. The pseudonym came about because the brothers worked for two competing media companies. They adopted the name to avoid the appearance of a conflict of interest. See Jean A. Boyd, *Dance All Night: Those Other Southwestern Swing Bands, Past and Present* (Lubbock: Texas Tech University Press, 2012), 109.

6. Carroll Wilson, *Playing by Heart: Leon Gibbs and the Miller Brothers Band* (Wichita Falls, TX: Midwestern State University Press, 2003), 73. While country groups like the Texas Playboys, Lefty Frizzell, Ray Price, and Ernest Tubb all played the Corral, so too did the big bands of Lionel Hampton, Tommy Dorsey, and Harry James. In the mid-fifties, the Corral also became an important stop for rock 'n' roll bands, and Fats Domino, Elvis Presley, Little Richard, Jerry Lee Lewis, Chuck Berry, and others played there.

7. Pascal Williams, whose name is sometimes listed as Paschalle Williams, had his own short recording career, which included two singles: "Crazy in Love" backed with "Biding Time" for Jay Records and "Who Flung That 'Mater?" backed with "I Believe in You" on Gold Standard Records.

8. It is also worth noting that, by this time, the group was officially endorsed by Rickenbacker, who supplied them with complimentary lap steel guitars and amplifiers. In Figure 14, Williams is shown playing a Fender bass through a Rickenbacker amp. Rickenbacker would not start manufacturing electric basses until 1957.

9. "Country Poll Winners," *Cash Box,* June 18, 1955, 40; "Country Poll Winners," *Cash Box,* July 14, 1956, 38.

10. "The Final Count for 1956 Poll!," *Cash Box,* December 8, 1956, 5; "The Final Count for 1957 Poll!," *Cash Box,* December 8, 1957, 9.

11. Joe Carr and Alan Munde, *Prairie Nights to Neon Lights: The Story of Country Music in West Texas* (Lubbock: Texas Tech University Press, 1995), 66.

12. Boyd, *Dance All Night,* 114.

13. Diane Pecknold, *The Selling Sound: The Rise of the Country Music Industry* (Durham: Duke University Press, 2007), 85–94.

14. Quoted in Rich Kienzle, *Southwest Shuffle: Pioneers of Honky-Tonk, Western Swing, and Country Jazz* (New York: Routledge, 2003), 168.

15. Quoted in Daniel Cooper, "Being Ray Price Means Never Having to Say You're Sorry," *Journal of Country Music* 14, no. 3 (1992): 27.

16. Cooper, "Being Ray Price," 27. According to Cooper, "Strictly speaking, the second bass was a six-string electric bass guitar, probably played by [guitarist] Jack Pruett." It is possible that the instrument was a Danelectro UB-2 (discussed in Chapter Four), but it difficult to know for certain.

17. Kienzle, *Southwest Shuffle,* 157.

18. Manuel Peña, *The Texas-Mexican Conjunto: History of a Working-Class Music* (Austin: University of Texas Press, 1985), 72–73.

19. Joe Holley, "Tony De La Rosa Dies," *Washington Post,* June 19, 2004, https://www.washingtonpost.com/archive/local/2004/06/19/tony-de-la-rosa -dies/d5027cec-9377-4a1b-861d-22f7b1568ef9/

20. Cathy Ragland, *Música Norteña: Mexican Migrants Creating a Nation between Nations* (Philadelphia: Temple University Press, 2009), 68.

21. Quoted in Ragland, *Música Norteña,* 69.

22. Peña, *The Texas-Mexican Conjunto,* 86.

23. Peña, *The Texas-Mexican Conjunto,* 85–88, 95–97.

24. Ragland, *Música Norteña,* 69.

25. Guadalupe San Miguel Jr., "The Rise of Recorded Tejano Music in the Post–World War II Years, 1946–1964," *Journal of American Ethnic History* 19, no. 1 (Fall 1999): 43.

26. Clayton T. Shorkey, "La Villita Dance Hall," *Handbook of Texas Online,* https://www.tshaonline.org/handbook/entries/la-villita-dance-hall

27. Peña, *The Texas-Mexican Conjunto,* 99.

28. Maldonado joined his first conjunto in 1956, recorded with Gilberto Lopez in 1957, and eventually formed his own band, with which he performed for decades. Photographs from his early career show him playing a Kay K-162 Electronic Bass.

Chapter 3

1. "Rock Around the Clock" reached No. 1 on July 9, 1955. The song's success came from its inclusion in the 1955 MGM film *Blackboard Jungle,* a juvenile delinquent drama that featured the song underneath the film's title sequence and closing credits. It had originally been released as a B-side in May 1954 but only became a hit after *Jungle*'s release in April 1955. No one had predicted

this development, least of all MGM: for its use in *Jungle*, it had licensed "Rock Around the Clock" for $5,000; Decca had offered the entire rights to the song for just $7,500, but the studio declined. See R. Serge Denisoff and William D. Romanowski, *Risky Business: Rock in Film* (New Brunswick, NJ: Transaction Publishers, 1991), 11.

2. David E. James, *Rock 'n' Film: Cinema's Dance with Popular Music* (New York: Oxford University Press, 2016), 43.

3. For a longer discussion of the Bellboys' career, see Wayne Russell, liner notes to Freddie Bell & the Bellboys, *Rockin' Is Our Business*, Bear Family Records, BCD 15901, 1996, CD.

4. The Bellboys and the Treniers were apparently on good terms; see Russell, liner notes to *Rockin' Is Our Business.*

5. Steve Waksman, *Live Music in America: A History from Jenny Lind to Beyoncé* (New York: Oxford University Press, 2022), 299; see also Richard A. Peterson, "Why 1955? Explaining the Advent of Rock Music," *Popular Music* 9, no. 1 (January 1990): 97–116.

6. Ian Inglis, "Introduction: History, Place and Time: The Possibility of the Unexpected," in *Performance and Popular Music*, ed. Ian Inglis (New York: Routledge, 2006), xv.

7. Bartholomew's career is detailed in John Broven, *Rhythm & Blues in New Orleans*, 3rd ed. (Gretna, LA: Pelican Publishing, 1995).

8. Quoted in Charles White, *The Life and Times of Little Richard: The Authorised Biography*, 2nd ed. (London: Omnibus press, 2003), 48.

9. Broven, *Rhythm & Blues*, 38. For a description of a typical Fats Domino recording session, see Broven, *Rhythm & Blues*, 68–69.

10. According to James Miller, "Richard discovered that 'Tutti Frutti' worked best in the whites-only clubs. 'He only did "Tutti Frutti" in white clubs,' one old friend has recalled, 'cause you see, Blacks were a little more sensitive than whites.' Richard, too, remembers a difference in the crowd's reaction: 'White people, it always cracked 'em up, but Black people didn't like it that much. They liked the blues.'" This points to an important demographic shift in early rock 'n' roll as the music's appeal was directed less at adult Black audiences and more at white teenagers. See James Miller, *Flowers in the Dustbin: The Rise of Rock and Roll, 1947–1977* (New York: Simon & Schuster, 1999), 110–111.

11. This rhythmic feel can be found on a host of hits from the mid-fifties, including Chuck Berry's "Rock and Roll Music" (1957) and Elvis Presley's "Jailhouse Rock" (1957); what all of these recordings speak to, ultimately, is an evolutionary moment where the aesthetics of rock 'n' roll were still in flux—here situated somewhere between the swing styles of the previous generations and the rock music of the sixties. For a broader discussion of the overlapping swing and straight rhythms of early rock 'n' roll, see Alexander Stewart, "'Funky Drummer': New Orleans, James Brown and the Rhythmic Transformation of American Popular Music," *Popular Music* 19, no. 3 (2000): 293–318; and Matt Brennan, "Creative Drummers, Artistry, Virtuosity, and Playing Time," in *Kick It: A Social History of the Drum Kit* (New York: Oxford University Press, 2020).

12. Quoted in Broven, *Rhythm & Blues*, 93–94.

13. White, *Life and Times*, 57–58.

14. Charles Connor, *Keep a Knockin': The Story of a Legendary Drummer* (Grapevine, TX: Waldorf Publishing, 2015), 62.

15. Connor, *Keep a Knockin'*, 50–52.

16. Roberts, *American Basses*, 73.

17. Walter Carter, *The Gibson Electric Guitar Book: Seventy Years of Classic Guitars* (San Francisco: Backbeat Books, 2007), 53.

18. Connor, *Keep a Knockin'*, 67–68. Connor also describes how Robinson got his moniker: "Richard found a guy named Olsie Robinson to fill in the job. But the guys, y'know, thought that Olsie was a funny name, so we just called him Basie."

19. Quoted in White, *Life and Times*, 74.

20. The film also features musical performances by Johnny Olenn and the Jokers, Gene Vincent, Fats Domino, the Platters, and the Treniers. The electric bass is well represented among the acts: it is shown being played by Bobby Gene Baker with Olenn, by Jimmy Johnson with the Treniers, and by Basie Robinson.

21. Guitarist B. B. King recalls the effect of seeing these Black bands in a full color, major studio production: "*The Girl Can't Help It* was the first film I can remember that was accepted as an A1 movie featuring Blacks. It had Fats Domino, Little Richard and several other Blacks and presented them in a beautiful way. I mean with a lot of class." Quoted in Rob Burt, *Rock and Roll: The Movies* (New York: New Orchard Editions, 1986), 21.

22. For more on Brown's life story, see his memoir: J. W. Brown, *Whole Lotta Shakin'* (Savannah, GA: Continental Shelf Publishing, 2010).

23. Brown claims to have played rhythm guitar during this session, but this is difficult to verify. See Brown, *Whole Lotta Shakin'*, 38. He also claims that Sam Phillips's shoddy bookkeeping cost him royalties that he should have earned: "The logs of recording sessions were kept in the same way that Sam kept his ledgers, with dates guesstimated, session musicians substituted, added or deleted, and sums paid to union labor falsified. I recorded seventeen sessions at Sun— some 70 or 80 songs—but was never paid a penny in session wages. In order to avoid having to pay me for session work, Sam substituted my name with Sun Studio session men that were already on the payroll, which meant that not only was I cheated out of union wages, I was cheated out of the credit on some of the biggest hits ever to come out of Sun Records." See Brown, *Whole Lotta Shakin'*, 53.

24. Brown, *Whole Lotta Shakin'*, 55.

25. Brown, *Whole Lotta Shakin'*, 55.

26. Rick Bragg, *Jerry Lee Lewis: His Own Story* (New York: HarperCollins, 2014), 181.

27. Brown, *Whole Lotta Shakin'*, 84.

28. While in California filming *High School Confidential*, Brown was invited by Leo Fender to visit the Fender factory. Ever the tinkerer, Fender was most interested in Brown's assessment of his second-generation Precision Bass. As Brown recalls, "He wanted my feedback on what it was like to play his invention before thousands of screaming fans and whether I thought there was room for improvement in the design. . . . Then Leo took me to school on the split-humbucking pickup that he had recently introduced [on the third-generation Precision Basses], and the two single coil pickups he was contemplating, and asked me if

I would prefer a sleeker style with a slimmer neck. I was flattered that he asked me for my opinion, and was even more impressed that he paid careful attention to my comments." See Brown, *Whole Lotta Shakin'*, 124. The "sleeker style" bass discussed here is a reference to the Fender Jazz Bass, which would be released in 1960.

29. Although most sources claim that Phillips has been accurately quoted, what he meant is still being debated. For instance, Peter Guralnick claims that the quotation has been abstracted from Phillips's "underlying vision and irony" and thus has consistently been taken out of context; see Peter Guralnick, *Last Train to Memphis: The Rise of Elvis Presley* (Boston: Little, Brown, 1994), 500. For a thorough interrogation of the quotation, see Gilbert B. Rodman, "A Hero to Most? Elvis, Myth, and the Politics of Race," *Cultural Studies* 8, no. 3 (1994): 457–483.

30. For a discussion of the rockabilly slap bass style and how it changed after the electric bass was introduced into the genre, see Roy Brewer, "The Appearance of the Electric Bass Guitar: A Rockabilly Perspective," *Popular Music and Society* 26, no. 3 (2003): 351–366.

31. Quoted in Ken Burke and Dan Griffin, *The Blue Moon Boys: The Story of Elvis Presley's Band* (Chicago: Chicago Review Press, 2006), 24.

32. Guralnick, *Last Train to Memphis*, 95.

33. The sexual implications of Presley's "Hound Dog" and his various televised appearances in support of it are detailed in Robert Fink, "Elvis Everywhere: Musicology and Popular Music Studies at the Twilight of the Canon," *American Music* 16, no. 2 (Summer 1998): 135–179.

34. For more on Thornton, see Maureen Mahon, *Black Diamond Queens: African American Women and Rock and Roll* (Durham: Duke University Press, 2020), and Kimberly Mack, *Fictional Blues: Narrative Self-Invention from Bessie Smith to Jack White* (Amherst: University of Massachusetts Press, 2020).

35. For more on Presley's relationship with Las Vegas, see Brian F. Wright, "Elvis in Vegas: The King of Rock 'n' Roll and the City of Second Chances," in *The Possibility Machine: Music and Myth in Las Vegas*, ed. Jake Johnson (Urbana: University of Illinois Press, 2023).

36. Guralnick, *Last Train to Memphis*, 273.

37. See Russell, liner notes to *Rockin' Is Our Business*.

38. Roy Brewer analyzes this specific bass line and claims that it was largely responsible for introducing an Afro-Cuban feel into rockabilly music; see Roy Brewer, "The Use of Habanera Rhythm in Rockabilly Music," *American Music* 17, no. 3 (1999): 300–317.

39. See "Jerry Leiber and Mike Stoller: A Bridge Built on the Blues," in Paul Zollo, *More Songwriters on Songwriting* (Boston: Perseus Books, 2016), 37–40.

40. Quoted in Zollo, *More Songwriters on Songwriting*, 48.

41. Jerry Leiber and Mike Stoller with David Ritz, *Hound Dog: The Leiber and Stoller Autobiography* (New York: Simon & Schuster, 2009), 112–113.

42. It is often erroneously claimed that Bill Black played electric bass on the song "Jailhouse Rock." Leiber's recollections contradict that claim, as do the multiple accounts concerning the recording of "(You're So Square) Baby I Don't Care" discussed later.

43. Guralnick, *Last Train to Memphis*, 407–408.

44. D. J. Fontana, interview by Parke Puterbaugh, Rock & Roll Hall of Fame and Museum Oral History Project, March 3, 2012; emphasis added.

45. Quoted on James V. Roy, "1956 Fender Precision Bass," *Scotty Moore: The Official Website*, June 27, 2011, http://www.scottymoore.net/56PBass.html/, accessed November 1, 2012.

46. To accomplish a "hammer-on," the musician uses one hand to strike the string while fretting it with one finger on the other hand; then, without striking it again, they use a different finger on their fretting hand to forcefully press down at a higher fret, producing a second note.

47. "Presley Whips 12,000 into Near-Hysteria," *Spokane Review*, August 31, 1957; reprinted in Ger Rijff, *Long Lonely Highway: A 1950s Elvis Scrapbook* (Ann Arbor, MI: Pierian Press, 1987), 160.

48. In total, the instrument, amplifier, and case cost $637.06 (approximately $5,500 today). An invoice for the bass is reprinted at Roy, "1956 Fender Precision Bass."

49. Guralnick, *Last Train to Memphis*, 432. Interestingly, Guralnick alludes to Black playing electric bass on the aforementioned Christmas album: "Scotty and Bill protested that they had a deal, but [Tom] Diskin told them Colonel said they could do it another time and told everyone to pack up, unmoved by either their anger or protestations. Bill hit the roof, muttering to himself and slamming his *electric bass* into its case."

50. As told to Moore's friend Gail Pollock; see James V. Roy, "Amplifying Bill's Upright Bass," *Scotty Moore: The Official Website*, http://www.scottymoore.net/ampeg.html/, accessed December 15, 2016.

51. Philip Norman, *Rave On: The Biography of Buddy Holly* (New York: Simon & Schuster, 1996), 107–108.

52. Quoted in Jim Dawson and Spencer Leigh, *Memories of Buddy Holly* (Milford, NH: Big Nickel Publications, 1996), 32.

53. Dave Laing, *Buddy Holly* (Bloomington: Indiana University Press, 2010), 94–95.

54. Dawson and Leigh, *Memories of Buddy Holly*, 69.

55. This photo was copied from the "Bill Griggs Papers, 1926–2016," Southwest Collection/Special Collections Library, Texas Tech University, Lubbock, Texas.

56. John Gribbin, *Not Fade Away: The Life and Music of Buddy Holly* (Colchester: Icon Books, 2009), 136.

57. After Holly's death, Mauldin and the Crickets continued to tour on their own and as the backing group for other artists. Notably, they backed up the Everly Brothers on their first UK concert tour.

58. Quoted in Bill Mack, "The Life and Times of Blue Cap Bill Mack, Mr. Bassman," *Forgotten Hits*, February 11, 2012, http://forgottenhits60s.blogspot.com/2012_02_05_archive.html

59. Mack, "Life and Times."

60. Susan VanHecke, *Race with the Devil: Gene Vincent's Life in the Fast Lane* (New York: St. Martins, 2001), 52.

61. Mack, "Life and Times." Like Joe B. Mauldin with Buddy Holly, Marshall

Grant did eventually switch to playing electric bass with Johnny Cash, but only on the road. As Grant recalled, "There's a good reason I started playing the electric [bass]. It became a problem to transport the upright bass . . . It was so big. And it got to where when we flew I had to buy [the bass] a seat. And put it in beside me and it got a little expensive. So I started playing the electric bass." G. E. Light, "Marshall Grant Was Here, There, and Everywhere," *Perfect Sound Forever Magazine,* February 2008, https://www.furious.com/perfect/marshallgr ant.html, accessed November 1, 2010.

62. Derek Henderson, *Gene Vincent: A Companion* (Southampton: Spent Brothers Productions, 2005), 11–12, 161. Jones also wrote songs for Vincent, including "Baby Blue" (1958). See Bob Erskine and Roger Nunn, "Bobby Jones, a Gene Vincent Blue Cap," *Rockabilly Hall of Fame,* November 2011, http://www .rockabillyhall.com/gvbobbyjones.html/, accessed November 1, 2010.

63. Quoted in Bacon and Moorhouse, *The Bass Book,* 25.

64. For recent large-scale histories of live music, see Simon Frith, Matt Brennan, Martin Cloonan, and Emma Webster, *The History of Live Music in Britain,* vol. 1: *1950–1967* (Farnham: Ashgate, 2013) and *The History of Live Music in Britain,* vol. 2: *1968–1984* (London: Routledge, 2019); and Waksman, *Live Music in America.*

65. Lewis's marriage to Myra Brown came as an unwelcome surprise to J. W., who was unaware of Lewis's relationship with his daughter. After the truth was revealed, Brown apparently showed up at Sun Studio with a gun, intent on killing Jerry Lee. Instead, Sam Phillips convinced him that it was in his best interest to remain in the band. The Jerry Lee Lewis Trio's career, however, was irreparably damaged after the British press discovered the marriage, and the subsequent news coverage forced them to abandon their 1958 tour of England. See Bragg, *Jerry Lee Lewis,* 241, 268–285.

Interlude IV

1. Figures cited in Mike Rowe, *Chicago Blues: The City & the Music* (New York: Da Capo Press, 1975), 35.

2. Elijah Wald, *The Blues: A Very Short Introduction* (New York: Oxford University Press, 2010), 59.

3. Mitsutoshi Inaba, *Willie Dixon: Preacher of the Blues* (Lanham, MD: Scarecrow Press, 2011), 59.

4. Quoted in Willie Dixon, *I Am the Blues: The Willie Dixon Story* (New York: Da Capo Press, 1989), 96.

5. For a more detailed history of the electric guitar's early history in the Chicago Black music scene, see Waksman, *Instruments of Desire,* 113–166.

6. Robert Palmer, *Deep Blues* (New York: Penguin, 1981), 267.

7. Jas Obrecht, "Buddy Guy and Otis Rush: Chicago Blues—the Inside Story," *Guitar Player,* November 1994; reprinted in *Rollin' and Tumblin': The Postwar Blues Guitarists,* ed. Jas Obrecht (San Francisco: Miller Freeman Books, 2000), 437.

8. Bill Greensmith, "Below's the Name, Drummin's the Game," *Blues Unlimited,* nos. 131–132 (September–December 1978): 18.

9. Robert Gordon, *Can't Be Satisfied: The Life and Times of Muddy Waters* (Boston: Little, Brown, 2002), 154.

10. According to his brother, guitarist Louis Myers, after he and Dave left Little Walter's band, they joined up with Otis Rush, where they got to witness Willie D. Warren's electric bass playing firsthand. See Willie Leiser, "Willie Leiser, 'The Road Runner,' Returns to the BU Pages," *Blues Unlimited,* April 1973, 33–34.

11. D. Thomas Moon, "Dave Myers: Somebody Has to Live It First," *Living Blues,* November–December 1998, 40.

12. Moon, "Dave Myers," 40.

13. Moon, "Dave Myers," 40.

14. Bill Milkowski, "Blues Legend Dave Myers," *Bass Player,* December 1998, 18.

15. Sources disagree about the spelling of his last name. The recent Chess rereleases, for example, list it as "Meyers," while the 1965 Chess session contract for Koko Taylor's "Wang Dang Doodle" and the liner notes to Junior Wells's *Hoodoo Man Blues* LP list it as "Myers."

16. Jean-Claude Arnaudon, "Jack Myers," in *Dictionnaire du blues* (Paris: Filipacchi, 1977), 192–193.

17. "Obituaries: Jack Myers," *Living Blues* 213, vol. 42, no. 3 (June 2011): 75; Sebastian Danchin, *Earl Hooker: Blues Master* (Jackson: University Press of Mississippi, 2001), 110.

18. Alan di Perna, "Buddy Guy: A Man and His Blues," *Guitar World,* October 2005, reprinted at https://www.guitarworld.com/features/buddy-guy-man-and-his-blues/

19. Dan Forte, "Buddy Guy: Keeping the Blues Alive and Definitely Kicking," *Vintage Guitar,* May 2013, reprinted at https://www.vintageguitar.com/14777/buddy-guy-3/. For examples highlighting Meyer's bass playing, listen to "Ten Years Ago," "Watch Yourself," and "Skippin'," all of which are preserved on Buddy Guy, *The Complete Chess Studio Recordings,* Chess/MCA CHD2-9337, 1992, CD.

20. In 2003, *Down Beat* went so far as to rank *Hoodoo Man Blues* the number one blues album of the last fifty years; see Frank-John Hadley, "Blues Pantheon: The 50 Top Blues Albums of the Past 50 Years," *Downbeat,* September 2003, 61.

21. Although he was well known in Chicago, little information survives about Boyd and his career. My discussion of his biography is reconstructed from a 1984 feature in *Guitar Player* magazine, as well as an interview I conducted with his son, Reggie Boyd Jr.; see Larry Birnbaum, "Reggie Boyd: Chess Session Ace, Jazz & Blues Educator," *Guitar Player,* January 1984, 14–22.

22. "Obituaries: Reggie Boyd," *Living Blues* 210, vol. 41, no. 6 (December 2010): 67.

23. Larry Hoffman, "Robert Lockwood, Jr.," *Living Blues,* June 1995, reprinted in *Rollin' and Tumblin',* 180.

24. Birnbaum's article claims that Boyd's electric bass was a Kay, but Boyd's son recalls that he exclusively played a Fender Precision Bass, and surviving photographs from the era support his son's claims. Boyd's son also recalls that Chess paid his father around twenty to twenty-five dollars per session, which at the time was well below union scale. This aligns with Dixon's recollection that, while as

a rule Chess's session musicians were paid scale, "The union required the musicians be paid within fourteen days of the session, but most wanted their money the day they finished. Leonard would say, 'If you take half the money, I'll give it to you now.' They were paying something like $42.50 so he'd go over and say, 'I'll give you $22 and we'll call it even, okay?'" Dixon, *I Am the Blues*, 98.

25. Birnbaum, "Reggie Boyd," 18.

26. For more on the Watusi, see Robert Pruter, "Chicago Black Dance," in *Chicago Soul* (Urbana: University of Illinois Press, 1991), 187–210.

27. Some sources claim that Boyd had previously recorded with Berry in July 1959 and February 1960. However, these claims are disputed by the discographies on Chess's official releases and by the fact that Boyd didn't start playing electric bass until around October 1960.

28. Taking place on either January 10 or January 19, 1961, this session produced one single, "I'm Talking About You," and two album cuts, "Route 66" and "Rip It Up." All three recordings appear on Berry's 1961 LP *New Juke Box Hits*.

29. Birnbaum, "Reggie Boyd," 21.

30. Billy Boy Arnold, *The Blues Dream of Billy Boy Arnold* (Chicago: University of Chicago Press, 2021), 183.

31. Jan Mark Wolkin and Bill Keenom, *Mike Bloomfield: If You Love These Blues* (San Francisco: Miller Freeman Books, 2000), 86.

32. Susan Oehler Herrick, "Performing Blues and Navigating Race in Transcultural Contexts," in *Issues in African American Music: Power, Gender, Race, Representation*, ed. Portia K. Maultsby and Mellonee V. Burnim (New York: Routledge, 2017), 3–29.

33. Elijah Wald, *Dylan Goes Electric! Newport, Seeger, Dylan, and the Night that Split the Sixties* (New York: Dey St, 2015), 216.

34. Wald notes that Arnold's performance during Dylan's set was as a disaster, as the bassist repeatedly lost his place in the music and could not recover. For more on Butterfield Band at Newport, see Wald, *Dylan Goes Electric!*

35. Mick Houghton, *Becoming Elektra: The True Story of Jac Holzman's Visionary Record Label* (London: Jawbone Press, 2010), 174.

36. Keith Tillman, "Bringing It to Jerome," *Blues Unlimited*, no. 63, June 1969, 13. This appears to be Arnold's only published interview.

37. Dixon's last two notable upright performances were on Howlin' Wolf's "The Red Rooster" (1961) and Muddy Waters's "You Shook Me" (1962).

38. Wald, *The Blues*, 67.

39. For example, electric bassist Louis Satterfield played on many of Chess's midsixties soul hits, including Billy Stewart's "I Do Love You" (1965) and Fontella Bass's "Rescue Me" (1965). For more, see Pruter, "Chicago Black Dance."

Chapter 4

1. "Sugar Shack" may be the first hit song to feature a Rickenbacker electric bass. As detailed in Interlude I, in the thirties, the company had produced some of the first electric uprights. Despite those early innovations, however, the Rickenbacker of the fifties and sixties was a fundamentally different company.

Its original owner, Adolph Rickenbacker sold the company to F. C. Hall in late 1953. Having worked as a distributor for Fender, Hall was keenly aware of the growing interest in electric guitars, and he pushed Rickenbacker to concentrate more on that market. As part of that push, the company produced its first electric bass guitar, the 4000, in 1957. The 4001 that Stan Lark played on "Sugar Shack" was a revamped, two-pickup version that had first gone into production in 1961.

2. For more on Lark's career, see Brian F. Wright, "Interview with Fireballs' Bassist Stan Lark," 2021, https://www.brianfwright.com/interviews/stan-lark/

3. Based on the evidence that survives, it appears that most bassists in the fifties who played with their index finger used that finger alone and did not add in their middle finger. The two-finger approach would not become common until the early sixties.

4. Albin J. Zak III, *I Don't Sound Like Nobody: Remaking Music in 1950s America* (Ann Arbor: University of Michigan Press, 2012).

5. Zak, *I Don't Sound Like Nobody*, 153.

6. Travis D. Stimeling, *Nashville Cats: Record Production in Music City* (New York: Oxford University Press, 2020).

7. Stimeling, *Nashville Cats*, 121.

8. Rob Finnis and John P. Dixon, liner notes to Duane Eddy, *Twangin' from Phoenix to L.A.: The Jamie Years*, Hambergen, Germany, Bear Family Records, 1994, CD, 21.

9. Wheeler briefly mentions playing at this gig in Dave Acker, "Interview with Buddy Wheeler," http://tony50.tripod.com/interview-bwheeler.html/, accessed September 26, 2020.

10. Acker, "Interview with Buddy Wheeler."

11. For more on Hazelwood, see Michael Hall, "The Making of an Urbane Cowboy," *Texas Monthly*, September 16, 2019, https://www.texasmonthly.com/the-culture/lee-hazlewood-musician-texas/

12. Sill's previous label, Spark Records, had been a joint venture between him, Jerry Leiber, and Mike Stoller. Founded in 1953, Spark found its biggest success with the Robins, who had hits with the Leiber & Stoller songs "Riot in Cell Block #9" (1954) and "Smokey Joe's Café" (1955). The success of the latter recording proved to be too much for the small label to properly manage, so Spark partnered with Atlantic Records in 1955. Sill became Atlantic's national sales manager, Leiber & Stoller signed an independent production deal, and Carl Gardner and Bobby Nunn from the Robins started the Coasters.

13. Finnis and Dixon, liner notes to *Twangin' from Phoenix*, 16.

14. For more on Dick Clark and his behind-the-scenes music industry dealings, see John A. Jackson, *American Bandstand: Dick Clark and the Making of a Rock 'n' Roll Empire* (New York: Oxford University Press, 1997).

15. Zak discusses producers' use of echo chambers and reverb in the fifties in *Don't Sound Like Nobody*, 153–162.

16. Finnis and Dixon, liner notes to *Twangin' from Phoenix*, 22.

17. Finnis and Dixon, liner notes to *Twangin' from Phoenix*, 16.

18. Susan Schmidt-Horning, "Recording: The Search for the Sound," in *The Electric Guitar: A History of an American Icon*, ed. André Millard (Baltimore: John Hopkins University Press, 2004), 115.

19. Quoted in Finnis and Dixon, liner notes to *Twangin' from Phoenix*, 64.

20. Quoted in liner notes to Duane Eddy, *Twang Thang: The Duane Eddy Anthology*, Los Angeles, Rhino Records, 1993, CD, 10.

21. John Collis, *Gene Vincent and Eddie Cochran: Rock 'n' Revolutionaries* (London: Virgin Digital, 2011).

22. Julie Mundy and Darrel Highham, *Don't Forget Me: The Eddie Cochran Story* (New York: Billboard Books, 2001), 50.

23. Rob Finnis, liner notes to Eddie Cochran, *The Eddie Cochran Box Set: A Complete History in Works and Music, 1938–1960*, Hayes, Middlesex, England, Liberty, 1988, CD.

24. Information for this and Cochran's other sessions can be found in Finnis, liner notes to *Eddie Cochran Box Set*.

25. Session work was more plentiful in Los Angeles than New Orleans, so Palmer had relocated there in 1957.

26. Eddie Cochran and Guybo Smith appeared on the February 7, 1959, episode of the California country TV program *Town Hall Party*. In the surviving footage, Smith is shown playing a second-generation Fender Precision Bass with a pickup cover but no bridge cover.

27. Mundy and Higham, *Don't Forget Me*, 124.

28. Mundy and Higham, *Don't Forget Me*, 139.

29. "Summertime Blues" has notably been covered by the Who, Blue Cheer, T. Rex, Rush, and Alan Jackson. "C'Mon Everybody" has likewise been covered by Led Zeppelin, Humble Pie, UFO, the Sex Pistols, and Bryan Adams.

30. For more on Geisler's life story, see Gerhard Klußmeier, *Ladi: Weltstar aus Hamburg* (Hamburg: Tradition, 2014).

31. Julia Sneeringer, *A Social History of Early Rock 'n' Roll in Germany: Hamburg from Burlesque to the Beatles, 1956–1969* (London: Bloomsbury Academic, 2018), 36.

32. Klaus Nathaus, "The History of the German Popular Music Industry in the Twentieth Century," in *Perspectives on German Popular Music*, ed. Michael Ahlers and Christoph Jacke (London: Routledge, 2018), 250.

33. Quoted in Marc Boettcher, *Stranger in the Night: Die Bert Kaempfert Story* (Hamburg: Europäische Verlagsanstalt, 2002), 127–128. Translation mine.

34. Klußmeier, *Ladi*, 33. Translation mine.

35. Klußmeier, *Ladi*, 99; "Cash Box Pop DJ Poll Results," *Cash Box*, August 5, 1961, 49.

36. The connections between these styles were obvious to Harold Bradley, who once described the tic-tac sound by stating, "You would recognize the sound of it if you have never heard it before by listening to 'Wonderland by Night.'" See Jennifer Ember Pierce, "Harold Ray Bradley," in *Playin' Around: The Lives and Careers of Famous Session Musicians* (Lanham, MD: Scarecrow Press, 1998), 19.

37. Harold Bradley gave multiple in-depth interviews about his and his brother's career. See, for example, Harold Bradley, interview by John W. Rumble, September 15, 1988, Country Music Foundation, Frist Library and Archive of the Country Music Hall of Fame and Museum; Harold Bradley, interview by John W. Rumble, September 28, 1988, Country Music Foundation, Frist Library

and Archive of the Country Music Hall of Fame and Museum; Rich Kienzle, "Harold Bradley: Dean of the Nashville Session Pickers," *Journal of the American Academy for the Preservation of Old-Time Country Music* 1, no. 2 (April 1991): 22–34; Harold Bradley, interview by John W. Rumble, May 14, 1991, Country Music Foundation, Frist Library and Archive of the Country Music Hall of Fame and Museum; Pierce, "Harold Ray Bradley"; Harold Bradley, interview by Travis D. Stimeling, August 1, 2014, Nashville Sound Oral History Project.

38. Michael Kosser, *How Nashville Became Music City, U.S.A.: 50 Years of Music Row* (New York: Hal Leonard, 2006), 9–10.

39. Buddy Holly's Decca sessions also took place at this studio, though they did not produce any hits.

40. For more detailed discussions of the Nashville Sound, see William Ivey, "Commercialization and Tradition in the Nashville Sound," in *Folk Music and Modern Sound*, ed. William Ferris and Mary L. Hart (Jackson: University Press of Mississippi, 1982), 129–138; Joli Jensen, *The Nashville Sound: Authenticity, Commercialization, and Country Music* (Nashville: Country Music Foundation Press & Vanderbilt University Press, 1998).

41. Stimeling, *Nashville Cats*, 120.

42. Pierce, "Harold Ray Bradley," 18.

43. Bradley, interview by Stimeling, 8.

44. The UB-1 and UB-2 were the first commercially available six-string basses, and they were the direct precursor to the Danelectro Longhorn bass discussed at the beginning of this chapter.

45. More information on Danelectro's history can be found in Paul Bechtoldt and Doug Tulloch, *Guitars from Neptune: A Definitive Journey into Danelectro-Mania* (Fort Lauderdale: Guitar Broker, 1995), and Doug Tulloch, *Neptune Bound: The Ultimate Danelectro Guitar Guide* (Fullerton: Centerstream, 2009).

46. Joe Fisher, "Tales of a Dinosaur," unpublished memoir, reproduced at *Silvertone World*, https://www.silvertoneworld.net/amplifiers/1448/1448p2.html/, accessed May 4, 2016.

47. Harold Bradley later described his struggles with the instrument: "It won't tune to anything. You have to tune up to whatever key you're playing in. You have tuned in the key of F, and you play, that's fine, but then if you go along to B-flat or something else like C you have to tweak the tuning again." Bradley, interview by Stimeling, 9.

48. Bradley, interview by Stimeling, 9.

49. Bradley, interview by Rumble, May 14, 1991, 16.

50. Bradley, interview by Stimeling, 12.

51. Stimeling similarly analyzes the role of Harold Bradley's tic-tac bass on the recording; see *Nashville Cats*, 196.

52. Jensen, *The Nashville Sound*, 106.

53. For these sessions, Garland played a prototype of the Gibson EB-6 six-string bass, rather than his Danelectro UB-2. For more information, see Wolf Marshall, "Hank's Protos: How Hank Garland Helped Gibson Develop Two Models Not Called Byrdland," *Vintage Guitar*, September 2011, reprinted at https://www.vintageguitar.com/11719/hanks-protos/

Chapter 5

1. For more on the Ventures' history, see Del Halterman, *Walk-Don't Run: The Story of the Ventures*, 2nd ed. (Milton Keynes: Lulu, 2010).

2. Don Wilson, quoted in Halterman, *Walk-Don't Run*, 16.

3. Dan Forte, "The Ventures: Still Rockin' after All These Years," *Guitar Player*, September 1981, 90.

4. Jas Obrecht, "20 Essential Rock Albums," *Guitar Player*, January 1987, 109.

5. Peter Stuart Kohman, "Surf Bass: Out of the Doghouse," *Vintage Guitar*, May 1997, 100.

6. George Lipsitz, *Time Passages: Collective Memory and American Popular Culture* (Minneapolis: University of Minnesota Press, 1990), 120.

7. Lipsitz, *Time Passages*, 127.

8. All three descriptions taken from Glenn Altschuler, *All Shook Up: How Rock 'n' Roll Changed America* (Oxford: Oxford University Press, 2003), 161–184.

9. Figure cited in American Music Conference, *Report on Amateur Instrumental Music in the United States—1964* (Chicago: American Music Conference, 1964), 3. It is important to note that these figures do not differentiate between acoustic and electric guitarists, and certainly the folk revival of the late fifties and early sixties influenced guitar sales as well.

10. *Statistics on Amateur Music in the United States*, AMC Review (Chicago: American Music Conference, 1960); *1970 Review of the Music Industry and Amateur Music Participation*, American Music Conference, (Chicago: American Music Conference, 1970), 3.

11. Jack Feddersen, "Music Industry Promotion," *The Music Trades*, December 1956, 29.

12. American Music Conference, *Report on Amateur Instrumental Music in the United States—1965* (Chicago: American Music Conference, 1965), 1.

13. Quoted in Bacon and Moorehouse, *The Bass Book*, 33.

14. Quoted in Tom Wheeler, *American Guitars: An Illustrated History*, rev. ed. (New York: HarperPerennial, 1992), 65.

15. Fender, advertisement, *Down Beat*, January 19, 1961.

16. For a different perspective on the Danelectro Shorthorn bass, see Panagiotis Poulopoulos, "Reflecting the 1950s Popular Lifestyle: The Danelectro 3412 Short Horn Bass," in *Quand la guitare [s']électrise!*, ed. Benoît Navarret, Marc Battier, Philippe Bruguière, and Philippe Gonin (Paris: Sorbonne Université Presses, 2022), 63–98.

17. Liner notes to Johnny and the Hurricanes, *Johnny and the Hurricanes Featuring "Red River Rock,"* Warwick W2007, LP, 1959.

18. Jacqueline Warwick, *Girl Groups, Girl Culture: Popular Music and Identity in the 1960s* (New York: Routledge, 2007), 15.

19. Renée Minus White, *Maybe: My Memoir* (Pittsburgh: RoseDog Books, 2015), 32.

20. The song is reproduced on the compilation *Girls with Guitars 3: The Rebel Kind*, Ace Records CDCHD 1374, CD.

21. *Sears Fall and Winter Catalog* (Chicago: Sears, Roebuck and Company, 1959), 1289; *Sears Fall and Winter Catalog* (Chicago: Sears, Roebuck and

Company, 1966), 1370. Under Sears's "Easy Terms" financing, in 1964 (when the 1444 first became $0 down/$5 per month) the company would have added an extra $10 to the list price, allowing the consumer to gradually pay the $89.95 total over a maximum of eighteen months.

22. *Sears Fall and Winter Catalog* (Chicago: Sears, Roebuck and Company, 1960), 1289; *Sears Fall and Winter Catalog* (Chicago: Sears, Roebuck and Company, 1964), 1436.

23. For more, see Brian F. Wright, "Interview with the Royal's Bassist Bob 'Mole' Schmidt, Jr.," 2016, https://www.brianfwright.com/interviews/bob-sch midt

24. The Ventures themselves also played a role in the electric bass market. In the 1960s, the band entered into a partnership with Semie Moseley's Mosrite guitars, endorsing an entire line of "Ventures" model guitars and basses. The Ventures Mark X electric bass was introduced that same year for $310, making it one of the most expensive electric basses on the market.

25. Quoted in June Bundy, "Gals Best Disk & Phono Buyers in Teen-Age Bracket," *Billboard*, August 25, 1956, 15.

26. Quoted in a *New Yorker* profile of teen marketing guru Eugene Gilbert; see Dwight Macdonald, "A Caste, A Culture, A Market," *New Yorker*, November 22, 1958, 73.

27. American Music Conference, *Amateur Instrumental Music 1964*, 15; emphasis mine; American Music Conference, *Report on Amateur Instrumental Music in the United States—1967* (Chicago: American Music Conference, 1967), 8.

28. Bert Gardner, *Bert Gardner's Complete Course for Electric Bass* (n.p.: Music Exploitation Enterprises, 1957), n.p.

29. Gardner, *Bert Gardner's Complete Course*, back cover.

30. Anthony J. Manfredi and Joseph M. Estella, *Smith's Modern Electric Bass Guitar Method* (New York: WM J. Smith Music Co., 1959).

31. Manfredi and Estella, *Smith's Modern Electric Bass*, 1. Notably, in their discussion of technique, Manfredi and Estella show how to play the electric bass with a thumb and with a pick but not with an index finger.

32. Manfredi and Estella, *Smith's Modern Electric Bass*, 7.

33. Manfredi and Estella, *Smith's Modern Electric Bass*, 26.

34. In November 1979, Filiberto was awarded a plaque by Bay for having sold one million copies of the book; a picture of Bay presenting the award to Filiberto can be found in Ray Dankenbring, *The Mel Bay Story* (Pacific, MO: Mel Bay Publications, 1997). Filiberto's obituary in the New Orleans *Times-Picayune* quotes Bay as saying that "Mr. Filiberto's 'Electric Bass Method,' first published in 1963, has sold almost 2 million copies, making it the top-selling electric-bass instruction book in the world." See "Roger Filiberto, 94, Guitar Instructor," *Times-Picayune*, July 30, 1998.

35. A 1967 feature article on Bay in a music trade magazine states, "Today, Bay has 80 distributors, two men on the road to act as go-betweens, a warehouse in Toronto and an arrangement with Mills, Ltd., of London to distribute to England, Europe, Australia, Asia and Africa. His United States warehouse, located in Kirkwood, Mo., ships to South America." See "Creating Guitarists around the World—the Mel Bay Story," *The Music Trades*, June 1967, 184, 186.

36. Mel Bay, foreword to Roger Filiberto, *Mel Bay Presents the Electric Bass, Volume 1* (Kirkwood, MO: Mel Bay Publications, 1963), 1.

37. Filiberto, *Mel Bay Presents*, 18–19.

38. Filiberto, *Mel Bay Presents*, 31.

39. *Play Guitar with the Ventures* [vol. 1], Dolton Records BLP-16501, 1965, LP.

40. These sales figures are taken from *Play Guitar with . . .* creator Wilbur Savidge's records and firsthand account; see *Guitar Phonics: The Official Guitar Phonics Archival Web Site*, http://guitarphonics-playguitar.com/. The seven records in the series included five Ventures-based albums, as well as *Play Country Guitar with Jimmy Bryant* and *Play Guitar with Chet Atkins*.

41. Wilbur M. Savidge, "The Guitar Phonics Episode" (unpublished book manuscript), archived at at https://web.archive.org/web/20100423201139/ht tp://jukebox.au.nu/instromania/instro_monsters/chet_atkins/2.html/

42. *Play Guitar with the Ventures* [vol. 1], n.p. Note that in the first album, they had not yet created a dedicated four-string diagram appropriate to the electric bass.

43. The Ventures' amateur aesthetic ironically worked against them when recording *Play Guitar with the Ventures* [vol. 1], as they had difficulty recording their parts at a slower speed. Due to this difficulty, all subsequent *Play Guitar with the Ventures* albums featured session musicians instead of the actual band.

44. K. Paul Harris, "U2's Creative Process: Sketching in Sound" (PhD dissertation, University of North Carolina at Chapel Hill, 2006), Ann Arbor: UMI, 2007, 21.

45. *Play Electric Bass with the Ventures: Play Guitar with the Ventures Volume 4*, Dolton Records BST-17504, 1966, LP.

46. Their final American hit would come in 1968 with their popular theme song to the show *Hawaii Five-O*, although that record was actually made by LA session musicians who were part of the Wrecking Crew.

47. For the band's reception in Japan, see Michael Furmanovsky, "Outselling the Beatles: Assessing the Influence and Legacy of the Ventures on Japanese Musicians and Popular Music in the 1960s," *Ryukoku University International Cultural Society*, no. 14 (March 2010): 51–64.

48. "How to Promote with the Beatles," *The Music Trades*, May 1964, 32–33, 44.

49. Vox, advertisement, *The Music Trades*, October 1964, n.p.

50. Vox, advertisement, *The Music Trades*, June 1965, 195.

Interlude V

1. All UK chart data in this book comes from the Official Charts Company, which has compiled it from *Record Retailer*'s singles charts from the sixties. This chart was just one of many popular charts released weekly by UK music periodicals in this era.

2. Tony Bacon, "The British Guitar Embargo: When Brits Were Banned from Buying American," *Reverb*, April 5, 2018, https://reverb.com/news/the-british -guitar-embargo-when-brits-were-banned-from-buying-american/

3. A *Melody Maker* article from June 1959 reported on the end of the ban; see "Ban Lifted on U.S. LP, Instruments," *Melody Maker,* June 6, 1959, 1.

4. For more on Höfner's history, see Christian Hoyer, "120 Years of Service to Music: A History of the Karl Höfner Company, 1887–2008," *Vintage Höfner,* archived at https://web.archive.org/web/20220811151224/https://vintagehof ner.co.uk/christianhoyer/hofnerhist/hofnerhistory.html

5. Hoyer, "120 Years of Service."

6. For more on the expulsion, see R. M. Douglas, *Orderly and Humane: The Expulsion of the Germans after the Second World War* (New Haven: Yale University Press, 2012).

7. Hoyer, "120 Years of Service"; and Christian Hoyer, *Framus: Built in the Heart of Bavaria* (Markneukirchen: Framus, 2007), 145.

8. The instrument was named after a German group, Die Starlets, who provided feedback on the prototype and then included it in their act.

9. "A Short History of the Höfner 500/1 Violin Bass," *Höfner,* archived at https://web.archive.org/web/20220221195234/https://www.hofner.com/viol in_bass_history, accessed February 19, 2017.

10. Hoyer, *Framus,* 103.

11. Hoyer, *Framus,* 104.

12. For more on the history of skiffle, see Michael Dewe, *The Skiffle Craze* (Aberystwyth, Wales: Planet, 1998).

13. Quoted in Pete Frame, *The Restless Generation: How Rock Music Changed the Face of 1950s Britain* (London: Rogan House, 2007).

14. Quoted in Keith Goodwin, "Focus on Skiffle," *New Musical Express,* January 31, 1958, 10.

15. Mo Foster, *Play Like Elvis: How British Musicians Bought the American Dream* (Bodmin: MPG Books, 2000), 93.

16. Both recordings are available on *The Chas McDevitt Skiffle Group Featuring Nancy Whiskey and Shirley Douglas,* Bear Family BCD 16156, CD.

17. Frame, *The Restless Generation.*

18. Foster, *Play Like Elvis,* 126. Hampton's first tour of England took place October through November 1956. The electric bassist on the tour was New Orleans native Peter "Chuck" Badie, who had replaced Monk Montgomery in Hampton's band. Badie would go on to have a long career in rhythm & blues, including a stint with Sam Cooke, with whom he recorded "A Change Is Gonna Come" (1964).

19. See Foster, *Play Like Elvis,* 126, and Frame, *The Restless Generation.*

20. Cattini's story, including his musical relationship with Gregg, is detailed in Clive Smith and Bip Wetherell, *Clem Cattini: My Life, through the Eye of a Tornado* (n.p.: Mango Books, 2019).

21. Quoted in Frame, *The Restless Generation.*

22. Quoted in "Brian Gregg 'In the Snug' with Bulls Head Bob," *Brum Beat,* December 1, 2010, http://www.brumbeat.net/bgregg.htm/, accessed March 15, 2015.

23. "Brian Gregg," *Brum Beat.*

24. Mike Cook, *Cliffhanger: The Life and Times of Jet Harris* (Surrey: Grosvenor House Publishing, 2016), 43.

25. As Harris recalled, "Although skiffle was on the wane, [the Vipers] were a big name earning good money and I jumped at the chance when [group leader Wally Whyton] asked me to join them. The only tracks that went down for posterity with me in the lineup were 'Liverpool Blues' [a Vipers original] and 'Summertime Blues' . . . [The session] was produced by the man who'd already made a name for himself producing the Goons and other comedy records, and was to guide the Beatles to great heights years later—George Martin." Quoted in Mike Read, *The Story of the Shadows: An Autobiography* (London: Elm Tree Books, 1983), 52–53.

26. The Rocket's first single—and likely the first British rock 'n' roll single—was a cover of the Bellboys' "Teach You to Rock," a tune that Crombie had learned from the *Rock Around the Clock* film.

27. Tony Crombie, interview by Tony Middleton. August 22, 1995, British Library Oral History Collection, C122/127-C122/259.

28. Mike Read, *The Story of the Shadows*, 50. Another contender for being the first electric bassist in England was Fred Kirk, who performed as part of the John Barry Seven. Kirk was an upright bassist, but he was inspired to switch to the electric after witnessing Lionel Hampton's bassist playing one during one of the bandleaders late 1956 UK tour dates. Notably, Kirk was only allowed to use the electric bass during live performances; for the John Barry Seven's recordings, he was asked to play upright. See: Laurence Canty, "The First Bass Guitar in England," *Making Music*, March 1997.

29. Mark Windows, dir., *Jet Harris: From There to Here*, 07:00–07:25.

30. Windows, *Jet Harris*, 07:43–07:51.

31. Written by Harris, the song was itself a novelty, not only because it (mostly) lacked sung vocals, but also because he had written it explicitly as a solo vehicle for electric bass. As Harris recalled, "I only ever wrote one [song] on my own [while with the Drifters], and that was a thing called 'Jet Black.' It was so simple to play that we kept making mistakes and, this is true, it took us 95 takes." See *Jet Harris: From There to Here*, 20:25–20:43.

32. This LP was recorded a few months before the single version, and the sound of Harris's bass on the *Cliff* LP is much more overdriven. It is also worth noting that the very next song on the album is a cover of "(You're So Square) Baby I Don't Care," featuring Harris pounding away on the opening electric bass line.

33. The band had been aware of this conflict for some time (nearly as soon as "Cliff Richard and the Drifters" recordings had been commercially released in the United States in November 1958). To avoid any dispute, they had released the "Jet Black" in the United States under the name "The Four Jets."

34. "Reader's Poll," *New Musical Express*, October 28, 1960, 7.

35. As Welch recalled the concert, "On the show was this Black American band called the Treniers. Hank Marvin and I were at the back and we were really impressed at the way the sax players moved in unison . . . and we thought, 'We must do something like that because it looks so interesting from the front.'" See Spencer Leigh, "Claude Trenier: Singer with the Early Rock 'n' Roll Group the Treniers," *The Independent*, November 24, 2003, https://www.independent.co.uk/news/obituaries/claude-trenier-37514.html, accessed November 9, 2014.

36. "Reader's Poll," *New Musical Express*, December 1, 1961, 7.

37. Derek Johnson, "The *Real* Reason *Jet Harris* left the *Shadows*," *New Musical Express*, May 4, 1962, 8.

38. Aside from Harris, the most famous musicians to play a Fender VI were Jack Bruce, who used the instrument in the early sixties, and John Lennon.

39. Mike Hellicar, "*Jet* and *Duane* Have Similar Assets," *New Musical Express*, May 26, 1962, 2.

40. "Reader's Poll," *New Musical Express*, November 23, 1962, 7.

41. On this recording, Harris abandoned bass altogether and instead played a Fender Jaguar electric guitar. The rhythm guitarist on the recording was an eighteen-year-old Jimmy Page; it was his first session.

42. Shirley Douglas and Chas McDevitt, *Shirley Douglas' Easy Guide to Rhythm & Blues for Bass-Guitar* (London: Southern Music Publishing, 1960).

43. Douglas and McDevitt, *Shirley Douglas' Easy Guide*, 6. She concludes her introduction by saying, "So there you are, in a matter of weeks you could be a virtuoso of the bass-guitar."

Chapter 6

1. The earlier version of the song (titled "Help Me, Ronda") appears on the LP *The Beach Boys Today!*, which was released on March 8, 1965. The re-recorded version ("Help Me, Rhonda") was released as a single on April 5, 1965 and later appeared on the Beach Boys' next LP, *Summer Days (and Summer Nights!!)* from July 1965.

2. Brian Wilson with Ben Greenman, *I Am Brian Wilson* (Philadelphia: Da Capo Press, 2016), 174.

3. "Interview with Carol Kaye," *AlbumLinerNotes.com*, 2010, archived at https://web.archive.org/web/20200220160725/http://albumlinernotes.com /Carol_Kaye.html/, accessed January 14, 2019.

4. "Interview with Carol Kaye." This story is also recounted in Kent Hartman, *The Wrecking Crew* (New York: Thomas Dunne Books, 2012), 144–147.

5. "Interview with Carol Kaye."

6. Collectively these bassists' styles encapsulate different components of what Per Elias Drabløs refers to as "melodic electric bass." See Per Elias Drabløs, *The Quest for the Melodic Electric Bass: From Jamerson to Spenner* (Farnham, Surrey: Ashgate, 2015).

7. A note on terminology: I prefer the term "session musician" to "studio musician," as the former stresses the type of *work* these musicians do (playing on a session) rather than simply the *location* where they do it (the recording studio). In terms of their meaning, they are often treated as interchangeable.

8. James P. Kraft, *Stage to Studio: Musicians and the Sound Revolution, 1890–1950* (Baltimore: John Hopkins University Press, 1996).

9. A similar set of requirements is discussed in Richard A. Peterson and Howard G. White, "The Simplex Located in Art Worlds," *Urban Life* 7, no. 4 (January 1979): 411–439; and Robert R. Faulkner, *Hollywood Studio Musicians: Their Work and Careers in the Recording Industry*, 2nd ed. (New Brunswick, NJ: Aldine Transaction, 2013).

10. Isabel Campelo, "'The Extra Thing'—the Role of Session Musicians in

the Recording Industry," *Journal on the Art of Record Production* 10 (July 2015), http://www.arpjournal.com/asarpwp/that-extra-thing-the-role-of-session-music ians-in-the-recording-industry/. See also Alan Williams, "Navigating Proximities: The Creative Identity of the Hired Musician," *Journal of the Music & Entertainment Industry Educators Association* 10, no. 1 (2010): 59–76.

11. "Reuse" (or "new use") payments were paid anytime a recording featuring a union musician was "reused" in a different form of media than originally intended, such as in film or on television.

12. There is the potential for US courts to void these "work for hire" agreements and force record companies to share copyright with session musicians, although it is unlikely to happen. An argument in favor of this approach can be found in Alexandra El-Bayeh, "They Could Be Back: The Possibility of Termination Rights for Session Musicians," *American University Law Review* 64, no. 2 (2014): 285–336.

13. Charles Hughes, *Country Soul: Making Music and Making Race in the American South* (Chapel Hill: University of North Carolina Press, 2015), 6.

14. For more on this history, see Kraft, *Stage to Studio.*

15. As was AFM practice, 8 to 10 percent of these session fees were paid into the union pension fund.

16. Hal Blaine and Mr. Bonzai, *Hal Blaine & the Wrecking Crew: The Story of the World's Most Recorded Musician*, ed. David M. Schwartz, 3rd ed. (Alma, MI: Rebeats Publications, 2010), 50–51.

17. Carol Kaye, *Studio Musician: Carol Kaye, 60s No. 1 Hit Bassist, Guitarist* (self-published, 2016), 46. It is worth noting that Kaye has repeatedly dismissed Blaine's depiction of the Wrecking Crew as an exaggeration.

18. Little information survives about Pohlman's life and career, outside of the recordings he played on. My discussion of his biography is adapted from what appears to be his only extant interview: Martin Richards, "Ray Pohlman," *Jazz Journal International* 40, no. 12 (December 1987): 8–10.

19. Richards, "Ray Pohlman," 9.

20. For more on *Shindig!* and how it shaped rock 'n' roll performance practices, see Norma Coates, "Excitement Is Made, Not Born: Jack Good, Television, and Rock and Roll," *Journal of Popular Music Studies* 25, no. 3 (2013): 301–325.

21. In his memoir, drummer Hal Blaine credits demo work with allowing him to build his reputation and studio experience within the LA scene. Blaine, *Hal Blaine,* 43.

22. Lyle Ritz, "The Wrecking Crew, Lyle Ritz—Recording with Phil Spector's Wall of Sound & the Beach Boys," interview, Musicians Hall of Fame & Museum, YouTube, https://www.youtube.com/watch?v=md4P3xlbUGY/

23. "Lyle Ritz Talks about working with Sonny and Cher," Wrecking Crew, 2017, YouTube, https://www.youtube.com/watch?v=JuuQBdSH6gQ/

24. Kaye, *Studio Musician,* 145–146.

25. For a detailed discussion of Kaye's involvement with Motown, see Brian F. Wright, "Reconstructing the History of Motown Session Musicians: The Carol Kaye / James Jamerson Controversy," *Journal of the Society for American Music* 13, no. 1 (February 2019): 78–109.

26. Contrary to standard practice, Cocker insisted that the session musicians

be credited, so Kaye's name is listed on the LP sleeve for *With a Little Help from My Friends* (1969), the album on which "Feelin' Alright" appears.

27. "Carol Kaye: Session Legend Interview," *The Snapshots Foundation*, June 13, 2013, YouTube, https://www.youtube.com/watch?v=q4JWqK6r6N4/

28. "Carol Kaye: Session Legend Interview."

29. Chris Jisi, "Precision Memories," *Bass Player* 12, no. 10 (October 2001): 60.

30. As part of Nelson's band, Kirkland was an early endorsee of the Rickenbacker 4000 bass.

31. "Joe Osborn," *Bass Player Presents: Session Legends & Studio Gear*, special issue (2009): 28.

32. "Joe Osborn," *Bass Player Presents*, 28.

33. A lengthy yet incomplete list of Osborn's Top 40 credits can be found in "Joe Osborn: A Few (Hundred) Hits," *Vintage Guitar*, October 1998, reprinted at https://www.vintageguitar.com/2925/joe-osborn/

34. Quoted in "Precision Memories."

35. While West is playing electric bass on "The Beat Goes On," it was Carol Kaye that had originally suggested the bass line. Hartman, *The Wrecking Crew*, 165. "The Beat Goes On" bass line may have been influenced by the bass line in Donovan's "The Trip" (1966).

36. "Joe Osborn," *Bass Player Presents*, 28; Ken Sharp, *Sound Explosion: Inside L.A.'s Studio Factory with the Wrecking Crew* (Woodland Hills: Wrecking Crew LLC, 2015), 115.

37. Ronnie Spector with Vince Waldron, *Be My Baby: How I Survived Mascara, Miniskirts, and Madness, or My Life as a Fabulous Ronette* (Los Angeles: Words in Edgewise, 2015), 104.

38. Carol Kaye, "For those who don't know much about Studio Musicians and Studio Work . . . ," Facebook post, May 23, 2018, https://www.facebook.com/1038222976284207/posts/for-those-who-dont-know-much-about-studio-musicians-and-studio-work-in-hollywood/1449866678453166/, accessed May 1, 2021; and Carol Kaye, "Flirty String Player, How I Fixed Him," Facebook post, March 25, 2021, https://www.facebook.com/carol.kaye.1840/posts/926968354706432/, accessed May 1, 2021.

39. I should note that Kaye would likely dispute this framing. In interviews, she has repeatedly dismissed the idea that she was somehow different from the other musicians; as she told the Rock & Roll Hall of Fame: "I could outswear the guys if they wanted to swear . . . 'Well, screw you too!' That kind of thing. So I'd feed it back if somebody ever said something, but they didn't! The minute you start playing, they know that you're an accomplished musician and the professionalism spoke for itself. But we were all in it together, and as far as the guys go, I was one of the guys. I never thought of myself as a woman." "Oral History with Carol Kaye of the Wrecking Crew," Rock & Roll Hall of Fame, May 2005, YouTube, https://www.youtube.com/watch?v=F9WQTrr3GZ4/

40. For more, see Andrew Flory, "The Rise of the Motown Sound," in *I Hear a Symphony: Motown and Crossover R&B* (Ann Arbor: University of Michigan Press, 2017), 41–68.

41. Other early Motown bassists include Clarence Isabell, Tweed Beard, Willie

Green, and Joe Williams. See Allan Slutsky, *Standing in the Shadows of Motown: The Life and Music of Legendary Bassist James Jamerson* (Milwaukee: Hal Leonard, 1989), 12–13.

42. James Jamerson, interview by Dan Forte, *Guitar Player*, June 1979, reprinted in *Bass Heroes*, ed. Tom Mulhern (San Francisco: GPI Books, 1993), 154–156.

43. Jamerson, like the other Funk Brothers, often broke his "exclusive" contract with Motown when he could get away with it—appearing, for example, on Jackie Wilson's "Higher and Higher" (1967).

44. James Jamerson, interview by Nelson George, "Standing in the Shadows of Motown," reprinted in *Buppies, B-Boys, Baps, & Bohos: Notes on Post-soul Black Culture*, 2nd ed. (Cambridge, MA: Da Capo Press, 2001), 171–172.

45. Wolfrum invented his prototype for DI technology around 1960, while still a teenager in high school. He describes the process of its invention and how he came to sell it to Detroit recording studios in Ed Wolfrum, interview by Mike Dutkewych, Detroit Music Oral History Project, Wayne State University, November 18, 2015.

46. Wolfrum, interview by Dutkewych.

47. Flory, "Rise of Motown Sound," 61.

48. For more, see Brian F. Wright, "Interview with Motown Bassist Tony Newton," 2021, https://www.brianfwright.com/interviews/tony-newton/

49. Wright, "Interview with Tony Newton." In 1964, Newton appeared with the Miracles in the *T.A.M.I. Show* concert film.

50. Wright, "Interview with Tony Newton."

51. Tony Newton, *Gold Thunder: Legendary Adventures of a Motown Bassman* (Venice, CA: Quantum Media Publishing, 2011), 46.

52. Wright, "Interview with Tony Newton."

53. "Stop! In the Name of Love" and "Nowhere to Run" were recorded during the same session, and the contract lists the date as January 22, 1965; the contract for "Love Is Like an Itching in My Heart" is dated June 24, 1965; and the contract for "Reach Out I'll Be There" is dated July 8, 1966. All contracts are in the author's possession.

54. Newton's performances on this tour are preserved on *Recorded Live: Motortown Revue in Paris*, Motown, 1965, LP. During this tour, he also appeared in "The Sounds of Motown" special episode of the TV show *Ready, Steady, Go!*, which was largely responsible for popularizing Motown artists among British audiences.

55. Other electric bassists that recorded for Motown in the late sixties and early seventies include Wilton Felder, who played on the Jackson 5's "I Want You Back" (1969) and "ABC" (1970), Nathan Watts, who recorded with Stevie Wonder, and Leroy Taylor and Eddie Watkins Jr., who both played with the Temptations.

56. For more on Golden World and Babbitt, see David A. Carson, *Grit, Noise, & Revolution: The Birth of Detroit Rock 'n' Roll* (Ann Arbor: University of Michigan Press, 2006).

57. Jisi, "Precision Memories."

58. Babbitt addressed this issue himself in an editorial for *Bass Player* magazine; see Bob Babbitt, "Who Played Bass?," *Bass Player*, December 2002, 88.

59. Nelson George, *Where Did Our Love Go: The Rise and Fall of the Motown Sound*, 2nd ed. (Urbana: University of Illinois Press, 2007), 104–105. The first Motown releases to credit session musicians were Valerie Simpson's solo album *Exposed* and Marvin Gaye's *What's Going On?*, both of which were released in May 1971.

60. George, "Standing in the Shadows," 173.

61. Allan Slutsky, "Who Is Bob Babbitt and How Did He Get All Those Gold Records," *BobBabbitt.com*, 2003, archived at https://web.archive.org/web/20210 210204334/http://www.bobbabbitt.com/about.htm/

62. See George, *Where Did Our Love Go*, 198–200; and Graham Betts, "James Jamerson," in *The Motown Encyclopedia* (n.p.: AC Publishing, 2014).

63. Paul Justman, dir., *Standing in the Shadows of Motown*, Artisan Entertainment, 2002, DVD. Among bass players, Allan Slutsky's 1989 hybrid biography of Jamerson/transcription of his bass lines was also highly influential; see Slutsky, *Standing in the Shadows*.

64. Ben Turner and Gabe Turner, dirs., *Hitsville: The Making of Motown*, Motown the Film LLC, 2019, Blu-Ray.

65. James Cortese, "Clanging Cash Register Provides Background Music," *The Commercial Appeal*, January 7, 1968, Morning Edition, 31; Phyl Garland, *The Sound of Soul* (Chicago: H. Regnery, 1969), 121–122.

66. Rob Bowman, *Soulsville U.S.A.: The Story of Stax Records* (New York: Schirmer Trader Books, 1997), 9.

67. Bowman, *Soulsville U.S.A.*, 10.

68. Jerry Wexler was an outspoken proponent of Black music and had worked previously with Ray Charles, the Drifters, and Ruth Brown. Before becoming a partner at Atlantic, he had also been an editor for *Billboard*, where he coined the term "rhythm & blues" to replace the older designation "Race Records." See Jerry Wexler, *Rhythm and the Blues: A Life in American Music* (New York: St. Martin's Press, 1993).

69. Steinberg appears to have only ever given two long-form interviews about his career, the first to Rob Bowman and the second to David Less; see David Less, "Interview with Lewie and Morris Steinberg," Rock 'n' Soul Audiovisual History Project Collection, Archives Center, National Museum of American History, Smithsonian Institution.

70. Less, "Interview with Lewie," 32.

71. Less, "Interview with Lewie," 116.

72. Robert Gordon, *Respect Yourself: Stax Records and the Soul Explosion* (New York: Bloomsbury, 2013), 18.

73. Less, "Interview with Lewie," 28–29.

74. Less, "Interview with Lewie," 116.

75. Hughes, *Country Soul*, 56.

76. Hughes, *Country Soul*, 61–62.

77. Less, "Interview with Lewie," 121.

78. Hughes, *Country Soul*, 60.

79. In his memoir, Booker T. Jones expresses regret about how the situation was handled but admits that this incident was the final straw for Steinberg. Booker T. Jones, *Time Is Tight: My Life, Note by Note* (New York: Little, Brown, 2019), 83–84.

80. Jones, *Time Is Tight*, 104.

81. Bowman, *Soulsville U.S.A.*, 116.

82. Chuck Crisafulli, "Duck Dunn: He's a Soul Man," *Bass Player*, December 1994, 50.

83. Crisafulli, "Duck Dunn," 47.

84. Critics and the musicians themselves have both repeatedly commented on the "delayed" rhythmic feel of the Memphis Sound, in which Al Jackson Jr. and the rest of the band would create distinctive grooves by ostensibly playing beats 2 and 4 slightly out of time. Recently, however, musicologist Eric Smialek has disputed these claims, using a computer-based analysis to show that, in fact, on "In the Midnight Hour," "Beats 2 and 4 are not delayed but are almost exactly in time." He goes on to argue that the mythology surrounding Stax's delayed backbeat is part of a wider discourse of musical-racial authenticity that depicts Stax's music as "Blacker" than Motown's. Eric Smialek, "The Myth of the Delayed Backbeat in Southern Soul: Discourses of Rhythmic, Corporeal, and Racial Authenticity," 2020 Society for American Music Conference.

85. Rob Bowman, "The Stax Sound: A Musicological Analysis," *Popular Music* 14, no. 3 (1995): 310.

86. In recognition of their importance to the company, the MG's, along with songwriters Isaac Hayes and David Porter, were reportedly given a 10 percent producer royalty for the music they wrote and recorded, which they then split six ways. That number is deceiving, however, as their 10 percent came out of the minuscule 15 percent royalty rate that Atlantic was paying to Stax for their releases. This meant that, in that era, Dunn received approximately 0.1 percent of each song. This could still translate into some big paydays, such as with triple-platinum singles like Otis Redding's "(Sittin' On) The Dock of the Bay," but relatively it was quite a small share of the song's total profits.

87. Hughes, *Country Soul*, 70–74.

88. In the late sixties and early seventies, Stax began to rely more on electric bassist James Alexander of the Bar-Kays. For more, see E. E. Bradman, "The Bar-Kays' James Alexander," in *Bass Player Presents: The Funky Bass Book*, ed. Bill Leigh (Milwaukee: Backbeat Books, 2010), 44–46.

89. Tom Vickers, "Interview with Steve Cropper [1984]," Rock 'n' Soul Audiovisual History Project Collection, Archives Center, National Museum of American History, Smithsonian Institution. Quoted in Jonathan Gould, *Otis Redding: An Unfinished Life* (New York: Crown Archetype, 2017), 458.

90. For more, see Brian F. Wright, "Interview with Bassist Norbert Putnam," 2021, https://www.brianfwright.com/interviews/norbert-putnam/

91. Wright, "Interview with Norbert Putnam."

92. Norbert Putnam, *Music Lessons*, vol. 1: *A Musical Memoir* (Nashville: Thimbleton House Media, 2017), 16.

93. Putnam, *Music Lessons*, 18.

94. Hughes, *Country Soul*, 15.

95. Putnam played upright bass on "What Kind of Fool (Do You Think I Am)."

96. Wright, "Interview with Norbert Putnam."

97. Christopher M. Reali, *Music and Mystique in Muscle Shoals* (Urbana: University of Illinois Press, 2022), 46.

98. Putnam, *Music Lessons,* 55.

99. Wright, "Interview with Norbert Putnam."

100. Nashville in this era was still a relatively small scene, with still only a handful of top players on each instrument. Putnam recalls that his arrival was met with great enthusiasm from Nashville's first-call electric bassist, the multi-instrumentalist Charlie McCoy; Putnam recalled that at their first meeting McCoy threw his arms around him and said, "Thank god you're here! I'll never have to play the Fender bass again!" Putnam was happy to oblige and became, along with Henry Strzelecki, one of the top session electric bassists in Nashville. Putnam's career was described in detail as part of a 1971 feature on Nashville session musicians in *Rolling Stone;* see John Grissim, "The Nashville Cats," *Rolling Stone,* December 9, 1971, 30–32.

101. Dan Forte, "Bassist David Hood: Muscle Shoals: The Band Attitude," *Guitar Player,* November 1982, 38.

102. Reali, *Music and Mystique,* 43.

103. Forte, "Bassist David Hood," 39.

104. For more on the "Muscle Shoals Sound," see Reali, *Music and Mystique,* 86–112.

105. Roben Jones, *Memphis Boys: The Story of American Studios* (Jackson: University Press of Mississippi, 2010), 33.

106. Wexler, *Rhythm and the Blues,* 191.

107. Hughes, *Country Soul,* 77.

108. Ed Friedland, *The R&B Bass Masters: The Way They Play* (San Francisco: BackBeat Books, 2005), 38.

109. Rick Hall, *The Man from Muscle Shoals* (Monterey: Heritage Builders, 2016), 245.

110. In addition to Cogbill, Moman also utilized electric bassist Mike Leech (1941–2017) on sessions at American Studios.

111. Gene Santoro, "Session Bassist Jerry Jemmott: The Groovemaster," *Guitar Player,* May 1984, 72.

112. Santoro, "Session Bassist Jerry Jemmott," 74.

113. For more, see Brian F. Wright, "Interview with Session Bassist Jerry Jemmott," 2021, https://www.brianfwright.com/interviews/jerry-jemmott/

114. Quoted in Timothy R. Hoover, *Soul Serenade: King Curtis and His Immortal Saxophone* (Denton: University of North Texas Press, 2022). 153.

115. Wright, "Interview with Jemmott."

116. Jerry Jemmott, "I'm That Guy: The Life, Times, and Music of Jerry Jemmott," unpublished book manuscript.

117. Wright, "Interview with Jemmott."

118. Reali, *Music and Mystique,* 56.

119. Wright, "Interview with Jemmott."

120. Wright, "Interview with Jemmott."

121. Christopher M. Reali, "Making Music in Muscle Shoals" (PhD dissertation, University of North Carolina at Chapel Hill, 2014), 180–181.

122. When Skynyrd released "Sweet Home Alabama" in 1974, the musicians were known in the industry (and among themselves) as the Muscle Shoals Rhythm Section. The success of Skynyrd's song, however, popularized their des-

ignation as the "Swampers," and through a mix of rock mythology and public relations marketing, that is what they are often now known as.

123. Atlantic's support of MSSS was not altruistic. In 1969, Hall severed his ties with Atlantic in favor of a better distribution deal through Capitol Records. Not wanting to lose their profitable relationship with the Shoals, Atlantic loaned the musicians the seed money to start MSSS—in exchange for 50 percent of the publishing rights. Through this deal, Reali notes, "Atlantic recouped on their initial investment long before the owners of MSS paid back the loan." Reali, "Making Music," 56.

124. "David Hood," *Bass Player Presents: Session Legends*, 19.

125. Unfortunately, the history of reggae bass playing is beyond the scope of this book. For information on the development of reggae in general, see David Katz, *Solid Foundation: An Oral History of Reggae* (London: Jawbone Press, 2012).

126. After the Muscle Shoals Rhythm Section stopped working with Hall, he brought in yet another cohort of session musicians, known as the FAME Gang. Notably, compared to his previous house bands, the FAME Gang was almost entirely comprised of Black musicians, including bassist Jesse Boyce (1948–2017). With the support of the FAME Gang, FAME continued to produce hits, and in 1971, *Billboard* named Rick Hall Producer of the Year.

127. This problem appears to be genre specific, as much dedicated effort has been put into capturing the history of New York's jazz scene and the many records produced within it (see, for example, Tom Lord's *The Jazz Discography*).

128. Andrew Mall, "Concentration, Diversity, and Consequences: Privileging Independent over Major Record Labels," *Popular Music* 37, no. 3 (2018): 444–465.

129. For more on Curtis's career, see Hoover, *Soul Serenade*.

130. Roy Simonds, *King Curtis: A Discography* (Middlesex, England: self-published, 1983).

131. Simonds, *King Curtis*. Tyrell also played electric bass on LaVern Baker's Top 40 rhythm & blues hit version of "Fly Me to the Moon" (1965) and, later, played electric bass on Dizzy Gillespie's *Souled Out* (1970).

132. Released a year before the 5th Dimension's version of "Aquarius / Let the Sunshine In (The Flesh Failures)," the Original Broadway Cast Recording of *Hair* (1968) was a massive hit and makes for a good comparative counterpoint between Jimmy Lewis and Joe Osborn. On "Aquarius," Lewis actually plays a funk-inspired bass line that is much more virtuosic than Osborn's, but also much looser rhythmically; for "The Flesh Failures (Let the Sunshine In)," the roles are reversed, with Lewis's line being the more reserved one.

133. For more, see Brian F. Wright, "Interview with Session Bassist Chuck Rainey," 2021, https://www.brianfwright.com/interviews/chuck-rainey

134. Chris Jisi, "Groove Convergence: Will Lee Interviews Chuck Rainey, the 'Godfather of the Groove,'" *Bass Player*, February 1997, 46.

135. Dan Forte, "Chuck Rainey: An Outspoken Interview with the Top Studio Bassist," *Guitar Player*, September 1976, 10.

136. Forte, "Chuck Rainey," 10–11.

137. Jisi, "Groove Convergence," 46, 48.

138. Wright, "Interview with Rainey."

139. Forte, "Chuck Rainey," 11.

140. Wright, "Interview with Rainey."

141. Jisi, "Groove Convergence," 56.

142. Among these films are *Standing in the Shadows of Motown* (2002), *The Wrecking Crew* (2015), *20 Feet from Stardom* (2013), *Muscle Shoals* (2014), and *Hired Gun* (2016). As other scholars have noted, these films often reproduce inaccurate or overly simplistic narratives; see Andrew Flory, "20 Feet from Stardom: Entertainment or History?," *Musicology Now*, February 21, 2014, https://music ologynow.org/20-feet-from-stardom-entertainment-or-history/; and Christopher Reali, "Review of Muscle Shoals," *Journal of the Society for American Music* 11, no. 3 (August 2017): 384–387.

Chapter 7

1. Andrew Kellett, *The British Blues Network: Adoption, Emulation, and Creativity* (Ann Arbor: University of Michigan Press, 2017).

2. Jack Hamilton, *Just Around Midnight: Rock and Roll and the Racial Imagination* (Cambridge: Harvard University Press, 2016), 91.

3. Hamilton, *Just Around Midnight*, 92.

4. Hamilton, *Just Around Midnight*, 94.

5. Hamilton, *Just Around Midnight*, 90.

6. For more on the Teddy Boys, see Hamilton, *Just Around Midnight*, 99–105.

7. Dick Bradley, *Understanding Rock 'n' Roll: Popular Music in Britain, 1955–1964* (Buckingham: Open University Press, 1992), 56. More recent work by Gillian Mitchell has argued that this association between rock 'n' roll and juvenile delinquency has been overstated and that the generation gap in England was less entrenched than it is usually depicted; see Gillian A. M. Mitchell, "Reassessing 'the Generation Gap': Bill Haley's 1957 Tour of Britain, Inter-generational Relations and Attitudes to Rock 'n' Roll in the Late 1950s," *Twentieth Century British History* 24, no. 4 (2013): 573–605.

8. Richard Stakes, "These Boys: The Rise of Mersey Beat," in *Gladsongs and Gatherings: Poetry and Its Social Context in Liverpool since the 1960s*, ed. Stephen Wade (Liverpool: Liverpool University Press, 2001), 160–161.

9. Dave Laing, "Six Boys, Six Beatles: The Formative Years, 1950–1962," in *The Cambridge Companion to the Beatles*, ed. Kenneth Womack (New York: Cambridge University Press, 2009), 9–32.

10. Andy Babiuk, *Beatles Gear: All the Fab Four's Instruments from Stage to Studio* (Milwaukee: Backbeat Books, 2015), 74–79. For the second Hamburg residency, the band's pay had been raised to thirty-five deutsche marks per day, meaning that McCartney's Violin Bass cost him a little more than one week's wages.

11. Richard Buskin, "Norman Smith: The Beatles' First Engineer," *Sound on Sound*, May 2008, https://www.soundonsound.com/people/norman-smith-bea tles-first-engineer/

12. Babiuk, *Beatles Gear*, 103, 137, 153, 179–180.

13. Tony Webster, "I Don't Know a Thing about the Guitar Says Paul McCartney," *Beat Instrumental*, October 1964, 23.

14. Webster, "Don't Know a Thing," 23.

15. For more on the music recorded in this era, see Walter Everett, *The Beatles as Musicians: The Quarry Men through Rubber Soul* (New York: Oxford University Press, 2001).

16. For more on Hall and the development of Rickenbacker electric basses, see Richard R. Smith, *The History of Rickenbacker Guitars* (Fullerton, CA: Centerstream Publishing, 1987); and Paul D. Boyer, *The Rickenbacker Electric Bass: 50 Years as Rock's Bottom*, 2nd ed. (Milwaukee: Hal Leonard, 2017).

17. Babiuk, *Beatles Gear*, 221–222. McCartney's endorsement was such a key component of the instrument's success that starting in 1964 Selmer, Höfner's UK distributor, paid McCartney £5 (or roughly 10 percent of the retail price) for each Violin Bass sold in the UK.

18. "Growing Up at 33 1/3: The George Harrison Interview," *Crawdaddy*, February 1977, 36.

19. Barry Miles, *Paul McCartney: Many Years from Now* (London: Secker & Warburg, 1997), 271.

20. Hamilton, *Just Around Midnight*, 146.

21. Kevin Ryan and Brian Kehew, *Recording the Beatles: The Studio Equipment and Techniques Used to Create Their Classic Albums* (Houston: Curvebender Publishing, 2009), 397.

22. "Think for Yourself" actually features two separate McCartney bass lines: one that he contributed to the original backing track and an overdubbed bass line that he played through a fuzz pedal. Ryan and Kehew, *Recording the Beatles*, 397.

23. Geoff Emerick, *Here, There and Everywhere: My Life Recording the Music of the Beatles* (New York: Gotham Books, 2006), 115.

24. Hamilton, *Just Around Midnight*, 149.

25. Mark Lewisohn, *The Complete Beatles Recording Sessions: The Official Story of the Abbey Road Years, 1962–1970* (New York: Hamlyn, 2021), 74.

26. Emerick, *Here, There and Everywhere*, 170.

27. Ken Michaels, "Interview with Beatles' Engineer Geoff Emerick," *Total Access Live*, 2006, archived at https://web.archive.org/web/20060117180903/http://www.totalaccesslive.com/geoffemerick.htm/. It is unclear which amplifiers McCartney used on *Sgt. Pepper*; at the time, he still had access to the Fender Bassman, as well as new Vox 730 and 430 amps. There also remains a debate over to what extent DI was used on McCartney's bass during the *Sgt. Pepper* sessions. Emerick claims to have never used the DI to record bass, but according to Ryan and Kehew, "Studio documentation clearly proves otherwise," and Lewisohn specifically cites the song "Sgt. Pepper's Lonely Hearts Club Band" as having been recorded direct. It therefore seems that DI was likely used during the sessions, albeit infrequently. For more on the debate, see Ryan and Kehew, *Recording the Beatles*, 440; Lewisohn, *Complete Beatles Recording Sessions*, 95; and Babiuk, *Beatles Gear*, 389–390.

28. Walter Everett, *The Beatles as Musicians: Revolver through the Anthology* (New York: Oxford University Press, 1999), 106.

29. Quoted in Tony Bacon and Gareth Morgan, *Bassmaster: Paul McCartney Playing the Great Beatles Basslines* (Milwaukee: Backbeat Books, 2006), 59.

30. The other members of the Rolling Stones were born after 1939 and therefore were exempt from conscription.

31. Bill Wyman, *Stone Alone: The Story of a Rock 'n' Roll Band* (New York: Da Capo Press, 1997), 72.

32. Wyman, *Stone Alone*, 72.

33. Figures included in the original; see Bill Wyman, *Bill Wyman's Blues Odyssey: A Journey to Music's Heart & Soul* (New York: DK Publishing, 2001), 320.

34. As Babiuk and Prevost note, "The Tuxedo, which was introduced in the late 1950s and officially called the Tuxedo Electro Bass Guitar 4398 model, was one of the first bass guitars built in England. . . . The Dallas Tuxedo bass sold new for twenty-five guineas and was manufactured for Dallas by Stuart Darkins & Co. of Shoeburyness, a woodworking factory that advertised itself as 'makers of furniture and fancy good.'" Andy Babiuk and Greg Prevost, *Rolling Stones Gear: All the Stones' Instruments from Stage to Studio* (Milwaukee: Hal Leonard, 2013), 43.

35. Babiuk and Prevost, *Rolling Stones Gear*, 42–43.

36. Wyman, *Stone Alone*, 113.

37. Oliver Murray, dir., *The Quiet One*, Sundance Selects, 2019, 00:25:07–00:25:11.

38. Roberta Freund Schwartz, *How Britain Got the Blues: The Transmission and Reception of American Blues Style in the United Kingdom* (Burlington, VT: Ashgate, 2007), 93–95.

39. Sean Lorre, "British R&B: A Study of Black Popular Music Revivalism in the United Kingdom, 1960–1964" (PhD dissertation, McGill University, 2017), 175.

40. Schwartz, *Britain Got the Blues*, 74.

41. Kellett, *The British Blues Network*, 71–72.

42. Hamilton, *Just around Midnight*, 252.

43. Wyman, *Stone Alone*, 113.

44. Keith Richards, *Life* (New York: Little, Brown, 2010), 103–104.

45. Wyman, *Blues Odyssey*, 9.

46. Wyman, *Blues Odyssey*, 9.

47. As Sean Lorre explains, "The professional musicians that recorded R&B for record companies understood well that they were participating in a commodified and stereotyped arena of cultural production. While they may have represented themselves in a manner that at least cursorily reflected their inner desires and senses of self, they also projected an imagined/imaginary persona . . . that would help sell records." Lorre, "British R&B," 197.

48. Andrew Loog Oldham, *Stoned* (London: Vintage, 2001), 293–294.

49. Hamilton, *Just Around Midnight*, 256, 249.

50. Wyman bought his first Framus Star 5/150 Bass in September 1963, which he eventually replaced with a thin-line Deluxe model in November 1964. Initially, he played his basses through a Vox T60 bass amplifier (eventually paired with an AC-30 head), both live and in the studio, but by April 1964, he had replaced this with a newly designed Vox Foundation bass amp, which became a part of his default rig. See Babiuk and Prevost, *Rolling Stones Gear*, 78, 88, 104–106.

51. Wyman, *Blues Odyssey*, 305.

52. Davis Inman, "'Balls in the Bottom': A Q&A with Bill Wyman," *American Songwriter*, 2012, https://americansongwriter.com/balls-in-the-bottom-a-qa-with-bill-wyman/

53. *The Quiet One*, 00:22:10–00:22:45.

54. Mick Jagger, "The Rolling Stones Write for Melody Maker: We're *Not* on the Wagon," *Melody Maker*, March 21, 1964, 3.

55. Jagger, "Rolling Stones Write."

56. Later scholars have been divided about how to interpret the Stones' use of Black musicians as support acts. Martha Bayles, for instance, argues that it "implied that the Stones were more musically sophisticated than their Black opening acts—even though that wasn't true." Elijah Wald, by contrast, notes that "for some of [the older blues musicians] the 1960s really was a revival. They might be baffled by the audiences of young white kids acclaiming them as voices from a vanished world, but the money could be very good, and it was a pleasure to have one's work treated with such seriousness and enthusiasm . . . [T]he reward more than balanced the oddity of it all." See Martha Bayles, *Hole in Our Soul: The Loss of Beauty & Meaning in American Popular Music* (Chicago: University of Chicago Press, 1996), 186–187; Elijah Wald, *Escaping the Delta: Robert Johnson and the Invention of the Blues* (New York: HarperCollins, 2004), 246–247.

57. Wyman, *Stone Alone*, 216–217.

58. "The Rolling Stones: The Crusaders," *Rave*, August 1964.

59. While recording at Chess, the Stones met many of their heroes, including Willie Dixon, Chuck Berry, Buddy Guy, and Muddy Waters, who they all remember as being supportive. But when they arrived, the band was again confronted with the disconnect between their imagination and reality: at Chess, they were shocked to find that Waters had been reduced to doing odd jobs around the studio, including, as Richards recalls it, carrying the Stones' amplifiers into the studio. See Richards, *Life*, 158.

60. Wyman, *Stone Alone*, 227–228.

61. Richards, *Life*, 160–161.

62. "The Rolling Stones: 'Little Red Rooster'; 'Off the Hook," *Beat Instrumental*, December 1964, 28.

63. "Way Out Sound from Stones," *Record Mirror*, November 7, 1964.

64. Derek Johnson, "The Stones and Hermits can't go wrong," *New Musical Express*, November 13, 1964, 6; quoted in Lorre, "British R&B," 275; emphasis added.

65. "Way Out Sound."

66. Lorre, "British R&B," 3.

67. "Beat Instrumental's 1965 Gold Star Awards," *Beat Instrumental*, January 1966, 10. Notably, Paul McCartney came in third in the poll, beaten both by Wyman and by the Animals' Chas Chandler (who had a big hit in 1965 with the bass-heavy "We've Gotta Get out of This Place"). John Entwistle, discussed in the next section, came in eighth.

68. Roger Daltrey, *Thanks a Lot, Mr. Kibblewhite: My Story* (New York: Henry Holt, 2018), 56.

69. John Dougan, *The Who Sell Out* (New York: Bloomsbury, 2006), 41.

70. Steve Rosen, "John Entwistle: The Who's Great Bass Guitarist," *Guitar Player*, November 1975, 24.

71. Quoted in Paul Rees, *The Ox: The Authorized Biography of the Who's John Entwistle* (New York: Hachette Books, 2020), 9.

72. Chris Jisi, "John Entwistle: The Return of Thunderfingers," reprinted in Mulhern, *Bass Heroes*, 92.

73. Quoted in Rees, *The Ox*, 40–41. Note that Entwistle is likely misremembering the specific Höfner model, as Violin Basses were not commercially available in England until 1963.

74. Rees, *The Ox*, 42.

75. Daltrey, *Thanks a Lot*, 45–46.

76. Daltrey, *Thanks a Lot*, 52.

77. "Zoot Suit" was based on the Dynamics' "Misery" (1963), while "I'm the Face" was based on Slim Harpo's "I Got Love If You Want It" (1957). Both songs were popular in the mod scene at the time.

78. Jisi, "John Entwistle," 92.

79. Glenn Aveni and Steve Luongo, dirs., *An Ox's Tale: The John Entwistle Story*, Image Entertainment, 2006, 00:25:28–00:25:42.

80. Jisi, "John Entwistle," 92.

81. Introduced in 1959, the Epiphone Rivoli was a high-end, short-scale electric bass that was popular among British musicians in this era, including Tony Jackson of the Searchers, Karl Green of Herman's Hermits, and Ronnie Lane of the Small Faces. Perhaps most famously, bassist Chas Chandler played a Rivoli on the Animals' "We've Gotta Get out of This Place" (1965).

82. John Atkins, *The Who on Record: A Critical History, 1963–1998* (Jefferson, NC: McFarland, 2000), 14.

83. For more on the Who's relationship to pirate radio, see Dougan, *The Who Sell Out*.

84. Richard Green, "The Who: A Disturbing Group," *Record Mirror*, March 6, 1965; Richard Green, "The Who: The Group That Slaughters Their Amplifiers," *Record Mirror*, April 3, 1965; Alan Smith, "The Who Use Force to Get the Sound They Want!!," *New Musical Express*, June 18, 1965.

85. Jisi, "John Entwistle," 92.

86. Rosen, "John Entwistle," 28.

87. Nick Jones, "Every So Often, a Band Is Poised on the Brink of a Breakthrough. Word Has It It's . . . the Who," *Melody Maker*, June 5, 1965, 7.

88. Peter Stanfield, "The Who and Pop Art: The Simple Things You See Are All Complicated," *Journal of Popular Music Studies* 29, no. 1 (March 2017): 6.

89. Nick Jones, "Well, What Is Pop Art: Who Guitarist Pete Townshend Has a Go at a Definition," *Melody Maker*, July 3, 1965, 11.

90. Bass guitar strings are created using two wires, one that acts as a center core and another that is wrapped around it. For flatwound strings, the core is wrapped with a flat wire, making the string smooth to touch; flatwounds strongly emphasize fundamental tones and therefore produce a dead, thuddy tone that is somewhat similar to an upright. For roundwound strings, the core is wrapped with a round wire, which gives the string ridges; because they produce more harmonic overtones than flatwounds, roundwounds have more top end, which gives them a brighter sound. For tapewound strings (discussed later), a wire is wrapped around the core that is then wrapped with a thin layer of nylon tape;

although they are rarely used, tapewounds have a warm tonal character that is similar to flatwounds, if a bit more trebley.

91. Andy Neill and Matt Kent, *Anyway Anyhow Anywhere: The Complete Chronicle of the Who, 1958–1978* (New York: Friedman/Fairfax, 2002), 48.

92. Johnny Black, "Interview with the Who's John Entwistle," August 1994, *Rock's Backpages Audio*, 00:33:10–00:33:36.

93. Black, "Interview with Entwistle," 00:31:11–00:31:27. Entwistle goes on to state that the Who's *Live at Leeds* album (1970) came closest to capturing his bass sound.

94. Black, "Interview with Entwistle," 00:33:39–00:33:53.

95. Pete Townshend, *Who I Am: A Memoir* (New York: Harper Perennial, 2012), 92.

96. Black, "Interview with Entwistle," 00:37:46–00:37:33.

97. Black, "Interview with Entwistle," 00:37:46–00:37:33. First introduced in 1961, the Gibson EB-3 had two pickups and a double-cutaway body design that was based on the company's SG guitars. It was used, most famously, by Jack Bruce of Cream.

98. Johnny Black, *Eyewitness the Who: The Day-by-Day Story* (London: Carlton Books, 2001), 71.

99. For more on the Slab Precisions, see Barry Matthews, *Fender Bass for Britain: The History of the 1966 Slab-Bodied Precision Bass* (Milton Keynes: AuthorHouse, 2009). For detailed information about the equipment that Entwistle used over the course of his career, see "John Entwistle's Bass Guitar Gear," *Whotabs*, 2021, archived at https://web.archive.org/web/20210415222157/https://www.thew ho.net/whotabs/gear/bass/bass.html/

100. Mark Cunningham, "Spider Man: John Entwistle," *Bassist & Bass Techniques*, May 1995, 16.

101. Aveni and Luongo, *An Ox's Tale*, 00:00:25–00:00:47.

Interlude VI

1. James Brown, *James Brown: The Godfather of Soul* (New York: Macmillan, 1986), 43.

2. Brown, *James Brown*, ix. Early in his career, Brown occasionally filled in for Little Richard with Richard's group, the Upsetters, and Brown would later claim that it was the group's drummer, Charles Connor, who first "put the funk in the music." See RJ Smith, *The One: The Life and Music of James Brown* (New York: Gotham Books, 2012), 62–69.

3. Allan Slutsky, "The Rhythm Sections of Soul Brother No. 1," in *Bass Player Presents the Funky Bass Book*, ed. Bill Leigh (Milwaukee: New Bay Media, 2010), 10–11.

4. Allan Slutsky and Chuck Silverman, *The Great James Brown Rhythm Sections, 1960–1973* (Van Nuys: Alfred Publishing, 1997), 19.

5. This mistake was even more costly than usual. As RJ Smith notes, "Usually Brown fined his band five or ten dollars for making a mistake, but [for the *Live at the Apollo* recording], he put out the word that if you flubbed a note . . . it would be fifty to a hundred." Smith, *The One*, 110.

6. Brown, *James Brown*, 158.

7. Many critics and scholars situate Brown's rhythmic approach as part of wider Afro-diasporic traditions. For an analysis of the discourse surrounding funk and Blackness, see Anne Danielsen, *Presence and Pleasure: The Funk Grooves of James Brown and Parliament* (Middleton, CT: Wesleyan University Press, 2006), 20–36; for an analysis of the specific musical traditions that informed Brown's approach, see Stewart, "Funky Drummer."

8. Smith, *The One*, 136.

9. Drummer Melvin Parker has confirmed that it was Williams that played bass on "I Got You"; see Jim Payne, *Mel Bay Presents the Great Drummers of R&B, Funk, and Soul*, 2nd ed. (Pacific, MO: Mel Bay Publications, 2006), 48. Slutsky and Silverman note that "Williams is remembered as being more of a jazz bassist than the rest of the predominately blues and R&B bass players James Brown carried at that time. Before moving on in the summer of 1966, he got the chance to show off that side of his musical personality when he also played on a JB instrumental for Smash Records appropriately entitled 'Hooks.'" See Slutsky and Silverman, *Great James Brown Rhythm*, 34.

10. James Brown, *I Feel Good: A Memoir of a Life of Soul* (London: New American Library, 2005), 80–81.

11. Rickey Vincent, *Funk: The Music, the People, and the Rhythm of the One* (New York: St. Martin's Press, 1996), 74.

12. Danielsen, *Presence and Pleasure*, 40.

13. Also, rather than being in a standard major or minor key, "Cold Sweat" is in a Dorian mode, which, as Danielsen notes, "allows for a more circular or nondirected temporal feel." Danielsen, *Presence and Pleasure*, 41.

14. For a broader discussion of the Dapps' career, see Chris Richardson, "The Dapps at King Records," *Zero to 180*, https://www.zeroto180.org/the-dapps-at-king-records/, accessed August 15, 2023.

15. Brown, *James Brown*, 192.

16. Smith, *The One*, 208.

17. The story of this concert is detailed in the documentary *The Night James Brown Saved Boston*, dir. David Leaf, Shout Factory, 2009, DVD.

18. Around 1967, Brown secured an endorsement deal for his musicians to use Vox instruments.

19. Brown, *I Feel Good*, 156.

20. After leaving Brown's band, Drummond became a session musician, eventually recording with artists such as Neil Young, Bob Dylan, Don Henley, Paula Abdul, Neil Diamond, Eric Clapton, Jewel, and more.

21. ". . . der Hitmaker hinter dem Godfather: 'Sweet' Charles Sherrell," *Bass Professor*, [date unknown], 19. Translation mine.

22. ". . . der Hitmaker," 19. Translation mine.

23. Brown, *James Brown*, 200.

24. Matt Rowland, "For Sweet People from Sweet Charles," *Wax Poetics* 5 (Summer 2003): 23.

25. Brown, *James Brown*, 198.

26. Steve Olson, "Interview with Bootsy Collins," *Juice Magazine* 66, vol. 6, no. 1 (2009): 124.

27. Bill Leigh, "Bootsy Collins: James Brown, Parliament, Bootsy's Rubber Band," *Bass Player*, December 1998, 34.

28. Tony Bolden, *Groove Theory: The Blues Foundation of Funk* (Jackson: University Press of Mississippi, 2020), 24.

29. Thomas Sayers Ellis, "From the Crib to the Coliseum: An Interview with Bootsy Collins," in *The Funk Era and Beyond: New Perspectives on Black Popular Culture*, ed. Tony Bolden (New York: Palgrave Macmillan, 2008), 92.

30. Danielsen, *Presence and Pleasure*, 77.

31. Olson, "Interview with Bootsy Collins," 125.

32. Jimmy Leslie, "Super Bad: Playing Bass with James Brown," in Leigh, *Bass Player Presents*, 16. Sherrell rejoined Brown's band in 1973, playing multiple instruments. He then stayed for twenty years and eventually became the group's musical director.

33. See Michael J. Hove et al., "Feel the Bass: Music Presented to Tactile and Auditory Modalities Increases Aesthetic Appreciation and Body Movement," *Journal of Experimental Psychology: General* 149, no. 6 (2020): 1137–1147.

Chapter 8

1. Nadya Zimmerman, *Counterculture Kaleidoscope: Musical and Cultural Perspective on Late Sixties San Francisco* (Ann Arbor: University of Michigan Press, 2011).

2. See David Brackett, "Improvisation and Value in Rock Music, 1966," *Journal of the Society for American Music* 14, no. 2 (May 2020): 197–232.

3. For more, see Brian F. Wright, "Interview with Jefferson Airplane Bassist Jack Casady," 2022, https://www.brianfwright.com/interviews/jack-casady/

4. After he became an electric bassist himself, he encountered the instrument's disreputability firsthand. As he recalled, "I was always put down kind of, by my jazz friends, for playing the electric bass." Ralph Gleason, *The Jefferson Airplane and the San Francisco Sound* (New York: Ballantine Books, 1969), 198.

5. Gleason, *The Jefferson Airplane*, 198.

6. Jack Casady, interviewed by Jeff Tamarkin, Rock & Roll Hall of Fame and Museum Oral History Project, February 9, 2012.

7. "The Jack Casady Interview," *The Jake Feinberg Show*, May 17, 2015, http://www.jakefeinbergshow.com/2015/05/the-jack-casady-interview/

8. Wright, "Interview with Casady."

9. For a detailed account of the band's career, see Jeff Tamarkin, *Got a Revolution: The Turbulent Flight of Jefferson Airplane* (New York: Atria Books, 2003).

10. Gleason, *The Jefferson Airplane*, 194. Looking back on it, Casady told me, "In retrospect, I wouldn't change a thing today. Because that was the truth. That was how I played [at that time]." The band, as he sees it, was still developing. Wright, "Interview with Casady."

11. The other notable electric bass player in the San Francisco scene was the Grateful Dead's Phil Lesh, who ultimately came to develop his own melodic, improvisatory approach; see Phil Lesh, *Searching for the Sound: My Life with the Grateful Dead* (New York: Little, Brown, 2005).

12. Of course, not everyone was thrilled about rock's potential ascent up the cultural hierarchy. Jazz critic Leonard Feather—who years earlier had been one of the most vocal proponents of the electric bass—reviewed Jefferson Airplane's performance at the 1966 Monterey Jazz Festival, noting that the band's "sledge-hammer rhythm, monotonous melodious concepts and almost nonexistent harmony had all the delicacy and finesse of a mule team knocking down a picket fence." See Leonard Feather, "Hard Rock Stones Sweet Sound of Monterey Festival," *Los Angeles Times*, September 19, 1966, 26. The band enjoyed this description so much that they later incorporated it into their own marketing materials.

13. Zimmerman, *Counterculture Kaleidoscope*, 7.

14. "The Hippies: Dropouts with a Mission," *Newsweek*, February 6, 1967, 95.

15. Wright, "Interview with Casady."

16. Wright, "Interview with Casady."

17. Chris Jisi, "Jefferson Airplane's 'Somebody to Love' (Live)," *Bass Player*, Holiday 2011, 70.

18. As Zimmerman notes, "White Rabbit" was not necessarily an attempt to literally invoke a "Spanish" sound, but rather was part of the counterculture's wider (and problematic) adoption of exoticism to represent the hallucinogenic experience. Zimmerman, *Counterculture Kaleidoscope*, 67.

19. Wright, "Interview with Casady."

20. Months later, when *Surrealistic Pillow* peaked at No. 3 on the Billboard album chart, it was *Sgt. Pepper* that held the No. 1 position.

21. Quoted in Barbara Rowes, *Grace Slick: The Biography* (New York: Doubleday, 1980), 98–99.

22. The concert also helped further popularize Otis Redding and Booker T. and the MG's, who followed Jefferson Airplane's Saturday night set.

23. Tony Bacon, "Interview: Jack Bruce Talks Cream, Ornette Coleman & Self-Expression," *Reverb*, May 14, 2020, https://reverb.com/news/interview-jack-bru ce-talks-cream-ornette-coleman-and-self-expression-bacons-archive/

24. Gleason, *The Jefferson Airplane*, 198.

25. Tom Philips, "Jefferson Airplane," *Jazz & Pop*, January 1969, 17.

26. Wright, "Interview with Casady."

27. Chris Jisi with Anthony Jackson, "The Heroic Bass of Jack Casady," *Bass Player*, September–October 1993, 47.

28. Wright, "Interview with Casady."

29. Jisi and Jackson, "Heroic Bass."

30. The same week that the band was in New York to perform these sets at the Fillmore East, Casady also participated in a recording session with Jimi Hendrix, whom he had previously jammed with in San Francisco. Using his new Guild Starfire, Casady played bass on the fifteen-minute version of "Voodoo Chile" from *Electric Ladyland*. Some of Casady's later live performances with the Jimi Hendrix Experience are also preserved on the 2011 *Winterland* box set.

31. Patricia Kennealy, "Review of *Crown of Creation*," *Jazz & Pop*, October 1968, 45. As Patrick Burke has extensively detailed, Jefferson Airplane's politics were complicated and often problematic. For example, when the band played "Crown of Creation" on *The Smothers Brothers Comedy Hour*, Slick attempted to make some

sort of political statement by donning blackface. For more, see Patrick Burke, "Blue Eyes and a Black Face: Jefferson Airplane and the Rock Revolution," in *Tear Down the Walls: White Radicalism and Black Power in 1960s Rock* (Chicago: University of Chicago Press, 2021), 45–68.

32. Jorma Kaukonen, *Been So Long: My Life and Music* (New York: St. Martin's Griffin, 2018), 133.

33. Wright, "Interview with Casady."

34. Jisi, "Somebody to Love," 69.

35. For a full breakdown of the song's bass line, see Jisi, "Somebody to Love," 69.

36. In 1969, Casady's modified Guild was stolen. He subsequently had a second, even more elaborate version built, this time by Stanley and Ron Wickersham. Joining with luthier Rick Turner, Stanley and Wickersham would eventually form the company Alembic and design high-quality musical instruments. Their first original, company-branded instrument was an electric bass for Casady.

37. "Best Individual Artists of 1968," *Jazz & Pop*, February 1969, 22; "Best Individual Artists of 1970," *Jazz & Pop*, February 1971, 22. He lost out to Jack Bruce in the 1969 poll.

38. James Gordon Williams, *Crossing Bar Lines: The Politics and Practices of Black Musical Space* (Jackson: University Press of Mississippi, 2021), 11.

39. The members of Sly and the Family Stone disagree about how much they were a part of San Francisco hippie culture. Bassist Larry Graham, for his part, appears to see a direct connection: "It depends on a person's definition of the word ["hippie"]. But, for a lot of people, we would fit in with that, which was really a lot about love and peace. And we didn't necessarily even dress like other segments of society back then." See George Varga, "Larry Graham: Woodstock, Prince & Beyond," *San Diego Union-Tribune*, September 17, 2014, https://www.sandiegouniontribune.com/entertainment/music/sdut-bass-great-larry-graham-talks-music-and-more-2014sep17-htmlstory.html/

40. "Reflections with Larry Graham," *Reflections in Rhythm*, August 8, 2010, https://reflectionsinrhythm.wordpress.com/2010/08/08/reflections-with-larry-graham/

41. "Reflections with Larry Graham." Although it was rebranded as "St. George" for sale in the United States, Graham's bass was an import that had actually been designed and manufactured by the Japanese company Teisco.

42. Jon Liebman, "Interview with Larry Graham," *For Bass Players Only*, October 1, 2021, https://forbassplayersonly.com/interview-larry-graham/. Graham is right that he was not the first to develop a slap bass style (there was, in fact, a long tradition of upright slap bass players in both jazz and country music). However, for electric bassists, Graham's approach would be, by far, the most influential.

43. Bill Leigh, "Father Funk: Larry Graham Thumps Straight from the Heart," *Bass Player*, July 1999.

44. Leigh, "Father Funk."

45. For a more detailed overview of Stone's biography and the Family Stone's career, see Jeff Kaliss, *I Want to Take You Higher: The Life and Times of Sly and the Family Stone* (Milwaukee: BackBeat Books, 2009).

46. Rick Suchow, "Larry Graham: Godfather of Funk Bass," *Bass Musician*, November 2010, reprinted at https://bassmusicianmagazine.com/2010/11/bass-musician-magazine-featuring-larry-graham-november-2010-issue/

47. Craig Werner, *A Change Is Gonna Come: Music, Race, and the Soul of America*, rev. ed. (Ann Arbor: University of Michigan Press, 2006), 103–104.

48. Frank Kofsky, "Review of *Dance to the Music*," *Jazz & Pop*, November 1968.

49. "Interview with Sly Stone," February 9, 1969, Sue Cassidy Clark Collection, Library and Archives, Rock and Roll Hall of Fame and Museum.

50. Greil Marcus, *Mystery Train: Images of America in Rock 'n' Roll Music*, 5th ed. (New York: Plume, 2008), 69.

51. Sly and the Family Stone, *Live at the Fillmore East: October 4th & 5th, 1968*, Epic, 2015, CD.

52. E. E. Bradman, "Full Circle: 360 Degrees of the Acoustic 360," *Bass Player*, May 2013, 30.

53. Similarly, the Ampeg SVT ("Super Vacuum Tube") bass amplifier was also explicitly designed to compete with the intense volume of Marshall guitar amps. Introduced in 1969, it had an output of 300 watts, and just as the B-15 had been celebrated as the best studio bass amp in the sixties, the SVT became the standard amp for large-scale live performance in the seventies. For more, see Hopkins and Moore, *Ampeg*, 181–184.

54. Tom Mulhern, "Larry Graham: Bass Popping Pioneer," *Guitar Player*, March 1980, 18.

55. Unfortunately, despite supplying the most crucial part of the composition, Graham was not given writing credit for "Thank You." As with all the Family Stone's recordings, the song was attributed solely to Sly Stone.

56. Mulhern, "Larry Graham," 18.

57. Jimmy Leslie, "Larry Graham: Trunk of the Funk Tree," *Bass Player*, May 2007, 32.

58. Rickey Vincent, *Funk: The Music, the People, and the Rhythm of the One* (New York: St. Martin's Press, 1996).

59. Vincent, *Funk*, 31.

60. Leigh, "Father Funk."

61. For more on the connections between Jefferson Airplane and progressive rock, see John Covach, "The Hippie Aesthetic: Cultural Positioning and Musical Ambition in Early Progressive Rock," in *Rock Music*, ed. Mark Spicer (New York: Routledge, 2016), 65–75.

Conclusion

1. Steven Johnson, *Where Good Ideas Come From: The Natural History of Innovation* (New York: Riverhead Books, 2010), 28–29. My conception of the adjacent possible is indebted to Josh Scott's discussion of it within the context of electric guitar history; see Josh Scott, "6 Guitar Inventions Explained," *The JHS Show*, 2023, https://thejhsshow.com/articles/6-guitar-inventions-explained/

2. Johnson, *Good Ideas*, 31.

Bibliography

Acker, Dave. "Interview with Buddy Wheeler." http://tony50.tripod.com/intervi
ew-bwheeler.html/. Accessed September 26, 2020.

"'All-Electric' Bands Cause Big Rivalry in New York." *Down Beat.* October 1, 1939.
6.

Altschuler, Glenn. *All Shook Up: How Rock 'n' Roll Changed America.* Oxford:
Oxford University Press, 2003.

American Music Conference. *Report on Amateur Instrumental Music in the United
States—1964.* Chicago: American Music Conference, 1964.

American Music Conference. *Report on Amateur Instrumental Music in the United
States—1965.* Chicago: American Music Conference, 1965.

American Music Conference. *Report on Amateur Instrumental Music in the United
States—1967.* Chicago: American Music Conference, 1967.

Ampeg. Advertisement. *Down Beat.* June 17, 1946. 16.

Arnaudon, Jean-Claude. "Jack Myers." In *Dictionnaire du blues.* Paris: Filipacchi,
1977. 192–193.

Arnold, Billy Boy *The Blues Dream of Billy Boy Arnold.* Chicago: University of Chicago Press, 2021.

Atkins, John. *The Who on Record: A Critical History, 1963–1998.* Jefferson, NC:
McFarland, 2000.

Babbitt, Bob. "Who Played Bass?" *Bass Player.* December 2002. 88.

Babiuk, Andy. *Beatles Gear: All the Fab Four's Instruments from Stage to Studio.* Milwaukee: Backbeat Books, 2015.

Babiuk, Andy and Greg Prevost. *Rolling Stones Gear: All the Stones' Instruments from
Stage to Studio.* Milwaukee: Hal Leonard, 2013.

Bacon, Tony. "The British Guitar Embargo: When Brits Were Banned from Buying American." *Reverb.* April 5, 2018. https://reverb.com/news/the-british
-guitar-embargo-when-brits-were-banned-from-buying-american/

Bacon, Tony. "Interview: Jack Bruce Talks Cream, Ornette Coleman & Self-
Expression." *Reverb.* May 14, 2020. https://reverb.com/news/interview-jack
-bruce-talks-cream-ornette-coleman-and-self-expression-bacons-archive/

Bacon, Tony and Barry Moorhouse, *The Bass Book: A Complete Illustrated History of
Bass Guitars.* 2nd ed. San Francisco: Backbeat, 2008.

Bacon, Tony and Gareth Morgan. *Bassmaster: Paul McCartney Playing the Great Beatles Basslines*. Milwaukee: Backbeat Books, 2006.

"Ban Lifted on U.S. LP, Instruments." *Melody Maker.* June 6, 1959. 1.

"Bass Lines: Crystal Gazing with a Bonanza of Experts." *Down Beat.* January 27, 1977.

Bass Player Presents: Session Legends & Studio Gear [special issue]. 2009.

Bayles, Martha. *Hole in Our Soul: The Loss of Beauty & Meaning in American Popular Music*. Chicago: University of Chicago Press, 1996.

"Beat Instrumental's 1965 Gold Star Awards." *Beat Instrumental.* January 1966. 10.

Beaumonte, Eddie. "'We'll Starve the Mickey Mouse Bands': Lionel Hampton, for the First Time, Reveals Exactly What He Wants." *Down Beat.* November 15, 1940. 4.

Bechtoldt, Paul and Doug Tulloch. *Guitars from Neptune: A Definitive Journey into Danelectro-Mania*. Fort Lauderdale: Guitar Broker, 1995.

Berton, Ralph. "Ralph Berton Writes Some More Notes on Lionel Hampton." *Melody Maker.* October 17, 1953. 13.

"Best Individual Artists of 1968." *Jazz & Pop.* February 1969.

"Best Individual Artists of 1970." *Jazz & Pop.* February 1971.

Betts, Graham. *The Motown Encyclopedia*. N.p.: AC Publishing, 2014.

Birnbaum, Larry. "Reggie Boyd: Chess Session Ace, Jazz & Blues Educator." *Guitar Player.* January 1984. 14–22.

Black, Johnny. *Eyewitness the Who: The Day-by-Day Story*. London: Carlton Books, 2001.

Black, Johnny. "Interview with the Who's John Entwistle." August 1994. *Rock's Backpages Audio.*

Blaine, Hal and Mr. Bonzai. *Hal Blaine & the Wrecking Crew: The Story of the World's Most Recorded Musician*. Ed. David M. Schwartz. 3rd ed. Alma, MI: Rebeats Publications, 2010.

Blecha, Peter. "Tutmarc, Paul (1896–1972), and His Audiovox Electric Guitars." *HistoryLink.* http://www.historylink.org/File/7479/. Accessed March 27, 2019.

Boettcher, Marc. *Stranger in the Night: Die Bert Kaempfert Story*. Hamburg: Europäische Verlagsanstalt, 2002.

Bolden, Tony. *Groove Theory: The Blues Foundation of Funk*. Jackson: University Press of Mississippi, 2020.

Bowman, Rob. *Soulsville U.S.A.: The Story of Stax Records*. New York: Schirmer Trader Books, 1997.

Bowman, Rob. "The Stax Sound: A Musicological Analysis." *Popular Music* 14, no. 3 (1995): 285–320.

Boyd, Jean A. *Dance All Night: Those Other Southwestern Swing Bands, Past and Present*. Lubbock: Texas Tech University Press, 2012.

Boyer, Paul D. *The Rickenbacker Electric Bass: 50 Years as Rock's Bottom*. 2nd ed. Milwaukee: Hal Leonard, 2017.

Brackett, David. *Categorizing Sound: Genre and Twentieth-Century Popular Music*. Oakland: University of California Press, 2016.

Brackett, David. "Improvisation and Value in Rock Music, 1966." *Journal of the Society for American Music* 14, no. 2 (May 2020): 197–232.

Bradley, Dick. *Understanding Rock 'n' Roll: Popular Music in Britain, 1955–1964.* Buckingham: Open University Press, 1992.

Bradley, Harold. Interview by John W. Rumble. May 14, 1991. Country Music Foundation. Frist Library and Archive of the Country Music Hall of Fame and Museum.

Bradley, Harold. Interview by John W. Rumble. September 15, 1988. Country Music Foundation. Frist Library and Archive of the Country Music Hall of Fame and Museum.

Bradley, Harold. Interview by John W. Rumble. September 28, 1988. Country Music Foundation. Frist Library and Archive of the Country Music Hall of Fame and Museum.

Bradley, Harold. Interview by Travis D. Stimeling. August 1, 2014. Nashville Sound Oral History Project.

Bradman, E. E. "The Bar-Kays' James Alexander." In *Bass Player Presents: The Funky Bass Book.* Ed. Bill Leigh. Milwaukee: Backbeat Books, 2010. 44–46.

Bradman, E. E. "Full Circle: 360 Degrees of the Acoustic 360." *Bass Player.* May 2013. 28–45.

Bragg, Rick. *Jerry Lee Lewis: His Own Story.* New York: HarperCollins, 2014.

Brehm, Simon. "Roligast Hittills—men mycket fin musik också." *Estrad.* Oktober 1953. 4.

Brennan, Matt. *Kick It: A Social History of the Drum Kit.* New York: Oxford University Press, 2020.

Brewer, Roy. "The Appearance of the Electric Bass Guitar: A Rockabilly Perspective." *Popular Music and Society* 26, no. 3 (2003): 351–366.

Brewer, Roy. "The Use of Habanera Rhythm in Rockabilly Music." *American Music* 17, no. 3 (1999): 300–317.

"Brian Gregg 'In the Snug' with Bulls Head Bob." *Brum Beat.* December 1, 2010. http://www.brumbeat.net/bgregg.htm/. Accessed March 30, 2015.

Broven, John. *Rhythm & Blues in New Orleans.* 3rd ed. Gretna, LA: Pelican Publishing, 1995.

Brown, J. W. *Whole Lotta Shakin'.* Savannah, GA: Continental Shelf Publishing, 2010.

Brown, James. *I Feel Good: A Memoir of a Life of Soul.* London: New American Library, 2005.

Brown, James. *James Brown: The Godfather of Soul.* New York: Macmillan, 1986.

Bundy, June. "Gals Best Disk & Phono Buyers in Teen-Age Bracket." *Billboard.* August 15, 1956. 15.

Burke, Ken and Dan Griffin. *The Blue Moon Boys: The Story of Elvis Presley's Band.* Chicago: Chicago Review Press, 2006.

Burke, Patrick. *Tear Down the Walls: White Radicalism and Black Power in 1960s Rock.* Chicago: University of Chicago Press, 2021.

Burt, Rob. *Rock and Roll: The Movies.* New York: New Orchard Editions, 1986.

Buskin, Richard. "Norman Smith: The Beatles' First Engineer." *Sound on Sound.* May 2008. https://www.soundonsound.com/people/norman-smith-beatles -first-engineer/

Butcher, Mike. Liner notes to Lionel Hampton, *Lionel Hampton's Paris All Stars.* Vogue L.D.E. 063. 1954. LP.

Butters, Rex. "Howard Rumsey: The Lighthouse All Star." *All About Jazz.* August 2007. https://www.allaboutjazz.com/howard-rumsey-the-lighthouse-all-star-howard-rumsey-by-rex-butters__3876/. Accessed December 22, 2021.

"The Byrds Top Hot 100 Chart." *Billboard.* June 26, 1965. 1.

Campelo, Isabel. "'The Extra Thing'—the Role of Session Musicians in the Recording Industry." *Journal on the Art of Record Production* 10 (July 2015). http://www.arpjournal.com/asarpwp/that-extra-thing-the-role-of-session-musicians-in-the-recording-industry/

"Carol Kaye: Session Legend Interview." June 13, 2013. *Snapshots Foundation.* YouTube. https://www.youtube.com/watch?v=q4JWqK6r6N4/

Carr, Joe and Alan Munde. *Prairie Nights to Neon Lights: The Story of Country Music in West Texas.* Lubbock: Texas Tech University Press, 1995.

Carson, David A. *Grit, Noise, & Revolution: The Birth of Detroit Rock 'n' Roll.* Ann Arbor: University of Michigan Press, 2006.

Carter, Walter. *The Gibson Electric Guitar Book: Seventy Years of Classic Guitars.* San Francisco: Backbeat Books, 2007.

Casady, Jack. Interview by Jeff Tamarkin. February 9, 2012. Rock & Roll Hall of Fame and Museum Oral History Project.

"Cash Box Pop DJ Poll Results." *Cash Box.* August 5, 1961. 49.

Chevan, David. "The Double Bass as a Solo Instrument in Early Jazz." *Black Perspective in Music* 17, nos. 1–2 (1989): 73–92.

Chilton, John. *Let the Good Times Roll: The Story of Louis Jordan and His Music.* Ann Arbor: University of Michigan Press, 1994.

Clawson, Mary Ann. "When Women Play the Bass: Instrument Specialization and Gender Interpretation in Alternative Rock Music." *Gender & Society* 13, no. 2 (April 1999): 193–210.

Coates, Norma. "Excitement Is Made, Not Born: Jack Good, Television, and Rock and Roll." *Journal of Popular Music Studies* 25, no. 3 (2013): 301–325.

Collis, John. *Gene Vincent and Eddie Cochran: Rock 'n' Revolutionaries.* London: Virgin Digital, 2011.

Connor, Charles. *Keep a Knockin': The Story of a Legendary Drummer.* Grapevine, TX: Waldorf Publishing, 2015.

Cook, Mike. *Cliffhanger: The Life and Times of Jet Harris.* Surrey: Grosvenor House Publishing, 2016.

Cooper, Daniel. "Being Ray Price Means Never Having to Say You're Sorry." *Journal of Country Music* 14, no. 3 (1992): 22–31.

Cortese, James. "Clanging Cash Register Provides Background Music." *The Commercial Appeal.* January 7, 1968. Morning Edition. 31.

"Country Poll Winners." *Cash Box.* July 14, 1956. 38.

"Country Poll Winners." *Cash Box.* June 18, 1955. 40.

Covach, John. "The Hippie Aesthetic: Cultural Positioning and Musical Ambition in Early Progressive Rock." In *Rock Music.* Edited by Mark Spicer. New York: Routledge, 2016. 65–75.

Cox, Billy. Interview Richard Johnston. *Bass Player.* July 2007. 38–46.

"Creating Guitarists around the World—the Mel Bay Story." *The Music Trades.* June 1967. 184, 186.

Crisafulli, Chuck. "Duck Dunn: He's a Soul Man." *Bass Player.* December 1994. 44–50.

Crombie, Tony. Interview by Tony Middleton. August 22, 1995. British Library Oral History Collection. C122/127-C122/259.

Cunningham, Mark. "Spider Man: John Entwistle." *Bassist & Bass Techniques.* May 1995. 12–18.

Dahl, Bill. Liner notes for The Treniers, *Rock.* Bear Family Records. 2010. CD.

Daltrey, Roger. *Thanks a Lot, Mr. Kibblewhite: My Story.* New York: Henry Holt, 2018.

Danchin, Sebastian. *Earl Hooker: Blues Master.* Jackson: University Press of Mississippi, 2001.

Danielsen, Anne. *Presence and Pleasure: The Funk Grooves of James Brown and Parliament.* Middleton, CT: Wesleyan University Press, 2006.

Dankenbring, Ray. *The Mel Bay Story.* Pacific, MO: Mel Bay Publications, 1997.

Dawe, Kevin. "The Cultural Study of Musical Instruments." In *The Cultural Study of Music: A Critical Introduction.* Ed. Martin Clayton, Trevor Herbert, and Richard Middleton. 2nd ed. New York: Routledge, 2012. 195–205.

Dawson, Jim and Spencer Leigh. *Memories of Buddy Holly.* Milford, NH: Big Nickel Publications, 1996.

Dean Martin & Jerry Lewis Collection. Mill Creek Entertainment. 2018. DVD.

Delaney, Kevin. "The Electric Upright: Common Ground for Bassists." *International Society of Bassists* 19, no. 1 (1993): 48–56.

Denisoff, R. Serge and William D. Romanowski. *Risky Business: Rock in Film.* New Brunswick, NJ: Transaction Publishers, 1991.

". . . der Hitmaker hinter dem Godfather: 'Sweet' Charles Sherrell." *Bass Professor.* n.d.

De Souza, Jonathan. *Music at Hand: Instruments, Bodies, and Cognition.* New York: Oxford University Press, 2017.

Determeyer, Eddy. *Rhythm Is Our Business: Jimmie Lunceford and the Harlem Express.* Ann Arbor: University of Michigan Press, 2010.

Dewe, Michael. *The Skiffle Craze.* Aberystwyth, Wales: Planet, 1998.

di Perna, Alan. "Buddy Guy: A Man and His Blues." *Guitar World.* October 2005. Reprinted at https://www.guitarworld.com/features/buddy-guy-man-and -his-blues/

Dixon, Willie. *I Am the Blues: The Willie Dixon Story.* New York: Da Capo Press, 1989.

Dougan, John. *The Who Sell Out.* New York: Bloomsbury, 2006.

Douglas, R. M. *Orderly and Humane: The Expulsion of the Germans after the Second World War.* New Haven: Yale University Press, 2012.

Douglas, Shirley and Chas McDevitt. *Shirley Douglas' Easy Guide to Rhythm & Blues for Bass-Guitar.* London: Southern Music Publishing Co., 1960.

Dowdall, Peter. *Technology and the Stylistic Evolution of the Jazz Bass.* New York: Routledge, 2018.

"Down Beat Critics' Poll Results." *Down Beat.* August 6, 1959. 19–22.

Drabløs, Per Elias. *The Quest for the Melodic Electric Bass: From Jamerson to Spenner.* Farnham, Surrey: Ashgate, 2015.

El-Bayeh, Alexandra. "They Could Be Back: The Possibility of Termination Rights for Session Musicians." *American University Law Review* 64, no. 2 (2014): 285–336.

Ellis, Thomas Sayers. "From the Crib to the Coliseum: An Interview with Bootsy Collins." In *The Funk Era and Beyond: New Perspectives on Black Popular Culture.* Ed. Tony Bolden. New York: Palgrave Macmillan, 2008. 89–103.

Emerick, Geoff. *Here, There and Everywhere: My Life Recording the Music of the Beatles.* New York: Gotham Books, 2006.

"Eric in the Evening: Alan Dawson Interview." June 6, 1994. *WGBH Media Library & Archives.* http://openvault.wgbh.org/catalog/2ae258-eric-in-the-evening -alan-dawson-interview/. Accessed May 2, 2014.

Erskine, Bob and Roger Nunn. "Bobby Jones, a Gene Vincent Blue Cap." *Rockabilly Hall of Fame.* November 2011. http://www.rockabillyhall.com/gvbobbyjo nes.html/. Accessed November 1, 2010.

Everett, Walter. *The Beatles as Musicians: Revolver through the Anthology.* New York: Oxford University Press, 1999.

Everett, Walter. *The Beatles as Musicians: The Quarry Men through Rubber Soul.* New York: Oxford University Press, 2001.

Everett, Walter. *The Foundations of Rock: From "Blue Suede Shoes" to "Suite Judy Blue Eyes".* New York: Oxford University Press, 2009.

Faulkner, Robert R. *Hollywood Studio Musicians: Their Work and Careers in the Recording Industry.* 2nd ed. New Brunswick, NJ: AldineTransaction, 2013.

Feather, Leonard, ed. *Encyclopedia of Jazz.* New York: Horizon Press, 1960.

Feather, Leonard. "Hamp-lified Fiddle May Lighten Bassists' Burdens." *Down Beat.* July 30, 1952. 22.

Feather, Leonard. "Hard Rock Stones Sweet Sound of Monterey Festival." *Los Angeles Times.* September 19, 1966. 26.

Feddersen, Jack. "Music Industry Promotion." *The Music Trades.* December 1956. 29.

Fender. Advertisement. *Down Beat.* January 19, 1961. 7.

Fender. Advertisement. *Down Beat.* May 1, 1958. 3.

Fender. Advertisement. *Down Beat.* October 31, 1957. 22–23.

Fender. Advertisement. *The Music Trades.* April 1952. 55.

"Fender Bass and Amplifier Replace Old Style in 1/6 Size." *The Music Trades.* April 1952. 54.

Filiberto, Roger. *Mel Bay Presents the Electric Bass, Volume 1.* Kirkwood, MO: Mel Bay Publications, 1963.

"The Final Count for 1956 Poll!" *Cash Box.* December 8, 1956. 5.

"The Final Count for 1957 Poll!" *Cash Box.* December 8, 1957. 9.

Fink, Robert. "Elvis Everywhere: Musicology and Popular Music Studies at the Twilight of the Canon." *American Music* 16, no. 2 (Summer 1998): 135–179.

Finnis, Rob. Liner notes to Eddie Cochran, *The Eddie Cochran Box Set: A Complete History in Works and Music, 1938–1960.* Liberty. 1988. CD.

Finnis, Rob and John P. Dixon. Liner notes to Duane Eddy, *Twangin' from Phoenix to L.A.: The Jamie Years.* Bear Family Records. 1994. CD.

Fisher, Joe. "Tales of a Dinosaur" [unpublished memoir]. Reproduced at *Silvertone World.* https://www.silvertoneworld.net/amplifiers/1448/1448p2.html. Accessed May 4, 2016/.

Fitten, Ronald K. "Obituary: Lorraine Tutmarc, Lived the Light, the Hope, and the Love of Christ." *Seattle Times.* December 23, 1992. https://archive.seattle times.com/archive/?date=19921223&slug=1531578/. Accessed June 3, 2023.

Fletcher, Tim. "The First Electric Bass Guitar Player." *Bass Musician.* February 17, 2020. https://bassmusicianmagazine.com/2020/02/the-first-electric-bass-gu itar-player/. Accessed May 1, 2023.

Flory, Andrew. "20 Feet from Stardom: Entertainment or History?" *Musicology Now.* February 21, 2014. https://musicologynow.org/20-feet-from-stardom -entertainment-or-history/

Flory, Andrew. *I Hear a Symphony: Motown and Crossover R&B.* Ann Arbor: University of Michigan Press, 2017.

Flückiger, Otto. *Discography of Lionel Hampton and His Orchestra: 1951–1953.* Reinach: Jazz-Publications, 1961.

Folkins, Gail. *Texas Dance Halls: A Two-Step Circuit.* Lubbock: Texas Tech University Press, 2007.

Folkins, Gail. "Texas Dance Halls: History, Culture, and Community." *Journal of Texas Music History* 6 (2006): 1–9.

Fontana, D. J. Interview by Parke Puterbaugh. March 3, 2012. Rock & Roll Hall of Fame and Museum Oral History Project.

Forte, Dan. "Bassist David Hood: Muscle Shoals. The Band Attitude." *Guitar Player.* November 1982. 33–42.

Forte, Dan. "Buddy Guy: Keeping the Blues Alive and Definitely Kicking." *Vintage Guitar.* May 2013. Reprinted at https://www.vintageguitar.com/14777 /buddy-guy-3/

Forte, Dan. "Chuck Rainey: An Outspoken Interview with the Top Studio Bassist." *Guitar Player.* September 1976. 10–11, 38, 40.

Forte, Dan. "The Ventures: Still Rockin' after All These Years." *Guitar Player.* September 1981. 90–98.

Foster, Mo. *Play Like Elvis: How British Musicians Bought the American Dream.* Bodmin: MPG Books, 2000.

Frame, Pete. *The Restless Generation: How Rock Music Changed the Face of 1950s Britain.* London: Rogan House, 2007.

Fratallone, Stephen. "Super Salesman: Lighthouse All-Stars Founder Howard Rumsey Sold Millions on West Coast Jazz." *Jazz Connection Magazine.* May 2005. Archived at http://archive.fo/1HCGv/

Friedland, Ed. *The R&B Bass Masters: The Way They Play.* San Francisco: BackBeat Books, 2005.

Frith, Simon, Matt Brennan, Martin Cloonan, and Emma Webster. *The History of Live Music in Britain.* Vol. 1: *1950–1967.* Farnham: Ashgate, 2013.

Frith, Simon, Matt Brennan, Martin Cloonan, and Emma Webster. *The History of Live Music in Britain.* Vol. 2: *1968–1984.* London: Routledge, 2019.

Fullerton, George. *Guitars from George & Leo: How Leo Fender and I Built G&L Guitars.* Milwaukee: Hal Leonard, 2005.

Furmanovsky, Michael. "Outselling the Beatles: Assessing the Influence and Legacy of the Ventures on Japanese Musicians and Popular Music in the 1960s." *Ryukoku University International Cultural Society,* no. 14 (March 2010): 51–64.

Gardner, Bert. *Bert Gardner's Complete Course for Electric Bass.* N.p.: Music Exploitation Enterprises, 1957.

Garland, Phyl. *The Sound of Soul.* Chicago: H. Regnery, 1969.

George, Nelson. "Standing in the Shadows of Motown." Reprinted in *Buppies, B-Boys, Baps, & Bohos: Notes on Post-soul Black Culture.* 2nd ed. Cambridge, MA: Da Capo Press, 2001. 165–174.

George, Nelson. *Where Did Our Love Go: The Rise and Fall of the Motown Sound.* 2nd ed. Urbana: University of Illinois Press, 2007.

Gioia, Ted. *West Coast Jazz: Modern Jazz in California, 1945–1960.* Oxford: Oxford University Press, 1992.

Gitelman, Lisa. *Always Already New: Media, History, and the Data of Culture.* Cambridge: MIT Press, 2006.

Gleason, Ralph. *The Jefferson Airplane and the San Francisco Sound.* New York: Ballantine Books, 1969.

Gleason, Ralph. Liner notes to Lionel Hampton, *Lionel Hampton.* Contemporary C 3502. 1955. LP.

Gleason, Ralph. Liner notes to The Mastersounds, *Jazz Showcase Introducing The Mastersounds.* World Pacific Records PJM-403. 1957. LP.

Goffman, Erving. *Stigma: Notes on the Management of Spoiled Identity.* New York: Simon & Schuster, 1963.

Goodwin, Keith. "Focus on Skiffle." *New Musical Express.* January 31, 1958. 10.

Gordon, Robert. *Can't Be Satisfied: The Life and Times of Muddy Waters.* Boston: Little, Brown, 2002.

Gordon, Robert. *Respect Yourself: Stax Records and the Soul Explosion.* New York: Bloomsbury, 2013.

Gould, Jonathan. *Otis Redding: An Unfinished Life.* New York: Crown Archetype, 2017.

Green, Richard. "The Who: A Disturbing Group." *Record Mirror.* March 6, 1965.

Green, Richard. "The Who: The Group That Slaughters Their Amplifiers." *Record Mirror.* April 3, 1965.

Greensmith, Bill. "Below's the Name, Drummin's the Game." *Blues Unlimited,* nos. 131–132 (September–December 1978): 18.

Grendysa, Peter. Liner notes to Louis Jordan, *Let the Good Times Roll: The Complete Decca Recordings, 1938–1954.* Bear Family Records. 1992. CD.

Gribbin, John. *Not Fade Away: The Life and Music of Buddy Holly.* Thriplow: Icon Books, 2009.

Grissim, John. "The Nashville Cats." *Rolling Stone.* December 9, 1971. 30–32.

"Growing Up at 33 1/3: The George Harrison Interview." *Crawdaddy.* February 1977.

Guralnick, Peter. *Last Train to Memphis: The Rise of Elvis Presley.* Boston: Little, Brown, 1994.

Hadley, Frank-John. "Blues Pantheon: The 50 Top Blues Albums of the Past 50 Years." *Downbeat.* September 2003.

Hall, Michael. "The Making of an Urbane Cowboy" *Texas Monthly.* September 16, 2019. https://www.texasmonthly.com/the-culture/lee-hazlewood-musician-texas/

Hall, Rick. *The Man from Muscle Shoals.* Monterey: Heritage Builders, 2016.

Halterman, Del. *Walk-Don't Run: The Story of the Ventures.* Milton Keynes: Lulu, 2010.

Hamilton, Jack. *Just Around Midnight: Rock and Roll and the Racial Imagination.* Cambridge: Harvard University Press, 2016.

"Hampton Now Has Electric Band." *Metronome.* November 1940. 9.

Harris, K. Paul. "U2's Creative Process: Sketching in Sound." PhD dissertation, University of North Carolina at Chapel Hill, 2006.

Harris, Steven D. *The Kenton Kronicles: A Biography of Modern America's Man of Music, Stan Kenton.* Pasadena, CA: Dynaflow Publications, 2003.

Hartman, Gary. *The History of Texas Music.* College Station: Texas A&M University Press, 2008.

Hartman, Kent. *The Wrecking Crew.* New York: Thomas Dunne Books, 2012.

Harvey, Karen. "Introduction: Historians, Material Culture, and Materiality." In *History and Material Culture: A Students' Guide to Approaching Alternative Sources.* Ed. Karen Harvey. 2nd ed. New York: Routledge, 2018. 1–26.

Hellicar, Mike. "*Jet* and *Duane* Have Similar Assets." *New Musical Express.* May 26, 1962. 2.

Henderson, Derek. *Gene Vincent: A Companion.* Southampton: Spent Brothers Productions, 2005.

Herrick, Susan Oehler. "Performing Blues and Navigating Race in Transcultural Contexts." In *Issues in African American Music: Power, Gender, Race, Representation.* Ed. Portia K. Maultsby and Mellonee V. Burnim. New York: Routledge, 2017. 3–29.

Hill, Matthew W. "George Beauchamp and the Rise of the Electric Guitar up to 1939." PhD dissertation, University of Edinburgh, 2013.

"The Hippies: Dropouts with a Mission." *Newsweek.* February 6, 1967. 92.

Hitsville: The Making of Motown. Directed by Ben Turner and Gabe Turner. Motown the Film LLC, 2019. Blu-Ray.

Hoffman, Larry. "Robert Lockwood, Jr." *Living Blues.* June 1995.

Holley, Joe. "Tony De La Rosa Dies." *Washington Post.* June 19, 2004. https://www .washingtonpost.com/archive/local/2004/06/19/tony-de-la-rosa-dies/d502 7cec-9377-4a1b-861d-22f7b1568ef9/

Hoover, Timothy R. *Soul Serenade: King Curtis and His Immortal Saxophone.* Denton: University of North Texas Press, 2022.

Hopkins, Gregg and Bill Moore. *Ampeg: The Story Behind the Sound.* Milwaukee: Hal Leonard, 1999.

Houghton, Mick. *Becoming Elektra: The True Story of Jac Holzman's Visionary Record Label.* London: Jawbone Press, 2010.

Hove, Michael J., et al. "Feel the Bass: Music Presented to Tactile and Auditory Modalities Increases Aesthetic Appreciation and Body Movement." *Journal of Experimental Psychology: General* 149, no. 6 (2020): 1137–1147.

"How to Promote with the Beatles." *The Music Trades.* May 1964. 32–33, 44.

Hoyer, Christian. *Framus: Built in the Heart of Bavaria.* Markneukirchen: Framus, 2007.

Hoyer, Christian. "120 Years of Service to Music: A History of the Karl Höfner Company, 1887–2008." *Vintage Höfner.* Archived at https://web.archive.org /web/20220811151224/https://vintagehofner.co.uk/christianhoyer/hofne rhist/hofnerhistory.html

Hughes, Charles. *Country Soul: Making Music and Making Race in the American South.* Chapel Hill: University of North Carolina Press, 2015.

Hull, Everette. Interview by Dorothy Gable. March 12, 1968. Frist Library and Archive of the Country Music Hall of Fame and Museum Oral History Collection, OH325.

Inaba, Mitsutoshi. *Willie Dixon: Preacher of the Blues.* Lanham, MD: Scarecrow Press, 2011.

Inglis, Ian. "Introduction: History, Place and Time: The Possibility of the Unexpected." In *Performance and Popular Music.* Ed. Ian Inglis. New York: Routledge, 2006. xii–xvi.

Inman, Davis. "'Balls in the Bottom': A Q&A with Bill Wyman." *American Songwriter.* 2012. https://americansongwriter.com/balls-in-the-bottom-a-qa-with-bill-wyman/

"Interview with Carol Kaye." 2010. *AlbumLinerNotes.com.* Archived at https://web.archive.org/web/20200220160725/http://albumlinernotes.com/Carol_Kaye.html/. Accessed January 14, 2019.

"Interview with Sly Stone." February 9, 1969. Sue Cassidy Clark Collection. Library and Archives. Rock and Roll Hall of Fame and Museum.

Ivey, William. "Commercialization and Tradition in the Nashville Sound." In *Folk Music and Modern Sound.* Ed. William Ferris and Mary L. Hart. Jackson: University Press of Mississippi, 1982. 129–138.

"The Jack Casady Interview." *The Jake Feinberg Show.* May 17, 2015. http://www.jakefeinbergshow.com/2015/05/the-jack-casady-interview/

Jackson, John A. *American Bandstand: Dick Clark and the Making of a Rock 'n' Roll Empire.* New York: Oxford University Press, 1997.

Jagger, Mick. "The Rolling Stones Write for Melody Maker: We're *Not* on the Wagon." *Melody Maker.* March 21, 1964. 3.

Jamerson, James. Interview by Dan Forte. *Guitar Player.* June 1979. Reprinted in *Bass Heroes.* Ed. Tom Mulhern. San Francisco: GPI Books, 1993. 154–156.

James, David E. *Rock 'n' Film: Cinema's Dance with Popular Music.* New York: Oxford University Press, 2016.

Jemmott, Jerry. "I'm That Guy: The Life, Times, and Music of Jerry Jemmott" [unpublished book manuscript].

Jensen, Joli. *The Nashville Sound: Authenticity, Commercialization, and Country Music.* Nashville: Country Music Foundation Press & Vanderbilt University Press, 1998.

Jet Harris: From There to Here. Directed by Mark Windows. 2012.

Jisi, Chris. "Groove Convergence: Will Lee Interviews Chuck Rainey, the 'Godfather of the Groove.'" *Bass Player.* February 1997. 46.

Jisi, Chris. "Jefferson Airplane's 'Somebody to Love' (Live)." *Bass Player.* Holiday 2011. 68–75.

Jisi, Chris. "John Entwistle: The Return of Thunderfingers." Reprinted in *Bass Heroes.* Ed. Tom Mulhern. San Francisco: GPI Books, 1993. 90–97.

Jisi, Chris. "Precision Memories." *Bass Player* 12, no. 10. October 2001.

Jisi, Chris with Anthony Jackson. "The Heroic Bass of Jack Casady." *Bass Player.* September–October 1993. 40–48.

"Joe Osborn: A Few (Hundred) Hits." *Vintage Guitar.* October 1998. Reprinted at https://www.vintageguitar.com/2925/joe-osborn/

"John Entwistle's Bass Guitar Gear." *Whotabs.* 2021. Archived at https://web.arch ive.org/web/20210415222157/https://www.thewho.net/whotabs/gear/ba ss/bass.html/

Johnson, Derek. "The *Real* Reason *Jet Harris* left the *Shadows.*" *New Musical Express.* May 4, 1962. 8.

Johnson, Derek. "The Stones and Hermits Can't Go Wrong." *New Musical Express.* November 13, 1964. 6.

Johnson, Steven. *Where Good Ideas Come From: The Natural History of Innovation.* New York: Riverhead Books, 2010.

Jones, Booker T. *Time Is Tight: My Life, Note by Note.* New York: Little, Brown, 2019.

Jones, Nick. "Every So Often, a Band is Poised on the Brink of a Breakthrough. Word Has It It's . . . the Who." *Melody Maker.* June 5, 1965.

Jones, Nick. "Well, What Is Pop Art: Who Guitarist Pete Townshend Has a Go at a Definition." *Melody Maker.* July 3, 1965. 11.

Jones, Quincy. *Q: The Autobiography of Quincy Jones.* New York: Doubleday, 2001.

Jones, Roben. *Memphis Boys: The Story of American Studios.* Jackson: University Press of Mississippi, 2010.

Jost, Kévin. "La basse électrique: Son histoire, sa facture, son rôle et ses apports à la musique populaire depuis 1960." MA thesis, Année universitaire, 2007–2008.

Kaliss, Jeff. *I Want to Take You Higher: The Life and Times of Sly and the Family Stone.* Milwaukee: BackBeat Books, 2009.

Katz, David. *Solid Foundation: An Oral History of Reggae.* London: Jawbone Press, 2012.

Kaukonen, Jorma. *Been So Long: My Life and Music.* New York: St. Martin's Griffin, 2018.

Kaye, Carol. "Flirty String Player, How I Fixed Him." Facebook post. March 25, 2021. https://www.facebook.com/carol.kaye.1840/posts/926968354706 432/. Accessed May 1, 2021.

Kaye, Carol. "For those who don't know much about Studio Musicians and Studio Work." Facebook post. May 23, 2018. https://www.facebook.com/10382 22976284207/posts/for-those-who-dont-know-much-about-studio-musicians -and-studio-work-in-hollywood/1449866678453166/

Kaye, Carol. *Studio Musician: Carol Kaye, 60s No. 1 Hit Bassist, Guitarist.* Self-published, 2016.

Kaye, Lenny. "Hey, Mr. Bassman." *Fusion.* September 19, 1969.

Kellett, Andrew. *The British Blues Network: Adoption, Emulation, and Creativity.* Ann Arbor: University of Michigan Press, 2017.

Kelly, Martin, Terry Foster, and Paul Kelly. *The Golden Age of Fender: 1946–1970.* London: Cassell Illustrated, 2010.

Kennealy, Patricia. "Review of *Crown of Creation.*" *Jazz & Pop.* October 1968. 45.

Kernodle, Tammy L. "Diggin' You Like Those Ol' Soul Records: Meshell Ndegeocello and the Expanding Definition of Funk in Postsoul America." *American Studies* 52, no. 4 (2013): 181–204.

Kienzle, Rich. "Harold Bradley: Dean of the Nashville Session Pickers." *Journal of the American Academy for the Preservation of Old-Time Country Music* 1, no. 2 (April 1991): 22–34.

Kienzle, Rich. *Southwest Shuffle: Pioneers of Honky-Tonk, Western Swing, and Country Jazz.* New York: Routledge, 2003.

Klußmeier, Gerhard. *Ladi: Weltstar aus Hamburg.* Hamburg: Tredition, 2014.

Kofsky, Frank, "Review of *Dance to the Music.*" *Jazz & Pop.* November 1968.

Kohman, Peter Stuart. "Surf Bass: Out of the Doghouse." *Vintage Guitar.* May 1997. 100.

Kosser, Michael. *How Nashville Became Music City, U.S.A.: 50 Years of Music Row.* New York: Hal Leonard, 2006.

Kraft, James P. *Stage to Studio: Musicians and the Sound Revolution, 1890–1950.* Baltimore: John Hopkins University Press, 1996.

Laing, Dave. *Buddy Holly.* Bloomington: Indiana University Press, 2010.

Laing, Dave. "Six Boys, Six Beatles: The Formative Years, 1950–1962." In *The Cambridge Companion to the Beatles.* Ed. Kenneth Womack. New York: Cambridge University Press, 2009. 9–32.

Lange, Jeffrey J. *Smile When You Call Me a Hillbilly: Country Music's Struggle for Respectability, 1939–1954.* Athens: University of Georgia Press, 2004.

LeBlanc, Eric S. and Bob Eagle. *Blues: A Regional Experience.* Santa Barbara, CA: Praeger, 2013.

Leiber, Jerry and Mike Stoller with David Ritz. *Hound Dog: The Leiber and Stoller Autobiography.* New York: Simon & Schuster, 2009.

Leigh, Bill. "Bootsy Collins: James Brown, Parliament, Bootsy's Rubber Band." *Bass Player.* December 1998. 32.

Leigh, Bill. "Father Funk: Larry Graham Thumps Straight from the Heart." *Bass Player.* July 1999.

Leigh, Spencer. "Claude Trenier: Singer with the Early Rock 'n' Roll Group the Treniers." *The Independent.* November 24, 2003. https://www.independent.co.uk/news/obituaries/claude-trenier-37514.html/. Accessed November 9, 2014.

Leiser, Willie. "Willie Leiser, 'The Road Runner,' Returns to the BU Pages." *Blues Unlimited.* April 1973. 33–34.

Lesh, Phil. *Searching for the Sound: My Life with the Grateful Dead.* New York: Little, Brown, 2005.

Leslie, Jimmy. "Larry Graham: Trunk of the Funk Tree." *Bass Player.* May 2007. 30–37.

Leslie, Jimmy "Super Bad: Playing Bass with James Brown." In *Bass Player Presents the Funky Bass Book.* Ed. Bill Leigh. Milwaukee: Backbeat Books, 2010. 10–19.

Less, David. "Interview with Lewie and Morris Steinberg." Rock 'n' Soul Audiovisual History Project Collection. Archives Center. National Museum of American History. Smithsonian Institution.

Lewisohn, Mark. *The Complete Beatles Recording Sessions: The Official Story of the Abbey Road Years, 1962–1970.* New York: Hamlyn, 2021.

Liberace TV Classics. Film Chest. 2013. DVD.

Liebman, Jon. "Interview with Larry Graham." *For Bass Players Only.* October 1, 2021. https://forbassplayersonly.com/interview-larry-graham/

Light, G. E. "Marshall Grant Was Here, There, and Everywhere." *Perfect Sound Forever Magazine.* February 2008. https://www.furious.com/perfect/marsha llgrant.html/. Accessed November 1, 2010.

Liner notes to Duane Eddy, *Twang Thang: The Duane Eddy Anthology.* Rhino Records. 1993. CD.

Liner notes to Johnny and the Hurricanes, *Johnny and the Hurricanes Featuring "Red River Rock."* Warwick W2007. 1959. LP.

Lipsitz, George. *Time Passages: Collective Memory and American Popular Culture.* Minneapolis: University of Minnesota Press, 1990.

Lorre, Sean. "British R&B: A Study of Black Popular Music Revivalism in the United Kingdom, 1960–1964." PhD dissertation, McGill University, 2017.

Love, Preston. *A Thousand Honey Creeks Later: My Life in Music from Basie to Motown.* Hanover, NH: Wesleyan University Press, 1997.

"Lyle Ritz Talks about Working with Sonny and Cher." Wrecking Crew. 2017. YouTube https://www.youtube.com/watch?v=JuuQBdSH6gQ/

Macdonald, Dwight. "A Caste, A Culture, A Market." *New Yorker.* November 22, 1958. 72–76.

Mack, Jimmy. "Refutes Claim of First Electric Bass." *Down Beat.* November 1, 1939. 10.

Mack, Kimberly. *Fictional Blues: Narrative Self-Invention from Bessie Smith to Jack White.* Amherst: University of Massachusetts Press, 2020.

Mahon, Maureen, *Black Diamond Queens: African American Women and Rock and Roll.* Durham: Duke University Press, 2020.

Mairants, Ivor. "The Electric Bass." *Melody Maker.* November 14, 1953. 13.

Mairants, Ivor. "Instrumental Intelligence." *Melody Maker.* November 21, 1953. 11.

Mall, Andrew. "Concentration, Diversity, and Consequences: Privileging Independent over Major Record Labels." *Popular Music* 37, no. 3 (2018): 444–465.

Malone, Bill C. and Tracy E. W. Laird. *Country Music USA.* 50th Anniversary ed. Austin: University of Texas Press, 2018.

Manfredi, Anthony J. and Joseph M. Estella. *Smith's Modern Electric Bass Guitar Method.* New York: WM J. Smith Music Co., 1959.

Marcus, Greil. *Mystery Train: Images of America in Rock 'n' Roll Music.* 5th ed. New York: Plume, 2008.

Marshall, Wolf. "Hank's Protos: How Hank Garland Helped Gibson Develop Two Models Not Called Byrdland." *Vintage Guitar.* September 2011. Reprinted at https://www.vintageguitar.com/11719/hanks-protos/

Matthews, Barry. *Fender Bass for Britain: The History of the 1966 Slab-Bodied Precision Bass.* Milton Keynes: AuthorHouse, 2009.

Meehan, Don. "Truth about Simon and Garfunkel Sounds of Silence." *Roughmix-Don Meehan.* Updated November 30, 2014. https://roughmixdon.com/2014/05/11/simon-garfunkels-s-s-truth/. Accessed January 20, 2015.

Michaels, Ken. "Interview with Beatles' Engineer Geoff Emerick." 2006. *Total Access Live.* Archived at https://web.archive.org/web/20060117180903/http://www.totalaccesslive.com/geoffemerick.htm/

Miles, Barry. *Paul McCartney: Many Years from Now.* London: Secker & Warburg, 1997.

Milkowski, Bill. "Blues Legend Dave Myers." *Bass Player.* December 1998. 18.

Miller, James. *Flowers in the Dustbin: The Rise of Rock and Roll, 1947–1977.* New York: Simon & Schuster, 1999.

Mitchell, Gillian A. M. "Reassessing 'the Generation Gap': Bill Haley's 1957 Tour of Britain, Inter-generational Relations and Attitudes to Rock 'n' Roll in the Late 1950s." *Twentieth Century British History* 24, no. 4 (2013): 573–605.

Moon, D. Thomas. "Dave Myers: Somebody Has to Live It First." *Living Blues.* November–December 1998. 32-41.

Montgomery, Monk. Interview by Maggie Hawthorn. 1980. Jazz Oral History Project. Rutgers Institute of Jazz Studies, Newark, NJ.

Morris, Jeremy Wade. *Selling Digital Music, Formatting Culture.* Oakland: University of California Press, 2015.

Mulhern, Tom. "Larry Graham: Bass Popping Pioneer." *Guitar Player.* March 1980. 16–25.

Mundy, Julie and Darrel Highham. *Don't Forget Me: The Eddie Cochran Story.* New York: Billboard Books, 2001.

Myers, Marc. "Interview: Howard Rumsey." *JazzWax.* September 2, 2009. https://www.jazzwax.com/2009/09/02/

Nathaus, Klaus. "The History of the German Popular Music Industry in the Twentieth Century." In *Perspectives on German Popular Music.* Ed. Michael Ahlers and Christoph Jacke. London: Routledge, 2018.

Neill, Andy and Matt Kent. *Anyway Anyhow Anywhere: The Complete Chronicle of the Who, 1958–1978.* New York: Friedman/Fairfax, 2002.

Nevard, Mike. "Hampton Band in Britain . . . but Only for 8 Hours." *Melody Maker.* November 28, 1953. 7.

Newman, Mike. "Monk Montgomery: The First Man to Record on Bass Guitar." *Guitar Player.* September 1977. 26–27.

Newton, Tony. *Gold Thunder: Legendary Adventures of a Motown Bassman.* Venice, CA: Quantum Media Publishing, 2011.

Nicolausson, Harry. "Tjo Och Tjim Och Lite Annat: Hampton motsvarade sitt rykte." *Orkester Journalen.* Oktober 1953. 14.

The Night James Brown Saved Boston. Directed by David Leaf. Shout Factory. 2009. DVD.

1970 Review of the Music Industry and Amateur Music Participation. American Music Conference. Chicago: American Music Conference. 1970.

Norman, Philip. *Rave On: The Biography of Buddy Holly.* New York: Simon & Schuster, 1996.

"Obituaries: Jack Myers." *Living Blues* 213, vol. 42, no. 3 (June 2011): 75.

"Obituaries: Reggie Boyd." *Living Blues* 210, vol. 41, no. 6 (December 2010): 67.

Obrecht, Jas. "20 Essential Rock Albums." *Guitar Player.* January 1987.

Obrecht, Jas, ed. *Rollin' and Tumblin': The Postwar Blues Guitarists.* San Francisco: Miller Freeman Books, 2000.

Oldham, Andrew Loog. *Stoned.* London: Vintage, 2001.

Olson, Steve. "Interview with Bootsy Collins." *Juice Magazine* 66, vol. 6, no. 1 (2009). 124–127.

"Oral History with Carol Kaye of the Wrecking Crew." Rock & Roll Hall of Fame. May 2005. YouTube. https://www.youtube.com/watch?v=F9WQTrr3GZ4/

An Ox's Tale: The John Entwistle Story. Directed by Glenn Aveni and Steve Luongo. Image Entertainment. 2006. DVD.

Palmer, Robert. *Deep Blues*. New York, Penguin, 1981.

Panassié, Hugues. "Review of Lionel Hampton, *Jazz Time Paris*." *Bulletin du Hot Club de France*. December 1953. 11–12.

"Paul Tutmarc & the Mystery behind Who Invented the Electric Guitar." *Jive Time Records Presents: Northwest Music History*. May 3, 2018. https://jivetimerecords .com/northwest/paula-tutmarc. Accessed April 13, 2019/.

Payne, Jim. *Mel Bay Presents the Great Drummers of R&B, Funk, and Soul*. 2nd ed. Pacific, MO: Mel Bay Publications, 2006.

Pecknold, Diane. *The Selling Sound: The Rise of the Country Music Industry*. Durham: Duke University Press, 2007.

Peña, Manuel. *The Texas-Mexican Conjunto: History of a Working-Class Music*. Austin: University of Texas Press, 1985.

Peterson, Richard A. "Why 1955? Explaining the Advent of Rock Music." *Popular Music* 9, no. 1 (January 1990): 97–116.

Peterson, Richard A. and Howard G. White. "The Simplex Located in Art Worlds." *Urban Life* 7, no. 4 (January 1979): 411–439.

Philips, Tom. "Jefferson Airplane." *Jazz & Pop*. January 1969.

Pierce, Jennifer Ember. *Playin' Around: The Lives and Careers of Famous Session Musicians*. Lanham, MD: Scarecrow Press, 1998.

"Pity Him No More—New Type Bull Fiddle Devised." *Seattle Post-Intelligencer*. February 17, 1935. 7.

Play Electric Bass with the Ventures: Play Guitar with the Ventures Volume 4. Dolton Records BST-17504. 1966. LP.

Play Guitar with the Ventures [Volume 1]. Dolton Records BLP-16501. 1965. LP.

Port, Ian S. *The Birth of Loud: Leo Fender, Les Paul, and the Guitar-Pioneering Rivalry That Shaped Rock 'n' Roll*. New York: Scribner, 2019.

Poulopoulos, Panagiotis. "Reflecting the 1950s Popular Lifestyle: The Danelectro 3412 Short Horn Bass." In *Quand la guitare [s']électrise!* Ed. Benoît Navarret, Marc Battier, Philippe Bruguière, and Philippe Gonin. Paris: Sorbonne Université Presses, 2022. 63–98.

"Presley Whips 12,000 into Near-Hysteria." *Spokane Review*. August 31, 1957. Reprinted in Ger Rijff. *Long Lonely Highway: A 1950s Elvis Scrapbook*. Ann Arbor, MI: Pierian Press, 1987. 160.

Pruter, Robert. *Chicago Soul*. Urbana: University of Illinois Press, 1991.

Putnam, Norbert. *Music Lessons*. Vol. 1: *A Musical Memoir*. Nashville: Thimbleton House Media, 2017.

The Quiet One. Directed by Oliver Murray. Sundance Selects. 2019. DVD.

Ragland, Cathy. *Música Norteña: Mexican Migrants Creating a Nation between Nations*. Philadelphia: Temple University Press, 2009.

Read, Mike. *The Story of the Shadows: An Autobiography*. London: Elm Tree Books, 1983.

"Reader's Poll." *New Musical Express*. December 1, 1961. 7.

"Reader's Poll." *New Musical Express*. November 23, 1962. 7.

"Reader's Poll." *New Musical Express*. October 28, 1960. 7.

Reali, Christopher M. "Making Music in Muscle Shoals." PhD dissertation, University of North Carolina at Chapel Hill, 2014.

Reali, Christopher M. *Music and Mystique in Muscle Shoals.* Urbana: University of Illinois Press, 2022.

Reali, Christopher M. "Review of Muscle Shoals." *Journal of the Society for American Music* 11, no. 3 (August 2017): 384–87.

Rees, Paul. *The Ox: The Authorized Biography of the Who's John Entwistle.* New York: Hachette Books, 2020.

"Reflections with Larry Graham." *Reflections in Rhythm.* August 8, 2010. https://reflectionsinrhythm.wordpress.com/2010/08/08/reflections-with-larry-graham/

Richards, Keith. *Life.* New York: Little, Brown, 2010.

Richards, Martin. "Ray Pohlman." *Jazz Journal International* 40, no. 12 (December 1987): 8–10.

Richardson, Chris. "The Dapps at King Records." *Zero to 180.* July 5, 2020. https://www.zeroto180.org/the-dapps-at-king-records/

Richardson, Sarah Deters. "Instruments of War: The Impact of World War II on the American Musical Instrument Industry." PhD dissertation, University of South Dakota, 2010.

"Rickenbacker Electric Bass." *Vintage Guitar.* February 2007. https://www.vintageguitar.com/3399/rickenbacker-electro-bass/. Accessed April 19, 2015.

Rijff, Ger. *Long Lonely Highway: A 1950s Elvis Scrapbook.* Ann Arbor, MI: Pierian Press, 1987.

Roberts, Jim. *American Basses: An Illustrated History & Player's Guide.* San Francisco: Backbeat Books, 2003.

Roberts, Jim. *How the Fender Bass Changed the World.* San Francisco: Backbeat Books, 2001.

Rodman, Gilbert B. "A Hero to Most? Elvis, Myth, and the Politics of Race." *Cultural Studies* 8, no. 3 (1994): 457–483.

"Roger Filiberto, 94, Guitar Instructor." *Times-Picayune.* July 30, 1998.

"The Rolling Stones: 'Little Red Rooster'; 'Off the Hook.'" *Beat Instrumental.* December 1964. 28.

"The Rolling Stones: The Crusaders." *Rave.* August 1964.

Rosen, Steve. "John Entwistle: The Who's Great Bass Guitarist." *Guitar Player.* November 1975. 24–28.

Rosenberg, Neil V. and Charles K. Wolfe. *The Music of Bill Monroe.* Urbana: University of Illinois Press, 2007.

Rowe, Mike. *Chicago Blues: The City & the Music.* New York: Da Capo Press, 1975.

Rowes, Barbara. *Grace Slick: The Biography.* New York: Doubleday, 1980.

Rowland, Matt. "For Sweet People from Sweet Charles." *Wax Poetics* 5 (Summer 2003). 18–38.

Roy, James V. "1956 Fender Precision Bass." *Scotty Moore: The Official Website.* June 27, 2011. http://www.scottymoore.net/56PBass.html/. Accessed November 1, 2012.

Roy, James V. "Amplifying Bill's Upright Bass." *Scotty Moore: The Official Website.* http://www.scottymoore.net/ampeg.html/. Accessed December 15, 2016.

Russell, Wayne. Liner notes to Freddie Bell & the Bellboys, *Rockin' Is Our Business.* Bear Family Records. BCD 15901. 1996. CD.

Ryan, Kevin and Brian Kehew. *Recording the Beatles: The Studio Equipment and Techniques Used to Create Their Classic Albums.* Houston: Curvebender Publishing, 2009.

San Miguel, Guadalupe, Jr. "The Rise of Recorded Tejano Music in the Post–World War II Years, 1946–1964." *Journal of American Ethnic History* 19, no. 1 (Fall 1999): 26–49.

Santoro, Gene. "Session Bassist Jerry Jemmott: The Groovemaster." *Guitar Player.* May 1984.

Savidge, Wilbur M. "The Guitar Phonics Episode" [unpublished book manuscript]. Archived at at https://web.archive.org/web/20100423201139/htt p://jukebox.au.nu/instromania/instro_monsters/chet_atkins/2.html/

Schmidt-Horning, Susan. "Recording: The Search for the Sound." In *The Electric Guitar: A History of an American Icon.* Ed. André Millard. Baltimore: John Hopkins University Press, 2004. 105–122.

Schneeberger, Mario. "The European Tour of Lionel Hampton and His Orchestra, 1953: Band Routes." *Names and Numbers*, no. 68 (January 2014). http://www.jazzdocumentation.ch/mario/lionel-hampton-bandroutes-europe-195 31.pdf/

Schneeberger, Mario. "The European Tour of Lionel Hampton and His Orchestra, 1953: The Recorded Concerts." *Names and Numbers*, no. 64 (January 2013). http://www.jazzdocumentation.ch/mario/hamprecords.pdf/

Schroeder, Joan V. "Patsy in Appleland." *Blue Ridge County.* September–October 1992. Archived at http://www.oocities.org/icanseeanangel1961/patsyinappl eland.html/

Schwartz, Roberta Freund. *How Britain Got the Blues: The Transmission and Reception of American Blues Style in the United Kingdom.* Burlington, VT: Ashgate, 2007.

Scott, Josh. "6 Guitar Inventions Explained." *The JHS Show.* 2023. https://thejhs show.com/articles/6-guitar-inventions-explained

Sears Fall and Winter Catalog. 1960. Chicago: Sears, Roebuck and Company.

Sears Fall and Winter Catalog. 1964. Chicago: Sears, Roebuck and Company.

Sharp, Ken. *Sound Explosion: Inside L.A.'s Studio Factory with the Wrecking Crew.* Woodland Hills: Wrecking Crew LLC, 2015).

Shorkey, Clayton T. "La Villita Dance Hall." *Handbook of Texas Online.* Updated August 8, 2018. https://www.tshaonline.org/handbook/entries/la-villita-da nce-hall/

"A Short History of the Höfner 500/1 Violin Bass." *Höfner.* Archived at https:// web.archive.org/web/20220221195234/https://www.hofner.com/violin_ba ss_history. Accessed February 19, 2017.

Simonds, Roy. *King Curtis: A Discography.* Middlesex, England: Self-published, 1983.

Slutsky, Allan and Chuck Silverman. *The Great James Brown Rhythm Sections, 1960–1973.* Van Nuys: Alfred Publishing, 1997.

Slutsky, Allan. "The Rhythm Sections of Soul Brother No. 1." In *Bass Player Pres-*

ents the Funky Bass Book. Ed. Bill Leigh. Milwaukee: New Bay Media, 2010. 10–11.

Slutsky, Allan. *Standing in the Shadows of Motown: The Life and Music of Legendary Bassist James Jamerson.* Milwaukee: Hal Leonard, 1989.

Slutsky, Allan. "Who Is Bob Babbitt and How Did He Get All Those Gold Records." 2003. BobBabbitt.com. Archived at https://web.archive.org/web/20210210204334/http://www.bobbabbitt.com/about.htm/

Smialek, Eric. "The Myth of the Delayed Backbeat in Southern Soul: Discourses of Rhythmic, Corporeal, and Racial Authenticity." Society for American Music Conference, 2020.

Smith, Alan. "The Who Use Force to Get the Sound They Want!!" *New Musical Express.* June 18, 1965.

Smith, Clive and Bip Wetherell. *Clem Cattini: My Life, through the Eye of a Tornado.* Mango Books, 2019.

Smith, Richard R. "Arlis McMinn and the California Playboys." *Vintage Guitar.* December 2013. https://www.vintageguitar.com/17470/arliss-mcminn-and-the-california-playboys/

Smith, Richard R. *Fender: The Sound Heard 'Round the World.* Milwaukee: Hal Leonard, 2003.

Smith, Richard R. *The History of Rickenbacker Guitars.* Fullerton, CA: Centerstream Publishing, 1987.

Smith, RJ. *The One: The Life and Music of James Brown.* New York: Gotham Books, 2012.

Sneeringer, Julia. *A Social History of Early Rock 'n' Roll in Germany: Hamburg from Burlesque to the Beatles, 1956–1969.* London: Bloomsbury Academic, 2018.

Spector, Ronnie with Vince Waldron. *Be My Baby: How I Survived Mascara, Miniskirts, and Madness, or My Life as a Fabulous Ronette.* Los Angeles: Words in Edgewise, 2015.

Standing in the Shadows of Motown. Directed by Paul Justman. Artisan Entertainment. 2002. DVD.

Stanfield, Peter. "The Who and Pop Art: The Simple Things You See Are All Complicated." *Journal of Popular Music Studies* 29, no. 1 (March 2017): 1–17.

Stakes, Richard. "These Boys: The Rise of Mersey Beat." In *Gladsongs and Gatherings: Poetry and Its Social Context in Liverpool since the 1960s.* Ed. Stephen Wade. Liverpool: Liverpool University Press, 2001. 157–167.

Statistics on Amateur Music in the United States. AMC Review. Chicago: American Music Conference, 1960.

Stephens, Vincent L. *Rocking the Closet: How Little Richard, Johnnie Ray, Liberace, and Johnny Mathis Queered Popular Music.* Urbana: University of Illinois Press, 2019.

Stewart, Alexander. "'Funky Drummer': New Orleans, James Brown and the Rhythmic Transformation of American Popular Music." *Popular Music* 19, no. 3 (2000): 293–318.

Stimeling, Travis D. *Nashville Cats; Record Production in Music City.* New York: Oxford University Press, 2020.

Sting. Interview by Vic Garbarini. *Bass Player.* April 1992. 32.

Stubbs, Eddie. Liner notes to Little Jimmy Dickens, *Country Boy*. Bear Family Records. 1999. CD.

Suchow, Rick. "Larry Graham: Godfather of Funk Bass." *Bass Musician Magazine*. November 2010. Reprinted at https://bassmusicianmagazine.com/2010/11/bass-musician-magazine-featuring-larry-graham-november-2010-issue/

Tamarkin, Jeff. *Got a Revolution: The Turbulent Flight of Jefferson Airplane*. New York: Atria Books, 2003.

Taylor, S. Gordon. "The 1940 Sound." *Service*. February 1940. 17–18.

Tesser, Neil. "The Electric Guitar and Vibraphone in Jazz: Batteries Not Included." In *Oxford Companion to Jazz*. Ed. Bill Kirchner. Oxford: Oxford University Press, 2000. 642–652.

Théberge, Paul. *Any Sound You Can Imagine: Making Music / Consuming Technology*. Hanover, NH: Wesleyan University Press, 1997.

Théberge, Paul. "'Plugged In': Technology and Popular Music." In *The Cambridge Companion to Pop and Rock*. Ed. Simon Frith, Will Straw, and John Street. Cambridge: Cambridge University Press, 2001. 3–25.

Tillman, Keith. "Bringing It to Jerome." *Blues Unlimited* 63. June 1969. 13.

Tolinksi, Brad and Alan Di Perna. *Play It Loud: An Epic History of the Style, Sound, and Revolution of the Electric Guitar*. New York: Doubleday, 2016.

Townshend, Pete. *Who I Am: A Memoir*. New York: Harper Perennial, 2012.

"A Tribute to Gene Vincent . . . and the Blue Caps." *Forgotten Hits*. February 11, 2012. http://forgottenhits60s.blogspot.com/2012_02_05_archive.html

Tulloch, Doug. *Neptune Bound: The Ultimate Danelectro Guitar Guide*. Fullerton, CA: Centerstream, 2009.

Tutmarc, Paul H. "The True Facts on the Invention of the Electric Guitar and Electric Bass." In *The Hawaiian Steel Guitar and its Great Hawaiian Musicians*. Compiled by Lorene Ruymar. Anaheim Hills, CA: Centerstream, 1996. 126–127.

VanHecke, Susan. *Race with the Devil: Gene Vincent's Life in the Fast Lane*. New York: St. Martins, 2001.

Varga, George. "Larry Graham: Woodstock, Prince & Beyond." *San Diego Union-Tribune*. September 17, 2014. https://www.sandiegouniontribune.com/entertainment/music/sdut-bass-great-larry-graham-talks-music-and-more-2014sep17-htmlstory.html/

Vermont, Jackie. "Lionel Hampton au Palais du Chaillot." *Jazz Hot*. October 1953. 17.

Vickers, Tom. "Interview with Steve Cropper [1984]." Rock 'n' Soul Audiovisual History Project Collection. Archives Center. National Museum of American History. Smithsonian Institution.

Vincent, Rickey. *Funk: The Music, the People, and the Rhythm of the One*. New York: St. Martin's Press, 1996.

Vivi-Tone. *Electrically Energized Musical Instruments: A Revolutionary Development in the Field of Music*. Catalog. 1934.

Vox. Advertisement. *The Music Trades*. October 1964. N.p.

Vox. Advertisement. *The Music Trades*. June 1965. 195.

Waksman, Steve. *Instruments of Desire: The Electric Guitar and the Shaping of Musical Experience*. Cambridge: Harvard University Press, 1999.

Waksman, Steve. *Live Music in America: A History from Jenny Lind to Beyoncé.* New York: Oxford University Press, 2022.

Waksman, Steve. "Reading the Instrument: An Introduction." *Popular Music and Society* 26, no. 3 (2003): 251–261.

Wald, Elijah. *The Blues: A Very Short Introduction.* New York: Oxford University Press, 2010.

Wald, Elijah. *Dylan Goes Electric! Newport, Seeger, Dylan, and the Night That Split the Sixties.* New York: Dey St, 2015.

Wald, Elijah. *Escaping the Delta: Robert Johnson and the Invention of the Blues.* New York: HarperCollins, 2004.

Warwick, Jacqueline. *Girl Groups, Girl Culture: Popular Music and Identity in the 1960s.* New York: Routledge, 2007.

"Way Out Sound from Stones." *Record Mirror.* November 7, 1964.

Webster, Tony. "I Don't Know a Thing about the Guitar Says Paul McCartney." *Beat Instrumental.* October 1964. 22–23.

Weir, Jonathan. "Amplified Fiddle Leads Way to Big-Time Music Business." *Newark Sunday News.* October 23, 1968. D2–D4.

Wenner, Jann S. "The Rolling Stone Interview: Dylan." *Rolling Stone.* November 29, 1969.

Werner, Craig. *A Change Is Gonna Come: Music, Race, and the Soul of America.* Rev. ed. Ann Arbor: University of Michigan Press, 2006.

Wexler, Jerry. *Rhythm and the Blues: A Life in American Music.* New York: St. Martin's Press, 1993.

Wheeler, Tom. *American Guitars: An Illustrated History.* Rev. ed. New York: HarperPerennial, 1992.

Wheeler, Tom. "Leo Fender: An Exclusive GP Interview." *Guitar Player.* May 1978. 32–34; 106–109.

Wheelwright, Lynn. "Vivi-Tone" [unpublished manuscript].

White, Charles. *The Life and Times of Little Richard: The Authorised Biography.* 2nd ed. London: Omnibus Press, 2003.

White, Forrest. *Fender: The Inside Story.* San Francisco: BackBeat Books, 1994.

White, Renée Minus. *Maybe: My Memoir.* Pittsburgh: RoseDog Books, 2015.

Wiley, Clete. "Lionel Is Cool, Crowd Is Small for Band Show." *Waterloo Daily Courier.* December 13, 1951. 22.

Williams, Alan. "Navigating Proximities: The Creative Identity of the Hired Musician." *Journal of the Music & Entertainment Industry Educators Association* 10, no. 1 (2010): 59–76.

Williams, James Gordon. *Crossing Bar Lines: The Politics and Practices of Black Musical Space.* Jackson: University Press of Mississippi, 2021.

Williams, Mark. "Liberace Show, The." In *Encyclopedia of Television.* Ed. Horace Newcomb. 2nd ed. London: Taylor & Francis, 2014. 1356.

Wilson, Brian with Ben Greenman. *I Am Brian Wilson.* Philadelphia: Da Capo Press, 2016.

Wilson, Carroll. *Playing by Heart: Leon Gibbs and the Miller Brothers Band.* Wichita Falls, TX: Midwestern State University Press, 2003.

Winquist, Sven. "Hampton Knocks 'Em Out at Oslo Debut." *Melody Maker.* September 12, 1953. 16.

Wolfrum, Ed. Interview by Mike Dutkewych. November 18, 2015. Detroit Music Oral History Project. Wayne State University.

Wolkin, Jan Mark and Bill Keenom. *Mike Bloomfield: If You Love These Blues.* San Francisco: Miller Freeman Books, 2000.

"The Wrecking Crew, Lyle Ritz—Recording with Phil Spector's Wall of Sound & the Beach Boys." Interview with Lyle Ritz. Musicians Hall of Fame & Museum. April 15, 2020. https://www.youtube.com/watch?v=md4P3xlbUGY/

Wright, Brian F. "The Bass Guitar in Popular Music." In *Cambridge Companion to the Electric Guitar.* Ed. Jan-Peter Herbst and Steve Waksman (forthcoming).

Wright, Brian F. "Elvis in Vegas: The King of Rock 'n' Roll and the City of Second Chances." In *The Possibility Machine: Music and Myth in Las Vegas.* Ed. Jake Johnson. Urbana: University of Illinois Press, 2023.

Wright, Brian F. "Interview with Bassist Norbert Putnam." 2021. https://www.brianfwright.com/interviews/norbert-putnam/

Wright, Brian F. "Interview with Fireballs' Bassist Stan Lark." 2021, https://www.brianfwright.com/interviews/stan-lark/

Wright, Brian F. "Interview with Jefferson Airplane Bassist Jack Casady." 2022. https://www.brianfwright.com/interviews/jack-casady/

Wright, Brian F. "Interview with Motown Bassist Tony Newton." 2021. https://www.brianfwright.com/interviews/tony-newton/

Wright, Brian F. "Interview with Royal's Bassist Bob 'Mole' Schmidt, Jr." 2016. https://www.brianfwright.com/interviews/bob-schmidt/

Wright, Brian F. "Interview with Session Bassist Chuck Rainey." 2021. https://www.brianfwright.com/interviews/chuck-rainey/

Wright, Brian F. "Interview with Session Bassist Jerry Jemmott." 2021. https://www.brianfwright.com/interviews/jerry-jemmott/

Wright, Brian F. "Jaco Pastorius, the Electric Bass, and the Struggle for Jazz Credibility." *Journal of Popular Music Studies* 32, no. 3 (September 2020): 121–138.

Wright, Brian F. "Reconstructing the History of Motown Session Musicians: The Carol Kaye / James Jamerson Controversy." *Journal of the Society for American Music* 13, no. 1 (February 2019): 78–109.

Wright, Brian F. "Transvaluing Adam Clayton: Why the Bass Matters in U2's Music." In *U2 Above, Across, and Beyond: Interdisciplinary Assessments.* Ed. Scott Calhoun. Lanham, MD: Lexington Books, 2014. 17–30.

Wyman, Bill. *Bill Wyman's Blues Odyssey: A Journey to Music's Heart & Soul.* New York: DK Publishing, 2001.

Wyman, Bill. *Stone Alone: The Story of a Rock 'n' Roll Band.* New York: Da Capo Press, 1997.

Zak, Albin J., III. *I Don't Sound Like Nobody: Remaking Music in 1950s America.* Ann Arbor: University of Michigan Press, 2012.

Zimmerman, Nadya. *Counterculture Kaleidoscope: Musical and Cultural Perspective on Late Sixties San Francisco.* Ann Arbor: University of Michigan Press, 2011.

Zollo, Paul. *More Songwriters on Songwriting.* Boston: Perseus Books, 2016.

Index

Page numbers in italics indicate figures.